THE **ALMIGHTY LATIN KING** AND **QUEEN NATION**

THE **ALMIGHTY LATIN KING** AND **QUEEN NATION**

David C. Brotherton and Luis Barrios

STREET POLITICS AND THE TRANSFORMATION
OF A NEW YORK CITY GANG

Columbia University Press   New York

COLUMBIA UNIVERSITY PRESS
Publishers Since 1893
New York   Chichester, West Sussex

© 2004 Columbia University Press
All rights reserved

Design by Brady McNamara
All photographs in this text are by Steve Hart.

Library of Congress Cataloging-in-Publication Data
Brotherton, David.
    The Almighty Latin King and Queen Nation : street
    politics and the transfomation of a New York City gang /
    David C. Brotherton and Luis Barrios.
        p.   cm.
    Includes bibliographical references and index.
    ISBN 0-231-11418-4 (cl : alk. paper)—
    ISBN 0-231-11419-2 (pbk. : alk. paper)
        1. Almighty Latin King and Queen Nation—History.
    2. Gangs—New York (State)—New York—Case studies.
    3. Gangs—New York (State)—New York—History.
    4. Hispanic American youth—New York (State)—New
    York—Social conditions.   5. African American youth—
    New York (State)—New York—social conditions.
    6. Youth with social disabilities—New York (State)—
    New York.   7. New York (N.Y.)—Social conditions.
    I. Title: Street politics and the transformation of a
    New York City gang.   II. Barrios, Luis.   III. Title.

    HV6439.U7N432 2003
    364.1'066'097471—dc22
                                                2003061751

Columbia University Press books are printed on permanent
and durable acid-free paper.
Printed in the United States of America
c 10 9 8 7 6 5 4 3 2 1
p 10 9 8 7 6 5 4 3 2 1

To my mother, father, wife, Lisa, and children, Gijs, Mia, and Aidan—DB

To my compañera, Minerva, my mother, Maria Inés, and my children, Mónika, Jonathan, Joseph Omar, and Mekael Antonio—LB

CONTENTS

ACKNOWLEDGMENTS

The first people to thank for the completion and publication of this project are the men and women of the Almighty Latin King and Queen Nation. To all of those who opened their hearts and minds to our questions, who took us to spaces and places that were an ethnographer's dream, who were generous with their time and honest with their answers, we are eternally grateful. In the annals of street research, we are hard pressed to think of another group of individuals who have so embraced the potential of social science, seeing in it a way to record and learn from history even if we, "the outsiders," are doing the writing. In particular, wewant to recognize the contributions of two individuals, Antonio Fernández, aka King Tone, and the late Héctor Torres. King Tone was and is a remarkable leader of the barrio poor, who kept his word from start to finish and risked much on our behalf. Héctor was a stalwart who helped to arrange many of the interviews and provided countless insights into the manifold ways resistance emerges among the voiceless.

We want to thank the research team: our two primary field researchers, Juan Esteva and Camila Salazar, who stayed with the project for almost three years and who never lost their focus or wilted under the enormous difficulties that accompany working in this environment. We also want to acknowledge Lorine Padilla, María Isabel Santiviago, and Marcia Esparza, for their support in the field when it was vitally needed; Rose Santos for the endless hours spent transcribing in both English and Spanish; Mindy Johnson, for keeping the project going through thick and thin; Qusai Hussein, for research support; Michael Flynn, for his inspirational probings, editorial suggestions, and psychological commentary; and Louis Kontos, for sharing with us his work on Long Island, a unique suburban setting for a street subculture, and for providing us with his field notes, interviews, analyses, and editing skills on the collective manuscript ("Gangs and Society: Alternative Perspectives.").

At the institutional level, we would have fared poorly without the long-term financial support of the Spencer Foundation, which, through its Small and Major Grants Programs, underwrote numerous research proposals over the past eight years, all of which have contributed to this final project. In the same vein, we should also mention the role of the National Academy of Education, which has given continued encouragement to Brotherton to pursue the connections between formal educational institutions and the street, an area that is still largely absent from the literature and one that both authors are seeking to develop in current and future-planned endeavors. We also want to recognize our union's research funding arm, PSC-CUNY, for providing several small grants over the years that have enabled us to pursue tangential lines of inquiry to the central focus of the study.

We would also like to thank the City University of New York (CUNY) Dispute Resolution Consortium, the William T. Grant Foundation, the General Board of the Global Ministry-United Methodist Church, the CUNY Vice-Chancellor's Office, and Henry Chalfant for supporting our series of conferences on street empowerment issues in which members of street subcultures are as valued as academics, social workers, community leaders, school teachers, media workers, lawyers, correctional officers, and representatives from law enforcement.

Finally, our home institution, John Jay College of Criminal Justice, must also share some of the blame/credit for accommodating us all these years, giving us the kind of students that can relate to our quest for socially responsible research and teaching agendas and the quality of faculty that know no bounds in their collegiality and intellectual insights. Among our friends at John Jay and CUNY we want to single out: Ric Curtis, Bill Kornblum, President Gerry Lynch, José Luis Morín, Barry Spunt, Jim Vrettos, Michael Blitz, Gerald Markowitz, Maria Volpe, Susan Rosenburg, and Basil Wilson. Aside from our home institutional colleagues, we also want to mention Dwight Conquergood, whose extraordinary accomplishments in the field have long set the standard for critical ethnography; John Michel, the senior executive editor at Columbia University Press, whose patience we have exhausted but who has stuck with us until the end; David Diefendorf and Ron Harris, from Columbia University Press, who masterfully copy edited this manuscript; Jeanie Lu, also of Columbia University Press; Brian Powers, whose grasp of research as praxis should be known to many more; and our dear friends and comrades in Los Angeles, California, Tom Hayden, Bloodhound, Michael Zinzun, and Homies Unidos, all of whom are beacons of hope for street youth across the United States and beyond. Last but not least, Brotherton wants to pay homage to his ex-colleague, the late Dan Waldorf, who, in such a short span, taught him more about ethnography than could have possibly been learned at graduate school, and Barrios wants to compliment the members of St. Mary's Episcopal Church (Manhattanville), who, despite the many challenges they faced, continued to create a church that was not afraid.

We also want to mention that parts of chapters 7, 9, and 10 have appeared in the *Review of Pedagogy/Education/Culture* (Winter 2002) and *Gangs and Society: Alternative Perspectives* (Columbia University Press, 2003).

I don't think that youth programs will help the Bloods, the Crips, the Latin Kings, the Zulu Nation, MS13. These are gangs that begin in jail and in prison. These are violent repeat career criminals and I don't think that giving them sewing lessons is going to help.

Mayor Giuliani of New York City during mayoral debates, as reported in the *New York Times,* Metropolitan Desk 1997:B-4

The press are driving us mad here. Everyday they want to do something on us—tell a bunch of lies about what we do and never want to say anything that tells it like it is—to be real. They don't want that. Just today, Channel 9 was here and this woman comes up to me and asks, "Where's the guns?" I said, "We don't have any. This is a meeting. This is who we are. " So, you know what? She wasn't interested anymore and she left. She was all like disappointed that we couldn't produce the kind of negative publicity that she was looking for. All they want to show us as is something crazed, out-of-control, a group of hoodlums. So when they can't show us in a bad light, maybe when we are no longer 'news,' then maybe they'll leave us alone and we can live in peace and go on about our business."

King N. of the ALKQN, 10/19/96

As youth street gangs throughout this century have ebbed and flowed, largely organized around class, racial, ethnic, and gender configurations, their relationship to the problems of society has been consistently framed by the most powerful interests in society. The ex-mayor of New York City, quoted above, is just one example of the almost visceral reaction that representatives of the dominant social and economic order exhibit when asked to discuss the "gang question." It is as if the gang today had achieved an unassailable status among the panoply of demons that the keyholders to our moral economy would have us expunge.

From Los Angeles to New York and from Chicago to Miami, the street gang is generally perceived as one of the most intractable problems of delinquency and crime that society is facing. It is said not only that gangs are more numerous and violent than at any time since World War II, but also that the age at which youth are joining gangs is younger, the length of time members stay in gangs is longer, and gangs themselves have moved beyond their big city confines to small towns in the suburbs and even to unsuspecting rural communities (Office of Juvenile Justice and Delinquency Prevention 1998).

As these qualitative and quantitative changes have occurred, so society has also changed the way it has reacted to the problem (Spergel 1995). For most of the twentieth century, the street gang was primarily considered a social and economic issue that was best dealt with by interventions designed to reintegrate youth and adults back into society's mainstream. These models of delinquency and adult crime prevention were reflective of "good society " values and paradigms at the time (Bellah 1986) and varied according to the progressive, "pastoral" (Sarup 1983) and/or welfare state strategies that were then in vogue. From urban experiments such as the 1930s' community-mobilizing Chicago Project, to the 1950s' social work concept of street outreach workers, to the 1960s' policies of providing expanded opportunities, a long line of pragmatic solutions was tried with varying levels of success. Ultimately, however, the so-called gang problem continued, returning to public scrutiny every few years in what Gilbert (1986) has called "cycles of outrage."

Departing from the reform-minded, more humanistic interventions of the past, crime control and gang prevention nowadays have reverted to a previous century, when individuals were thought to be endowed with pathological properties and the citizenry was divided into "good" and "bad" elements (Spergel 1995:173). Today, the methods most often used to respond to gangs and their members are heavily weighted in favor of suppressive law-enforcement techniques and the punitive sanctions of the incarceration industry—with some of the most coercive means reserved for minorities in the poorest districts of the nation. In terms of social policies and fiscal budgets, this translates into far more resources being channeled into curfews, mass arrests, mandatory sentences, anti-combination laws, and conspiracy indictments, than into social services that could support and empower gang-related youths or the kinds of information for schools, neighborhoods, political parties, churches, and family networks that promotes understanding and humanistic responses rather than fear and loathing. The street gang, therefore, despite the absence of a universal definition, is a subject about which the government and the state seem to have reached a consensus: first, it is above all a crime problem; and second, the solution to the problem lies in the eradication of the gang.

Much of what is known about the Almighty Latin King and Queen Nation ("ALKQN"), the subject of our study, is derived from local, crime-fighting law-enforcement agencies, state and federal prosecutors, defense lawyers, and media scribes. King N.'s insider perspective, above, accurately describes the specific symbolic reality (Berger and Luckman 1966)[1] in which the ALKQN found itself during the late 1990s in New York City. For the most part, it is also the accepted view of the dominant culture within which criminologists in particular, and social scientists in general, have approached "gangs."

> The emphasis on the study of gangs "as a crime problem" allows criminal justice researchers to study gang members as felons, or law violators, and not as part of the community.... Variables of race, sex, age, and class are used solely to explain behavior which violates the law. Broader concerns about social and economic structures or community processes are not seen as important.
>
> (Hagedorn 1988:27)

In our study, which has arisen out of concerns similar to those of Hagedorn, we attempt to show precisely this "other" side of gang life.

Consequently, when one of the most notorious and most criminally pursued gangs in the United States, the Almighty Latin King and Queen Nation of New York City, declares that it is a social movement acting on behalf of the dispossessed, renouncing violence, refusing to be associated with the underground economy, and making school attendance a criterion of membership, it is time to take a closer look at the gang phenomenon. Using the specific case study of the ALKQN in New York City, focusing primarily on its social, cultural, spiritual, and political transformation between the years 1995 and 1999, we will show the limitations of both criminological and criminal-justice assessments of gangs. We will argue that gangs and their members are not simply the result of discrete processes of social adaptation or, worse still, of social and individual pathologies. Instead, they reflect the contradictory, misunderstood, and often ignored outcomes of sociohistorical agency. We will further demonstrate how and why the gang, or in this case the street organization, in the face of intense counter-insurgency operations by the police, can still manifest far-reaching examples of urban social and cultural resistance to control and domination.

The Evolution of the Almighty Latin King and Queen Nation

I'm the leader of the Almighty Latin King and Queen Nation Incorporation, our goal is a very hard goal to reach and that's to change.... So right now the ALKQN, as I see it, is a lighthouse to the rest of the country of how gangs can make a transition.... We took the step to tell the kids "drop the gun, leave the corners on the drug market and learn that there's a better way." Stop looking at TV and admiring Michael Jordan's sneakers, it ain't his feet that's gonna get you somewhere its your head. So, as we instill this in our youth, they recognize that yes, the ALKQN has an answer, and that doesn't mean you have to be deprived to join us or a loser. You have to be a man with a vision.... Youth are joining us now not because they want to have a clique and somebody to defend them, now they got a voice to be heard and that's what we represent in New York.

Antonio Fernández, aka King Tone, Inca and Leader of the Almighty Latin King and Queen Nation, New York State, 10/30/96

This quote, taken from an early interview with the ALKQN's leader, reflects the activist orientations of the group during its transformative period. A brief chronology of the group's history shows the twists and turns in this development.

1986: Group is founded by Luis Felipe (King Blood) together with two others in Collins Correctional Facility, New York State. Blood writes the New York State manifesto for the Latin Kings, based on the teachings of the "Motherland" (Chicago), describing himself as Inca and Supreme Crown. In the early days, the group is only for Latinos and excludes gays.

1991: The group moves from being primarily prison-based to the streets of New York City's barrios. The group also attracts a small contingent of women called Latin Queens.

King Blood returns to prison after breaking parole—he is charged with receiving stolen goods.

1993: The group continues to expand, particularly in prison. Few media report on the group during this time.

1994: A fierce internal power struggle takes place. Seven Kings are murdered between July 1993 and February 1994. In June 1994, King Blood and nineteen others are indicted for racketeering and murder (eight slayings altogether). By the end of 1995, thirty-nine Kings and one Queen have been indicted under the Racketeering in Industrial Organizations Act.

1995: Antonio Fernández, aka King Tone, the head of the Brooklyn tribe, becomes Supreme Crown and Inca of the New York State and New Jersey Almighty Latin King and Queen Nation. He is blessed by King Blood. King Tone declares that the group has to renounce its violent past to survive and begins a campaign to reform the organization into a community movement. Media reports estimate the group to have 3,000 members in prison and 4,000 more on the streets. In May, King Tone is arrested for possession of a handgun but beats the charge. In September he is rearrested on a federal gun charge and released in February 1996 when the judge dismisses the case.

1996: The trial of King Blood begins and hundreds of Kings and Queens attend the hearings. During the year, the ALKQN are regularly present at political demonstrations in support of the Latino community. The group now holds all its monthly meetings at St. Mary's Episcopal Church (Manhattanville), in West Harlem; approximately 500 to 600 are regularly in attendance. New instructions are added to the old manifesto; these include the ending of the death penalty, new procedures for grievances and charges, and an attempt to bring parliamentary procedure to meetings.

1997: All sentences are handed down. Of the forty Latin Kings and Queens indicted, thirty-nine plead guilty; only King Blood elects to go to trial. The average sentence for the thirty-nine is twenty years. King Blood receives 250 years with the first forty-five to be spent in solitary confinement—the harshest federal sentence since World War II.

New Jersey is taken out of King Tone's hands. There is talk that Chicago, the leading branch in the Nation, sees Tone as too ambitious.

In October, during New York City's mayoral race, the Special Commissioner of Investigation for Schools releases a report charging the Latin Kings with infiltrating the public school system. A Latin King school security guard is dismissed after 5 years' service for unprofessional conduct.

In November, King Tone and thirty-one Latin Kings are arrested after a meeting on the Lower East Side. Twenty-four are charged with disorderly conduct and unlawful assembly. King Tone is released.

In December, King Tone is arrested by the FBI for domestic violence and held until April 1998.

During 1997, the ALKQN are featured on both "Nightline" with Ted Koppel and "Prime Time." The *New York Times, Daily News, Newsday,* and *New York Post* all run articles on the reform of the group.

1998: In April, King Tone is released after his female partner drops charges of domestic violence. The ALKQN makes their own documentary in collaboration with two Harvard film graduates.

In May, approximately 1,000 members of the FBI, NYPD, INS, New York State Police, and Federal Drug Enforcement Agency, under code name Operation Crown, arrest ninety-two suspected members of the ALKQN during early-morning raids. The *New York Times* calls this the biggest "sweep" in the city since prohibition. More than 50 percent of those arrested are charged with misdemeanors. The ALKQN leadership maintains that less than half of those arrested are actual members. The cost of the raid is estimated at more than $1 million.

Four days after being arrested King Tone is brought to court and the judge sets the bail at $350,000. Community and group members pledge their salaries, their cars, and their houses to meet King Tone's bail and he is placed under house arrest. Of the ninety-two arrested, only forty appear to be Latin Kings. Charges range from drug dealing and firearm possession to conspiracy. No charges of homicide result from the nineteen-month investigation.

Between June and November, King Tone is allowed to attend St. Mary's Church in Harlem on Sundays. Monthly meetings are held after the service and once again 500 to 600 are in attendance. The group's newsletter, *El Grito*, goes color and the organization decentralizes to develop new leadership structures in the different tribes. The Queens are reorganized and the old leadership is purged in an effort to bring new, more "political" Queens forward. The group estimates that its New York State membership is still around 5,000, both free and incarcerated.

1999: In January, King Tone goes to federal court in Brooklyn and pleads guilty to conspiracy to sell and distribute heroin during the summer of 1996. King Tone's lawyer has advised him that with his ten criminal history points, he faces twenty-five years under federal statutory guidelines if he fails to win his case in a jury trial. By pleading guilty he can receive a lesser sentence of 13 to 15 years. King tone is taken into custody after the hearing.

In June, King Tone is sentenced to thirteen years in federal detention. If he maintains a record of good behavior he can be released in ten years.

He is held at the Manhattan house of detention while the federal bureau of prisons finds a suitable location.

In November, King Tone is sent to Leavenworth Federal Penitentiary in Kansas, the oldest maximum security prison in the United States, and he is placed under segregated administration (solitary confinement) in the facility's Special Housing Unit. The prison administration argues that he is an "at risk" inmate because of his group connections and history. He is allowed one five-minute phone call every thirty-one days, a one-hour trip to the exercise yard in the early morning, no television, and no participation in any work or educational programs.

2001: In May, at the "Globalizing the Streets" conference held at John Jay College, a Latin King denounces the "culture of snitching" perpetrated by the criminal justice system. The New York *Daily News*, under the headline, "Lunacy at John Jay," denounces the conference in a Sunday editorial. The paper argues that Latin Kings "belong behind bars or in looney bins" and should not be given an opportunity to speak openly at a public university.

In June, King Tone is moved to a federal penitentiary in Louisiana, where he is finally placed in the general population.

2002: In March, the ALKQN tries to hold its first major general meeting since the imprisonment of King Tone at its old meeting place, St. Mary's Church in Harlem. More than 500 members attend the event but there is open friction between tribes and no legitimate leadership emerges for the entire group.

The Organization of the Book

We have divided the book into three parts. In part 1 (chapters 1-3), we outline the central concerns, parameters, and methodology of the study, followed by a discussion of the theories that have shaped social-scientific discourses on street gangs and working-class youth subcultures primarily in the English-speaking world and that lead us to draw on a very different literature within the social movements tradition. This unusual theoretical journey through schools of thought anchored in such diverse geographical locales as Chicago, Birmingham (England), Paris, Madrid, and various intellectual capitals of Latin America has been necessary in order to extend our analytical sweep and provide us with the interpretive tools demanded by our rich and extensive data. Thus, in this section we lay out a definitional model of what we call the street organization phenomenon, which essentially provides the framework for the rest of the text.

In part 2 (chapters 4-7), we begin the presentation of our data based on the model, devoting a great deal of attention to the diverse roles of subcultures in the creation of the Almighty Latin King and Queen Nation. Thus, in chapter 4, we delineate and interpret the range of influences that come from what Latin Kings refer to as the Chicago Motherland. Chapter 5 discusses the early origins and subcultural history of the New York franchise and the symbolic functions that King Blood, one of the six founders of the New York Latin Kings and Queens, has had on the movement. Chapter 6 deals with the emergence of the reformed ALKQN's charismatic leader, King Tone, and the final section of part 2, chapter 7, traces the non-gang subcultural influences on the ALKQN such as the Black Panthers, the Young Lords, and other community movements.

Part 3 (chapters 8-12), the final part of the book's empirical analysis, is devoted to the other five properties of the definitional model. In chapter 8 we discuss the group's level of organization, while in chapter 9 we look at the types of members who joined and led the ALKQN during its reformist path, and include an in-depth description of some of the key players upon whose shoulders the group's development was largely being sustained. Chapter 10 explains the importance of ethnic and cultural identity both in the moral careers of individual members and in the sociopolitical evolution of the organization. Chapter 11 contrasts the rhetoric of the group with the goals it has accomplished and shows both the successes of the transition and why it was so difficult to integrate the lessons of experience into a new praxis. The last chapter in this section, chapter 12, focuses on the enemies of the organization as perceived by its members. Here we investigate the roles of law enforcement and the systematic use of "snitches," the politics of the state's gang-repression tactics, the emergence of renegade bodies of Latin Kings, predations by other street groups, and the contradictory influence of the media.

The final chapter of the book, chapter 13, is devoted to concluding arguments. In this we reiterate our earlier conclusions about the ALKQN and make a final plea both for new theoretical directions in future gang research and for fresh policies in the fields of education, politics, and criminal justice that empower the marginalized rather than condemn them.

PART I

TOWARD A THEORY OF THE GANG AS
A SOCIAL MOVEMENT

CHAPTER 1

THE STUDY

The Method

It is probably safe to say that the majority of studies of inner city inhabitants, particularly those that focus on members of youth gangs, have been carried out within the tradition of positivistic social science.[1] With natural science as the paradigm of good research, a premium has traditionally been placed on the value neutrality of the observer, the scientific rigor of the methodology, the unpolluted character of the data, and the generalizability of the findings, all with the aim of proving or disproving testable hypotheses (see Lincoln and Guba 1985). In this way, the gang phenomenon, whether it is understood as a delinquent organization (Klein 1971), an interstitial peer association (Thrasher 1927) or a violent near-group (Yablonsky 1963), has consistently been treated as an objectified unit of analysis and the subject of an ever-growing list of truth claims.[2] Few researchers, however, ever openly discuss the underlying assumptions contained in their written accounts of gangs and gang members, even though, for the most part, they occupy completely different racial and class worlds from those of their subjects.

In contrast to this scientistic conception of knowledge production and social investigation, what Mills (1959) and others have termed "abstract empiricism," replete with its male, white, middle-class biases and its discursive appropriation in the service of bureaucratic agencies (Foucault 1977), we have chosen an unabashedly critical approach to the ethnographic study of gangs and their members. Basing our work on the philosophical critiques of normative social-science practices, especially those which emanated from within the neo-Marxian traditions of the Frankfurt School (e.g. Adorno 1973, 1976; Benjamin 1969; Marcuse 1960, 1964, 1978) and later developed by an array of poststructuralist and postmodernist discourses (see Kincheloe and McLaren 1994), our interrogation problematizes relations between the researcher and the researched and resists the authority of mainstream social science. Thus, rather than accept as given the working definitions, normative value systems, and categories of social and cultural action that are implicit in orthodox gang canons, our orientation begins from the premise that all social and cultural phenomena emerge out of tensions between the agents and interests of those who seek to control everyday life and those who have little option but to resist this relationship of domination. This fundamentally critical approach to society seeks to uncover the processes by which seemingly normative relationships are contingent upon structured inequalities and reproduced by rituals, rules and a range of symbolic systems. Our approach, therefore, into the life of the ALKQN, is a holistic one, collecting and analyzing multiple types of data and maintaining an openness to modes of analysis that cut across disciplinary turfs.

In addition, we have chosen a collaborative mode of inquiry in order to expressly participate with the subjects in an active, reciprocal and quasi-democratic research relationship (Touraine 1981).[3] By this approach, we mean the establishment of a mutually respectful and trusting relationship with a community or a collective of individuals which: (1) will lead to empirical data that humanize the subjects, (2) can potentially contribute to social reform[4] and social justice, and (3) can create the conditions for a dialogical relationship (Bakhtin 1981; Freire 1970) between the investigator(s) and the respondents.[5]

In the Right Place at the Right Time

Our relationship with the ALKQN began in 1996, at a time when the ALKQN was reeling from the arrest and indictment of its leader, Luis Felipe, aka King Blood, and another thirty-five members of the group's hierarchy. It was clear to a number of the free and incarcerated leaders that the police and political establishments of the federal government, the state, and the city would not stop their assault on the organization regardless of how many leaders were successfully prosecuted. Certainly, this was an accurate assessment of current police thinking and as long as the group remained committed to its gangster past it gave the combined forces of the state every legal and social justification to destroy the organization. Thus, the new leadership, under Antonio Fernández, began to come to terms with this highly threatening situation and, with the support of King Blood, set about looking to accomplish at least two immediate goals: (1) to establish ties with activist members of the community, particularly Latinos, who would be willing to work in a supportive, nonjudgmental way with the group, and (2) to find public or private spaces where the group could meet, safe from the constant surveillance and harassment of the police.

FIGURE 1.1 The two authors with Latin Kings and Queens.

It was at this time that one of the coauthors, Luis Barrios, was approached about offering the ALKQN a space to have their meetings.[6] Barrios agreed that his church could be used for this purpose as long as the group: (1) allowed him to be present during the meetings; (2) agreed to open the meetings to the public; and (3) was serious about involving the group in the community's social and political issues. The ALKQN concurred with all the stipulations and became officially part of the Latino/Latina ministry of St. Mary's Episcopal Church in Manhattanville, Central Harlem in 1996.

Following this development, one of the rare occasions that a church in New York City (or anywhere else) had opened its doors to the group, Barrios, with the approval of the ALKQN leadership, invited his colleague,

Brotherton, to the church with a view to studying and documenting this movement in its early stages. For Brotherton, the rich description that Barrios offered of this organization and its proposed sociopolitical agenda was in marked contrast not only to what he had observed on the West Coast,[7] but to what he had found in the current literature on gangs. It was, to quote Burawoy (1991), an "anomalous outcome," and appeared to contradict the theoretical paradigms within which nearly all gang-focused social scientists were working.

Negotiations, Negotiations, and More Negotiations

We're not gonna let ourselves be represented by academics like we were born in the barrio yesterday. We ain't fish in a bowl to be looked at and dissected—you better get that straight! We're not here in your laboratory, doing your bidding, helping your careers. We ain't nobody's fools and we're not gonna be used by no poverty pimps. If you wanna work with us that's fine but you ain't gonna take us for granted. We don't care what the rules of the games are. . . . We gonna change the game.

[Informal interview with King H.]

After further meetings with the leaders of the ALKQN, in which we talked about our preliminary findings, the authors developed a research proposal that the group could work with, similar to the research strategy that Lincoln and Guba (1985) call the "hermeneutic-dialectic."[8] Thus, we would focus on the learning development of the membership and the role that the organization was playing as a site of informal education. We felt that most studies of gangs were overly focused on acts of delinquency and crime and neglected, almost entirely, the relationship that all young people have with myriad systems of knowledge, be it school-based training and socialization processes or the inculcation of values, norms, and symbolic codes that comes with gang membership.

At each stage of the research process, however, we were involved in intense negotiations with different members of the group regarding the shape that the research would take, its claims to authenticity, its uses, and its ownership. Who would benefit from the knowledge? Who would do the writing? What questions could be asked and of whom? Such issues were constantly raised by the group's leading members and the researchers' long discussions with them often took the form of power plays between the organization and the researchers. This was particularly so now that the group was taking its public self very seriously and was attempting to control and reappropriate its image in the face of what the group's Spiritual Advisor (Santo) called the "academic-correctional-industrial complex."

These exchanges and debates, which centered on the nature and boundaries of the research, were complex and multi-layered, not least because many of the members still resisted the idea of the organization's research and media involvement. For even though the organization was moving rapidly to open its doors to more scrutiny and was adopting radical political positions that, in time, would push it to the forefront of the city's grassroots resistance to welfare and education cuts, many members were loath to compromise the autonomy that came with the group's old practices of complete secrecy. Furthermore, the research was taking place during a time when the organization was under some form of surveillance virtually twenty-four hours a day (see chapter 12).

Eventually, in 1997, Brotherton, Barrios, and the leaders of the ALKQN, principally Antonio Fernández and King H., agreed that the study would be a viable way for the organization to (1) tell its story (in a way that the media were unlikely to do) and (2) document this transitional phase not only as a service to the ALKQN but to the Latino/a community in general. This consensus meant that we could now interview a cross-section of the membership and attend a variety of meetings that included weekly branch meetings of the youth section(s) (known as the Pee Wees) and the womens' section (known as the Latin Queens), monthly general meetings called "universals" (which have all been recorded either on audio or video tape), and socials, such as weddings, baptisms, funerals, and birthdays. It was also agreed that we would collect and collate all the monthly newsletters of the organization, all music recordings distributed under the organization's name, and that we would develop a database of media stories dating back to the early 1980s. In addition, the leadership was keen to have designated Latin Kings and Queens help us to "map" areas, which included photographing local neighborhoods where large numbers of the membership were living.

Flexible Data Collection and Innovative Methods

A thousand law enforcement officials fanned out across New York City before dawn yesterday and struck what the authorities called a crippling blow to the Latin Kings gang, seizing 94 members and associates, including top leaders, on charges ranging from possessing guns and drugs to conspiring to commit murders. . . . While more than half of the state and Federal charges filed yesterday were felony charges, there were no homicide allegations, and many of the charges were misdemeanors.

New York Times, 5/15/98:B3

The quote above from the *New York Times* gives some indication of the rapidly changing social and political terrain within which the project was taking place. As participant observers in the action of the group we, of course, needed to follow as closely as possible the multiple forms of struggle that were being waged between the state and its agents and the group's members. Consequently, we had to be prepared to gather our data in whatever set of circumstances were presented to us without becoming embroiled in the internal politics of the group or, alternatively, being made timid by the relentless encroachments of the police and members of the security state.

We chose, therefore, to hire a leading member of the group to consult with us throughout the project's duration. In practical terms this ensured: (1) the continuity of the project, (2) the permanent and mutually understood presence of a "gatekeeper," (3) the provision of a cultural broker to help us interpret unfamiliar meaning systems, and (4) the project's ethical integrity with the targeted community. To this end, we hired the leader of the ALKQN, Antonio Fernández, who worked as a part-time paid research assistant during six months from July 1998 (when he was under house arrest) until just prior to his incarceration in January 1999.[9] In addition to Fernández, several other Kings and Queens, among them King H., King M., Queen D., and Queen N., helped in the recruitment of respondents from both the adult and youth sectors of the group. Further, both Fernandez and King H. consistently responded to our analyses of the data, offering their own interpretations while also suggesting new research areas.

The interviews, most of which were in English with twelve in Spanish, were carried out by Brotherton and Barrios, along with three field researchers, Juan Esteva, Camila Salazar, and Lorinne Padilla, and a fourth affiliate researcher working on his own independent Latin Kings' project on Long Island, Louis Kontos.[10] Various sites were used to do the interviews, nearly all of which were tape recorded and later transcribed, but the majority took place at St. Mary's Episcopal Church in Harlem, in members' homes, at John Jay College in Manhattan, in local diners, or at outdoor sites during group meetings (only one interview was done in prison). Each participant was provided with a voluntary consent form before the interview, assured of the confidentiality and anonymity of the interview process, and paid twenty-five dollars, which was deposited in a general fund administered by the organization's leadership. Throughout this book we have adhered to the principle of disguising both Kings and Queens by identifying them only by an initial, with the exception of King Tone. We found it almost impossible to conceal his identity in the text and so, with his agreement, we have printed his name in full.

The project yielded sixty-seven individual life history interviews covering a range of the group's membership, i.e., males and females, young and old between the ages of sixteen and forty-eight, longstanding members and new recruits, members in the leadership and those in the rank-and-file. In addition, several leading members who were at the heart of the changes in the organization were interviewed multiple times throughout the research period. Further, we interviewed a wide variety of "outsiders," i.e., those who had interacted with the group in different capacities. Outsiders included nongroup family members, members of the clergy, leaders of nonprofit community groups, defense lawyers, public high school teachers and administrators, correctional officers, journalists, ex-members of the city's gang task force, and filmmakers. Unfortunately, no active members of law enforcement agreed to be interviewed, nor did any members of the specialized gang unit with the city's correctional department.

We have also collected a large archive of documents related to the group's practices and history, including letters used during the Luis Felipe trial; organization-produced newsletters; copies of manifestos from New York and other affiliates; Web-site representations of the group; hundreds of pages of participatory and nonparticipatory observational field notes; photographs taken at the group's branch and at city-wide meetings, political rallies, and social events; photographs of individual members in their home settings; and media coverage of the group through the years 1995–2000. Together these data provide a detailed historical and multilevel account of the group's transitional stages of development while offering a rare insight into the lives and perspectives of both its rank-and-file and leading members.

Below we provide a detailed description of the social and economic context in which our research narrative takes place. Our aim is to highlight primarily the life chances of the Puerto Rican and Dominican population, particularly those who find themselves among the lower or working classes of these communities.

The Setting

New York: A Tale of Two Cities

During the late 1990s, it was still possible to read seemingly depression-era reports about New York City's consistently high rates of child poverty (Terry 2000:A-10) or the wretched living conditions for most of its black and Hispanic immigrants (Hevesi 1998:B-8). Such reports flew in the face of the images painted by the city's political establishment and its legions of public relations firms. For most outsiders, New York was and is a city on the mend, where the urban nightmares depicted in such 1970s films as *Mean Streets* and *Taxi Driver*, or in the best-selling book *Bonfire of the Vanities* during the

1980s, were replaced by a booming, stable, universally prosperous atmosphere in the 1990s. Gone were the graffiti-riddled subways, the unkempt Central Park, the crack heads and shooting galleries, and the profligate chicanery of Wall Street. In its place was constructed an image of New York as once again "under control," though still very much a multicultural mecca where grateful, entrepreneurial immigrants from Colombia, Mexico, the Dominican Republic, Jamaica, India, Pakistan, Nigeria, and Russia struggled for their piece of the "American Dream" alongside native-born residents (Sachs 2001).

Certainly, a great deal changed during that last decade, with crime rates, particularly homicide, sharply down (less than 1,000 homicides per year), and unemployment at the lowest rate since the late 1960s. Yet, despite the longest U.S. expansion in history, the purported increase in efficiency and professionalism at the police department, the creation of new high-tech industries, and the frenzied pace of real estate development, the city, as much as ever, was a polarized community, split along race and class lines more trenchantly than at any time since World War II. Thus, while New York could justly claim to be many cities, it could also be described as two cities, with the rich, predominantly white, upper and upper-middle classes leading distinctly different lives from the poor, predominantly nonwhite lower classes, such as those families described by Kozol (1995:4) in a South Bronx neighborhood during the mid-1990s:

> In some cities, the public reputation of a ghetto neighborhood bears little connection to the world that you discover when you walk the streets with children and listen to their words. In Mott Haven, this is not the case. By and large, the words of the children in the streets and schools and houses that surround St. Ann's more than justify the grimness in the words of journalists who have described the area. . . . The houses in which these children live are often as squalid as the houses of the poorest children I have visited in rural Mississippi, but there is none of the greenness and the healing sweetness of the Mississippi countryside outside their windows, which are often barred and bolted as protection against thieves.

And what is experienced in the South Bronx as a particularly vicious clustering of urban ills is similarly observed, albeit with a different mix of "at-risk" indices, in Washington Heights, Central and East Harlem, East New York, Bushwick, Bedford Stuyvesant, and Jamaica (Queens), among other neighborhoods. These are the neighborhoods where most of the ninety-seven failing public schools are located (Hartocollis 1998): reading levels are the lowest and class sizes are the highest in the state; infant mortality is at Third World levels; AIDS, chronic asthma, and/or tuberculosis plague most families; and residents who are either unemployed, underemployed, or working poor constitute the majority of the inhabitants (Citizen's Committee for Children of New York 1998; Hevesi 1998:B-8).

It is also in these areas that most of the participants in this study resided, grew up, and attempted to make their futures. In the following, we have compiled statistics, primarily from the second half of the 1990s, that give an indication of the "quality of life" enjoyed by Dominicans and Puerto Ricans, the two most prominent ethnic groups within the ALKQN (comparing them where possible with both white and black populations of the city[11]). To reduce this information to more manageable levels, we have synthesized the data into four composite areas: Population and Health; Family and Housing; Education, Occupation, and Income; and Imprisonment.

Population and Health

At a population of more than three million, Latinos/as make up more than a third of New York City and are now its largest ethnic group. Although often grouped together under the umbrella terms Latino or Hispanic, the community represents a host of different cultures and origins, which approximately break down as follows: 36.5 percent Puerto Ricans, 18.8 percent Dominicans, 8.6 percent Mexicans, 4.7 percent Ecuadorians, and 3.6 percent Colombians. The expansion of the Latino/a population in New York has been ongoing since World War II and mirrors changes that are occurring in both New York State and the U.S. as a whole, where Latinos and Latinas constitute one of the largest and most rapidly growing ethnic populations.[12]

The healthy development of children is a crucial building block for any society, yet in a nation so riven with class and racial cleavages as ours, it should be no surprise to find that the condition of Latino/a youth and adults in the city reflects their relatively low rankings in other indices of well-being. According to 1999 figures for Puerto Ricans, 50.5 percent stated that no one in their household had health insurance, compared to 22.8 percent for whites and 45.6 percent for African-Americans. While definite strides were made through the state's child insurance plan (Child Health Plus), more than 370,000 children still remained outside the program with no health care coverage at all.[13] But Latino/a children and adults in the city are at risk not only because of inadequate insurance but because of at least two diseases that plague their communities: AIDS and Asthma (Puerto Rican/Hispanic Task Force 2001).

Family and Housing

There have been tremendous pressures exerted on both Puerto Rican and Dominican family structures due to intergenerational poverty, the withdrawal of the state from welfare and educational supports, and the many issues related to transnational population shifts brought about by globalized capitalist development in general and U.S. economic domination in particular (Sassen 1998). As a result, each family unit in both communities has had to: (1) adapt to and sustain a great many changes in its life circumstances that were frequently outside of its control, and (2) still be the bedrock of social and community life.

Consequently, it should not be surprising that many families have not been able to remain intact. In 1996, for example, 63.2 percent of Puerto Rican families were female-headed and only 27.3 percent of Puerto Rican children had both parents present (U.S. Department of Commerce 1996) while, for Dominicans in the same year, more than 50 percent of the children lived in single-family homes, a 10-percent increase in less than seven years (Hernández and Rivera-Batiz 1997). It should also be mentioned that roughly a third of the 29,453 child neglect and abuse cases reported to authorities in 1999 were Latino/a. Although this figure is about equal to the percentage of Latino children in New York City, it is still a strong indication of the level of stress within Latino families given that much of the culture highlights the centrality of family and children in the organization of daily life.

For a city like New York, where the majority of the residents do not own their own homes, the rental market and the ways in which it is regulated are of critical importance. As the Puerto Rican/Hispanic Task Force (2001:7) report states, "Despite the increase in the number of new housing units, decent and affordable housing remains out of reach of too many Hispanic households, who must devote precariously high percentages of their incomes to simply paying for rent." According to one interesting statistic, by 1999 the percentage of Puerto Ricans living in housing projects (30.6 percent) was higher than that of African-Americans (24.7 percent) and, of course, dwarfed that of whites (2.1 percent). The fact is, the 1990s saw a tremendous loss in affordable housing as Manhattan and many of the outer boroughs became increasingly gentrified, rent regulations were weakened, and the Giuliani regime did almost nothing to invest in the low-cost housing stock of the city.

Education, Occupation, and Income

In a report on at-risk youth in New York, the authors described the public education system as

a two-tier system that has essentially given up on the neediest students. . . .
While culture and language differences are crucial considerations in the education of the Latino child, racism, poverty, and political powerlessness continue to play a central role in shaping the poor educational outcome of the
schools in these communities.

Task Force on the Education of Children and Youth at Risk, 1996

This constant reference to the inadequate provision of a quality education to
the children of the city's poor and minority families has been at the center of
political debates in New York for much of the last thirty years, yet little has
changed in all that time, and the city still spends less per pupil ($8,171 in
1997) than New York State ($9,321) or any of the city's surrounding coun-
ties (e.g., Westchester, Nassau, and Suffolk counties, which all spent more
than $11,500 per pupil in 1997). In the following quote, taken from an an-
nual report on the state of New York City's children, the authors detail some
of the educational "outcomes":

New York City public elementary and middle school students learn in difficult conditions, including schools that are overcrowded and dangerous. . . .
Instead of full-time teachers, temporary per diem teachers teach many students in elementary and middle schools. These conditions lead to more than
half of the students in New York City not being able to read at grade level,
and 4 of every 10 students unable to do mathematics at grade level. . . . High
school dropout rates remain problematic especially among Latino(a) students, nearly 21 percent of whom dropped out of high school in 1997. . . .
For those who graduated, the four-year rate decreased from 51 percent in
1993 to 48 percent in 1997, and the percentage of students graduating in five
to seven years increased from 19 to 36 percent.

The Citizens' Committee for the Children of New York, 1999:11

These descriptions of the learning environment for so many Latino children,
more than thirty years after the Bakke decision on separate but equal education, obviously point to a troubling picture for both present and future generations. But the level of the crisis is particularly acute when we consider that
in 1996, 53.6 percent of adult Puerto Ricans (i.e., over 25 years of age) had
not earned a high school diploma, while 19 percent had experienced no high
school at all; and among Dominicans, 54.7 percent had no diploma and 25
percent had less than high school (U.S. Dept. of Commerce 1997).[14] Further,
looking at the higher end of the educational attainment mill, the overall status of both groups is just as dismal. The percentages in 1996 of those with at

least a college education among different ethnic groups were as follows: Puerto Ricans, 7.2 percent; Dominicans, 4 percent; African-Americans, 10.1 percent; and whites, 37 percent. Thus, white New Yorkers were more than five times as likely to be attending college than Puerto Ricans and eight times as likely as Dominicans, which highlights the degree to which these two groups can successfully compete in a labor market increasingly dominated by knowledge-based industries. At the same time, however, we should not dismiss the level of educational motivation that still persists in both communities despite the social, economic, and cultural difficulties. According to New York City student surveys, almost 70 percent of Dominicans provided responses that showed high levels of interest in their schooling (Hernández and Rivera-Batiz 1997), while between 1976 and 1996, the number of Latinos enrolled in undergraduate education nationwide increased by 202 percent (Puerto Rican/Hispanic Task Force 2001), compared to 13 percent for whites and 44 percent for African-Americans.

While the occupational status of many Dominicans is heavily skewed toward blue-collar professions and low- and unskilled jobs, compared to other ethnic groups in the city, Puerto Ricans have moved away from their lower occupational designation: "heavy reliance on unskilled and semi-skilled manufacturing jobs, the historical hallmark of Puerto Rican employment, is no longer apparent" (New York City Department of Planning 1994). Thus, in 1990, 18.6 percent of Latinos and 25.7 percent of Dominicans were involved in manufacturing, compared to 10.9 percent of whites and 8.2 percent of African-Americans; and in the trade sector, the Latinos made up 22.5 percent of the work force compared to the Dominicans' 27.6 percent, whites' 17.9 percent, and African-Americans' 14.1 percent (Hernández and Rivera-Batiz 1997).

This racial-ethnic segmentation of the work force can be partially explained by the varying levels of educational opportunities available to different ethnic groups; the types of cultural capital each generation infuses in its offspring; the city's long history of racial and ethnic discrimination in hiring (preventing many Latinos/as from acquiring union jobs in the building trades, the fire department, the police, and so on); the point of entry for the immigrant group vis-à-vis the host society's economic needs; and the many factors that promote or impede rates of assimilation. Whatever the differences in occupational mobility at the bottom, both groups found it extremely difficult to penetrate positions at the top. In 1990, 13 percent of Puerto Ricans were in managerial and professional positions compared to 29 percent for the rest of the city, whereas in 1997, only 8.4 percent of Dominicans were in managerial or executive occupations compared to 30.2 percent for the overall population of New York (Hernández and Rivera-Batiz 1997; New York City Department of Planning 1994).

By the middle to late 1990s, despite the longest economic boom in postwar history, the life chances for many Puerto Ricans and Dominicans were still grim. In 1996, 44.8 percent of Puerto Ricans and 45.7 percent of Dominicans were still living in households below the poverty line (U.S. Department of Commerce 1996; Hernández and Rivera-Batiz 1997) compared to 31.1 percent of African-Americans and 11.6 percent of whites. While the 1990s saw a decrease in the rates of poverty for nearly all ethnic groups, for Dominicans, the reverse was the case, with the poverty rate increasing almost 10 percent during the years 1989–1996 (Hernández and Rivera-Batiz 1997). Nonetheless, whether income levels for adults went up marginally or not, the risks of poverty for Latino/a children in general remained staggeringly high (see table 1.1 below).

TABLE 1.1   Comparative Rates of Child Poverty Across New York City Ethnic Groups

Indicator	African-American	Latino/a	Asian	White
Children born into poor families	58.3%	73.1%	47.8%	20.1%
Children (0–17 years) below poverty	51.0%	59.8%	DNA	12.2%

Citizens' Committee for Children of New York, Inc. 1999.

Imprisonment

A close examination of the Bureau of Justice Statistics shows that Hispanics constituted the fastest growing minority group in prison from 1980 to 1993. Confirming this finding, Donziger (1996:104) states that "the proportion of inmates of Hispanic origin increased from 7.7 percent to 14.3 percent and the rate of imprisonment for Latinos/as more than tripled, from 163 to 529 prison inmates per 100,000 Latino/a residents." During the last twenty years the prison population of New York State has gone from approximately 22,000 in 1980 to 71,500 in 1999, an increase of more than 300 percent.[15]

Among the major factors behind the prison explosion are: the draconian Rockefeller Drug Laws of 1973; the "get tough on crime" platforms of both Democratic and Republican politicians; the "war on the poor" (Gans 1995); the prison-industrial complex (Wacquant 1998; Parenti 1999); the crusade against youth, particularly youth of color (Correctional Association of New York 2000); endemic and increased racism of the criminal justice system (Miller 1996); and the sentencing counter-revolution (Donziger 1996). In a recent summary of inmates' needs, it was found that 14 percent of incoming female prisoners and 5 percent of incoming males are infected with HIV; 23 percent of incoming female inmates and 14 percent of incoming males have hepatitis C; 75 percent of inmates are self-reported substance abusers; 11 percent of inmates have been diagnosed as "significantly, seriously, or persistently mentally ill"; and more than 50 percent lack a high school diploma or equivalent degree (Correctional Association 2002). Bearing in mind the often appalling physical and mental state of many inmates, the ending of many educational and vocational programs for inmates, and the ever-increasing use of disciplinary housing (approximately 8 percent of inmates are kept in solitary conditions), it should not be surprising that the recidivism rate is around 50 percent, which means that approximately 15,000 inmates will be back in prison within three years of their release.

The Sample

What follows are some of the basic demographics and characteristics of our "snowball" (Biernacki and Waldorf 1981) and "selective" (Lincoln and Guba 1985) sample of sixty-seven respondents. This empirical summary is based on life history interviews with each of the subjects. Later, in chapter 8, we provide a more thorough analysis and interpretation of four of these background areas: family, school, street life, and prison.

Age, Race, and Ethnicity

The ages of the Kings and Queens in the sample ranged from as young as fourteen to as old as forty-eight years. Based on observations of the group as a whole, the majority were between sixteen and twenty-one years old approximately, which is in accord with many other studies of street youth cultures (see Curry and Decker 2003[16]) in which youth are the dominant age group. As explained earlier, those members of the group under eighteen were members of the Pee Wees, i.e., the coeducational youth section of the organization, which had its own leadership, meetings, and activities. At the same time, there was a substantial number of older members, i.e., people in their thirties and forties, which reflects what Moore has called the quasi-institutional role that gangs have come to play in communities ravaged by high rates of incarceration and disinvestment.

Correlated with the age of the members seemed to be the length of time they had been in the organization. Of the members less than eighteen years old, only three Kings and one Queen had been involved for more than twelve months. Among sample members in their twenties, approximately half had been in the organization for more than a year.

In terms of ethnicity, eighteen respondents, i.e., just over 25 percent of the total sample, were born outside of the United States with equal numbers (seven) born in Puerto Rico or the Dominican Republic. The category "other" included such Latin American countries as Mexico, Ecuador, and Guatemala. In contrast, the parents of these first- and second-generation children were born mostly outside the U.S. mainland, with thirty-seven born in Puerto Rico and ten born in the Dominican Republic. With the majority of the sample coming from the first generation, it is not surprising that only four respondents stated that they spoke little Spanish, and only two self-identified as "American" (one male and one female), with the rest identifying themselves as Nuyorican, Puerto Rican, Dominican, or "mixed" (i.e., Black and Hispanic, Puerto Rican and Dominican, or Puerto Rican and Italian). The preponderance of members in the group from relatively recently immigrated families accords well with the early writings of Thrasher (1927), who found many immigrant youth among the gangs of Chicago's interstitial inner city.

TABLE 1.2 Ages of Respondents

	Ages 14–18	19–25	Above 26 Years Old
Kings	15	14	10 (oldest 41 yrs old)
Queens	6	17	5 (oldest 45 yrs old)

TABLE 1.3 Respondents' National Birth Place

	United States	Puerto Rico	Dominican Rep.	Other
Kings	25	3	7	4
Queens	24	4	–	–

TABLE 1.4 **Parents' Birth Place**

	United States	Puerto Rico	Dominican Rep.	Other
Kings	M 3 F 4	M 17 F 18	M 5 F 5	M 3 F 3
Queens	M 6 F 4	M 18 F 14	M 4 F 5	–

Family and Residence

Perhaps counterintuitively, a two-parent family situation was the dominant type for most of the sample, although a one-parent family, some kind of guardianship, or a group home was the norm for 40 percent of the respondents. Further, the size of the families for most respondents was quite modest, with most respondents reporting only one or two siblings in their household while twelve respondents stated that they came from relatively large families with four or more children.

In terms of residentiality, the data are much closer to what one might assume. Nearly all the respondents reported growing up in one of the barrios or ghettos of New York City, among them the Lower East Side, East Harlem, and Washington Heights in Manhattan; Bushwick and East New York in Brooklyn; Jackson Heights in Queens; and Mott Haven and Morrisania in the Bronx. Twenty-nine described particularly high rates of residential mobility, moving both within and between low-income neighborhoods in New York, and some ten respondents reported frequent travel between Puerto Rico or the Dominican Republic and the U.S. mainland. In other descriptions and recollections of their immediate environment, forty-five said that they lived for most of their lives in neighborhoods where interpersonal violence and drug use were common, while only eight regarded their neighborhoods either in the past or the present as relatively safe (all females reported drugs and/or violence in their local environment).

Education and Social Class

As might be expected with respondents from backgrounds of little economic and cultural capital, schooling was viewed as a mixed blessing and for many, especially the males, it was difficult to stay through the twelfth grade. Not only did a number of respondents (see chapter 9) express a mutual disinterest in school as a socializing institution, but dramatic changes in their

TABLE 1.5 **Types of Family for Respondents**

	Two Parents	One Parent	Guardians/ Grandparents/ Relatives	Group Home/ Foster Care
Kings	18 (plus 3 with stepfathers/mothers	11 (10 M, 1F)	3	2
Queens	13 (plus 2 with stepfathers/stepmothers)	9 (8 M, 1F)	2	1

life circumstances could also end their school career prematurely, e.g., imprisonment, the death of a parent, sudden decline in family finances, etc. While the dearth of educational attainments among the respondents would be in keeping with findings in most of the literature, some respondents showed another side that is more atypical of youths in street subcultures. For, as we see below in table 1.6, a high number of Kings were still in school, and most of these were in "good standing." Further, more than twice as many Queens graduated from high school than dropped out, and almost 20 percent of the respondents were either attending college or had received some kind of college-level instruction (see table 1.7).

TABLE 1.6 **Educational Backgrounds of Respondents**

	In School	Graduated H.S.	Dropped Out	GED
Kings	11	12	16 (6 reached 8th grade)	2
Queens	3	18	7	3

Not surprisingly, the vast majority of Kings and Queens, according to descriptions of their own economic status during their youth, were from the lower or lowest socioeconomic groups, with only ten respondents describing the material conditions in which they were raised as "comfortable" or "well off" (see table 1.8).

In social class terms, this would designate most of the sample as working-class, which is also borne out in the blue-collar occupational statuses of most of their parents (see table 1.9), who worked as building superintendents, construction workers, taxi drivers, factory hands, and correctional officers. It is worth noting that in comparison to several recent gang studies, this sample

TABLE 1.7 **Types of Educational Institution Respondents Attended**

	Public School	Private School (including Catholic)	Both	Other	College
Kings	33	1	1	4	6
Queens	18	7	3	–	6

TABLE 1.8 **Descriptions of Economic Standing During Childhood**

	Poor/Very Poor	Getting By	Comfortable/Well Off
Kings	22	12	5
Queens	12	11	5

TABLE 1.9 **Occupational Status of Parent(s)**

	Blue Collar	White Collar	Unemployed	Welfare	Armed Forces
Kings	M 13 F 21	M 1 F 2	F 1	M 4	M 1 F 1
Queens	M 10 F 8	M 4 F 3		M 3	F 3

TABLE 1.10 **Occupational Status of Respondents**

	Blue Collar	White Collar	Other	None	Unemployed	Welfare	Disability
Kings	16	5	9		7	–	2
Queens	12	5	–	4		7	

group does not contain a significantly large number of prototypically underclass youth and adults. In data on the parents provided by the respondents, only seven described them as "on welfare," while among the total of sixty-seven respondents, seven males described themselves as "unemployed" and seven females described themselves as "on welfare."[17] Thus, more than half of the sam-

TABLE 1.11   **Self-reported Criminal Histories of Respondents**

	Arrested	Not Arrested	Juvenile Inst.	Adult Inst.
Kings	24	7	2	16
Queens	11	17	5	3

TABLE 1.12   **Most Severe Self-reported Criminal Charges**

	Murder	Attempted Murder	Robbery	Drug Assault	Sales	Possession of Weapon	Shop-lifting	Status Offense
Kings	1	1	4	3	14	1	–	–
Queens	–	–	2	1	5	–	2	1

ple were gainfully employed not only in blue-collar jobs like their fathers and mothers but also in white-collar occupations. Among these were bank telling and retail assistants (for females), and computer programming, nonprofit management, counseling, school security, and car maintenance (for males).

Criminal History

Of the Kings who answered questions on their criminal histories (one could argue that the eight that refused to answer were somewhat guarded about revealing their past), the majority said that they had been arrested at least once, compared to a minority of the Queens who declared the same. This accords with other studies of street subcultures and gangs, where the vast majority of male respondents have been processed by the criminal justice system at least once while females have generally been able to remain free of a criminal record. Further, in line with more recent studies, drug sales are the primary reason for arrest in both males and females. However, unlike some other studies, homicide is only self-reported in one case, which indicates either that: (1) the respondents were not being truthful, (2) New York City intergroup rivalry was less intense and less deadly than in other cities,[18] and/or (3) the extraterritorial basis of the ALKQN and its conflict-resolution skills were keeping violent incidents to a minimum.

Method of Joining the Organization

As in many other studies of street subcultures, respondents came into the organization via a variety of institutional contexts and social networks. For the Kings, the favored entree was through a male friend who was already in the Nation or through the enforced social relationships developed in prison. The Queens, on the other hand, mostly came into the group via male members of their family, be it an uncle, cousin, brother, or spouse.[19] These are important gender differences and, in many respects, show the increasing influence of incarceration on collective street behavior for males and the overarching role of the family for females (see chapter 9). In addition, thirty respondents, almost half of the sample, reported that they had multiple family members in the organization.

TABLE 1.13 **Respondents' Introductions into the Group**

	Nonmember Friend	Family	Member Friend	Other (e.g., in Prison)
Kings	6	6	13	14
Queens	–	18	7	3

The Issues

Above we have summarized how the study came into existence and introduced the reader to our methodological approach and the basic demographic characteristics of the sample. In the final section of this chapter, we delineate the major issues that the book attempts to address and highlight some of the leading arguments we will be making throughout. We have divided them into the following themes: (1) seeking an alternative definition of "the gang"; (2) the social movement possibilities of gang members; (3) the form and content of gang reforms; (4) societal reactions to the group's transformation; and (5) lessons from this case study.

Seeking an Alternative Definition of the Gang

An early, process-based definition of the gang, which dominated the literature during its infancy, is contained in the pioneering work of Frederic Thrasher (1927:46). He described the phenomenon as: "an interstitial group originally formed spontaneously and then integrated through conflict. . . . The result of this collective behavior is the development of tradition, unreflective internal structure, esprit de corps, solidarity, morale, group awareness, and attachment to a local territory." In more recent times, a favored or influential definition (Bursik and Grasmick 1996) emerges from Klein's early work (1971:13) where he describes a street gang as "any identifiable group of youngsters who (a) are generally perceived as a distinct aggregation by others in their neighborhood, (b) recognize themselves as a denotable group (almost invariably with a group name), and (c) have been involved in a sufficient number of delinquent incidents to call forth a consistent negative response from neighborhood residents and/or law enforcement agencies." In our view, both definitions are tied to notions of middle-class rule-breaking and fail to take into account the dynamic social, cultural, spiritual, and political trajectory of some contemporary street subcultures. As an alternative, we have developed the following definition of a street organization as:

A group formed largely by youth and adults of a marginalized social class which aims to provide its members with a resistant identity, an opportunity to be individually and collectively empowered, a voice to speak back to and challenge the dominant culture, a refuge from the stresses and strains of barrio or ghetto life, and a spiritual enclave within which its own sacred rituals can be generated and practiced.

In table 1.14 (see also Brotherton 1999), we compare the period during which most of the Latin Kings would have self-identified as gang members with the period during which the group was attempting to foster a new image and create a new praxis.

The Social Movement Possibilities of Gang Members

Based on our analysis of the data covering the period from 1996 to 1999, we found that both individual gang members and the group itself were clearly on the path toward the creation of a social movement. The group, therefore, was in transition, i.e., moving from the gang world—complete with its secret codes of loyalty, involvement in inter- and intragroup violence, and underground economic practices—to a set of behaviors and goals, such as voter registration and culture classes, that befit a postindustrial social movement. This transitional process, however, was never a smooth one, particularly since there is and was a dynamic tension between the older, prison-based members who joined a gang on the "inside" (i.e., prison) and those younger members who

TABLE 1.14 **A Comparison of Street Organizations and Gangs**

	Street Organizations	Gangs
Period	1996-	1985–1995
Structure	vertical with increasing level of decentralization	vertical with limited level of local autonomy
Territory	extra-territorial	situationally territorial
Ideology	communitarian/utopian/spiritual	street survivalism/entrepreneurial/cultish
Education	pro-school rhetorically and in practice	anti-school in practice but rhetorically pro-school
Delinquency	although some individuals do engage in delinquency, this is not sanctioned by the group	rhetorically anti-delinquent but high tolerance in practice
Conflict management	mostly negotiation and mediation in inter- and intra-group conflicts with physical solutions as a last resort	negotiation and mediation used but confrontational and retributional solutions to inter- and intra-group conflict are common
Attire	beads and colors often situationally displayed	colors universally displayed and also artifacts of conspicuous consumption
Integration	high solidarity maintained through moral and political group pressure	loyalty maintained through physical threats and group pressure
Duration	long-term commitment; exiting and entering the group through signed mutual consent	long-term commitment; entering through mutual consent, exiting more difficult and may include physical penalties
Communication	local and general meetings; newsletters; face-to-face meetings	local, general, and face-to-face meetings but many decisions made through secret missives

were drawn to the organization specifically because it was different from the typical gangs in their neighborhood. After this period, however, the group lost much of its reformist leadership and, very importantly, the sanctuary of the church where it was meeting. While not returning necessarily to its former "gang" days, the organization did not maintain a social movement momentum that bore out the other side of the group's transitional nature.

We view this dynamic of positive social change in the organization as similar to that of some political movements when there is an abrupt break with the past and new ideas and leadership styles signal a movement's reinvention, e.g., democratic reform movements inside bureaucratized trade unions and political parties. In the case of the ALKQN, it is important to understand: (1) the role of the leadership as change agents, and (2) the niche filled by the group as virtually the only political force left in the barrio that had not given up on the "incorrigibles," and the educational "failures."

In terms of what lay behind this development, we point to a confluence of factors: (1) the involvement of radical intellectuals, (2) the evolution of new leadership strata, (3) the prison-to-street trajectory that avoids parochial turf wars, (4) the political development of and demands of the female members, (5) the coexistence of an anticolonial consciousness in the barrio, and (6) the absence of any radical, alternative, political and social movements for the Latino/a working class.

The Form and Content of Gang Reforms

The group ended many of the punitive disciplinary procedures that were used to bind the organization in an obsessive and parochial fashion. Turning its attention to the substantive problems of its members, it set about mobilizing its abundant human resources. This was done by promoting an educational ethic among school-age members and setting up self-help programs such as tutorial classes, AIDS outreach, Alcoholic Anonymous and Narcotics Anonymous meetings, and domestic violence counseling. While the major changes in the group came from their street members, these changes began to influence the workings of the organization in prison. Although it might be argued that the ALKQN's members were not simply victims of the revolving door of justice but perpetrators of it (i.e., because of their large incarcerated membership), we found that the organization was actively and effectively helping to counteract recidivism.

Societal Reactions to the Group's Transformation

There were diverse reactions to the group's most recent development. From the perspective of many grassroots community movements, the shift of the group was welcomed and supported. However, there were many institutional actors in social control positions who refused to countenance the changes and were skeptical about or dismissive of the group's transformation.

Lessons from This Case Study

It has been a long time since we as a society have learned anything from new and emerging social movements, especially those that originate among the inner-city poor and working classes. One reason for this, as suggested by Finnegan's (1999) concept of "secular consumerism," is that the materialist, corporate culture of the United States effectively obliterates history as a form of consciousness and as a guide to practice. A second reason is the pervasive presence of racism, which misrepresents and invalidates "other" cultures and their modes of resistance. A third reason is that many groups that chart a course of opposition to the mainstream are often issue- and/or identity-based, making them susceptible to co-optation and the fickleness of the media and its public.

Although the reformist era of the ALKQN only lasted a few years, it represented a formidable experiment among the poor and the marginalized. It should not be forgotten that the ALKQN was waging a struggle against the most powerful "establishment" in modern history in an era of welfare-state destruction, rampant anticommunism, and the biggest assault on civil rights legislation since the 1930s. If nothing else, the efforts of the ALKQN and its members are an extraordinary testimony to the poor's collective will and to the indefatigable spirit of youth.

In this chapter we have laid down the groundwork for the rest of the book. Our methodology, based on our interpretation of the practice of critical ethnography, was discussed along with the reasons why we believe this to be the best approach to research of this nature. This was followed by a short description of the sample and many of the demographic characteristics that are to be analyzed more fully in chapter nine. Further, we have highlighted some of the most important issues that a study of this nature brings to the table, as well as some brief answers to questions that have been asked of us during our time in the field.

Much of the rest of the book is devoted to providing a deeper explanation on a number of different levels, using the words and experiences of the subjects to authenticate the interpretation. Finally, we have given the reader an idea of the setting in which the research has taken place. Without this context, the research could have been assumed to have been gathered almost anywhere. On the contrary, in many ways it is specific to a particular time and place, even though the social processes and the principles upon which movements like this take shape are generalizable.

CHAPTER 2

THE THEORY OF GANGS

To come to terms with the evolution of the ALKQN, to explain its appearance and its transformation, requires a rigorous engagement with those theories that purport to provide us with the analytical tools for just such an undertaking. In the event, however, that the dominant paradigms fail to serve our purpose—a predicament similar to what Cohen (1955) refers to as the need for "facts the theory must fit"—then we must search for alternative conceptual schemas to make sense of our data. This process of theoretical testing is similar to the approach of Burawoy (1991), which he describes as the "extended case study approach." In the following discussion, we trace the archaeology of gang theory, first through its initial appearance as an offshoot of juvenile psychology and then through its own sui generis development largely within the discipline of sociology. After making a case for the political shortcomings of historical and contemporary gang theory we will offer an alternative social-movement-based paradigm that more accurately explains what we have witnessed and which is ultimately more useful in the prediction of future trends.

From Delinquent Youth to Delinquent Gangs

The concept of the gang had its roots in Scottish and meant "a walk for cattle." Later, in old English, it became more actively applied to group formation as in "a number going in or forming a company, as a gang of sailors." Quite clearly from these two early definitions the term is tied to the historical context; that is, an agricultural society in the first definition and a mercantile society in the second. In time, the term "gang" was applied to certain groups of people socially displaced by the industrial revolution in England (Geis 1960; Sheldon 1997; Thompson 1963), as in "a company of persons acting together for some purpose, usually criminal, as a gang of thieves." And finally, "gang" becomes used in conjunction with another type of political and economic society, as in "a group of persons associated under the same direction, as a gang of slaves." Therefore, the etymology of the word "gang" clearly illustrates the importance of understanding the materialist culture from which the word arises in any particular epoch. This is as true of the term's usage in the eighteenth century as it is in the 1990s.

By the turn of the century, "the gang" had already been well established in Europe as a peculiarly pejorative term for a group and its behavior. Meanwhile, in the United States, a similar negative label was also being attached to the gang phenomenon. After first being used to describe groups of slaves for sale in North American auction houses, the term "gang" was then used to describe professional collectives of working-class thieves—that is, thugs (Asbury 1927), and adolescent bands or "hoodlums" in the early years of New York City's "rowdy republican universe" (Burrows and Wallace, 1999:998). The first time, however, that "the gang" appears as an analytical concept in narrative descriptions of marginalized youth and deviant subcultures is in the Los Angeles–based work of Bogardus (1926) and the Chicago studies of Thrasher (1927).

The Psychogenic View of Delinquency

It is hard to separate the terms under which youth gangs have been examined sociologically in the United States from the discourse of juvenile delinquency. Historically, discussions of the two subject areas have constantly intersected, and in many ways their governing paradigms have suffered from the same upper- and middle-class white biases that dominate the social sciences in general (Collins 1989; Ladner 1973; Platt 1969; Spitzer 1975; Schlossman 1978).[1]

The most salient early work on the concept of juvenile delinquency is the collection of legendary psychogenic accounts of youth development by G. Stanley Hall (1904). In Hall's now classic two-volume study *Adolescence: Its Psychology and Its Relations to Physiology, Anthropology, Sociology, Sex, Crime, Religion, and Education*, the leading U.S. psychologist of his time argues that storm and stress are the chief impulses in youth development and goes on to assert that adolescents are actually a race apart, similar to the "natives" of the then colonized world.

For all of Hall's legitimated knowledge claims and his "pioneering" work in the field, which were clearly a construction of a biologically determinist mind-set (Gould 1981), he provided little scientific evidence to show that the hormone-bound adolescent, caught between childhood and adulthood, is likely to be any more confused, irrational, or unstable than at any other stage of his/her psychosocial development. Indeed, this narrative of adolescence had more to do with the paternalistic domination of adult society and with the particularistic world-view of the middle-class professional than any physiological laws of nature (see also Coffield, Borrill, and Marshall 1986).

Nonetheless, based on these social-Darwinistic concepts of youth deviance, an impressive array of legislation and bureaucratic apparatuses were rationalized (Platt 1969) and established. In later years, the study of delinquency moved away from the individualized purviews of physiology and psychology to the more social and cultural realms of sociology and, in particular, to studies of the socializing conditions under which youth were being raised.

The Sociology of the Gang

In sociology, street gangs have generally been defined by and compared across the following group characteristics: (1) structure, (2) crime/delinquency, (3) territory, (4) integration/cohesion, (5) conflict, (6) antisocial agenda, and (7) community perceptions (Arnold 1966). Frederic Thrasher (1927) is usually credited with being the first sociologist to study, and to conceive of, the gang as a phenomenon in and of itself and came to define it as: "an interstitial group, originally formed spontaneously, then integrated through conflict" (p. 46).

Thrasher's work, based on the Chicago traditions of empiricism and pragmatism,[2] made a number of sociological assumptions about gangs that have continued to orient the field:

1. Gangs are not necessarily criminogenic units, though they tend to predispose members to lives of crime.
2. Gangs are largely male domains.
3. Gangs are expressive subcultures that range in their degree of sophistication.
4. Street gangs are mainly a working- or lower-class phenomenon, conditioned by the spatial and social ecological development of any given area.
5. Gangs emerge over a competition for scarce economic, social, and political resources.
6. Most gang members experience a nonvalidation of their class and ethnic-racial cultures in schools and other mainstream socializing institutions.
7. Gangs are prominent in areas marked by intergenerational racial and class segregation.

8. Gangs are both products of and contributors to the social disorganization of their communities.
9. The presence of gangs is symptomatic of the lessening of social controls due to or resulting in culture conflict.

Although criminal and/or delinquent deviance was one focus of Thrasher's research, equal if not more emphasis was placed on uncovering the conditions from which gang members emerged. This early emphasis on the environmental factors underlying gang behavior has become an ongoing focus of research, and the results have provided some of the major conceptual thrusts in the study of delinquency since World War II.

To better appreciate the continuity and discontinuity of gang research during the twentieth century, we have constructed table 2.1, in which we have divided the study of gangs into four time periods:[3] 1920–30s, 1950–60s, 1970–80s, and 1990s (there were no studies of gangs in the 1940s). For each time frame, we have located several major conceptual and theoretical approaches that dominated the research approach to street gangs. Below, we briefly survey each of these periods and discuss some of the leading ideas that typified each of the approaches.

1920s and 1930s: Disorganization, Conflict, and Strain

Thomas and Znaniecki's (1920) early work on the acculturation of Polish peasants to the urban environment of Chicago first gave rise to the notion of

TABLE 2.1 Periods and Paradigms of Gang Research

1920s and 1930s	1950s and 1960s	1970' and 1980s	1990s
*Social disorganization (e.g., Shaw and McKay 1969 (orig. 1942)	*Subcultural theory (Cohen 1955, Miller 1958)	*The theory of the underclass (Moore 1978, 1991; Vigil 1988; Hagedorn 1988; Taylor 1990; Padilla 1993; Huff 1991; Jankowski 1991; Anderson 1990; Klein 1995)	*Social and economic contingency (Sullivan 1989, Venkatesh 1997, 2000)
*Cultural conflict (e.g., Thrasher 1927)	*Opportunity structure (Cloward and Ohlin 1960)		
*Strain theory (Merton 1938, 1949)	*Labeling theory (Werthman 1969)		
	*Near-group theory (Yablonsky 1963)		

social disorganization in sociological literature. Rejecting both the individu-alistic pathological and rational-choice views of deviant behavior, these early practitioners of urban sociology looked to the natural social processes of norms and values to explain nonconformity. In their view, rapid social change brought about by technology, immigration, and urbanization were the chief causes of normative conflict or dissension, which, in turn, led to noncon-forming values and actions. Thus, disorganization was essentially the term given to the disruption of society's imagined equilibrium. For Thrasher, then, the rise of the gang was

> one manifestation of the disorganization incident to cultural conflict among diverse nations and races gathered together in one place and themselves in contact with a civilization foreign and largely inimical to them. At base the problem is one of reconciliating these divergent heritages with each other and with America. If there has been any failure here, it can hardly be laid at the door of the immigrant [Thrasher 1927:154].

However, what happens when society is out of kilter? Can it be self-corrected or does it require major interventions from the outside? In the op-timistic post-World War I opinions of the Chicago School, what was required was a scientific approach to social problems and the application of progres-sive, well-thought-out reforms to bring society back into balance. It is this theory and implicit practice that were embraced by both Thrasher (1927) and Shaw and McKay (1969) in their studies of gangs in the Chicago area.

In time, the gangs would recede as the natural processes of integration combined with the enlightened policies of social control reined in the non-conformists. The gang, therefore, would eventually succumb to social engi-neering even though Thrasher's own data point to the persistence of struc-tural antagonisms in society at large that would undermine the process, e.g., racial segregation and poverty.[4]

A decade or so later, this socially optimistic view of gangs and delinquen-cy (this is certainly so if compared with the current cynicism) was revised when social science began to focus on the hitherto invisibility of the black popula-tion in U.S. cities and beyond (Myrdal 1944; St. Clair and Clayton 1962; Warner 1938 and Cox 1942). This attention to structured and historical con-ditioning was reflected in McKay and Shaw's (1969) reconsideration of ghet-to deviance. Based on their longitudinal empirical studies, McKay and Shaw concluded that social disorganization does not necessarily wane over time but appears both entrenched and systematically enforced. They went on to con-clude that, denied the housing, jobs, and educational opportunities enjoyed by the white "mainstream," communities will develop "traditions" to cope with their deprivations. These traditions will include criminal and gang subcultures which are culturally transferred from generation to generation. In the following, the authors discuss the relationship between the experience of schooling by black adolescents and their eventual recourse to a youth gang:

> If the adolescent fails in school or drops out, or for other reasons finds school's role unsatisfactory or unplayable, he finds himself in an institutional void. He is not wanted in industry or commerce, he is too young for military service, and odd jobs traditionally available to his age group are decreasing in numbers. The problem is complicated enormously by the fact that, where racial or ethnic barriers to employment are encountered, nonparticipation in economic roles may be extended into young adulthood. The result is that youth gangs in the city may include both boys and young men [McKay and Shaw 1939:383].

By the end of the Depression, Robert Merton (1938, 1949) shifted the discussion away from strict concerns about the "settled" versus "unsettled" nature of a community and launched his now classic postulations on societal strain and the resulting emergence of adaptive subcultures. His work, although not formally integrated into gang theory for another decade, provided a sharper focus on the influence of structural properties such as class and, to a lesser extent, race. Influenced by Durkheim's anomie theory, he pointed out that while strains between differentially empowered groups were common to most societies, it was a particular problem in the United States, where members of the lower orders were supposed to be more upwardly mobile, provided they took advantage of institutional opportunities to ascend into the middle classes. The problem, he asserted, was the tension that arises between goals and means, especially when the lower classes do not have the opportunities decreed in myths about the "American Dream."

1950s and 1960s: Subcultures, Opportunities, and Pathology

During the 1950s and 1960s, a number of delinquency theorists followed Merton's lead and reformulated explanations for the continued discontent among urban lower-class youth (Gilbert 1986). Specifically addressing the reemerging gang phenomenon, this time focusing on class and subculture, Cohen (1955) discussed the problem in terms of status frustration and reaction formation, while Miller (1958) conjured up the notion of an alternative value system of the lower-class adolescent. Their work, in part an attempt to address the consternation and fear felt by the United States' white, upper-class Establishment toward the more expressive, multiracial, postwar youth generations,[5] sought to explain how certain working-class youth could be so resistant to their socially assigned roles (see Parsons 1957).

Perhaps reflecting the ascendancy of middle-class conservatism in the postwar United States, Yablonsky (1963) completely dispensed with sociology's more structurally inclined analyses and returned gang theory to the clinical psychological and highly pathological reading of the youth gang participant. His interventionist and research work among New York City street youth led him to conclude that they were so lacking in areas of emotional and cognitive development that they were even incapable of forming the reciprocal social bonds that a gang required. Consequently, the closest they could come to a collective formation was a "near-group" created spontaneously and ephemerally for the purpose of fighting.

In a particularly Mertonian reading of the gang problem, Cloward and Ohlin (1960) returned the discourse back to more traditional sociological territory, claiming that what was being witnessed in delinquency-plagued neighborhoods was none other than attempts by marginalized lower-class and minority youth to seek a way through their blocked opportunities. They argued that the type of subculture that emerges depends on the level of criminal and noncriminal opportunity structures that exist in the community at the time. Cloward and Ohlin (1960) described these ideal typical gangs as criminal, conflict, or retreatist. This new model of delinquency was a theoretical advance over the classical social disorganization explanations, not least because it brought back the race/class dialectic left untheorized by both Thrasher and the "subculturalists."

In many ways, Cloward and Ohlin's early accounts of inner-city youth prefigured a debate that raged around the plight of poor African-American and Chicano youth during the urban rebellions of the 1960s and continues to this day in issues related to the emergence of an "underclass" (Wilson 1987):

> What remains in the community is a residual of "failures"—persons who have not succeeded in the search for higher socioeconomic status. The old forms of social organization begin to break down, and with them opportunities for upward mobility diminish. . . . Once again the young find themselves both cut off from avenues to higher status and free from external restraint. This is a period, then, in which we should expect a resurgence of violent modes of delinquent adaptation [p. 199].

Finally, as the 1960s were drawing to a close, Werthman (1969) began to advance some of the clearest, empirically based descriptions of urban gang behavior from within the labeling perspective (Becker 1963; Tannenbaum

1938). His interactional field studies in San Francisco included the systematic observations of relations between the police and young black gang members. Based on his data, he was able to discern the process by which identities, both deviant and mainstream, were mutually constructed and reinforced, and how the "career paths" of gang youths were first constituted.

1970s and 1980s: The Underclass Debate

With the revolt of the 1960s a distant memory and the myriad experiments at social reform giving way to a conservative revanchism,[6] there emerged a massive increase in the numbers of young people joining gang subcultures. Part of the explanation for this proliferation derived from the development of a class of impoverished and disenfranchised youths and adults who had failed to adapt to the "new times" (see Hall and Jacques 1990) of free market hegemony. This class, identified by Wilson (1987) as an "underclass," a term borrowed both from Myrdal (1944) and Glasgow (1981), consisted primarily of urban residents within census tracts where poverty rates exceeded 40 percent (Wilson 1987). For Wilson, the extent of the underclass was determined by four variables: (1) the out-migration of the middle class, (2) the shift in industrial modes from manufacturing to service, (3) the segregation of minorities, and (4) the failure of the educational system. In short order, not least because of the ideological war being waged on the poor, the underclass notion took on a life of its own, both in social-scientific and popular media discourses (Acland 1995).[7] But what was its explicit relationship to the gang phenomenon?

While the underclass literature has many contributors, we discuss two related though distinct perspectives grouped under the umbrella terms: (1) gangs as oppositional institutions, and (2) gangs as integrative organizations.

Gangs as Oppositional Institutions

In their analyses of gangs in the "postindustrial" era, Hagedorn (1988), Moore (1988), and others[8] see in the underclass the main reason behind the "astounding proliferation of U.S. street gangs" (Klein 1995:205) during the late 1980s and early 1990s. In their various studies, they have noted how members of this class could find their only economic recourse in welfare and/or crime, particularly in the burgeoning illicit drug market (e.g., Bourgois 1995; Barrios and Curtis 1998b; Inciardi 1990), which perfectly complemented the cultural and social support networks that came from the expanding worlds of street gangs. The underclass paradigm was applied both to young inner-city blacks in the rust belts of the Midwest and to Latinos/as in the so-called booming metropolises of the West. Nonetheless, despite the different populations to whom the phenomenon is applied, the result is similar: underclass gang subcultures reproduce behaviors and value systems that are in opposition to those of the dominant culture.

Commenting both on the Chicano gangs of East Los Angeles and on their African-American counterparts in Milwaukee, Moore (1991) contrasts contemporary gangs to those of the past using the underclass as a primary marker of difference:

> It is also important to remember that these [contemporary gangs] are overwhelmingly black and Hispanic youth. They are not the ethnic Europeans of the gangs of the 1920s, whose marginality lasted only one generation. Nor are they the working-class youth of so many studies, but rather they are increasingly a fraction of the urban underclass. In short, when we talk about gangs we are talking about quasi-institutionalized structures within the poorer minority communities.

Gangs as Integrative Organizations

In contrast to the exclusionary and somewhat pathological interpretation of the gang-underclass relationship above, a more positive reading of the same concept is provided by Jankowski (1991). Based on his multisite, bicoastal field research spanning more than ten years, Jankowski concludes that enduring gangs: (1) are first and foremost sophisticated organizations rationally responding to economic and social deprivation, (2) are fully integrated into the community, and (3) manage to contain their members' defiant individualist characters. In Jankowski's definitional terms, a gang is distinguished from other delinquent groups to the extent that it is: "an organized social system that . . . plans and provides not only for the social and economic services of its members, but also for its own maintenance as an organization" (1991:29).

Thus, according to Jankowski, the key to a gang's longevity is the strength of its dialectical relationship with the community. If the gang consistently goes against the accepted norms of the local neighborhood, then the residents will no longer tolerate the gang's operations and will begin to provide intelligence reports to antigang law enforcement agencies and generally be complicit in the state's attempts to eradicate the group. In other words, the neighborhood engages in a kind of cost-benefit analysis and decides that despite the range of gang-related services (i.e., protection, illicit economic access, sponsored social gatherings, and so on), the payoff is not worth it.

1990s: Gangs as Social and Economic Actors in the "New World Order"?

By the end of the 1980s, some researchers saw a tendency toward cultural and economic determinism in gang studies using the underclass concept as if it were a catchall variable. If the underclass concept was to retain its explanatory power it needed to be constantly reexamined in light of changing local, national, and global conditions; analyzed as part of a contingent and reflexive relationship between gangs and the external society; and set alongside the agency of social actors. Two researchers who approached these issues with perhaps the most thoroughgoing theoretical critique, recognizing that more grounded questions needed to be asked about the gang-underclass connection, were Sullivan (1989) and Venkatesh (1997, 2000).

Sullivan's research, based on ethnographic data from comparative samples of delinquent White, Black, and Latino/a youth in three New York City neighborhoods, employed a range of analytical paradigms to disentangle the complex forms of delinquency in different economic and social terrains. Combining Cloward and Ohlin's (1960) abstract theory of opportunity structure with two "nonmainstream bodies of economic theory" (Sullivan 1989:10)—namely, segmented labor theory and redistributionist theory—Sullivan concluded that the criminal career paths of his subjects were: "the collective choices of those in similar structural situations who refuse to accept the impossible contradictions of these situations" (1989:247).

But what explained the different forms of group-based delinquency across different neighborhoods? To answer this question Sullivan looked at the intersection of formal and informal economies and concluded that a range of local economic and social forces mediate between individuals and their surrounding structures which provide marginalized youth with different options for collectively coping with external constraints.

Venkatesh (1997), in a different though related vein, argues that certain contemporary gangs in Chicago, far from settling for their fatalistic trajectory into the annals of local outlaw legend, have also actively engaged the American Dream in the ghetto with varying levels of success. In his study of black gangs in a housing project, he describes their myriad efforts to respond to their social and economic disenfranchisement of the ruling classes through their own forms of illicit capital accumulation, and through joining with other community associations to enhance the quality of life of their impoverished neighborhood. He describes this process as corporatization, a term he uses to describe the range of interdependency in the economic and social relationships between the gang and the community. But Venkatesh's major contribution is his novel analysis of the way the community is reconstituted through a process that he calls "built social space" (see Lefebvre 1971).

From the previous discussion, we would expect gang theory to be developing much in line with the constant emphases on structural conditioning and marginalizing contexts in sociological gang research as it has throughout most of this century. Yet the relationship between gangs and delinquency has emerged as the central, if not the only focus of inquiry in funded research at the turn of the millennium. This viselike grip that crime has had on the sociological and criminological imagination is not new (Goode 1984), but it has taken many contemporary gang studies further and further away from the more social, problem-based concerns of earlier researchers. As Bursik and Grasmick (1996:11) have commented: "The implications of this shift in focus are much more important than they may first appear, for illegal behavior is considered to be a definitional aspect of gang activity, whereas for Thrasher it was an empirical question."

Consequently, current trends in criminological gang research—while continuing to address important issues such as the dynamics of delinquent gang processes, rates and variations in gang delinquency, the economic determination of the delinquent gang milieux, and the specific contextual properties of neighborhoods in gang delinquency—have paid relatively little attention to questions of political substance. Thus, there is a signal failure to discuss what might be called the "political possibilities" of gangs, which include such issues as: spirituality in gang culture; the making and remaking of resistant subcultures over time; the role of capitalist schooling in a gang member's identity; and the struggle by gangs for spatial and social autonomy.[9] In the next chapter, we will discuss these "oversights" in the criminological literature and embark on the next stage of our theoretical journey, advancing beyond the borders of criminology and into the turf of social movements theory.

CHAPTER 3

POLITICS AND GANGS

Rather than the withering away of gangs as their ethnic group assimilates and joins the middle class, gangs stabilize as different kinds of social, economic, and political structures within an immobile community. Gangs in late modernity don't go away, they become part of the landscape.

Hagedorn 2001:103

It is perhaps surprising that, while so much has been written on the liberal-humanistic side of the causation debate, little has been forthcoming on the political capacity of gangs to actually change their environment and thereby, to use a Marxian argument, change themselves. In the following, we offer an alternative theoretical approach to the study of "street organizations" (see chapter 1). By this term we primarily mean that gangs and gang members can be (1) change agents as well as adaptive social animals/groups in the world of highly unequal power relations, and (2) active repositories of knowledge of sociocultural resistance as well as reproducers of the dominant cultural value system. To make this analysis, we first review the orthodox criminological literature on gang politics, before moving to a treatment of gangs in the area of performance studies, and finally to social movements theory.

The Delinquent Gang and the End of Politics

There are six themes that run consistently through the gang-politics discussion in the research literature. Below, we have delineated these arguments which together form a consensus that gang members cannot remain members of their own subculture and consciously oppose the dominant culture and its structural foundations.

Gangs as Goon Squads

The political boss finds gangs . . . ingratiates himself by means of money for camping, uniforms . . . children's picnics . . . to "get him in good" with potential voters . . . . To repay the politician for putting gang members on official pay-rolls, and providing subsidies, protection, and immunities from official interference, the gang often splits . . . the proceeds of its illegitimate activities; controls for him the votes of its members . . . and performs for him various types of "work" at the polls, such as slugging, intimidation, vandalism (tearing down signs), ballot fixing, repeating, stealing ballot boxes [Thrasher 1927:452, 477; quoted in Spergel 1995:121].

The preceding classic formulation of Thrasher[1] sums up most considerations of gangs and their relationship to politics. Basically, gangs have been viewed as the pliant tools of corrupt, powerful city players of machine politics. When required, gang members can be brought in to perform criminal acts that can be plausibly denied by the true conspirators. Then, just as quickly, the low-level thugs-for-hire can be summarily dismissed from the scene, usually after election time or some other period of intense political competition. This function of the gang in interethnic and spoils-driven politics has persisted throughout much of the literature until recently, when gangs after the 1970s have rarely been considered as political entities at all (as an exception see Whyte [1943]). Jankowski (1991) offers two explanations for this: one is that the political machines of the cities disappeared or lost much of their former influence, and the second is that gang studies have nearly always focused on working-class adolescents who have never been particularly associated with politics, even in the so-called youth decade of the 1960s.

Gangs, Politics, and the Mass Society

In Jacobs's seminal study (1977) of an Illinois prison during the late 1960s and early 1970s, he witnessed the introduction of Chicago street gangs into the facility. Adopting the methodological case study approach of the Chicago school and the analytical framework of "the mass society," Jacobs set about tracing the prison's movement in society from "the periphery to the center." For Jacobs, central to understanding this shift was the relationship between two value systems: that of the organization of the inmates and that of the institution. One of the most important findings in Jacobs' work is his description of new forms of prisoner self-organization that he called the supergangs.

> Not only are the supergangs larger and more violent than their predecessors of the past several decades, but their location at the intersection of the civil rights movement, the youth movement, and a reconstructed relationship between the federal government and grassroots society suggests a divergence from the traditional street gang [p. 139].

While Jacobs was careful to point out the historical juncture in which the contemporary prison system was emerging, he could find little in the massive contradictions that were unsettling the social order of the day to thwart the ultimate return to institutional equilibrium, not even the "supergangs." Thus, outside their embrace of black radical rhetoric, what he calls a "justificatory vocabulary" (see Miller 1976), the supergangs were incapable of mounting a truly oppositional force to society's structures.

But why was the prison and/or street gang so necessarily doomed to reproduce itself and the oppressive structures from which it emerged? The key to this question lay in the conceptual straitjacket of the status system, an argument that will be repeated until the present day:

> To the extent that the gang structure provides a status system for its membership, there exists a highly vested interest in its perpetuation for its own sake. Radical politics requires commitment to transcendent values and leaves less opportunity for achieved status for the average youth. Gang leaders from these organizations think less of acting on behalf of their neighborhoods than acting on behalf of their membership [1977:145].

The Underclass Gang Will Not Be Party to the Revolution

In concurring, for the most part, with Jacobs (above), a number of researchers have distanced themselves from the notion that the gang under any circumstances can be viewed as a "progressive" political entity and, in fact, may exhibit tendencies that are more in common with conservative and even counter-revolutionary groups. These researchers, for all their diversity, tend to view the gang as primarily an underclass phenomenon and hence its class nature and its alienation from most community structures preclude it from acting in behalf of broader community interests.

Moore, for example, found that while Chicano gangs in Los Angeles have continued to be socially opposed to white, middle-class cultural value systems, they have not developed into a social or political orientation that reflects the objective interests of their members' subaltern race and class locations. Similarly, in Milwaukee, Hagedorn (1988) also found an apolitical current prominent among the members of the mainly black gangs in his research: "Gangs of the 1980s are rebellious, but they are quite unlike the civil rights organizations of the 1960s. Milwaukee gangs have caused some serious harm to their communities" (p. 144) and "we believe gangs have a rebellious aspect, but the rebellion, unlike the 'class consciousness' or 'racial solidarity' predicted by Cloward and Ohlin, is often cynical and directed against the gang's own community" (p. 164).

This consensus is shared by almost all other underclass-gang theorists although their central explanations for the apolitical nature of gangs and gang members varies. Some, like Klein (1995), argue that the gang is too inherently *unstable* and that gang members are too tied to a pathological gang culture. Others, such as Short (1967), saw and continue to see gangs as simply *indifferent* to politics.

While most of these aforementioned researchers see little evidence of any political potential in gangs, there are other researchers who argue that the politics that do exist among these subcultures are not radical but conservative, a finding that is consistent with the underclass view that gang members' consciousness is either lacking or "false."[2] One variant of this perspective was presented by Oscar Lewis in his research on the Puerto Rican poor during the 1950s. Although his work was not focused on youth gangs per se, his argument about the political limitations that emerge from the culture of poverty bears a close resemblance to many "underclass" gang inquiries (see, for example, Campbell 1991):

> My own studies of the urban poor in the slums of San Juan do not support the generalizations of Fanon.[3] I have found very little revolutionary spirit or racial ideology among low-income Puerto Ricans. On the contrary, most of the families I studied were quite conservative politically and about half of them were in favor of the Republican Statehood Party [Lewis 1965:xlvi].

Finally, Katz (1988) is most explicit in seeing a relationship between what he calls "street elites" and their affinity for fascistic or aristocratic forms of social and political authority.

> The tensions in collective youth deviance are shaped in dialectical relationship to the unspeakable fears in their elders' lives. Thus, middle-class youths represent dirt, the violation of all neat boundaries, lower-class rebellion, insidious

esthetic attacks on the conventions of bourgeois, rule-manipulating, rationality-celebrating classes. In contrast, working-class youths embrace fascist forms that give a surreal, lock-step representation to the mechanical institutional disciplines that threaten to constrain their parents; and ethnic-minority lower-class youths strut in the style of aristocratic authority, acting out a version of historical caste sentiments of humility and indignation that remain vivid for their elders [p. 158].

Gangs Fill a Low-Level Political Void

A gang's primary involvement in politics, according to Spergel, is a result of the social breakdown of a community (i.e., its social disorganization). The connection comes about, he asserts, "at times of crisis" when "gangs act out many of the aspirations, feelings, and legitimate and illegitimate interests of populations in communities that are weakly organized" (1995:120).

In this reading, the contemporary gang inches toward political action almost spontaneously and without history, inexplicably gravitating toward the vacuum left by traditional community and neighborhood organizations which have presumably disintegrated, failed to emerge in the first place, or been left without connections to the resource-granting mainstream. Consequently, where gangs have been observed in political action, such as the Chicago phenomena of the Black Gangster Disciples and their involvement in the grassroots organization during the early 1990s (Muwakkil 2000) or the Vice Lords' relationship with the urban renewal programs of the 1960s (Dawley 1992), it is either because they are the only organized community vehicle remaining with whom outsiders can work, or because they are the only viable force left inside the ghetto that can claim access to informal versions of the "American Dream" (see also Jankowski 1991; Padilla 1992; Spergel 1995; and Venkatesh 1997).

Nonetheless, while there exists a certain potential in gangs for social action, and some even refer to the gang at times as a "social movement" (Spergel 1995:123), there is little theoretical or empirical development of this position. Consequently, the possibility of gangs emerging with their own alternative political, economic, or even cultural agenda is never given serious consideration.

Instrumental Politics and the Community

Jankowski (1991) is one of the few recent researchers, other than Moore (1991) and Jacobs (1977), to discuss the role of politics among his respondents based on empirical data. As part of his general thesis that gangs are part of the overall organization of lower-class communities, Jankowski sees the gang operating politically through a system of what he calls expedient and prudential exchange relations.

In this paradigm, gang relations with street-level politicians and bureaucrats are based on the perceived needs of both parties and come about when politicians require physical and social support at the most grassroots level. However, Jankowksi concludes that gangs cannot go further than what the current consensus of the community demands. Therefore, the gang is unlikely to fulfill any kind of vanguard political role. Rather, much like the findings of Suttles (1968), the gang can play a paradoxical self-regulatory community role in which it is as much a function of equilibrium as it is a cause of disequilibrium.

There Are No Gang Politics in the Absence of a Radical Culture

In the late 1970s, the sociologist Erlanger (1974) argued that the increase in youth gangs was the direct result of the failure of 1960s radical political movements to successfully address the long-term needs of the barrios and ghettos of the USA. To Erlanger, although gang members were a force readily recruited into grassroots political struggles, without an ongoing radical movement that could win concessions and effectively change the balance of power in urban areas, lower-class youth gangs would become mired in parochial turf wars and fail to realize their potential. As Shoemaker (1985) has stated, "it has been seen as an interesting piece of speculation but one that could not be tested empirically." Let us now consider this issue of gang politics by drawing on paradigms that are frequently outside the boundaries of mainstream criminological discourse.

Gangs, Street Performances, and the Moment of Postmodern Resistance

Conquergood's long-term in situ documentation of neighborhood Latin Kings in Chicago has produced a number of highly innovative cultural interpretations of the customs, rituals, and symbolic universes of gang members (Conqergood 1997, 1993, 1992, 1990). Borrowing equally from the British school of cultural resistance studies (i.e., Hall et al. 1978; Hall and Jefferson 1975; Willis 1977), from the labeling theories of Becker (1963), and from the interdisciplinary discourses of performance studies (e.g., Turner 1977; Rosaldo 1989; Clifford 1988; Bakhtin 1981; and Geertz 1983), Conquergood alerts us to the actively produced and reproduced worlds of gangs. For him, gang members are not viewed as typically adapting either fatalistically or pathologically—or even innovatively—to their environment but rather as consciously making their culture in between the structures and crevices of an imposed bourgeois social order. As Conquergood phrases it:

> The homeboys are keenly aware of class difference in communication style, and are critical of what they take to be the tepid, distant, interpersonal mode of the middle class. . . . Against a dominant world that displaces, stifles, and erases identity, the homeboys create, through their communications practices, a hood: a subterranean space of life-sustaining warmth, intimacy, and protection [1993:47].

Conquergood's work stands in direct contrast to the bulk of prior gang studies, not least because he requires us (the author, the observer, the listener, etc.) to unearth the hidden and the opaque and to question our own expert positionality (Rosaldo 1989). In a series of probing questions, Conquergood asks:

> What are the differences between reading an analysis of fieldwork data, and hearing the voices from the field interpretively filtered through the voice of the researcher? For the listening audience of peers? For the performing ethnographer? For the people whose lived experience is the subject matter of the ethnography? What about enabling the people themselves to perform their own experience? [1997:190]

Thus, Conquergood calls upon the research community to see gangs as cultural agents who function both as subjects and objects in their own theater of operations as well as in the gaze of the researcher. For a variety of reasons, however, Conquergood's perspective of gangs is considered heretical, evidenced by the fact that, with the exception of Venkatesh (1997), not a single major gang theorist has seen fit to reference his considerable theoretical and empirical oeuvre![4]

In table 3.1 we have summarized some of these conceptual differences between Conquergood's approach and those of mainstream criminology across the analytical categories of (1) social agency; (2) processes of cultural construction; (3) presumed character of society; and (4) perceived relations between the gang and the community.

In Conquergood's conceptual approach we see the most sophisticated interdisciplinary effort to understand and analyze the multiple meaning systems of gangs. Nonetheless, Conquergood can only accomplish theoretically that which his empirical data allow him to reveal. Thus, while he painstak-

TABLE 3.1   **Comparison Between Conquergood's Approach to Gangs and That of Orthodox Criminology Across Four Analytical Categories**

	(I) Social Agency	(II) Cultural Processes	(III) Character of Society	(IV) Gang-Community Relations
Conquergood	Active, purposive, resistant, empowering, and spatially transformative	Symbolically appropriating from dominant, hostile culture Rational self-articulating Learned in interactions with juveniles and adults Regenerative	Capitalist mode of production, Class- and racial-based hierarchies Coercive apparatuses of bourgeois state control used to exclude, demonize and contain lower class "other"	Organically emergent Contradictory
Orthodox criminology	Adaptive Reproducing itself pathologically	Learned criminal deviance Cultures and subcultures of poverty Apart lower class cultural milieu, mainly juvenile peer-influenced	Nondefined, modern, industrial, disorganized, rapidly changing, naturally poverty-producing, transhistorical	Strained with mainstream, reflective of community pathologies, fundamentally anomic

ingly shows how the Latin Kings in Chicago produce an impressive and hitherto unexplored range of symbolic and linguistic resistances, he cannot point to the level of political development we have witnessed with the same group in the New York City area. Therefore, it is to the studies of collective behavior and social movements that we turn for some theoretical guidance.

Social Movements: From Irrationalism and Elite Controls to Postmodern Empowerment

Since gangs have never been considered as a "collective enterprise to establish a new order of life" (Blumer 1971), they have rarely been approached from a social movements perspective. To do so, however, adds not only a much needed historical dimension to the analysis but allows a broader political framework for interpreting group dynamics that is sorely missing from the deviance-centered gang literature. In the following, we will review some of the dominant paradigms in the social movement literature and then focus on three analytical areas that, in many ways, bridge the conceptual gap between the two literatures (i.e., gangs and social movements).

The Classical and Resource Mobilization Models (RM)

In the classical model of movement emergence (Smelser 1962; Kornhauser 1959; Selznick 1960, 1970), oppositional groups are said to arise during specific historical epochs under abnormal structural conditions (usually brought about by rapid social change). These societal tensions undermine the normative workings of pluralist-based societies and have a destabilizing impact on individuals and their attendant psychological states. Under the variations of this classical model, which include mass society, status inconsistency, and structural strain paradigms (McAdam 1982), despite their differences, the processual sequence of movement emergence is remarkably similar.

Thus, according to the classical school, what gives rise to a social movement is not organized individuals seeking political goals related to their perceived common interests but individuals attempting to "manage the psychological tensions of a stressful situation" (McAdam, 1982). This belief in the masses' psychopathological nature is a basic tenet of the classical model and logically leads to the notion that movements of resistance such as those studied by a variety of analysts of the counterculture during the 1950s and 1960s (e.g., Keniston 1960; Flacks 1971; Roszak 1969; Yinger 1982) are an irrational response to opposition and marginalization.

Succeeding the classical school as the dominant social-movements paradigm in the 1970s was the work of so-called resource mobilization theorists (RM). Basing their theories of movement emergence on a more critical appraisal of society, particularly the U.S. version, the RM proponents were convinced that the phenomenon of protest and social unrest was a result of society's elite-centered and elite-maintained contradictions. Their guiding assumptions were that marked differences in access to economic and social power, caused by the elite's hold on interlocking networks of governance, resulted in tactical efforts by the marginalized to gain meaningful inclusion in society. However, they argued, the excluded were so lacking in resources they had little chance of success in challenging the status quo unless the elites intervened and provided them with the support necessary to wage an effective struggle.

This focus on the interplay between identifiable resources, collective movements' strategies, and the responses of the elite provided for a more radical understanding of society's power dynamics than did these classical theorists, who assumed modern capitalistic societies to be pluralistic, self-correcting models of democracy (see Dahl 1970; Schumpeter 1942). Thus, researchers working within the RM approach found society to be mired in a constant state of conflict between the entrenched interests of the powerful and the challenges of the powerless. In fact, they saw these tensions as one of the most salient characteristics of a society, and considered them part of that society's objective conditions.

Nonetheless, for all the RM's improvement on the conservative classical model, it too had a number of flaws. First, it failed (unlike the classical school) to sufficiently weigh the importance of ideas and beliefs in movement mobilizations. Second, with its emphasis on elite largesse and self-interested involvement, it overlooked more fundamental resources among highly deprived populations which are difficult to quantify, such as kinship networks, individual self-sacrifice, social solidarity, and collectively organized, indigenous problem-solving (see Morris 1984). Third, it was nonreflexive and placed too much faith in the elite's ability to constantly overwhelm, co-opt, or crush any form of insurgency from below. Finally, although the emergence of social movements should be expected based on the unequal nature of objective conditions that lead to "social incongruities" (Rosaldo 1989), they could not explain why deprived populations varied in their appraisal of these objective conditions—that is, why would people revolt in one era rather than another when conditions were much the same? In the following, we delineate the three key social-movement concepts that speak directly to this issue of subterranean revolt and resistance and which will become central analytical themes in the unraveling of our data.

The Politics, Reflexivity, and Identity of Lower-Class Social Movements

Although traditional political parties and social movements of the industrial era have seen their mass appeal decline, a plethora of issue, identity, and lifestyle movements have emerged to reinvigorate the notion of democratic citizenship. This section draws on the work of several well-known social movement analysts to help us rethink the task and scope of sociocultural resistance and what amounts to history-making from below.

Politics

As we have seen with the gang literature, the question of politics has been strangely absent from most of the gang discourse throughout this century. Oddly enough, the same could also be said of the social movement literature in terms of appreciating and analyzing the indigenous politics and organizations of the subaltern or lower classes. In the wake of the civil rights years two sociologists, in separate studies—McAdam (1982) and Morris (1984)—took on this task and began their work, guided by the following formulations:

> The crucial question, then, is: what set of circumstances is most likely to facilitate the transformation from hopeless submission to oppressive conditions to an aroused readiness to challenge those conditions? (McAdam 1982:34)

> Did the major events and confrontations of the movement [the civil rights movement] arise from spontaneous explosions, or were they the products of skillfully organized efforts and preexisting institutions? [Morris 1984:xii]

Both McAdam's and Morris's study of the black civil rights movement during the 1960s represented a sharp break from the early social-psychological models of collective behavior and from the power elite orientations of resource mobilization theorists. Their sociohistorically grounded study of the evolution of the protest movement among the Southern poor led them to make the following correctives to the dominant frameworks in social movement discourse:

1. Oppositional movements to the status quo are not irrational responses by alienated individuals but reflect a rational necessity given the constantly unresolved social problems based in systems of unequal power and distribution.
2. Movement actors and leaders do not suddenly arrive on the historical scene but rather they are nurtured over time and emerge out of a long-drawn-out process of collective resistance traditions, including charismatic leadership traditions and multiple movement centers (see Morris 1984).
3. Much of the resources for social movements do not come from the coffers of generous outside benefactors[5] but from the development of a network impetus and the already existing indigenous organizations that create social and cultural resources to meet the demands of the situation.[6]

Thus, for McAdam and Morris, movement members were essentially political actors who saw themselves struggling against and potentially transcending contemporary historical power lines. This precondition of social movement genesis McAdam calls "cognitive liberation," and for him it is one of the most crucial factors behind a movement's success, even though it is difficult to measure. For Morris, in turn, what is critical for success in movement building and movement sustainability is the intervention of indigenously trained social activists who are able to "read" accurately the possibilities within politically loaded social conditions.

Reflexivity

Earlier, in the introductory chapter, we talked about the need for reflexivity in the research act, but equally important is an understanding of reflexivity that focuses on the fluctuating relationship between a movement and its community, and between a movement and its own set of actions. Touraine's theory of social movements is probably the most developed, reflexively based analysis in the literature and is based on three separate studies: the student movement of France in the late 1960s, the antinuclear social movements in France during the 1970s, and the prodemocracy movements in Poland during the same period. Despite the seemingly reactionary trends of the postindustrial age, Touraine argues that social movements are the key to social change. They contain what he calls "class actors," members of movements who are "fighting for control of historicity, i.e., control of the great cultural orientations by which a society's environmental relationships are normatively organized" (p. 26).

For Touraine, and like McAdam, there always exists a dynamic reflexivity between a social movement and its allied community which serves to generate and to regenerate a movement's momentum and at the same time help shape and influence its agenda.[7] Moreover, Touraine also considers two other aspects of the reflexive process: (1) the roles that social movements play not only in promoting and generating social change itself but in revealing the underlying structures of the formal institutions with which social movements are in conflict, and (2) the culture that is created by the social movement, which in turn generates more social action.

Touraine's approach is extremely insightful in the context of movements that arise from seemingly atypical sociopolitical actors. Specifically, his work helps us to understand: (1) how collectivized social actors struggle for alternative visions of a society or, at least, of certain aspects of its culture, despite facing overwhelming opposition from society's elites; and (2) the reverse dynamics of oppression, i.e., those developmental processes of an oppositional movement which occur not despite an increase in the levels of oppression but because of them.

Identity

The third analytical lesson to be drawn from social movement theory is the crucial importance of identity as it is constructed by marginalized movement populations in the postmodern period. This concept is exhaustively discussed and rehearsed in a range of contemporary works on social movement analysis (see Melucci 1996). However, for the specific purposes of this study, we want to focus on the work of researcher/theorists who have discussed the importance of this approach for social movement actors in highly marginalized locations.

In Castells's 1997 work *The Power of Identity*, the author applies the theories of Touraine to the Information Age—characterized as a Network Society. Castells uses a highly eclectic theoretical framework to explain the myriad resistance movements that sprang up in the 1980s and 1990s which were notable not for their commitment to structural change but for their struggles to acquire their own social and cultural spaces within the shifting boundaries of the newly globalized and decentered nation state. [See also the critique by Harvey (2000).]

But what is identity in the social movement context? For Castells it is a process of meaning construction both for individuals and for collectivities by which certain "sources of meaning" (p. 6) are prioritized over others and eventually internalized. Castells sees three different types of identity that all have to be factored into social movement development. These he calls legitimizing, resistance, and project identities (Castells, p. 8) and it is the interplay between these identities that largely underscores the complexity of the social movement process. For each identity, Castells lays out the following set of guidelines:

> Legitimizing identity: introduced by the dominant institutions of society to extend and rationalize their domination vis-à-vis social actors. . . .
>
> Resistance identity: generated by those actors that are in positions/conditions devalued and /or stigmatized by the logic of domination. . . .
>
> Project identity: when social actors, on the basis of whichever cultural materials are available to them, build a new identity that redefines their position in society and, by so doing, seek the transformation of overall social structure [1997:8].

While the first identity obviously refers to the condition of domination, in a Gramscian sense, the other two are strictly associated with oppositional movement development. However, it is to the concept of resistance identity that Castells attaches most weight given the postmodern context. Below, Castells outlines why this formulation should require so much emphasis:

> The second type of identity-building, identity for resistance, leads to the formation of communes, or communities, in Etzioni's formulation. This may be the most important type of identity-building in our society. It constructs forms of collective resistance against otherwise unbearable oppression, usually on the

basis of identities that were, apparently, clearly defined by history, geography, or biology, making it easier to essentialize the boundaries of resistance [p. 9].

Thus, the concept of identity is a critical aspect of social movement analysis, not least because it reveals the process by which individuals and their respective affiliations both come to believe in certain self-representations and act upon them accordingly. Taking into account these three central analytical concepts—politics, reflexivity, and identity—we are now able to construct the models that will guide the ensuing analysis.

From Gangs to Social Movements to the Street Organization

If the earlier definition of a social movement provided by Blumer (1971) is not sufficient and if the models of both classical theorists and the RM theorists fail to inspire confidence, how do we define or come to recognize when a social movement exists? Touraine's answer is to devise a tripartite schema to understand the range of movements which occur in the postindustrial era. The construct is broken down into three separate "principles" of identity, opposition, and totality, which Castells (1994) has succinctly interpreted to mean the following:

> Identity refers to the self-definition of the movement of what it is, on behalf of whom it speaks. Adversary refers to the movement's principal enemy, as explicitly identified by the movement. Societal goal refers to the movement's vision of the kind of social order, or social organization, it would wish in the historical horizon of its collective [p. 71].

We have found this more contemporary definition of a social movement to be the most applicable to our own data and to the conceptual construct we have previously referred to as a street organization. Therefore, combining concepts from both the research on gangs and the social movements literature, we have arrived at the configurations shown in figure 3.1.

Explanation of the Definitional Model

The definitional model draws from a range of sources and inspirations, e.g. Touraine's (1981) schema as discussed earlier, Thrasher's humanistic treatment of gangs in the urban context, Jankowsi's (1991) organizational analysis, both the U.S. and British notions of subculture (see chapter 3), and our

FIGURE 3.1 Definitional model.

own understanding of the importance of membership properties. We describe each aspect of the model as follows:

Subcultural Traditions: The group is built on a certain history that melds gang, radical-political, and street subcultures.

Level of Organization: The group's organization should reflect the complexity of its operations and its democratic designs. Paramount in this category is the level of training being given by the group and the responsibilities and accountability of the leadership.

Membership: What is the class membership of the group? Typically, for the group to go beyond the parochial designs of the street gang its membership should reflect a more working-class contingent.

Identity: This is the process by which a group comes to accept and define itself as a movement actor and therefore as something other than the pejorative label imposed on it by the dominant society which, in turn, is reinforced by its own actions. Important in this category is the group's development of an ideological belief system.

Goals versus Acts: This refers, on the one hand, to the stated social and political agenda of the group and the practical measures it takes to accomplish it, and, on the other, to all its actions, whether or not they comply with its goals. In order for the group to be defined as a street organization with social movement properties, the group's political and oppositional actions must significantly outweigh the importance of its criminally deviant actions.

Perceived Adversaries: These are the common enemy(ies) which give the group a political focus. Hence, it must have gone beyond the normal gang turf syndrome.

I n this chapter we saw how the research into gangs has treated the issue of human agency. Either it is overlooked entirely, collapsed into an aggregate of attitudes (Venkatesh 1997), or it is viewed as a mode of adaptation to prevailing social and economic realities. Rarely are gangs understood within a set of individual and collective practices that resist, transform, or transcend society's structures. In other words, rarely are these groups considered political entities.

However, even when they are, their treatment is still very much dominated by the top-down, middle-class understandings of politics as a form of institutional engagement, co-optation, or manipulation. More recently, a new literature has emerged that goes beyond these paradigms and focuses on the contradictory daily life struggles of gang members and their quest not only for economic sustenance and social power but for meaning and possibility within communities that have long histories of political and cultural resistance. Consequently, it seems appropriate to look beyond gang theory and consider other conceptual frameworks that specifically address collectivized action through processes of identity formation and communal transcendence. Hence, we have begun a dialogue with social movements theory and emerged with a new model which integrates both gang and social movement constructs. It will be this model that will provide the framework for the analysis that follows, and it will thereby set out in empirical detail why and how a new era has dawned for street gang collectives and their potential reinvention.

PART II

THE MAKING OF THE ALKQN:
SUBCULTURAL TRADITIONS

CHAPTER 4

WHO ARE THE ALMIGHTY LATIN KING
AND QUEEN NATION?

Saying that only extraordinary restrictions can prevent a Bronx gang leader from con-
tinuing murderous enterprises from behind bars, a Federal judge sentenced the head
of the state's Latin Kings street gang yesterday to a life sentence that must be served
in solitary confinement and with severely limited visits from family members and his
lawyer. . . . "This defendant has no regard for human life and obviously enjoys a god-
like role in determining who should live and who should die," Judge Martin said in
sentencing Mr. Felipe, 34. "This defendant has forfeited any right to human contact."

Hoffman 1997

Youth are joining us now not because they want to have a clique and somebody to
defend them, now they got a voice to be heard and that's what we represent in New
York City. A strong Latino voice that is not muzzled by these sell-out politicians that
are Latinos and Black Africans that sold out the community for years. The Latin Kings
wants to be something that stays in the community, for the people, by the people,
with the people.

Antonio Fernández, aka King Tone, Supreme Crown of the New York State Almighty Latin
King and Queen Nation

In part 2 we will concentrate on an analysis of the data, principally organized into themes developed from the model outlined above. This model has
been drawn from the literature and represents the most accurate conceptual
framework for the type of hybrid, dynamic organization we are studying.
Some readers may object, saying that we are trying to fit the organization into
a preconceived paradigm, thus effectively departing from the traditions of induction. We would argue that this model provides us with both descriptive

and hermeneutic devices that have emerged directly from the data collected, which have then been compared to previous findings and theories. There is no real significance given to the order of the chapters other than that they flow sequentially from the logic of the analysis and it should not be implied that any one factor or property is more of a determinant than any other.

Subcultural Traditions

What can we make of the vastly different public reactions to this group of mostly poor, working-class Latino/a youth from the most impoverished districts in New York City? To some they are indigenous leaders, fighters against injustice and unafraid to defend their social and cultural autonomy even against the overwhelming power of the state. To others, they are nothing more than the criminal sum of their arrest records, their only reasons for coming together being to plot, scheme and conspire against the law-abiding citizens of this fair city. Many of the reasons for these conflicting claims and beliefs reside in the group's history of subcultural influences. For example, there is the notoriety of the parent organization, the Latin Kings of Chicago, the stigma of criminally deviant pasts that many members carry with them, and the not-too-distant memory of the villainy associated with the New York State Latin Kings themselves.

At the same time, there are other subcultural and community traditions associated with the group that are not gang- or crime-related but derive from the long history of political and cultural resistance among barrio residents. For example, the radicalism of the Young Lords Party and the Black Panthers is frequently mentioned in the ALKQN literature and at its meetings; many members have had long associations with cultural guerrillas such as street rappers and graffiti artists; and we should not discount the influences of labor and community-organizing experiences that are part of any high-functioning poor community. Finally, there are the traditions that the organization was attempting to establish during its reformist incarnation. In this chapter we will focus on these traditions in more detail, tracing their appearance in the respondents' interviews and in the documents, speeches, poetry, letters, and observations of the group and its members.

Gang Traditions

As noted earlier, gangs have long been part of the urban landscape. But interpretations as to what gangs constitute have been almost as varied as the gangs themselves. Based on our reading of the literature, most approaches to gangs concern themselves at least to some degree with the cultural significance of the gang phenomenon. Our approach builds on this tradtion while noting a number of critical developments.

The Notion of Subculture

In gang theory, the early fieldwork-based notion of subcultural traditions is primarily understood in relation to crime, the onset of delinquency, and/or inter-generational cleavages in poor neighborhoods. Shaw and McKay (1931), for example, the pioneers of this culturalist approach to crime, saw them in the following context:

> Membership in such groups is an important contributing factor in many cases [of delinquency], since it is found that very often the boy's contact with the delinquent group marks the beginning of his career in delinquency and that his initial delinquencies are often identical with the traditions and practices of the group [McKay and Shaw 1931:256, quoted in Empey and Stafford 1991].

Meanwhile, Whyte observed them emerging within a range of social group possibilities:

> The younger generation has built up its own society relatively independent of the influence of its elders. Within the ranks of the younger men there are two main divisions: corner boys and college boys. Corner boys are groups of men who center their social activities upon particular street corners, with their adjoining barbershops, lunchrooms, poolrooms, or clubrooms. They constitute the bottom level of society within their age group, and at the same time they make up the great majority of the young men of Cornerville. During the depression most of them were unemployed or had only irregular employment. Few had completed the eighth grade [Whyte 1943:xviii].

These interpretations, though rich in descriptive detail, emphasized the existence of subcultures as largely independent of the historical, economic, and ideological contexts of capitalist social relations (Snodgrass 1976). Later, Cohen (1955) and then Miller (1958) looked again at the appearance of youth gang subcultures in the post-World War II period and linked their emergence more explicitly to a class- and generation-bound society. Locating them among the "continuities and breaks between dominant and subordinate value systems" (Hebdige 1979:77), Cohen argued that the youth gang subculture constituted a set of lower-class behaviors and goals that compensated for the elusive achievements of the middle-class straight world, while Miller saw the gang subculture as the repository of core values passed on by the youths' parent class.

Nonetheless, despite the renewed attention paid to the shaping of these subcultures, these treatments failed to consider (1) the historical conditions under which specific subcultures arise, or (2) the nature of the community(ies) from which the generic subculture(s) were supposedly emerging. A strong analytical corrective, therefore, was needed and this was finally provided across the Atlantic in the work of Phil Cohen (1972).

In Cohen's insightful interpretation of the skinhead phenomenon in London's East End, he defined subculture as a "compromise solution between two contradictory needs: the need to create and express autonomy and difference from parents . . . and the need to maintain the parental identifications." Cohen saw a content that went beyond the limited culturalist designs of a reaction formation and the generational reenactment of lower-class traditions and invoked the latent function of what he called the "magical solution." Such a concept attempted to explain phenomenologically the multiple ways in which youth were appropriating and mixing representational styles that spoke directly to their alienation. At least theoretically, Cohen recognized that these youth subcultures contained a much greater degree of agency than was appreciated in the literature, and he argued that what appeared to be a chaotic canvas of youth representations to "outsiders" was, in fact, limitless ways to "resolve the contradictions which remain hidden or unresolved in the parent culture"(Cohen 1972), and systems of values and cultural forms that were both organized and homologous (Willis 1977).

Hebdige (1979) picked up where Cohen and others left off, infusing both semiotic and spatial theories of Barthes and Lefebvre into the analysis. According to Hebidge, subcultures are:

> expressive forms but what they express is, in the last instance, a fundamental tension between those in power and those condemned to subordinate positions and second-class lives. This tension is figuratively expressed in the form of subcultural style [Hebdige 1979:132].

Based on our data we have come to a somewhat different reading of the subculture phenomenon, which builds on both U.S. and British versions by addressing the following shortcomings: (1) a failure to recognize that subcultures may have designs on the larger culture; (2) a lack of attention to inter-generational subcultures; (3) a failure to assess the ability of a subculture to generate and regenerate its own community, and (4) a failure to recognize that street youth are shaped by experience and contribute to a range of subcultures, only some of which can be classified as delinquent or criminally deviant. Table 4.1, in general terms, compares these two schools of thought with our own working concept of subculture as used throughout the book.

TABLE 4.1 Comparative Approaches to Youth Subcultures

Source	USA Model	British Model	Street Organizational Model
Class values	Lower class, proletarian and subproletarian	Specific to the working-class and middle-class history of the subculture	Working-class and subproletarian strongly infused with specific racial and ethnic experiences
Relation to mainstream or dominant class structure	Adaptive and/or rejectionist	Subversive and "magically" oppositional but never transformative	Subversive, partly adaptive, partly oppositional, intentionally transformative
Observable deviance from the prototypical "mainstream"	Mainly delinquent involving group organized fighting, crime, drugs and other antisocial behaviors	Heavily aesthetic and stylistic, some drug use, some fighting	Stylistic, political and ideological, members recruited from both working and subworking classes
Historical contingency (i.e., does the analysis take pains to dialectically and historically situate the phenomena)	Mostly transhistorical; however, there are exceptions, such as the work of Hagedorn (the black underclass) and Moore and Vigil (the Latino underclass)	Rooted in specific historical conditions	Highly historical, shaped by discrete resistances from below and social control processes from above
Representational forms	Socially organized, displays of turf allegiance, some later attention to attire and both body and verbal language	Wide range of symbolism involving music, attire, and language	Wide range of symbolism involving music, graffiti, physical and verbal language, attire and written texts

As should be clear from the above, there are many differences between the three approaches, even though each school of thought might conceivably be focusing on the same phenomenon. The consequences of this divergence are important, as we have already stated, since how one approaches the problem will often determine what one will eventually find. Even so, there may be instances when the empirical data are so powerful that they burst through the constraining nature of the paradigm. Certainly, in the street-organizational approach this is more likely since all activities engaged in by the subjects are considered worthy of study and interpretation.

Back to the Data

Below, we discuss five clusters of traditions that were prominent in the activities and the thinking of the members and which created part of the cultural landscape against which the organization attempted to elevate its social and political missions. Thus we have organized the data as follows: (1) the organizational and representational rituals coming from Chicago; (2) the mobilizing yet ultimately self-destructive practices of Luis Felipe and the early New York Latin Kings; (3) the youthful experiences of gangs and posses among the members; (4) the nongang traditions of liberationist groups such as the Black Panthers and the Young Lords Party; and (5) new traditions during the reform era.

Chicago: The Motherland

Chicago is the Motherland of the Mother chapter of the Latin Kings. "Amor de Rey" originated in Chicago. The Latin Kings are 360 degrees strong in knowledge, Understanding, and Respect. 360 degrees completely strong, whole, and unbreakable.

From text of the ALKQN bible

The passage above, taken from an early section of the ALKQN's bible, clearly shows the importance placed on the relationship between the ALKQN and the Latin Kings from Chicago. References to Chicago are made in nearly all meetings (i.e., in prayers and speeches at "universals," at local chapter meetings, and at public rallies), and many of Chicago's rules and lessons are included in the ALKQN's manifesto. It would be impossible, therefore, to examine the evolution and makeup of New York's Kings and Queens without understanding at a deeper level the influence that Chicago has had on this process.

The Traditions of Chicago: Secrecy, Lessons, Rules, Sanctions, Prayers, Record-keeping, and Representing

While the tradition of gangs keeping their members in check through written rules and regulations is not new, the degree to which the Chicago Kings have developed an elaborate system of secret laws, homespun philosophies, political theses, and codes for member-only interactions has few parallels outside of Masonic lodges and underground revolutionary movements. In the following we examine some of the major Chicago traditions that have been transmuted to fit the specific conditions of the New York City and State chapter.

Secrecy

The first of these traditions we have termed secrecy, or the premium placed by the organization on reserving knowledge of its affairs for the eyes and ears of members only. In the introduction of the ALKQN bible, the following appears:

> You are now entering into the depths and secrets of the ALKQN. This secret elite society is made up of great men of honor, courage, boldness, selfrespect, pride, and most importantly—"*silence.*"

This tradition of silence originated with the Chicago Latin Kings and has been adopted by the New York chapter. In one of Conquergood's (1992) first articles based on his Chicago research, he describes the rule of secrecy and the context in which it was finally broken:

> "Do you know what's in there, Dwight?" Chico asked, pointing to the stereo speaker on top of his bedroom dresser. Cued by the teasing tone in his voice, punctuated by the playful arch of his eyebrows, I played along. After three years of fieldwork I now understood that "play," "playing around"—"playing with you, bro"—often signaled entry into sensitive space, the preamble to intimate disclosures. I tentatively fingered the surface of the speaker and responded, guilelessly: "No, I don't know what's in here. Do you have something in here, Chico?"
>
> Wordlessly, Chico removed the speaker cover, pulled out a crumpled sheaf of papers, and handed it to me. I unfolded the typescript and read the all-caps underlined title, *THE KING MANIFESTO.* Penned in longhand and encircled at the top right-hand corner of the title page was this enjoinder "For real Latin Kings only." Realizing that this dog-eared manuscript was the

secret "Book," the closely guarded "Laws," that are kept hidden from the uninitiated and revealed only to the inner circle of gang members, I sucked in my breath and exclaimed, "Wow!"

I had been in the field almost a year before I even had heard about "the Book," and then it was always shrouded in secrecy. Once a sister had confided to me that she had accidentally discovered "the laws" while cleaning her brother's room, and two recently initiated Kings had slipped me a single page from "the Book" that they had been given as part of their initiation. Intermittently I came across references to this secret manuscript, but I never expected to see a copy. "You read that and you'll be a real gangbanger," Chico teasingly avowed [1992:1].

The extreme emphasis placed by the Chicago Latin Kings on ensuring that group-based knowledge and rituals remained subterranean is powerfully present among the Latin Kings and Queens of New York City, though it has been considerably modified because the new leadership (see chapter 8) has attempted to promote openness both within the organization and between the organization and the community. In fact, it could be said that this tension between openness and secrecy represents one of the biggest challenges to New York's reform efforts.

Despite these differences in New York, we too, like Conquergood in Chicago, were subject to a number of constraints placed by the organization on our ability to collect data. For example, we were not allowed to see any of the lessons from the bible, or indeed the bible itself, during most of the research period. Consequently, we had to infer from the interviews and the speeches of the leaders how the principles and rules of membership were actually written. Further, although the general meetings were open to invited guests, and throughout the research period we were invited (except for times when the research was suspended due to conflicts with the leadership[1]) to more than twenty general meetings, there were entire periods during these meetings when all guests were required to leave so that internal business could be conducted. And finally, although most of the central leadership was in agreement with the aims of the research, we had great difficulty gaining access to branch members or observing branch events due to opposition from leaders at the local level.

Of course, there are various ways to interpret the need for such secrecy. Some would consider it another example of the group's essential conspiratorial nature, implying that the organization's communitarian rhetoric and practices were fronts for its nefarious core activities (i.e., planning present and future illicit acts or developing strategies to expand its criminal reach). As one researcher has described this position with regard to the Chicago Kings:

Apparently, there is another side about gang life in America that has not emerged in anthropological studies of younger gang members who may not be at all knowledgeable of this larger picture. "Shorties" or "Peewees" as associates of a real gang might be easily approached by such anthropological techniques, but these type [sic] of data sources are the least likely to actually be knowledgeable about the larger financial and economic issues of gang life today [Knox 1997:68].

Others, however, might interpret such secrecy more benignly. For example, Conquergood argues that the same Chicago Latin Kings described by Knox (above) are best seen as a border culture, existing in an actively negotiated terrain that separates them not only from other gangs but from the incursive actions of the dominant culture:

The need for silence, secrecy, and circumspection is intensified because the line between insiders and outsiders is slippery and shifting. Once one looks closely at gangs, it becomes evident that borders are constructed on multiple and mobile fronts. Actually, borders absolutely crisscross the entire domain of gang culture because gangs set themselves apart from mainstream society, as well as from one another [Conquergood 1993:29].

Based on our data in New York, we similarly locate the role of secrecy within the organization's broad web of internal and external societal relations. Thus, on the one hand it has to do with the vertical organization of the group; its origins as a resistance movement; and the tolerance of members who are still involved in the illicit economy. On the other hand, it is a rational response to: (1) the threat of law enforcement agencies whose openly stated mission, after all, is to disband the group (Gang Intelligence Task Force 1999, chapter 12); (2) the predations of other groups; (3) the natural distrust of barrio youth toward "outsiders," especially considering the consistent demonization of the group and its members in the press; and (4) the rampant use of "informants" by law enforcement.

Moreover, from the perspective that the group is not so deviant, it could be argued that corporate or trade-union business meetings are also usually for the eyes and ears of members only and that the group, therefore, is following the examples of the so-called "mainstream."

In the following field notes, we see how important it is to situate the practice of secrecy in the New York context. We should add that the author of these notes had only been attached to this branch of the ALKQN for less than a month, though he had been working with another branch for the previous six months:

Since it was very cold I decided to go into a local pizzeria, which is directly across from the gas station where we were supposed to meet. I decided to wait because I wanted to at least talk to either King M., the chapter leader, or King L., the Suprema. A group of youths are hanging out at the corner. I approach them and ask if they are Kings. One of them sees me (from the Universals I guess) and says "Hi." He starts talking to me and I ask him the whereabouts of King M. and King L. All of a sudden, another King approaches and tells the other Kings to "shut up." He seems upset, angry, and very distrustful of me. He says "No, we don't know no one." He is very hostile and as I start to talk to him he tells me "We are not talking. "We don't know anything. Keep walking!"

I decided to just drop it and to clarify things later when either King M. or King L. could be present. I went back home very upset about the incident. I thought about it and although I understood the Kings' defensive attitude, I was upset that the leader did not even let me explain. Well, this is a perfect example of the unpredictability of field work. As a researcher who meets subjects in their natural habitat/milieu, I need to be prepared and to expect this type of situation. The Kings are responding to the fact that the police and the FBI have infiltrated them and have paid "snitches" to incriminate their leader King Tone who was going to jail. They were also reacting to the fact that although they do not consider themselves a gang, other gangs do consider them a gang and are constantly attacking them [JE, Field notes 1:12/8/1998].

Just over a month later, the same researcher encountered a very different situation. After he had become more accepted by the membership, particularly by the leadership, the issue of secrecy not only became more negotiable but its practice could be better appreciated as a mix both of the organization's custom of voluntary exclusion and its enforced geographic exclusion (Sibley 1992).

J. told me that he had to go but that I should continue waiting at that particular spot and that King M. would show up soon. King M. arrived about half an hour later. He took me across the street down a path through the woods to the riverbank. We were stopped by a couple of Kings on the way. They both had flashlights and lit us as we were walking down. King M. told them that I was "okay." The view was incredible. I felt like I was in the movies. The haziness of the scene combined with the massive structure of the Washington Bridge created a mystical and magical scenario. Down under this colossal body of concrete were a group of 30 kids lined up in a 360 [a circle formed by members in which the meeting takes place]. I realized why I could never have found this place by myself. Despite the almost freezing temperatures, despite the rain, and the darkness, they were there meeting right under this huge concrete structure, hidden from the public. According to King M., "I feel safe here, no one bothers us here" [JE, field notes 2:1/16/1999].

As we can see, the importance of secrecy is a primary concern of both groups and the influence of the Chicago tradition in this respect is very powerful. However, New York's practices of secrecy are much more situational, not only because of the reform movement but also because the New York chapter does not find itself immersed in the same competitive world of gang coalitions that exists between the Peoples and Folks Nations of Chicago.[2] In terms of the attention given to these groups by the police, both groups probably receive an equal amount of surveillance and intelligence gathering due to their pariah status in the eyes of law enforcement.

Lessons

The lessons contain the basic elements of the Chicago and New York City Kings and Queens moral, social, and political codes. As such, they function on a number of levels: as ideological doctrine, as guides to personal and collective behavior, and as personal goals for members.

The wide-ranging lessons and principles of Chicago have been considerably extended over the last thirteen years, first by King Blood and then by his successors. In the group's New York State constitution for the males, there are ten basic lessons that were adopted from the Chicago constitution, which have been augmented by a further twenty-six lessons that were inserted during King Blood's tutelage. For the females there are twenty-two lessons that were specifically adopted during the King Blood era, whereas in Chicago there is no reference to the Queens at all.

In both the male and female lessons of New York the five basic principles of the crown are similar to, though slightly different from, those in Chicago. In Chicago they are: respect, loyalty, love, wisdom, and obedience, which are also used by the New York Queens. However, the New York Kings have made respect, honesty, unity, knowledge, and love their five points (and these are slightly different again from the five points that appear in the Latin Kings' constitution in Connecticut). Each of these five points, or principles, as in the Motherland, have very specific meanings within Kingism. In addition to the five points there are five senses which are also known as the five diamonds or jewels in a King or Queen's crown. Both the points and the senses listed below are defined according to the New York bible.

Five Points (from the Kings' manifesto)

(1) Respect: Respect for your brothers, your crown, and your nation. A Brother will show high regards to his nation.

(2) Honesty: Honesty is marked by the truth. Your word is your crown and your crown is your nation. A King will live by his word.

(3) Unity: Unity is the condition of being united into a single whole. All for one and one for all. Our crown symbolizes our people, Latinos. Amor de Rey.

(4) Knowledge: Knowledge is the knowing of your lessons and prayers gained through experience and the studies of our nation.

(5) Love: Love is what you carry in your heart for your brothers your crown and your nation. Amor de Rey.

Five Points (from the Queens' manifesto)

(1) Respect: For your brothers, sisters, crown and nation. A Queen's respect will show high regards to her nation.

(2) Loyalty: Its [sic] my duty to be loyal to my brothers, sisters, crown and nation. I must uphold and live by our "code of silence." Betrayal of any kind will be considered a threat to the nation.

(3) Love: Is what we carry in our heart for our brothers, sisters, crown and nation. In order to live in peace we must feel love for all my 5 points.

(4) Wisdom: Its [sic] what we seek in our nation through the studies of our lessons and prayers. Its also what we must pass on to future Kings and Queens of our great nation.

(5) Obedience: We will obey all laws, rule or any order coming from our superior, Kings and Queens.

Five Senses (these apply equally to Kings and Queens).

(1) Seeing: To identify your Brother and see the Love and Respect in the Nation.

(2) Hearing: To hear your Brothers cry for help and listen to the message and purpose of the lessons.

(3) Touching: Your Brothers and your people with the joy of the Nation.

(4) Smelling: To immediately detect danger and any threats to the Nation.

(5) Tasting: To Taste the victory over the opposing forces that comes [sic] against the Nation.

But what exactly do these lessons mean to Latin Kings and Queens? Are they simply rhetoric, similar to the grandiose claims of so many political manifestos found in liberationist groups? According to the Chicago Kings, a member must constantly strive to live by his lessons and only to the extent that this is done can one succeed in becoming a true King. To understand the importance of these lessons for the organization, the relationship between the points and the senses, and how both the lessons and the senses are actively invoked in the everyday lives of members, consider the following exegesis provided by King Tone, the President or Inca of New York's Kings and Queens. The text comes from a diary that King Tone was keeping while he was under house arrest and working as a consultant on this project:

> Pity is not what I seek from my brothers and pity is not what I seek from my friends. It's respect, the respect that I would step out or step aside for anyone who comes in the name of the Holy Righteous Crown and the truth of the five stones that are placed upon it that stand for the leadership. I praise it because I know the diamonds live within my five senses and I can see, hear, smell, touch, and taste. But more than that. I got senses of spiritualities that no one could count, so if you're stuck on five senses, please arise from that slumber, for you got many more that must awaken. The sense of knowledge, the sense of knowing, the sense of history, the sense of bad, the sense of good, the sense of 360 strong, whole and unbreakable. This is what you should be thankful for, this is what you got, this is what the fuck you fight for, people! Don't let nobody mislead you or make you understand that this cause is about makin' a buck and getting you to retire and having a nice family to sit by you and a TV and watch the fuckin' football games on Sunday [12/9/1998].

Under the circumstances in which King Tone found himself, knowledge of the ALKQN's lessons provided him with a moral framework and a vision to continue to struggle against adversity. While the bible's primary lessons are quite specific in encouraging the notion of salvation and self-help through community attachment, there are literally hundreds of other lessons and aphorisms that are designed to help members through the darkest of moments and the most difficult of choices similar to those remembered by King Tone above. Below, we quote from several sections of what is called the "Kings Gnosis" in the New York bible. There are 360 points in the Gnosis, one for each of the 360 degrees that make up an ALKQN meeting circle. To our knowledge, this section is not contained in the Chicago manifesto and is unique to New York:

> 60°: I will have a Kings [sic] patience and not despair. We must know when to rest and when to attack. We will not break patience by leaping before it is time, for then we shall surely fall short.

> 61°: We will raise up our fallen and sustain our hungry to the best of our ability. We shall not turn our backs on our brothers or we will not be entirely pure and just on the last day of the beginning of infinity, when we take our thrones by the creator.

> 62°: Kings will perform acts of benevolence and love for our brothers with a generous heart, for to do these acts without want will be a false act and therefore you break your point of honesty, and when your honesty is broken you have violated your father and nation.

Rules

There is a range of very precise rules, many of which flow directly from the Chicago tradition, which spell out the obligations, the disciplinary norms, and the rights of all members and leaders. These include the proper way to conduct meetings; the physical and nonphysical sanctions that may be applied to certain infractions; the meanings behind the colors and the numbers of beads worn by rank-and-file members and officers; the structural hierarchy of the organization; the amount of dues to be paid by members and how the money should be used; and the prayers that must be said at the beginning and end of each meeting, at funerals, at initiations, at baptisms, and at weddings. To provide the reader with a better grasp of the sheer range of these rules we have divided them into four thematic subsections: comportment, social responsibility, engagement, and meetings. The issues of sanctions and prayers will be dealt with separately.

RULES OF COMPORTMENT The rules of comportment address the way that members interact with one another and with the community. The repertoire of bodily and verbal gestures that Kings and Queens employ in their exchanges are very precise and highly ritualistic. The crossing of arms and hands, the use of one hand or two hands to make a crown, the kissing of a crown before the reigning Inca, and even the level of composure that one is supposed to assume in certain settings, are examples of the degree to which the comportment of members is regulated, albeit ideal-typically. The following are some examples of rules which are practiced in Chicago and are used to guide behavior in the New York chapter.

A brother never crosses his arms with his left over his right. A King should never cover his right hand because his right hand represents his crown.

No member shall take the law into their own hands especially when he knows that what he did will reflect upon the nation and jeopardize the health and well-being of every member of the chapter.

No member shall conduct an interview with any person from the news media concerning nation affairs without the approval of Las Coronas.

No member shall use his membership or position in the nation to exploit anyone inside or outside the Nation.

When a member gives another member the Nation salute it should always be returned.

From the above, we can see that a King or Queen's behavior is highly circumscribed and that there is no laissez-faire attitude taken toward membership. But other than social conduct and interactional codes (see the section below on representation) there is a great deal of emphasis on what might be described as the practice of nation "citizenship."

RULES OF SOCIAL RESPONSIBILITY   At all times, Latin Kings and Queens are supposed to be examples both to other members of the organization and to members of the Latino community. This means that, depending on their age, they should be (1) employed or looking for work, (2) going to school, (3) showing responsibility in their family affairs, (4) free of hard drugs, and (5) taking an avid interest in their cultural history. Of course, these are all models of behavior to live up to and there is a great deal of variation among Kings and Queens in terms of the degree to which they conform to these standards. In the King's doctrine, it is only as one enters deeper into the King experience, evolving through certain stages of development, that one can achieve this heightened form of consciousness and practice which is the hallmark of true Kingism.[3]

To understand this more clearly, consider the analysis of a King's career or what is termed the three "cycles of nation life that constitute Kingism," as it appears in the ALKQN's bible. This section of the text, which is taken straight from the Chicago manifesto, describes the three stages of Kingism as: the primitive stage; the conservative or mummy stage; and the New King stage. Each of these stages is defined as follows:

(1) The Primitive Stage: [According to the bible this period of a King's membership is described as] that stage in life where the King warrior acts on impulse, executing his action without giving them the serious thought that they demand. A stage of immaturity where the King warrior's time is spent gang banging, getting high and being recognized as big and bad. . . This is the original stage of Kingism and from the roots of the primitive stage emerges the second stage.

(2) The Conservative or Mummy stage: [This stage is described as follows:] at this level the King warrior becomes tired of the primitive stage. He no longer wishes to participate in the senseless routine of gang fighting, hanging on the corner or being recognized as big and bad. Most often at this level the King warrior gets married and retires. It is inappropriate to call this stage the maturity stage due to the fact that the King warrior at this time does not really become mature in the sense of maturity. Instead he becomes mummified or reaches a level of accepting life as it has been taught to him by the existing system that exploits all people of color—dehumanizes them and maintains them under the economic and social yoke of slavery.

(3) The New King Stage: [After passing through the above stages and finally emerging from the conservative stage where "there are more Kings than at any other level," the member reaches the third stage, described as] the stage of awareness and decision. The new King recognizes that the time for revolution is at hand. Revolution of the mind! The revolution of knowledge! A revolution that will bring freedom to the enslaved, to all Third World people as we together sing and praise with joy what time it is—it is Nation time! . . . For him there are no horizons between races, sexes and senseless labels. For him everything has meaning, human life is placed above materialistic values. . . . When a man becomes a new King the will of the Nation becomes his will, for to be at variance with the Nation is one thing that cannot endure. The Almighty Latin King Nation requires wholehearted and complete devotion.

Thus, in entering this final stage one has shown both the highest commitment to Kingism and the greatest capacity to carry out one's social responsibilities on behalf of the Nation. In many ways, this final stage, the ultimate in the qualitative development of a Latin King's career, is tantamount to becoming a model citizen in the "imagined" (Anderson 1983) nation of the Latin Kings.

RULES OF MEETINGS Meetings are an extremely important activity of the ALKQN and are similarly taken very seriously by the organization in the Motherland. The functions of meetings are manifold but some of their major contributions to the organization are: (1) to inform members of group activities, (2) to collect dues for the organization, (3) to enforce discipline, (4) to debate internal issues of the organization, (5) to train members in Kingism, and (6) to recruit and hone the skills of new leaders. An indication of the primacy placed on this organizational practice is given by the following rules:

> Attendance of every regular scheduled weekly meeting is mandatory of every member of the ALKQN organization. These meetings are the absolute significance [sic] of our growth both physically and intellectually.
>
> No member is to enter any regular scheduled meeting under the influence of anything that impair or infringe [sic] upon the process of the meeting and or the normality there of its members.
>
> Members are required to vote but are not allowed to vote in absentia. The attempt to persuade, imitate or coerce votes are [sic] violations of the constitutional law.

Sanctions

There is a range of sanctions and procedures that are available to leaders of the organization which are designed to maintain cohesion and protect the group from outside interference. This aspect of norm enforcement has become somewhat legendary in the Latin Kings of Chicago. As one researcher describes it:

> A frequent activity of the gang is order maintenance: sanctioning its own members for infractions and not meeting financial obligations. Such sanctions typically are "violations" or monetary fines. The violations are beatings from up to four members of the gang lasting specific time limits: 30 seconds, 60 seconds, etc. The fines sometimes involve situations where the individual gang member may lose a gun owned by the gang, that is a gun purchased from its treasury money (i.e., paying a $50 fine for losing a $150 pistol) [Knox, 1997:67].

In the New York State chapter—although many of these disciplinary rituals are similar to those of Chicago, including physical punishments, social exclusion, and group shaming—their application varies both in frequency and intensity according to the quality of the leadership and the political development of the group at any given time. For example, as will be discussed in detail in chapter 11, many of the physical punishments in New York City were abolished during the reform period, including the most severe form, the death penalty or what was called TOS (terminate on sight). Below we have listed the different disciplinary actions and procedures as they still appear in the New York State's bible, many of which are carryovers from Chicago.

VIOLATIONS Bringing someone up on charges in the ALKQN is a tradition that comes from Chicago and in procedural terms is generally called a violation. In New York, this is defined as "a justice given by the first lady for abusing or breaking the law of the chapter for an act that doesn't represent a queen. A violation can be physical or a fine, but it can also be both" (Queen's Manifesto).

When someone is formally charged with wrongdoing a form is filled out and a charge is made describing the infraction; the form is given to the accused within seven days of the offense. According to the constitution, there has to be a hearing within 30 days of the formal complaint, at which time the accused has to put his or her case to the local leadership (called crowns). After the hearing, the crowns have to decide on a verdict and a punishment.

Figure 4.1 is a copy of a violation form. As can be seen, the system of punishment is highly rational, calculated, and bureaucratized. Thus, sanctions, at least theoretically, are not supposed to be meted out to individuals in an ad hoc fashion, i.e., at the whim of individual leaders. Certainly, in organizational terms, this makes sense for to do so would (1) undermine the moral authority of the collective leadership and its belief system, (2) make the power of individual members more unaccountable, arbitrary, and localistic, and (3) lead to random acts of uncontrolled aggression. All of these factors, of course, would bring increased instability to the group and undermine cohesion.

But what of the sanctions themselves? What do they consist of? How are they justified? In the following, we describe the nonphysical and physical punishments as they occur in the ALKQN's texts and/or in interviews with group members and, where possible, we show the relationship between norm violations and sanctions.

NONPHYSICAL PUNISHMENTS The following is a list of nonphysical punishments:

Probation: According to the bible, probation "is a period of no less than 2
    weeks or more than 2 months. Instead of a physical or fine you can also

Procedures for violation form

Name of member_____ Date _____

Type of violation _____
_____
_____
_____

Name of accuser _____

Crown hearing date _____ Place _____ Time _____

Crown members present:

1. _____   3. _____   5. _____

2. _____   4. _____

Version of the accused _____
_____
_____

      If you need more space please use the reverse side of this page.

Witnesses if any   1. _____
                      2. _____

Crown disposition _____
_____

FIGURE 4.1 Violation form.

be put on probation, but you can also get all three of them" (New York State Bible, 1994).

Fines: These can range from $10 to $30 and are more commonly known by their Spanish translation of "multa." Multas could be received for being late to meetings or missing meetings and were very common during the early 1990s. In the period during which our field research was carried out, multas were rarely imposed, though they were not unknown.

Stripping: This happens to members when they have threatened the security of the organization or disrespected the power structure and basically means that the beads and the rank of the member are taken away for a determined or sometimes indefinite amount of time. Once stripped, it is difficult for that member to ascend to the same position since he or she has been tested by the organization and is found to be morally wanting in some way. During the most recent period, there was a policy of forgiving members for certain infractions, even very serious ones, after a certain amount of time (see chapter 8). The reason for this was to prevent the disciplined member from becoming resentful and turning into an enemy of the organization.

Suspension: Of the serious punishments within the Nation, suspensions are the ultimate form of shaming without resorting to corporal punishment. The rules of suspension are very specific, as indicated by the document reprinted from the ALKQN's bible (see figure 4.2). From this document we can see that much thought has gone into both normalizing and formalizing punishment sanctions, almost as if they were part of an official legal system. In this case, members are punished mainly by being removed from all active offices (they are not allowed to wear their colors and hence their beads) and by being shamed, for example, by changing their "greetings" ritual to that of a novice. Note, however, that they are not being excluded from the meetings and, in fact, it is being implied that they should be present at the "360s" (i.e., the chapter and general meetings), which keeps the member close to the organization, preventing him or her from becoming too ostracized.

Community Service: During the most recent period, the leadership of the ALKQN began to move away from most of the corporal disciplining and toward sanctions that required a member to contribute to the community. This could take the form of working in a soup kitchen for several weekends, collecting clothes for the homeless, or working on voter registration in poor neighborhoods.

Rules under Suspension

In the name of the Almighty Latin King Nation & in compliance with all procedures of the A.L.K.Q.N. the following rules have been established for each member to adhere while under any form of suspension. The rules are to be followed entirely until the member has completed jis or her suspension.

When a member is under suspension he or she are authorized to & must:

1. Keep their colors but not permited to wear them during any period of suspension......

2. Automatically put their colors back on <u>after</u> the last day of suspension has been completed.

3. Not wear any clothing that bears the colors of the A.L.K.Q.N durring the entire period of suspension.....

4. Salute by making the sign of the probationary crown (using both hands) without any hand contact with another member during the entire peroid of suspension.

5. Not get involved in any questionable activity that may lead to or result in a new violation charge.....

6. Not wear any item of jewlery that signifies or represents the colors of the A.L.K.Q.N. during the entire period of suspension....

Note: all of the above six rules have been done keeping the 5 points in mind which this nation is founded & guided by. Be advised that no member male or female should be removed from the 360 unless they are on observation probation.....

2

FIGURE 4.2   Rules Under Suspension.

PHYSICAL PUNISHMENTS In the early history of the New York chapter, "physicals" were very common and took a variety of forms. From the data it is not clear when an infraction merited a corporal form of punishment other than to say that both the male and female leadership during this period was willing to have members beaten for quite minor forms of insubordination. The following list describes the range of corporal punishments that are either listed in the ALKQN bible or have been recorded in court-related documents during Latin King trials.

B.O.S.: This acronym stands for Beat on Sight, which is a form of punishment carried out by rank-and-file members or soldiers of the Nation who might, in turn, be supervised by a designated "Enforcer" (the third crown of the five crowns that make up the chapter leadership). At chapter meetings, soldiers would be chosen to go on "missions" with the gender of the violator usually matching the gender of those doing the punishing. The physical punishment could last for several minutes, although we have no specific data that point to either the length of time or severity of a B.O.S.

Three-minute physicals: These are carried out by three or more members of the Kings or Queens during meetings.

Five-point violations: These are physicals carried out by five members of the leadership, one for each point of the crown, and are meant as a serious punishment for a serious infraction.

T.O.S.: This acronym stands for Terminate on Sight and is an order of execution to be carried out on a member. This form of the death penalty is unique to the New York bylaws and was introduced by King Blood during his early imprisonment (see chapter 5). In various letters between King Blood and other leaders, this form of punishment is mentioned on a number of occasions but it is doubtful that all of the orders were ever carried out. According to court documents of Latin Kings' trials, the reasons for ordering such extreme action would be treason, overt homosexuality, and consistent challenges to the leadership.

Prayers

In all religions, the rituals of prayer are important spiritual exercises for the believers. They can cover petition, entreaty, expostulation, confession, thanksgiving, recollection, praise, adoration, meditation, or interception. However, a close study of prayer rituals in different religions uncovers significant discrepancies concerning the regulation of time, place, and posture.

Similarly, an analysis of the ALKQN's prayers reveals instructions only for place and posture, without emphasizing any particular time regulation. For the ALKQN prayers are a serious matter indicated by the 360 prayers in the "Kings' Gnosis" (this is a section of the ALKQN's manifesto which, roughly interpreted, means a King's way of knowing). Prayers, therefore, are established rituals for all convocations of the ALKQN. In fact, there is no meeting that members of the ALKQN can attend without prayers being said. Certainly, the origins of this tradition lie in the Chicago chapter and presumably their adherence to this practice is just as strong.

Below is the holy prayer of the Latin Kings printed in its entirety. This is an example of a prayer that is always recited at New York universals though it originated in Chicago.

> Almighty Father, King of Kings, Maker of the Universe and Foundation of life. Bring peace to our soul, to those here present, to those not present, to the young and the old. As an Almighty Nation under one sun protected by thine love and guidance we bring our right fist upon our heart for sincerity, love, wisdom, strength, knowledge and understanding. Three hundred-sixty degrees of strong king wisdom. Illuminate our minds and our hearts. Guide our thoughts with thine righteousness. Guide and protect the thoughts of our Coronas and all those holy and righteous lovers and followers of our beloved family and tribe—the Almighty Latin King and Queen Nation. Let the Manifesto of our departed brothers be the path to thee and let it be as it was in the beginning—strong King wisdom on both continents, Peace in Black and Gold. King Love! Yesterday, Today, Tomorrow, Always and Forever.

Bureaucracy and the Importance of Record Keeping

The organization has another social and textual tradition that separates it from most other comparable groups: it has a bureaucracy. More explicitly, this highly formal side of the organization is characterized by: (1) a strict hierarchy in which office holders have defined realms of power and paths of both ascension and descension; (2) decisions made by the organization's bodies that are recorded and filed; (3) a system of maintaining members' conduct and biographical records; (4) minutes and reports of group activities that are taken regularly; and (5) accounts of dues collections and outgoing expenditures which are supposed to be open to membership scrutiny. According to Knox, this kind of organizational efficiency is powerfully present in the Chicago Kings:

This type of gang is a rational, calculating, and self-supporting enterprise. . . . It has costs for maintaining its operations, it collects dues, and keeps accurate account of its gang treasury money, its income sources over time and its expenditures over time. . . . The gang has this general welfare benefit character by being able to provide money to its needy members in or outside of jail/prison. The gang does in this sense function as an economic benevolent society for its members in a small but very symbolic way [Knox 1997:67].

Noting a structure not unlike the Chicago group, we have observed a developed level of task delegation and specialization in New York City as well, with members serving as secretaries, treasurers, and media officers in addition to the crown structure with its regional leaders, spiritual advisors, enforcers, and vice-presidents. This bureaucratic culture is not only a direct manifestation of the Chicago tradition, it is also a reflection of the group's natural history. For, as it has grown from its early prison or street corner confines to a more multiregional agency, it has necessarily become more complex, more ambitious, and more rule-laden. In figures 4.3 and 4.4, we see two examples of this bureaucratic culture: the first is a recruitment form and the second is a report written by one of the Queens for her branch chapter.

The Role of Record Keeping

In the application process, as shown in figure 4.3, we can see what some might consider further evidence of the group's malevolent and violent world outlook. A close look at the recruitment document shows that the group not only wants to know the address of the applicant's next of kin, but it also has to know about his or her enemies, where he or she can be reached quickly, and so forth. On the other hand, in order to be an effective player in the fast-moving dramas that are the stuff of street subcultures, such knowledge has obvious merits. Quite simply, members need to be found at short notice especially when there are sworn enemies of the organization, as is the case in *The People v. Folks* feud in Chicago or in various neighborhoods throughout New York where conflicts between the ALKQN and a range of street-based groups erupt from time to time.

But aside from the social control functions and the self-defense rationales of these kinds of data, this kind of knowledge acquisition shows that the group is very conscious of its own development and takes itself very seriously. Approaching this tradition of record keeping through a paradigm of resistance, we could interpret the practice as the group's attempt to write its own history, thereby: (1) providing a powerful counter to the destructive ten-

APPLICATION FOR THE A.L.K.Q.N. MEMBERSHIP

NAME_____

D.O.B._____

PLACE OF BIRTH_____

ACTUAL ADDRESS_____

HOME ADDRESS_____

NAME_____

NAME_____

THREE RELATIVES ADDRESS:
1)_____
2)_____
3)_____

WIFE,COMMON IN-LAW OR GIRL'S ADDRESS:
_____

ENEMY'S_____
_____
_____

HOW MANY TIMES HAVE YOU BEEN IN JAIL AND WHY?_____
_____

IF YOU ARE NEEDED,WHERE TO FIND YOU
QUICKLY:_____
_____

TELEPHONE NUMBER____(____)_____

REASON WHY YOU CHOSE TO BECOME A KING:_____
_____
_____
_____
_____
_____

WHICH ARE YOUR GOALS AS A LATINO,AND WHAT KIND OF GOAL YOU
SEEK AS A KING:_____

(CONTINUE ON THE BACK)>>>>>>>>>>>>>>>>>>>>>>>>>>>>>>

FIGURE 4.3 Example of an ALKQN recruitment form.

S. J.

Daily Report
    Amor De Reins. Today is Sunday the 27th of February 1994. I'm coming to you with my right fist upon my heart with my willingness to die 360° strong.
    Queen Melisa called me, and ask me if she can be excuse because her stepfather had died, and she was going to Florida up to Saturday of March 5, 1994
    Queen Sina had an order from King Mike that she had to be home at 9:30 pm on week days, and on weekends 12:00 A.M. On Wednesday her father told her to be home at 12:00 A.M. she didn't listen she came home at 3:00 A.M. She didn't listen to the order King Mike 2nd Supreme Crown of New York State
    I'm coming to you with my right fist upon my heart and my willingness to die. 360° strong. Amor De Reins

Queen Jone - 4th crown

FIGURE 4.4 Example of a Daily Report from the Queens Section of the ALKQN (early 1994).

dencies of rumor; (2) making members more accountable both for their actions and for their ideas; and (3) reporting on the progress of the group in meeting its goals over time.

Whatever model we use to analyze this extraordinary phenomenon, there is no doubt that the group is following the rational-legal model of organizational development that Weber (1910) saw as the outgrowth of capitalist social relations. Further, the group is also following the intergenerational traditions of innumerable social and athletic clubs which have emerged in all social classes, but which are particularly plentiful in the old collectivized neighborhoods of the working classes.

Finally, the act of record keeping could be interpreted as a ritual that is both empowering and an expression of resistance for a group whose members have often come from the most marginalized classes and who have experienced the most substandard of educations. In other words, the effort to develop their own data resources, to add logic and rigor to group proceedings, to find a form of discipline in everyday life that is not dictated by the structures of poverty and segregation, can all be seen in the tradition of record keeping that the group seems to cherish.

Representing

The key term in gang communication is reppin', short for representing. It refers to a repertoire of communication practices whereby gang members enact, and thereby constitute, their gang identity. Reppin' encompasses everything from wearing the signifying gang colors, throwing up hand signs, and calling out code words to inscribing elaborate graffiti murals. However, there is a deeper meaning undergirding all of these representations. As one neighbor explained to me, It is throwing up your love—it is all about love.

Conquergood 1993:40

These subcultural traditions and practices described by Conquergood above are not specific to the Kings but exist among many other gangs in Chicago. However, it is fair to say that the Kings have taken the art and language of reppin' to a level that is extraordinarily complex and layered—so much so that it is difficult and practically impossible for outsiders to appreciate or understand.[4]

Whether it is graffiti, hand signals, symbolic mixes of clothing, verbal cues, or the ever-expanding lexicon of argot, each new generation of Kings builds on the subcultural traditions of the previous one in a milieu where marginality from the "mainstream" is a constant—only the ethnic origins of the members may change.

Physical Reppin'

The photograph in figure 4.5 of young members (Pee Wees) of the ALKQN tells us a great deal about the communication system of the group. There are at least five kinds of representations of the crown being displayed by the eight Kings, in an act that appears choreographed but in fact is completely spontaneous before the photojournalist's camera. This highly ritualized system of physical representation is one of the most valued traditions appropriated and handed down by the prescient maternal organization in Chicago. Every member of the group takes great pride in this tradition, which is evident in the energetic self-confidence and cocky attitudes displayed.

In the act of representing they are also engaging in what might be called a studied, or rehearsed, comradery, exemplified by the linking of hands to make a crown. As Conquergood has noted, in every first encounter between Kings and Queens each member is obliged to give the national salute, which is a fluid, complex gesture involving the making of a crown with the right hand, kissing it, and then hitting the heart, followed by the exclamation "amor de rey" or "amor de reina" (King Love or Queen Love). Sometimes this is also followed by the two members embracing each other or the two members putting their crowns together.

Finally, the photograph also depicts the powerful metaphor of sanctity, demonstrated by the draping of beads over the crown. In essence this gesture signifies both the righteous and blessed nature of the individuals who have taken the oath of Kingism and the spiritual protection that the nation enjoys as long as it is pursuing the cause of individual and collective liberation and empowerment.

Officially Representing

Thus far we have discussed several different forms of highly visible self-representations and collective representations which members of the ALKQN have appropriated from their Chicago counterparts. These representational forms have evolved over many years with the Chicago Kings tracing their continuity back as far as the 1950s on the streets and to the 1940s in the state prison system of Illinois. However, in New York there is another form of representation which is frequently used and which has been appropriated just as much from the "high" culture of the dominant classes as from the "low" culture of the streets of Chicago.

FIGURE 4.5 Example of New York Latin Kings physical reppin.'
(Courtesy of Steve Hart.)

D.B.: What did the ambassador do?

King S.: The ambassador was like an ambassador of the world. You know what ambassadors do. He was like the President. He was like the biggest one, you know?

D.B.: So you would represent the Kings?

King S.: I would represent, yeah, I would be Ambassador of the Nation. I would go to other states and stuff and I would preach Kingism.

D.B.: You'd talk to other people?

King S.: Other members, seminars, talk to people like you that were interested in the Latin Kings [Interview, 8/18/1997].

The above exchange demonstrates the role that diplomacy plays in the ALKQN, which is not so dissimilar from that of nation states. According to King S., he would travel to meet with leaders of the same organization or with other street organizations in different parts of the state and sometimes, when a matter was urgent, he would cross state lines even though this might have violated his parole terms. As the ALKQN grew in reputation and size, these visits to other groups became more necessary in order to mediate conflicts with local groups operating under the name of the New York franchise, to share information on law enforcement strategies and actions, or simply to establish ground rules for future acts of collaboration. At the same time, there were numerous representational visits from other groups to the heartland of the ALKQN. Some came to learn from ALKQN's reform movement; others were there to help mediate disputes between the group and some local unreformed gangs; and still others came simply to voice their support for the work that was gaining the group so much media attention.

Although the ALKQN members pay great homage to the example of their brothers in Chicago, this should not imply that Chicago is somehow controlling the New York City organization.[5] Quite the contrary, for some time the New York City organization was charting a course both similar and quite different from its maternal organization and it has gone so far as to break with a number of shibboleths held dear by its Chicago founders.[6] However, there is no doubt that Chicago has had and continues to have a tremendous influence on the New York chapter, in particular on the group's most basic rituals of internal organization, intragroup communications, and symbolic representations. In addition, the Chicago Motherland has handed down the fundamental goals of the New York branch and has framed much of the organization's street political agenda.

Nonetheless, from the point of view of the New York chapters, Chicago could not make good on its own political goals and, despite all its wisdom and experience, too many of its members were mired in the primitive stage of Kingism [i.e., gangbanging (the intergroup fighting rituals of gang membership) and "holding down the hood"]. For New York, therefore, during its reform period, it was the principles and concepts of the New King stage that the leaders attempted to instill in members and which were used as a framework for social movement building.

In the ensuing chapters we will elaborate on the other subcultural traditions, both gang and nongang, that have fueled ALKQN's growth, provided a constant state of tension within the organization, and ultimately caused it to be one of the most exciting youth subcultural developments to originate from America's streets since the 1960s.

CHAPTER 5

THE TRADITIONS OF KING BLOOD

You sentenced me to die day by day. . . . I don't mind my mail to be monitored, but you are telling me nobody can write to me, nobody can send money to me, nobody can care about me no more?

King Blood on being sentenced to a life term, with the first forty-five years to be spent in solitary confinement, quoted in Hoffman 1997

"Wassup?" he says, smiling as he takes a seat. Then the founder of the organization now known as the Latin Kings closes his eyes in a gesture of fatigue. "I've been in segregation for 38 months in the box," King Blood finally grunts in Spanish so the man with the walkie-talkie can't understand. "Before this, I was in Attica for 14 months." He pauses to look at his hands. "They say I have a lot of power with the Latino community and that I'm very dangerous."

Lucas Rivera, *Vibe* magazine, 1997

In this chapter we will discuss the role of the Latin Kings under King Blood's leadership during the period from 1986 to 1996. What kind of a group was it during this time? How did Luis Felipe become the most heavily sentenced federal inmate since World War II? Is or was he the "amiable sociopath," as his lawyer, Lawrence Feitell, described him? What kind of legacy did King Blood leave behind, such that he was revered by many in the organization as a Latino hero, an indestructible visionary, and someone of great courage who was willing to sacrifice his life for the sake of the movement? These questions will be addressed, and the highly contradictory impact that King Blood has had on the ALKQN's traditions will be discussed. It should be stated from the outset that the bulk of the data for this chapter is based on newspaper articles and letters between King Blood and his confederates both inside and outside the prison walls. Other data will come from interviews with King Blood's lawyers and prosecutors, correctional staff, and older Latin Kings who had relations with King Blood during this early period.

Who Is King Blood?

To understand a little about King Blood it is necessary to see his life in two stages. The first encompasses his early years up until he was about nineteen years old, during which time he is, for the most part, in civil society. The second includes his latter years, when he is mostly imprisoned.

The Early Years: Cuba, Miami, and the Road to Chicago

According to King Blood (see figure 5.1), his real name is Luis Felipe Fernández Mendez, born on May 11, 1961, in Havana, Cuba. Further details about Blood's early life are very few except that he had a mother, Esterina, who was a sex worker (Hoffman 1997:31); a father, Gilbert, who he never knew; a brother; a son named Duane; and an ex-wife named María. Currently, according to King Blood, other than his son, who lives with his grandmother in Spain, and his ex-wife, who lives in New York City, he "has no living relatives."

In a detailed interview, King Blood reveals other aspects of his early years, in particular his extraordinary journey to the United States:

> One morning in 1979, he [King Blood] was making his way home when he felt the cold barrel of a gun behind his ear. He escaped, ran behind a car, pulled out a .38 revolver, and fired several shots. "I shot the guy in the arm," he says. "But before I had a chance to run away from la policia, they arrested me and charged me with attempted homicide. I got 10 years."
>
> By the next year, Cuba seemed overtaken with lawlessness and desperation. That's when Castro opened his prison cells and freed the "undesirables." King Blood became one of the lucky ones, setting off across the Straits of Florida in a rickety boat made of inner tubes and old furniture. More than 100 refugees traveled together in a ragtag flotilla, their fate in nature's indifferent hands. He remembers seeing a fin cutting through the water just before the raft next to him was rammed, throwing an old man overboard. The sharks ripped him apart, filling the water with magenta clouds. "I felt like a prisoner of the sea," says King Blood. Six years later, he wrote in the Latin Kings' manifesto, "You don't even know if you will survive the present night.

8/18/93

My Name is, Luis felipe fernandez Mendez. King Blood #1 Supreme Crown(INKA) of New York State.

I was born in May 11 of 1961. My Sign is Taurus. My Parents are: Gilbert and Esterina.

I was the President of Brinmark and Winthrop in Chicago.

On the above day. I use the power of my rank to named our brother Alex Figueroa "King Alex" to became the #4 Supreme Crown(Treasure) of the State of New york.

His word is law in any Chapter of New york State. failure to fallow his orders will be a Violation the the Latin King's, Queen's Nation Constitution.

King Love!

I signing this with my right fist letting my heart making the sign of the almighty Crown as a representation of my willingness of Dil, for my brothers, sisters, Crown, and Nation

"King Blood"

#1 Supreme Crow (Inka) of New york Sta

FIGURE 5.1 Letter from Luis Felipe, AKA King Blood.

But the biggest risk of all is living and dying, and as a King this is our eternal companion."

Felipe landed in Miami two days later, traveled to Key West, then to Puerto Rico, and eventually wound up in Chicago. There he reapplied his street skills, dealing cocaine and heroin and developing a reputation for ruthlessness. . . . He joined a renegade faction called the Pee Wee Kings. "I was about gangbanging then," he says, "I shot people, I killed people, I have been shot and killed myself" [Rivera, 10/11/1997].

There, in "Chi-town," according to King Blood, he rose in the ranks of the Latin Kings to be the President of the Brynmar and Winthrop chapter, a working-class neighborhood in the gang's "North Side" homeland and since then, "I never been in no other club but the Latin Kings."

In 1981, King Blood moved to the South Bronx in New York City, an area that by then had become synonymous with poverty and racial discrimination and which was declared "the poorest congressional district in the United States" (Kozol 1990) by the U.S. government. In this environment, where joining a gang subculture was a relatively normal stage of teenage socialization (Fecher and Chalfant 1989; Collins 1979; Brotherton 1999), and where the streets were still smouldering from the landlord-inspired burning of working-class tenements begun during the early 1970s, it did not take long for King Blood to resume his criminal career. Committing what he has called a "drunken accident," King Blood was charged with shooting his girlfriend through a door and was convicted in 1982 of second-degree manslaughter; he received nine years in the state correctional system. After moving from institution to institution, King Blood eventually found himself in Collins Correctional Facility, a medium security prison with a reputation for brutality.[1] In this environment, King Blood felt surrounded by "an inmate system lorded over by black gangs and white guards" (Hoffman (1997:31). In 1986, after repeated clashes with the Five Percent Nation,[2] King Blood set about establishing the first branch of the Latin Kings in the New York State prison system, with himself as the Inca, First Supreme Crown, and President. In the following, King Blood recounts this history in his broken English:

> The Latin Kings start in New York City in Jan-20-1986. The reasons a sign of togetherness in Collins Correctional Facility a group of guys calling they self "gods" or "five percents" stab a Puerto Rican kid to take his belongings, this took place in side #1 a couple of days later, another Spanish guy also got jump by the same guys, and was send to Collins #2. At that time, I was in Collins two and I was planning already to do something about it, I use to hang out with this two Puerto Rican kids "Diablo and Chito" they also was mad about this situation, we desire to created the Nation in New York. I use to talk a lot with them about the Mother Land and how much respect the Latinos earn over there and why they always was looking for me to hear all the histories about the Kings of Chicago and I always enjoy talking about my Nation. . . . Well, they was my two first Kings brothers in New York City.

King Diablo and King Chito I teach them everything about our constitution, our lessons, prayers, allies, names, and enemies of the Mother Land [From "The History of the Latin Kings," written by King Blood in the ALKQN Manifesto].

Finally, in 1989, King Blood is paroled, but less than a year later he is rearrested for car theft and sent back "upstate" to Attica for another five years. It appears that during his prison stay King Blood was regularly disciplined by the authorities, and by 1993 he had already spent four years in "the box," i.e., a part of the prison that is segregated from the general population of inmates and where much of the time is spent in solitary confinement.[3] In fact, right up until his final conviction in 1996, King Blood spent almost half of his incarceration time under the prison regime's most punishing physical and psychological conditions. Below, a contemporary member of the ALKQN recounts both his experience of the segregation unit and his early memories of King Blood:

D.B.: How was it in the box?

King S.: I told you, I spent 2 years in there. It was hell, they used to torture you, you know mentally and physically. They treat you like an animal, you can't believe it.

D.B.: How do they try to break you?

King S.: For a start, the food is only cabbage and water, they do this just to let you have enough protein but no more. Then all the racist things they say to you, like "Spic, you're never gonna get outta here," "We're gonna kill you," and this kind of crap. After a while you get used to it and you're never gonna give in, but especially if you have the Nation behind you, that helps you.

D.B.: What about people coming to visit you?

King S.: No, very few people came but you know, you have to understand you can't try to live your outside life on the inside. It will kill you. If all you are doing is worrying about what's happening to your family, your wife and that kind of thing you'll break so you have to work on getting by on the inside and then you'll survive. It's all about survival. You have to do everything to survive. It's as simple as that [Interview, 8/18/1997].

By the time King Blood's final trial date approaches, he is thoroughly institutionalized. The only real source of meaning for him are his beloved Latin

Kings, who are no longer a small clique of Latino inmates in "the system" but a city-wide organization that is growing rapidly throughout the state as more and more inmates are released. Meanwhile, the many new, mostly young members are desperate to know their organization's founder and mysterious leader.

Public Enemy No. 1 and Prisoner Extraordinaire

When King Blood comes to trial for his final denouement in 1996, the "moral entrepreneurs" (Becker 1963) in local, state, and federal government have long been active in their crusades to eradicate the influence of street-organized gangs throughout the United States (Parenti 1999). State prisons built specially for gang members, such as Pelican Bay in California, have become commonplace; juvenile anticombination laws, particularly aimed at members of street gangs, have sprouted in most major states; curfews on youth who might be suspected of gang membership are in operation in large and small cities across the nation; and the Racketeering Influence and Corrupt Organizations Act, supposedly designed to bust the Mafia in the early 1970s, is now routinely used in injunctions against street gangs.

The above only describes the political and legal atmosphere in which King Blood was tried, so what exactly was King Blood charged with? During 1995, some fifty members of the Latin Kings were indicted by a federal grand jury on a series of charges, including: racketeering, extortion, and the murders of three Latin Kings and the attempted murder of four others during the years 1993 and 1994. However, King Blood during this period was incarcerated, so what was his role? According to the prosecution, he was guilty of conspiracy, for it was he and he alone, as day-to-day leader of the group, who could have ordered the executions and the attempted murders. The primary evidence against King Blood and the rest came from two star informers or "snitches," Alex Figueroa (King Al) and Nelson Torres[5] (King Nel), who were formerly leading members of the New York City organization and who themselves played a major role in all of the homicides. Figure 5.2 contains a partial list of the defendants taken from the court appearance list.

That these murders and attempted murders took place and were carried out by the Latin Kings was not in question. However, there were two extraordinary features of this case: (1) two of the major perpetrators of these crimes would be the ones who were essentially released into the witness protection program, complete with a new identity and tens of thousands of dollars of federal money, and (2) the authorities knew well in advance who was going to be murdered and when, yet, apparently, they did little to stop this from happening.

```
 1    UNITED STATES DISTRICT COURT
      SOUTHERN DISTRICT OF NEW YORK
 2    -----------------------------x

 3    UNITED STATES OF AMERICA,

 4              v.                              S7 94 Cr. 395(LMM)

 5    LUIS FELIPE, a/k/a "King Blood,"
      a/k/a "King Inka,"
 6    ZULMA ANDINO, a/k/a "Queen Zulma,"
      JOSE GABRIEL, a/k/a "King Teardrop,"
 7    JOSE CRUZ, a/k/a "King Blaze,"
      NELSON TORRES, a/k/a "King Nell,"
 8    MARIO QUINONES, a/k/a "King Bosco,"
      REYNALDO PEREZ, a/k/a "King Lil Rey,"
 9    FIDEL AYALA-MERCADO, a/k/a "King Ito,"
      ELQUIADES MORALES, a/k/a "King Apollo,"
10    SAMUEL SANTIAGO, a/k/a "King Sammy,"
      CARMELO GARCIA, a/k/a "King Mello,"
11    ALI FARES, a/k/a "King Tattoo,"
      JOSE TORRES, a/k/a "King Chino,"
12    ULYSSES CAMPOS, a/k/a "King Puti,"
      FELIX CORDERO, a/k/a "King Bear,"
13    DANIEL NAVARRO, a/k/a "King Scarface,"
      GILBERTO RIVERA, a/k/a "King Cano,"
14    RICHARD RIVERA, a/k/a "King Oreo,"
      WILSON CORTEZ, a/k/a "King Chino,"
15    CARLOS DONIS, a/k/a "King Mousey,"
      ANGEL FELICIANO, a/k/a "King Angel,"
16    a/k/a "King A,"
      ALBERTO FIGUEROA, a/k/a "King Drac,"
17    FRANCISCO TORRES, a/k/a "King Bollo,"
      ROBERTO PUENTE, a/k/a "King Manole,"
18    MICHAEL GONZALEZ, a/k/a "King Wolfie,"
      ANTONIO DELESTRE, a/k/a "King Tone,"
19    SAMMY FONSECA, a/k/a "King Green Eyes,"
      RICHARD ACEVEDO, a/k/a "King Richie,"
20    and JOHN DOE, a/k/a "King Julio,"

21
                    Defendants.
22
      -----------------------------x
23

24                                          August 10, 1995
                                            4:30 p.m.
25    C-2234


              SOUTHERN DISTRICT REPORTERS 212-637-0300
```

FIGURE 5.2 Partial list of the defendants taken from the court appearance list.

The prize for the authorities was the destruction of this "dangerous" and growing organization. One of Blood's lawyers explained the situation:

> Lawyer: It's like a contest, it's like a football game. If the two teams match up and whichever team wins, that's great, but if you have the players taking pay-offs, you know, that's not right, and that's basically what the government is doing. The government is paying off informants. They're paying them with their freedom and they're paying them with money.
>
> D.B.: But one of the things you said earlier was that the main witnesses were guilty of homicide?
>
> Lawyer: They were . . . and Mr. X. The three of them were, they were the culpable parties, the most culpable.
>
> D.B.: Because they admitted it?
>
> Lawyer: They got up on the stand and they admitted their participation. Mr. X. didn't because they didn't use him, but Sombra and Nell (the two witnesses), they got up on the stand and they admitted in very specific detail, how and what they did and the killing [2/17/1999].

The plea bargains arranged between the two informers and the prosecution effectively saved their lives but condemned those of their erstwhile *manitos* (brothers) to sentences ranging from fifteen to thirty years. Blood, however, decided not to go the way of his followers, and instead of pleading guilty like all the others, he opted to face a trial by his peers. Although ably defended by his public defense lawyers, the charge that he ordered the killings from his jail cell was overwhelmingly supported by: the testimony of the two federal witnesses; the copious letters he wrote to his colleagues (some 1,556 of them were intercepted, photocopied, and summarized by the prison authorities); and his phone calls, which were all taped. Figure 5.3 contains a facsimile of a page from one of the many hundreds of letters written by King Blood and used as evidence.

On September 9, 1997, at the United States District Court in Manhattan, King Blood was sentenced to life for the murder conspiracies (a total of 100 years) plus forty-five years for weapons possession. He would probably have received a death sentence, but this was not allowed under federal sentencing laws on conspiracy. Still, to spend the rest of one's natural life behind bars without the possibility of parole would seem punishment enough, but then the presiding federal judge outlined the following highly unusual stipulations for his incarceration: (1) the first 45 years of King Blood's sentence are

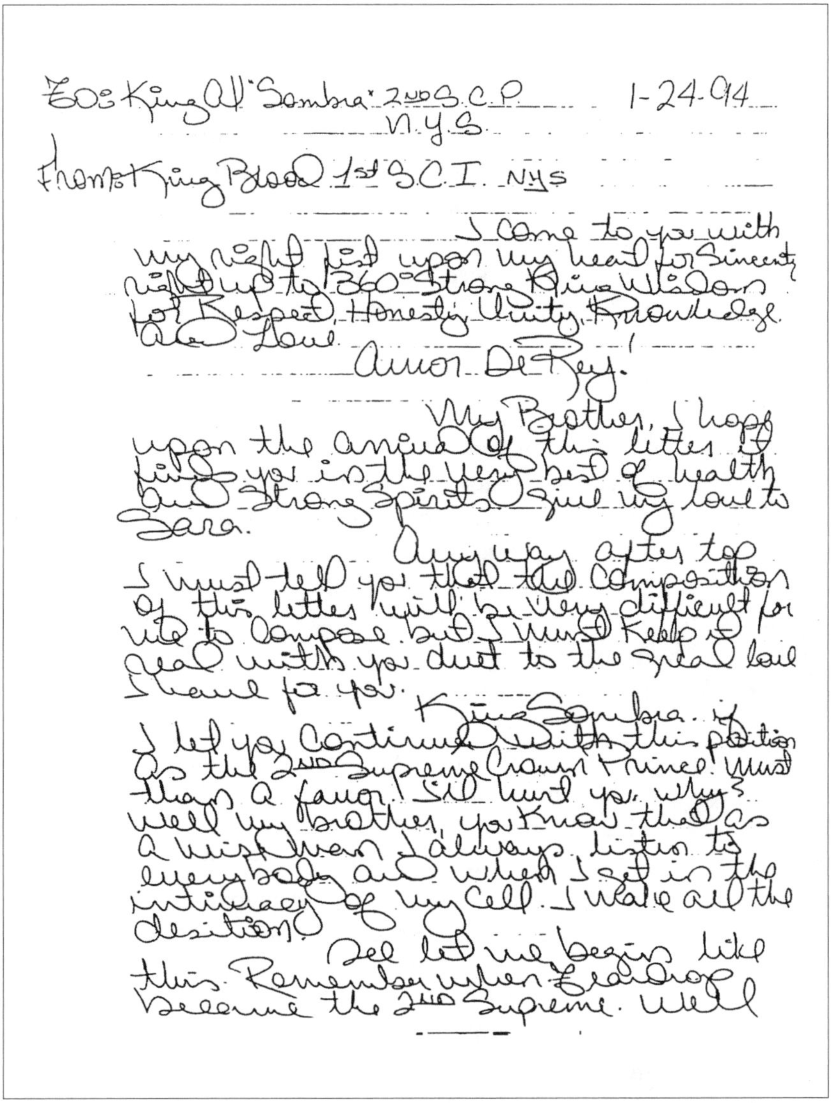

FIGURE 5.3 Facsimile of a page from a letter written by King Blood.

to be spent in solitary confinement; (2) there will be no mail between King Blood and anyone except through his lawyers; and (3) the only people who will be allowed to see King Blood are his two lawyers, Lawrence Feitell and Mr. L.; a paralegal secretary who works on the case in Manhattan; and Father Luis Barrios (coauthor of this book).[6]

The Judge, John S. Martin, a former United States attorney and defense lawyer and considered a "moderate" on the bench, explained the need for such restrictions: "some of the young men sitting in this court today who are supporters of Mr. Felipe might well be murdered in the future." Blood's only response was: "You sentenced me to die day by day. . . . I don't mind my mail to be monitored, but you are telling me nobody can write to me, nobody can send money to me, nobody can care about me no more?" (Hoffman 1997).

This act by the judge was a dramatic example of public degradation (Garfinkel 1963) and dehumanization by the criminal justice system. Serial killers, Mafia hit men and Godfathers, rapists, and other examples of "dangerous citizens" have rarely merited the kind of pre- and post-trial "shaming" that was reserved for King Blood—a point made repeatedly by King Tone during his subsequent leadership of the ALKQN.[7] Blood's lawyer, Lawrence Feitell, concurred with his client's self-described mental state and commented that, "he [King Blood] is not cerebrating normally. He has been in isolation for so long it's pushed him into never-never land" (Jane Gross, *New York Times*, 3/25/1999, B-2).

But the punishment and the demonization that necessarily accompanies it did not stop there. Rather, to complete the process, the state ruled that King Blood would keep company with the sickest, the most deviant, and the most violent of society's adjudicated individuals. From the time of his sentencing until the present, King Blood has been in Florence, Colorado, at an Administration Maximum Facility (ADX)—a "supermax" facility built by the Department of Corrections (Weissman and Cummings 1994). The facility contains an assortment of confinement units—the worst being the superisolation cells where King Blood is held for twenty-three hours a day along with Timothy McVeigh, one of the Oklahoma bombers; Ted Kaczynski, better known as the Unabomber from California; and Ramzi Ahmed Yousef, the so-called mastermind of the plot to blow up the World Trade Center. Some three years into King Blood's sentence, only Mr. L., one of his lawyers, has been able to visit him. Fr. Barrios has requested permission to visit King Blood on three occasions, but each time his request has been denied by the judge.[8]

The Multiple Personae of King Blood

In the following, we describe what we know of King Blood and the different roles and functions he has had during the Latin Kings and Queens' early years. Thereafter, we will interpret and provide the context to the traditions that seemed to abound in the ALKQN during the period 1990–1994.

King Blood: The Organizer

> First of all cuz I'm from Chicago and I never been in no other club but the Latin Kings. I also explain to them that who ever come out of this chapter will be 1 percent which mean that this is the first Division and to tell you the truth I never imagined that it will be as big as it is now [King Love].
>
> We start to regroup [recruit] more Spanish guys, at the beginning it was kind of complicated because lots of these guys were outlaws or from M.C. Clubs and what I was planning to do was a family thing.
>
> After a week we have nine (9) brothers. "Charlie Rock" which I made my enforcer then, "Chico" the first crown because his knowledge with the Latin Kings Nation, he was from Chicago, also, "Diablo" #2 Crown, Chito also Rock my person bodyguards and my other body, "B.K. and Babe King" who I named after our older brother from the Mother Land, "Rusty" the Crazy Cuban, "Speedy" an ex-Dirty One, these were the first Kings in New York.
>
> Well, Chico, Diablo, and Chito went to Collins #1 and took over that territory. They regroup many brothers over there also, like King Benny, King Barretto, Shorty Collins and many others.
>
> One day of the summer of 1987 this guy that has just came up from "Rikers Island" was one of the guys that jump in one of our brothers down there. When we find out that our brother "Jay" was in there and that he belong to the Latin Kings, he became over night a Muslim. I went to talk to the [Iman] of the Muslim community and explained to him the reason why this guy desire to become a Muslim. Well, he told that is nothing that he can do about it because the kid was already Muslim and that if we try to do anything to that guy they don't have a choice but to get involved. Well, what a better chance to find out how strong we really was at that time. So the shit hit the fence in the middle of the summer of 87 in Collins #2 yard [ALKQN Manifesto].

King Blood clearly saw that the Latino inmates were disorganized and dominated both by the guards and by the African-American inmates who, through the Nation of Islam and their respective prison gangs, gave them control of many of the resources, such as the television, the telephone, and various forms of contraband in the *sub rosa* economy (Parenti 1999). In this highly racialized setting, the lack of respect accorded the Latino inmate population caused enormous resentment, and as Blood says in his account of the early history, he was always talking to other Puerto Rican inmates about "how much respect the Latinos earn over there" (i.e., in Chicago).

But what kind of inmates did King Blood and his confederates recruit? And how did the organization grow so quickly and extensively? For King Blood, not just anybody could join the organization and only those who were willing to sacrifice their life for the *"causa"* could become members. "Snitches," "rapists," "gay men," and drug users (mainly by injection) were not recruitment material and neither were those who were joining mainly for the exercise of individual power. Rhetorically, at least, the Latin Kings were primarily about equality and respect for all Latinos/as:

The main purpose of this Nation (#1) is to show the world that we are equals and that together as one can claim the respect we deserve as human beings, (#2) to let them know that we are entitled as Latinos to been seeing as equals and we will do what must be necessary to obtain our goals [ALKQN Manifesto].

Thus, the organization was reserved for strong individuals who were willing and able to literally fight for their rights inside this perverse system of social control (Irwin 1982) against other inmates and the administration. Second, every member had to become a teacher and a student, serving as a mentor to others and as a serious seeker of truth to himself. Third, every member had to be able to take orders and respect authority although, he says, if a member sees that a leader is not being true to his crown, i.e., living the many lessons of the organization, then he has a right to reject that authority and "he will not be wrong in the eyes of the real kings." Fourth, all those who passed the tests of membership and were sworn into the organization were blessed "to have the power to open a chapter wherever they go." And finally, in early 1993, King Blood was the first Latin King leader to write a manifesto just for the women of the organization, which in theory gave female members more organizational autonomy, status, and power, while underscoring the role of the family in the group's praxis.

Within a short while, King Blood was seen by the facility's hierarchy as a major threat to its central authority[9] and, "a year later, the Administration put most of us in the boat to unknown places." But, of course, the only consequence this had for the Latin Kings was to spread them throughout the system as the members took their brand of Latino self-defense and self-help techniques to the growing numbers of alienated Latino inmates herded into the system courtesy of antidrug and antiviolence laws (see Parenti 1999; Donziger 1996). The Kings, then, spread not only throughout New York State but also to Boston, Connecticut, New Jersey, Massachusetts, Pennsylvania, and Florida, where they set up their franchises and wrote their own manifestos, integrating the basic philosophy and rituals of Chicago with local traditions. In 1993, King Blood reports that except for Connecticut and Florida, all the "nations" are all reporting to him and that Chicago is calling for a unity meeting between King Blood's representatives and the Connecticut leadership (whom King Blood refers to, in disparaging tones, as a bunch of "gangbusters"). The following letter to King Blood is from a leader in the Massachusetts correction system:

> Amor de Rey, Brother. Networking is todays topic. We have solid brothers in the streets and 2 solid people in both states can becom an issue of progress. We have Chicago support and contacts to back us up. Enough said Brother. I'm asking if its possible to have an intelligent solid Brother to prove as a messenger for some possible networking. It is something I'm sure you'd be interested in.

King Blood, then, in his early years, meshed this understanding of the human psyche with a penchant for self-discipline and a respect for intellectual growth (albeit a mixture of prison knowledge and official book knowledge). He was also someone who was able to go beyond the black, Latino, and white racial divide, and when he came to Attica in the late 1980s he began organizing a cross-racial coalition of forces to resist the prison authorities. This little-known chapter of King Blood's life is described by one of his lawyers and helps to explain more about the hero status that King Blood maintained among many of his followers:

> King Blood was like Cyrus, you know from that film, *The Warriors*. Because he wasn't just the leader of the Latin Kings, but he was tryin' in this grand effort to bring peace, to bring together all the gangs, 'cause he knew that if he could bring together all the gangs he could perhaps have an uprising against the institution or whatever his ultimate goal was. Or, to make demands, to change the way the conditions were. Because the conditions suck. I mean, Amnesty International, you know, they're coming after the U.S. They're saying that our prisons . . . and they are . . . they're terrible. Just because they don't torture people and kill them doesn't mean that the conditions are any

better than anywhere else. The conditions are horrible, and, you know, the isolation is the worst [Interview with Mr. L., a King Blood lawyer].

Had King Blood been successful, he would have been the first inmate to have united all the prisoner factions against their common enemy since the Attica uprising in 1971. Figure 5.4 is an example of King Blood being cited for organizing inmates in the Attica facility.

King Blood: The Teacher

D.B.: How did you talk to Blood in this time?

King S.: Through the vents, he would talk to me at all times of the day. Sometimes at 2 or 3 in the morning he would call a culture class, he was the first to get them going for Latinos in the state system. He demanded that we know our history. . . . They just wanted to let him have it at one prison but he demanded it throughout and we eventually got it. We used to talk a lot about our past. He used to read all the time and I used to always get things out of the library and try to understand where I came from cuz no one before had ever told me. No one really told me about Pedro Albizu Campos and Lolita Lebrón and these people. . . . You know, he's Cuban and these Cuban's are very strong. They'll never break him only if they send him crazy [Interview, 8/18/1997].

King S. above is describing the profound impact that King Blood had on him as an inmate. He discusses this influence not in terms of King Blood's ruthlessness and guile, as might befit a leader and founder of an organized crime outfit, but rather as a vital connector to a past which has been obliterated by the colonizer. It is King Blood, therefore, a Cuban, who pushes King S. to recognize the importance of Puerto Rican revolutionary heroes and heroines. It is King Blood who sets up the culture classes to teach reading and writing and revisit the ways in which the U.S. laid open the veins of Latin America and the Caribbean (cf. Galeano 1977). This emphasis on learning and self-edification is a powerful trait in the original Latin Kings in Chicago but it is taken to a new level in the King Blood version of the organization, not least because King Blood himself prizes the art of writing, debating, and waxing lyrical on a range of day-to-day topics:

There are many ways to prove to your self how much of a King you are. Not always you have to die in order to become a hero of the Nation. Just be a good teacher. Help those who most need that help. Teach our youngest the

DEPARTMENT OF CORRECTIONAL SERVICES   P.O.M. #3.404
APPENDIX "U"

ATTICA CORRECTIONAL FACILITY

CELL SHIELD ORDER RENEWAL

In accordance with NYCRR Title 7, Section 305.6, you, _Felipe_.

• _92A5674_, cell location _CW-8_ have had your cell shield

status reviewed and renewed from _9-24-93_ to _10-1-93_ because of the

following reasons:

On 9·22·93 you refused several orders to move And : · 1
threatened to harm C.O.s when you came out of cell
Also incited entire East galley to refuse any
given order

<u>Notice to inmate:</u>

You may write to the Deputy Superintendent for Security or his/her
designee to make a statement as to the need for continuing the cell
shield order.

Authorization

                                        Date 9/27/93
Deputy Supt. for Security

cc: Superintendent
       Guidance Unit
       SHU Sergeant
       Inmate

FIGURE 5.4 Form citing King Blood for organizing inmates in the
Attica facility.

same way we will teach our own kids. Learn how to be "under before you think about been in top." Give to your brother what you like to receive [ALKQN Manifesto].

Thus, King Blood understands only too well that to build the organization in these highly restrictive settings it is necessary to empower people by giving them hope, a new identity, and the social, organizational, and intellectual tools with which to survive. Therefore, the lessons have to be both practical and abstract, resonating with the life worlds of the members. They also have to be able to spark the imagination and transport people into a world that is free of the numbing contradictions of the present. In this way, King Blood constantly exhorts members to be "real" and not to be "fake," to be honest and not to deceive, to resist the opportunism and depravity inherent in prison life and not cave in to forces of evil.

We must remember where we come from. We created this for the 3rd oppressed world. And our oppressed peoples, even that they want to learn, they was blinded by the oppressor so they can't never learn. . . . You don't need a Degree when your heart is in the Nation. . . . Don't matter how slow you might be to learn what is written on paper if you really love your people you will die for them and this is what counts [King Blood, ALKQN Manifesto].

King Blood: The Leader

I warned you before about this but it seems like you ignore the facts that I'm the head leader and founder of the Nation in the State of New York and that to do things related with this Nation you must inform me before and not after decisions have been made [Letter to Queen L.].

To understand the legacy of King Blood for the nation is to appreciate his primary role as a leader. However, in King Blood's case, this role was more complicated than for most gang leaders since he was required to be both a leader for the incarcerated and for "the free," two very different kinds of constituents and organizational settings. Furthermore, he was a leader coming out of a Latino culture with an enormous emphasis on kinship rituals and obligations. But, before we begin to discuss and interpret the data, we might ask what the literature says about gang leadership, surely one of the most important areas of a group's development.

Curiously, empirical studies on gang leadership are very few. Most studies, because they are based on one-time interviews, focus primarily on the activities of gangs and give short shrift to the nature and qualities of legitimate authority.[10] Two researchers who have provided useful insights into this area are Campbell and Jankowski, who wrote on the hierarchical nature of New York City gangs during the 1970s (Campbell 1984) and the 1980s (Jankowski 1991).

Why was this pyramidal structure so prevalent? Jankowski argues that it is due to two primary factors: (1) gangs are rational organizations with short- and long-term goals aimed at improving their social and economic conditions, and this form of organization is the most efficient method of controlling and expanding their territory, and (2) gangs reflect their immediate cultural environment, which in New York City's case is characterized by a history of race and ethnic competitiveness that emphasizes the need of groups to be organized as a matter of survival.[11]

But what are the requirements of leadership itself? Jankowski argues that in gangs with powerful hierarchies, what he calls "vertical gangs," the characteristics of leaders are similar to those noted by Machiavelli. A successful gang leader must: attend to the needs and desires of the rank and file; maintain a "court" of loyalists; recruit and train a staff to carry out routine duties; be flexible in handling a range of personal and membership problems without appearing "weak"; and be fair in handing out justice (or at least be prudent and not reckless). Where and how does Blood measure up to these findings?

From Rational Leadership and Familialism to Ruthlessness

There are a number of problems in applying Jankowski's rational action or Campbell's dominant cultural model to King Blood's brand of leadership. While there are certainly aspects of each in the way that Blood exercised control over the organization, both the style and the substance of his leadership defy easy categorization.

First, in King Blood's own mind, leadership in the Kings is only achieved by: (1) being an honest individual, especially to all brothers and sisters; (2) never refusing to sacrifice for the Nation, even if it means losing one's life; and (3) passing on the wisdom of the organization to other deserving individuals. To this extent, Blood is what might be called a "righteous" leader, whose claims to leadership emerge as much from a moral calling as from any calculating strategies of gang leadership.

Second, while Blood certainly saw himself as head of a hierarchical organization, his thinking was shaped by a range of influences, not just those embedded in the localized culture, for example: the nature of the organization in Chicago; the requirements of the prison setting; and the memory of democratic centralism and the dominant role of the Communist Party in King Blood's home nation.

Third, this "vertical" organization was not, as Jankowski presumes, in strict contrast to "horizontal" organizations with their emphases on brotherly solidarity and the family. Quite the contrary, it is difficult to think of a group that is more influenced by family ties, family culture, and the powerful mind-set of *carnalismo* (a very physical form of camaraderie) than the ALKQN.

Fourth, while Jankowski is correct in that a vertical leadership encourages a limited degree of democracy and is not as prone to the "charismatic" irrationalism of leaders,[12] nonetheless, King Blood repeatedly displays a penchant for dictatorial *pronunciamentos*, and he is not shy about using his mystique to elevate his legitimacy.

Below are excerpts from many hundreds of letters to members. They give a more precise indication of the contradictions in King Blood's style of leadership. The letters themselves cover a range of topics but most of them focus on: the group's struggles against its external enemies (i.e., the police, the prison authorities, the media, and other prison and street groups); the group's battle with its internal enemies; the state of the group as an organization; and the welfare of individual members.

Battling the Enemies Without

Although King Blood was largely concerned with intrigues coming from within his organization, he was also focused on several external forces that seemed to be committed to his downfall.

THE PRISON REGIME   The Kings were caught between two worlds: on the one hand, competing with African-American inmates for prison power and, on the other, resisting the injustices of prison rules and punishments. Although King Blood was almost constantly kept in solitary, there is little mention in his letters either of his struggles with the authorities or of the punishments he received, except when he was given his life sentence.

> Well I'm here to try to nock this box time off. But these Devils [the prison authorities] are fucking with me like hell. I just went to my article 78[13] and lost it a bit. Fucked, its nothing but box time. I'll handle it.

> Listen, I don't know if King L. tell you we got into some conflict with the cops and they got us like "silence of the lambs" behind glass. They give him 60 more days of box time I'm still waiting for my hearing.

> "North Facility" = The door is open for retaliation against the devils. So you know the rest.

THE MEDIA Blood did not seem to know much about what the outside world was saying except when members wrote to inform him and they sent a clipping from an article. But he could be very clear on the reciprocal relations between the media and the social construction of crime and criminals (Baer and Chambliss 1997), and he certainly understood that the rules from Chicago forbade talking to journalists.

> Can you imagine how the police are looking at me? . . . They all know who I am. You know what they gonna do? They gonna tip the press with my name and who I am in the Latin King's Nation and you know what's gonna happen when this happen? Well they already made me C.M.C.[14] in jail cuz I'm a threat to the security of all prisons state wide, plus I am a menace to society. Well the next move when the media gets involved they will classify me public enemy #1 and when this happen I can kiss the street good by for ever [Letter to King A.].

THE ENEMY GANGS The Kings were at war mainly with different factions within the prison system (see also Parenti 1999) and there were constant fears of a group emerging to challenge their power, which eventually happened with the Bloods prison gang at Riker's Island during the period after 1993. However, these wars seemed to ebb and flow as victories were won, defeats were accepted, and the authorities responded by moving the leaders from prison to prison to destabilize the command structure of the organization. But there is little doubt that King Blood reveled in his presumed role as general of an army that was constantly facing down challenges and strategizing for supreme advantage in present or future battles.

> Right now our Nation is in the middle of a war. But because many brothers are talking they selves to death they not even know it. We have a war in New York against "Unity" or "Power Rules," in Rikers Island and upstate have been created also. Why? To challenge the Kings but we are too busy talking and fighting against each other to realize this.

> About the Muslims, be on point. The same weak move they try to pull after ramadan was what they try to pull on me in 86. So be on point.

Battling the Enemies Within

A great deal of the letters were devoted to rooting out the uncommitted and the traitors in the group. He often refers to the times he has been "flipped on," i.e., betrayed to the authorities by presumed allies, and he has little patience or compassion for any of his leaders who challenge his decisions or who are seen to abuse their power. The only exceptions to this were two or three leaders at Rikers Island who were able to negotiate certain areas with Blood[15] and one, in particular, who was able to compete with Blood on the production of knowledge for the organization.

"THE FAKES"

Listen my brother, if we have to start all over again we will but a lot of fakes will feel my strength. My brother, when I see you this week or better yet in our next visit we will talk some serious shit, lot of punks will drop like fly's but it's over with the games. I'm mad tired of sacrificing myself for some fake ass niggers that don't deserve it. . . . We gonna get into some real death squad. Like I said, lot of people gonna feel the heat but it will be necessary [King Blood, letter to King Al, 8/31/1993].

THE ABUSERS

Why do you think I got so many followers? Because I'm badest than everybody? No, its just because I'm fair and I treat everybody like a man. As long as a brother act like a man is how I treat him in return. . . . My brother, see, many leaders in history be overthrow by their own peoples. I'm talking about people in history like "Batista from Cuba" "Salvador Allende from Chile" "Trujillo from Santo Domingo." And you know why this happen to them? Because they suffering from power fever. My brother, the people give you the power when they choose to follow you. So they will take it away from you. . . . I love you and I'd never hesitated a bit to die for you. But, if our Nation fall because you be too stubborn or selfish to share your power with your crowns, my brother, all I can tell you is that you too will become my worse enemy [King Blood to King T., 9/12/1993].

The State of the Organization

The bulk of his letters focused on the ongoing struggles of the group to organize itself into an idealized prison/street movement with ideologically committed adherents, an unbreakable leadership, a fluid command structure, and a zest for "power." Thus, his letters are full of themes that range from the administrative to the instigative and always in a language that is deadly serious, laced with the syntax of war, religion, sports, and, of course, the street. However, what is probably most chilling about Blood's language is his routine way of giving someone a death sentence or a beating. Certainly, in these highly volatile interrelated worlds of the prison and the street the "live by the sword die by the sword" mentality (see also Anderson 1999;

Sanchez 2000) is commonplace but with King Blood it constitutes the core of his organizational theory. To him, and it is explicit in much of his manifesto, it is only through the purging of weak individuals that the organization can attain collective purity, a social-Darwinistic notion that is a characteristic of many messianic social movements as well as the military. Further, he views such actions as the hallmarks of strong, male leadership, and as salutary reminders to other members of the nation's unwavering mission, however that may be defined.

PROMOTIONS AND DEMOTIONS

Through your leadership as the 2nd crown you have made some mistakes that can be very dangerous to our Nation in general. . . . I don't try to know you for what you did. No, you have done a lot for being a rookie, but if I allow you to continue in there you will end up doing something very detrimental. So I must stop you in time [Letter to King A.].

ACTION AND IDEALISM

We are created in the image and likeness of God. We have god power. As much as the stars, the trees and the rivers, we are both the word and the voice of God. The mind, the word and the voice of god. The Mind, the Word, the Powers that give birth to our Universe are ours. All we have to do is claim them and use them to create the world we want [Letter to King R.].

NATION BUILDING

Listen, I want you to know that we are the role model of all Kings in the whole USA. No one are more disciplined that us believe me. Even with all the negative things we are getting from the media we are still more close to the 360 degrees goal than any one. Plus in Chicago they know that thanks to me we have new Kings in so many places cuase after I created the Nation in N.Y. all the rest of the States follow up [Letter to King B.].

PEACEMAKER

Latin King S. wrote me the other day talking about the hunger strike on the 17th. But he wasn't talking about a peaceful strike. He was talking about take the building over and all that stuff. I told him to chill and to report to you. So be on point [Letter to King D.].

RUTHLESSNESS AND DISCIPLINE

It's a brother named "King X" out there that fake the funk on our brother King L. Well accorded to what L. told me he doesn't desire to be one of us.

Now King L. coming out soon and I give him green light to take care of him. Correct me if I'm wrong [Letter to King B.].

Brothersito since you and E. left I can't help but worried about the way the mission of you know who went down. I hope if they do find him they can't identify him. Those brothers should take him out of there but its too late now, just hope for the best. One thing you brothers got to make sure is in the future don't leave loose ends like that again [this is in reference to the killing of Lil' Man; Letter to King S.].

He should know that from the get go, now is too late. Not because he's a threat, but because he shed our blood. I probably let him live, if he never touch one of us before. But he did. Plus we know that this are his true intentions. It looks to me like he knows that he doesn't have the best hand at the moment, so as a good general he fake weakness to make the enemy more arrogant. So he can buy time and regroup. *No,* I don't believe he's really coming from the heart. He must be T.O.S. cuz to let him live, he always gonna have to look behind. Remember my beloved brother, when is on is on until the end. Always remember, "I reward my friends and hate my enemies" [Letter to King M.].

FORGIVENESS

We have two kinds of beef. Personal beef and others that I called "shit happens." You know like I know that the beef wasn't . . . like you say it was 3 young Latin kids. Do you really think they know what they was doing? No. They just want to show up and kill something. And you was at the wrong place at the wrong time. I can't tell you, fuck, kill him cuz you know it's not right. Our duty is to help our young to no do nonsenses like this, to love our race, and to become better in life, not to destroy our own people [Letter to second-in-command at Rikers Island].

King Blood: The Isolated

Although King Blood liked to think he was in touch with the day-to-day activities of the group, it was evident that towards the end of his reign he was extremely marginalized and dependent.

A. the only thing I really treasure in this life is "loyalty" and I receive that from you and E. [both of whom became or tried to become key witnesses for the federal prosecution] so this is what you two will get from me, no matter what.

Now as my mind, body and soul in the outside world you two must always be aware of what is best for me. As you know I can very well take care of myself and survive in here, but out there I can't ever survive if you two don't guide me.

I need to hear everything about how we should run things when I get out there. See, from here I only can wish to run things the way I dream off but as a wise King I know that the real world must be run one day at a time [From Blood's letter to King Al].

King Blood not only became a master of prison survival skills but he turned his internment into a site of opportunity. In an extraordinary twist of punishment logic, he managed to derive power from the state's every effort to make him powerless, a fact that should not be lost on those who have a rapacious appetite for the role of incarceration in deterring crime.[16] At the same time, however, how rational can he be after so many years in "the hole"?

D.B.: How long has he been inside? I mean this time. Five, six years?

King T.: More. You gotta remember he did his sixteen years. He came out he did his parole board. 'Cause his first charge was murder. He claimed in front of the judge it was accidental . . . blah, blah, blah. He did his bid, came out. Stood out two weeks in the street. Got violated for use of drugs. And went in and continued his bid. Now by this time, Blood is actually almost incarcerated without that little month vacation—almost twenty years. See where I'm going?

In studies of isolation on the human psyche, one or all of several psychosocial tendencies have been noted: paranoia, anxiety, depression, and psychosis (Weinstein and Cummins 1996). A New York City prison psychologist who evaluates inmates awaiting trial articulates what many have found with long-term inmates or repeat offenders:

Many of them are comfortable here. It sounds crazy to say this, but they have gotten so used to the predictability of life, or they know their limits and they know what to expect . . . but when they're on the outside they can't handle it. There are too many choices, too many decisions to make, too many responsibilities. So what do they do? They break the law and come right back in. I interview them all the time, the ones who have spent much of their lives behind bars. There is little rehabilitation because they have psychologically adapted to this world in ways that are staggering and frightening [Ms. M., New York City Department of Corrections; Interview 3/18/1999].

Yet, despite Blood's many capabilities, he is utterly dependent on others to function as his "eyes and ears," and as his "body and soul," the terms he uses for those who reveal to him the everyday world of the ALKQN.[17] But he has few mechanisms to check on these renditions except through other secondary sources.

> They put him in isolation. Now, they claim they were monitoring his letters, but they were taking a copy and they didn't have the resources to read it. That's why they . . . what you saw in the letter came out in trial, Ok? But, basically he didn't know what was going on in the outside world. He didn't even know what was going on in the rest of the prison [Mr. L., King Blood's lawyer; interview, 2/17/1999].

These points about Blood's isolation are extremely important to appreciate, for a great deal of what Blood knows about the nation is "imagined" and constructed from the accounts of people who have a range of interests in the way they present each and every situation to him. This is particularly true as the organization comes under increasing pressure from individual ambition, the internal power plays, the police infiltrations, the conflicts with rival groups, the intelligence gathering, the criminal involvement of individual members, and the sensationalized treatments of the media. These tensions and contingencies invariably impact on Blood's information system, ensuring that what he receives is at best partial and at worst highly manipulative.

> L.B.: What went wrong exactly with the Nation?
>
> Queen F.: I think what went wrong was that a lot of people fed him things that they was not supposed to, and somebody being inside the penal system can't do nothing about people. What they feeding you is gonna make you do things that maybe you don't wanna do.

Of course, Blood is aware of this vulnerability, which is one reason why he places so much importance on the notion of loyalty. But there is nothing or very little that he can do from within a twelve- by eight-foot prison cell, locked up for twenty-three hours a day, one phone call a month, contacted by members who only want to be in his good graces and surrounded by correctional staff who watch his every move, befuddled by his power and the steady increase in membership throughout the system.

Yet the group's growth also throws into stark relief the problems of Blood's isolation. How can one man stay in control of an organization whose social and geographical complexity is intensifying with every new addition to the ranks? The answer is that he cannot and it is at this point that "Blood the isolated" is more prone than ever to misjudging the characters and intentions of his members, particularly his leaders, and misperceiving the path the nation is traveling. Essentially, the very traits that made him so successful in the earliest days of the Kings turned into their opposite in his hyperisolated and manipulatable state, eventually leading him to overreact to internal problems of discipline and commitment with threats of physical intimidation, expulsion, and execution. While Blood was fond of likening himself to a field general, commanding his army on the front lines, never far away from the action, by 1993 he had lost sight of the war he claimed he was always fighting. Instead of the "oppressor," "the system," and "the devils," he was singularly concerned with the "traitors" and the "fakes" within his own ranks. And certainly it appears from the letters that within his own ranks there was rampant abuse of power and that there were many Kings "in the system" and outside it who were flouting the basic principles of Kings membership, e.g., by using hard drugs, taking money from the box, or coveting other Kings' and even Blood's women.

> Most of the murders that occurred were people that messed with Blood's women, which is something that Mary Jo White [Federal District Attorney] doesn't say. All the murders were over women or power. Never for organization purposes. Always selfish members' purposes [King T.].

The Early Latin Kings: From Prison Gang to Street Gang

It started when Blood was in charge from the incarnation of the Nation. From the very beginning that was what was happening as soon as they would get out in the street. I mean, there are people, of course, that brought it out into the street. The first members, the first jail convicts to be released, they brought the gang into the streets, you know, and then they got followers, you know, and maybe they would go back to jail, maybe they would drop out, maybe they didn't wanna be crowned, they didn't want the responsibility—whatever they were doing. So, little by little these other guys moved in, just kids, and that was the basis for the whole trial and the murders that went on there. It was a power struggle. It wasn't about a money-making enterprise, as the government claims. It wasn't about drug dealing. They never found any drugs.

Mr. L., King Blood's lawyer

Mr. L is correct; the ALKQN that appeared on the streets in the early 1990s was not about drugs or other forms of "product" from which organized crime gets its capital; it was about filling an enormous vacuum in the barrio by seasoned inmates who took their prison subcultures to the marginalized youth of the outside world. Further, although King Blood originally began a highly motivated and disciplined prisoners' self-defense organization, there is little evidence to suggest that it was his intention for the same organization to spread to the streets as it did. If anything, it was the conditions created by the massive incarceration of African-Americans and Latinos/as as a result of the Rockefeller Drug Laws, the Federal three-strikes legislation, truth-in-sentencing laws, persistent impoverishment and underachievement of the lowest social orders, and the reaction of youth in the post-crack-epidemic years that fueled the Latin Kings and Queens expansion (Brotherton 1999; Curtis 1999). But grow they did, both in prison and on the streets, and by 1993 there were perhaps a thousand members attending meetings regularly throughout the New York City area, plus perhaps two thousand more in the prison system, and a thousand members in affiliated groups in the other northeastern states.

This expansion of the Kings poses several important questions. If the group in prison was principally about vying for prison power, uplifting the Latino/a inmate community, and contending with the dictatorial regime of the correctional administration, what was motivating the group's members on the outside? Moreover, did the street branches of the ALKQN show much inclination toward politics and community empowerment projects as we have seen in more recent years? We shall make some observations about this early period below and suggest some of the reasons for the internal warfare that emerged in the 1993–94 period, some of which we have already mentioned.

Street Organizations and the Context of the Early 1990s

In a previous article, Brotherton (1999) wrote that the organized cultures of the street took a qualitatively different path in the mid-1990s as youth and adults (especially those coming out of prison) joined up with groups like the ALKQN and began to retake their neighborhoods from the drug crews and posses. This type of organization in its early formation was certainly ganglike in that, to use Klein's (1989) definition, it was seen by others as a "distinct aggregation," recognized by its own members as a "denotable group" with its own language of representation, and it had engaged in sufficient illegal acts to gain the negative attention of law enforcement and neighborhood agencies. But there was more to the group's potential than its criminogenic properties. Queen Z., who becomes a leader after only five months' membership, expresses the sentiments of the nongang side of the organization:

> A little about myself. I am 30 years old. I'm married to King G. We are rais-ing 4 children together. I am in college at the present moment. I would like to become an AIDs counselor and to teach our children about drugs. That's one of my goals [Letter to King Blood, 10/31/1993].

But what were the social and economic circumstances in which this group emerged and developed along with other collective movements of the street (e.g., the Netas and the Zulu Nation, which were groups that also possessed a distinctive political allure)? Furthermore, if the group was expanding so eas-ily, moving increasingly between the prisons and the streets, what does this say about the relationships between oppression, exclusion, and violence in both "free" and "unfree" settings?

The Margins Are Still the Margins

The overwhelming changes imposed so rapidly on the formerly rural-based Puerto Rican population translate into high rates of unemployment, sub-stance abuse, broken families, and deteriorated health in New York's inner city. Few other ethnic groups, except perhaps Native American Indians, fared more poorly in official statistics than the 867,753 Puerto Ricans who lived in New York City at the time of the 1990 census [Bourgois 1995:53].

The early 1990s in New York City were for residents of the barrios and ghet-tos a time of both change and continuity regarding their economic, political, and social standing. But with the recession enveloping much of the United States in the late 1980s, the Latino/a community was particularly hard hit. By 1990, 19 percent of the city was living at or below the poverty line (i.e., $10,800 for a family of three) with the rate for Puerto Ricans more than 38 percent. Unemployment, which had begun to fall significantly during the late 1980s, climbed steadily at the turn of the decade, going from almost 6 percent in 1989 to over 10 percent in 1992. However, among Latinos/as, the percent-age of those without work increased even higher, with the unemployment rate doubling from 8 percent in 1985 to 16 percent in 1992 (Citizen's Committee for Children 1993) and with Puerto Rican joblessness remaining the highest of any ethnic group, averaging 14 percent through the years 1991–1993.

As poverty increased among the adults, then children (i.e., youth aged under 18 years) were even harder hit, particularly children of color. In 1989, approximately 30 percent of all the city's children were below the poverty line, an increase of 7 percent since the 1970s. Among African-American and Latino/a children, however, the rate was 52 percent and 46 percent respectively (versus 20 percent for white children). This very high number of Puerto Rican and Latino/a youth being raised in extremely poor settings correlated with the numbers growing up in female-headed families: by 1990, almost half of Puerto Rican children in the city were in such households [Department of City Planning 1994].

Of course, the increase in hardship for Latino/a youth and adults had a direct impact on their performance in the educational system. Although the percentage of Puerto Ricans with high school diplomas had increased from 35 percent in 1980 to 46 percent ten years later (compared to 69 percent in the general population), in 1991, Latinos/as made up the majority of the city's high school dropouts (42 percent Latinos and 39 percent African-Americans) and made up 41 percent of students in the city's special education classes (Citizen's Committee for Children 1993).

Meanwhile, the criminalization processes of Latinos/as were going on apace. Between 1986, when Blood first founded the "Nation," and 1993 the inmate population in New York State almost doubled, from 38,647 to 64,569 (Correctional Association Bulletin 2000) and the numbers entering the infamous city jail at Rikers Island tripled in less than twenty years (from 7,000 in 1970 to 21,000 in 1990; see Wynn 2001). In the early 1990s, the juvenile wing of Rikers Island Correctional Complex (the largest penal colony in the Western world, located on an island in the middle of New York City's East River), was said to be the most violent jail or prison facility in the United States. As a current correctional officer recounted:

> We used to come to work and there would be blood up the walls, inmates were being led out on stretchers and you didn't know when you would be going home. It was a war zone. . . . They was slicing each other up here without a second thought, and all we could do was write 'em up and send 'em to the bing [physical isolation cell]. Nobody was safe here then, nobody. It was out of control [Informal interview with Officer G.].

These combined conditions ensured that youth in the margins continued to proliferate in the barrio communities, which guaranteed a steady supply of members constantly applying to join. In contrast to much received wisdom on the subject, the ALKQN had no need to mount any recruitment campaign; "teenagers and young adults flocked to it" (Curtis 1998:8) out of generalized feelings of social exclusion. In fact, during both 1993 and 1994, the organization was specifically told by its leadership that it could not "crown" anybody, i.e., recruit people in the organization. In the following, a prospective Queen gives her reasons for wanting to join:

The reason why I am choosing to become a queen is because I would like to help my fellow latin brothers and sisters overcome the oppresion. I would also like the opportunity to educate them schoolwise and streetwise. . . . What I plan to do for this nation is to help out in any which way I can, to help society look at us as equals not as minorities [application to join the Latin Queens, undated but probably early 1994].

Street Leaders with Muscle but Little Vision

Besides the problem with 5-0, all is well with the family. Inca, I have a slight problem that I'd like to discuss with you. I'm having a slight problem with #3. You see he asked if he could borrow some gak's [guns, usually automatic weapons from Brooklyn and gave me his word that I would have it back in 3 days. It's now been two weeks and I still haven't received the two gak's I lent to the Bronx. My brother, you know I'm not one to talk shit about anyone, but a lot of times I call on #3 and he's not there for me. Two brothers got jumped in Brooklyn by a mob of Dominicans and we don't even have gak's so that we can step to them and I'm not going to send the hermanitos [brothers] in without any gak's [Letter from King T. to Blood, 11/23/1993].

In the letter above from King T. to Blood we read an account that is quite typical of the many "scribes" that Blood's leaders sent to him. As Blood himself says, only two of his leading people ever sent him letters wherein the narratives contained any thoughtful reflections on the group's development, problem-solving, or complementary additions to Blood's numerous "masterpieces," i.e., his manifestos. Most letters were filled with the "he says, she says" anecdotes of group members, the interpersonal duels common among street subcultures, the latest state of "the box" (i.e., the group's treasury), the obligatory statements of personal loyalty, and sometimes a reference to partnership issues.

Now let me give you a short report about the box. We had $1278.50 in the box and the money been go for thing in the Nation. Helping brother look for work and buying guns and stuff. . . . So my brother I must keep going back to one thing in my mind right now. I wish I could tell you or show you how faithful I am to you. I would kill anyone that try to hurt you even those white mother fuckers up there [King A. to Blood, 11/4/1993].

Like hundreds of reports Blood received from the outside, the writing skills themselves are clearly rudimentary, which could be one reason why the authors were unable to articulate the organization's mission. However, even with poor literacy, people can express themselves if they need to and none of the leaders seemed so self-conscious in their letters that they were holding something back. The only conclusion is that the street leadership's main concern was to hang on to their power within the organization, which, in turn, gave them power on the streets. To this degree, the leadership that he had chosen on the outside was in the traditional mold of "enforcers," people who could keep a certain amount of internal order by ensuring that the rules of the organization were followed, that members were paying their dues on time, that the accounts were relatively intact, and that the group's branches were meeting regularly. Further, these leaders played a social and economic role for Blood. They would visit him quite regularly and make sure that others did the same, they would be responsible for his commissary, usually sending him $100–$150 a month, and they could be relied upon to do Blood's bidding regarding his relationships with women.

> You know, Queen L. want to be with me but she doesn't do things the way a real Queen must do. I have to keep her until I get home 'cause she know too damn much and if she deside to flip I can't get away. You know what I mean?
>
> But I do need a "cutie" to hang with me for this year I have left now. If she is a Queen I must release "L" but if she is not then I can hold on to L. until I get home. So, can you do something for me? [King Blood to King T., 8/4/1993]

These leaders were, on the one hand, what Jacobs describes as status seekers in the gang world, with little thought to the "transcendent values" (Jacobs 1977:171) that Blood and some of the other Kings' leaders had written about. Certainly in their letters, a place where they had plenty of opportunity to try to impress their mentor, they gave no indication of being worldly or interested in anything outside of their parochial surroundings. This emphasis is similarly highlighted in the branch meetings. In a series of minutes taken at Queens' meetings during early 1994, we read page after page of details that primarily consist of: charges against members brought by leaders, punishments to be meted out for code violations, field reports of people claiming to be Queens, changes in the personnel structure of the organization, instructions about when and where members can openly adorn their beads, and upcoming social events. For example:

Queen Z. mentioned that Queen R. is to get a B.O.S. at the nation on the spot & a 5 point violation, also Queen Jeannie left a meeting without permission, Queen J. is getting a $30 multa [fine]. Queen Z. explain to us that she is going to read charges against Queen R. because this is a fair trial. Queen Z. mention that Queen Z. called Queen R. and said that she was coming and she didn't come. Queen R. also was going to leave the nation because of a #9 for a Ñeta [another street organization]. A rumor come to us that she was getting a B.O.S. at her next meeting. . . . Queen Z. mentioned that she called Queen R. and gave her a $20 multa & Queen R. said that she "don't got fucking money to pay a fucking multa" [Report from a universal meeting, 2/18/1994].

For the most part, therefore, the leaders of the different branches behaved as mid-level functionaries, even though they were in positions that gave them the power and authority to organize their members on many different levels. But this could hardly be otherwise in such a hierarchical organization, when the core male leaders on the street were themselves unsure of their role except in its most basic bureaucratic terms. Frequently complaining to Blood that too many Kings did not accept their authority as legitimate, even Blood himself was given to admit to his number-one supreme crown that "I know there are many that don't understand why I have you in this position."

In short, the street leaders during this period were not of the caliber that Jankowski (1991) thought he recognized in his more sophisticated vertical gangs a decade before, nor did they evidence the self-confidence and energy of some prison leaders in the same organization who, while certainly ruthless, could be extremely eloquent, charismatic, and innovative.

It is very important that as a King and leader one understands the importance of being in control and staying in a low profile status. The life of this nation depends on a code of silence that cannot be broken. "360." Extinction is our worse enemy. So we must fight wisely, cautiously, and intelligently.

"Chain of Command" has many purposes and must be followed to the extreme. The enemy cannot know "WHO" is sending out orders. For the simple fact that if the enemy knows "WHO" is sending out deadly orders, he will be a target, a target that will be attacked from all directions [many different opposing enemies] [King B. in a letter to King Blood, 1993].

Blood Letting and for What?

It is another thing to make a law out of violence—a contradictory position that would forget why we fight, that would remove all meaning from the

struggle by depriving it of truly political objectives, that would refuse revolutionary renewal sought by risks taken in common, and that would belittle
the will to become a collectivity of human beings as nothing more than the
bestial [or natural] "law" of a struggle for life" [De Certeau 1995:10, originally appeared in 1969].

With little else to occupy the organization other than its own internal business, and with the street leadership consumed with its own survival, it is little wonder that the group eventually was led down a path of self-destruction.
Similar to de Certeau's observation, above, about the apolitical impact of obsessive violence among certain social movements in the late 1960s, the
ALKQN allowed the subject of violence and the culture of intrigue to become the main foci of group life, thereby severely detracting from its commitment to create opportunities for social and cultural renewal that had originally attracted so many members. Below, King Tone remembers what it was
like to be at one of the universals during the high point of the ALKQN's
"crazy" period:

> I seen people get five slap violations. I seen people get that from King T. for
> jokes—like, let's say the circle was big, and they were youngsters. And this
> guy used to actually just pick a herb. "Yo, say he said this about me and bring
> him up on charges." And you would see kids just get beat up for that night's
> wreck. And every Saturday you knew in the circle that there was going to be
> at least five violations. You know, you already knew. The whole thing through
> the whole week was thinking if you were going to be the one. So, instead of
> a circle of love it was a circle of fear. You could feel it, the tension of every
> Saturday [Interview, 3/31/1998].

Of course, this culture of tyranny did not happen overnight and there
was a process at work. First, as leaders increasingly ruled through repression
rather than by consensus or by legitimate authority, members began to side
with one leader versus another, creating numerous factions. Second, the lack
of constructive leadership sharply affected the security of the organization by
turning community residents against the organization and making them
willing accomplices of the police and lowering the consciousness of the
members, which made them careless, unfocused, and lacking in thoughtful
rather than ritualized discipline. Finally, the combined effects of low morale
among the members and the increasing tally of arrests produced all the
"snitches" that the "authorities" needed for local, state, and federal prosecutors to build their case.

In this atmosphere of internal fratricidal warfare, a total of eleven Latin Kings were executed and another seventeen seriously assaulted. It was not "expressive," "symbolic," or "instrumental" violence (Block and Block 1993), the usual modes of group and interpersonal conflict associated with gang warfare. Rather, it was the social reproduction of racial, ethnic, gender, and class oppression at its worst, as members took out other members in the name of Latino/a unity and Latino/a pride. At this stage of its emergence, the Nation began more and more to resemble the pathological "near group" model of Yablonsky (1963) than the coherent, Latino prison and street organization that Jacobs described in his earlier study of a post-1960s Illinois state prison:

> The Latin Kings are the largest Latin gang in Chicago. They cannot be identified with any single neighborhood, as their chapters are sprawled across the city. Most of the Kings are Puerto Rican, but there are Mexicans as well. On Chicago's streets the Kings have also been involved in a number of economic enterprises. The Stateville Latin Kings constitute an autonomous and distinct chapter of the Latin King federation. Inside Stateville the Kings associate almost exclusively with Spanish inmates. Most of the staff members agree that "we never have any problems out of the Kings." Rarely does a King come before the disciplinary court for a serious rule infraction. Decisions for the Kings are made by a council of ranking chiefs [Jacobs 1977:148].[18]

Getting Involved with the Community

Not until the blood letting was over and many of the leaders were incarcerated did the ALKQN begin to resemble the street organization that we have been studying during the latter part of the 1990s. At that point, the question of whether it was a conscious decision by Blood and other leaders to engage in some public relations, or a critical mass of opinion within the organization that recognized that the Nation had to turn back to its political and communitarian roots, is difficult to answer. However, at this juncture in the group's history, it responded positively to overtures made by political activists in the Latino, mainly Puerto Rican, community to get involved in campaigns for City Council, voter registration drives, and even neighborhood cleanup campaigns (see figure 5.5).

Thus, in all the boroughs, we start to read in local papers that the Kings are turning over a new leaf and that they are seeking to change their image. Of course, this by itself means little unless these new actions and foci of the organization begin to result in new goals, rules, norms, and reciprocal relations vis-à-vis the community with which they interact. By the middle of

City of New York
Parks & Recreation

The Arsenal
Central Park
New York, New York 10021

Henry J. Stern
Commissioner

29 July 1994

TO THE ALMIGHTY LATIN KINGS QUEENS NATION,

On Saturday, 23 July and on Sunday, 24 July 1994, a beautiful thing happened in El Barrio.

Three playgrounds that used to look like hell were transformed. Poor Richard's Park at East 109 Street between 3rd and 2nd Avenues, White Park at East 106 Street between 3rd and Lexington Avenues and the basketball courts and playground at East 106 Street and the FDR Drive received a well deserved facelift.

Many people thought that something like this could never happen. Why did it happen? It happened because some people said, "We care." The people that said, "We care," are THE ALMIGHTY LATIN KINGS QUEENS NATION.

As everyone knows, the City has been faced with cutbacks. While the cutbacks are necessary, those of us in public service must still work to improve the quality of life in New York City. Through the efforts of Nelson Denis, an East Harlem community leader, the energy of The Latin Kings and the resources of the Department of Parks and Recreation were brought together, and the quality of life in three playgrounds was improved.

Many will say that this effort was a one shot deal. We in the Department of Parks know that this effort must be continued so that clean parks and playgrounds are the rule, not the exception.

On behalf of the Department of Parks and Recreation, I thank the ALMIGHTY LATIN KINGS QUEENS NATION for your effort to improve the community and I look forward to working with you again in the future.

Sincerely.

Richard Sedlisky,
Project Manager

FIGURE 5.5 Letter from New York City Department of Parks and Recreation.

1994, a new leadership started to emerge from the badly bruised corpse of the old conflict-ridden organization and it is in this new era that King Tone, Antonio Fernández, a charming, loquacious speaker and skillful street organizer from Brooklyn, begins to move into the spotlight and eventually becomes ordained as Inka by King Blood in early 1995. It is with King Tone's arrival that a fresh chapter begins for the ALKQN, and this we shall discuss in the ensuing pages of the book.

In the discussion above we see the enormous contradictions that beset the early Latin Kings in New York under King Blood's leadership. We have emphasized the range of talents that he possessed for organizing the kind of group that could flourish in settings that were highly complementary: the violent, oppressive regimes of the prison and the risky social and cultural worlds that make up life on the street. At the same time, we have shown the weaknesses of this man in his increasingly isolated state, believing that the organization could best be brought to order through fear and intimidation even if he, himself, rails against others for using the same methods and for assuming the same authoritarian roles.

We have also seen that King Blood was focused on the moral and organizational superiority of the Nation (as he interpreted it) and that, in his eyes, nothing could stop the power and unity of the most marginalized Latinos/as once they were able to cast aside their feelings of social inadequacy and cultural inferiority and discover the magical powers of the Latin Kings' credo. Nonetheless, it is the same King Blood who, despite his race and class consciousness, does the "devil's work" by making war in the prisons against other racially based gangs rather than against the administration itself.

Finally, we have shown how King Blood could be nurturing and capable of thinking great thoughts for "his people," and then we also encounter his criminal mindset, which cannot leave behind the seductive opportunities of the drug market and the political economy of the street. Perhaps, therefore, it is not too difficult to comprehend the extreme position that the judge took in his sentencing.[19] But this, of course, avoids the central question: Where did King Blood come from? What made him what he is? For all of King Blood's sociopathic tendencies and his predilection for individual power, we cannot escape a central conclusion: King Blood, in many ways, was made both directly and indirectly by the State. Ultimately, it was the United States and its longstanding political opposition to the Socialist Republic of Cuba that was the root cause of the Mariel boat lift which brought King Blood to the shores of Florida in the first place, and it was in state and federal prison that he rose to national and even international infamy.

CHAPTER 6

NONGANG TRADITIONS I

I think that the media and the government's afraid of what we represent. I mean, it was like the Young Lords in the '60s—they marched for Puerto Rican political rights and to free Puerto Rico, and I guess you could say that we're kind of like the Young Lords of the '90s, or the next millennium. But I think we're gonna take it further than that. we're not just marching for this and that. We're gonna be around, you know. We're not gonna die. We're gonna be around whether the government or the Bloods or anyone else got anything to say about it.

Interview with King Tone, 3/31/1998

Introduction

At the end of the previous chapter, we discussed how the ALKQN was turning in on itself. In the absence of any consistent external enemy to unify the membership[1] (such as the Chicago Latin Kings have in the many gangs that make up the People Nation in the "Motherland"), together with the isolation and increasing authoritarianism of King Blood and no clear set of political goals, the organization internally corroded. As King Blood himself often warned, the Kings will be their own worst enemy when they are not moving together as one and do not live by their "five points" (i.e., respect, love, honesty, knowledge, and truth).

It seems at this point in the ALKQN's development that most gang researchers would have been right in their predictions. The overwhelming traditions of the gang finally outweighed the possibilities of collective empowerment. At best, to borrow from Jacobs's analysis, the ALKQN could only be said to have achieved a semblance of the "social betterment" model of gang development before it ran afoul of its own internal and external limitations. Or, to draw on Jankowski's model of gangs, the ALKQN appeared to have reached its organizational limits when it started to act irrationally both toward its own members and toward the community. At that point, the efficiency of the group was diminished by no longer being able to provide the services to its members that it promised, by failing to produce a leadership with legitimate authority, and by ceasing to operate an exchange relationship with the community.

Nonetheless, however predictable the group's self-destructive development might have seemed, an important lesson we need to bear in mind with such groups is that we can never rule out the impact of new movement actors or of shifts in the external environment that could turn this stage into yet another phase of the group's uneven path of development. Two essential questions that remain to be answered are: What residual politics were still left in the ALKQN? and how would such politics relate to the reconstruction of the ALKQN in the post-King Blood period?[2] Below, we explore these empirical and conceptual lines of inquiry more fully. Our argument is that the group, once it acquired a more forward-looking leadership and an ambitious, more demanding membership, returned for a short period of time to its sociocultural roots and began to experiment in many different forms of activism and community building. As it did so, it learned that its new strength lay precisely in the practices, rationales, and worldviews that it had pragmatically adopted. Fundamentally, the group faced up to a truth its leadership had long denied: it was serving members who had vastly different orientations to everyday life and who lived within a completely different set of possibilities than the thousands of inmate members that comprised the majority of the old group's membership. Mr. L., one of King Blood's lawyers, makes this point, highlighting both the potential for transformation and the inevitable conflicts that would arise:

> There's like a dichotomy between these two factions of the Kings. There's the Latin Kings that joined in jail and there's the Latin Kings that joined in the street. Basically, the problem is with the power and who gets to make the decisions on which way the group is gonna go, and you're really dealing with two separate groups under the same name. The problem was that you had the Latin Kings who were jail convicts and who had been in the group for a few years and they were released onto the street. They were hardened criminals, a lot of them. Now, at the same time, you had people joining, people like King Tone or others, even like kids, fifteen, sixteen year olds, that had never been in trouble with the law before, or very minor misdemeanors. So, a guy

would get out of Attica perhaps, or Riker's or wherever he was and he goes back home to the Bronx and he's still a Latin King, wearing his colors proudly, and he starts going to meetings, you know. He hears about this community involvement and helping people and he just got through with knife fights in prison with other gangs. He's not gonna take orders from a 20 year-old kid who's never been to jail before. So, that's where the whole conflict arose with the power struggles [Interview with L., King Blood's lawyer, 2/17/1999].

It was obvious that the growing disputes between the members were bound to continue and, if left unaddressed, could easily spell the end of the ALKQN as a unified entity. The group's future, therefore, hinged on whether it could come up with solutions to a range of questions: How could the organization resolve its many internal and external tensions? How could it increase the quality of its leadership and reenergize its rank-and-file? How could it prove to the community that it was not a gang? And, finally, how could it stop providing law enforcement with the countless opportunities to pursue yet another "internal enemy" among the "minority communities"? We tackle these questions through the life history of the reform leader King Tone, through an analysis of the indigenous forms of community building that the ALKQN appropriated, and through a discussion of the practices that emerged from the group's newfound identity.

The Struggle for a New Inca and the Making of King Tone

In many ways, Tone's path to the top resembled what Jankowski (1991) found in his "vertical" gangs:

One fact that must be emphasized is that an extended period of time is required for a gang leader to rise to power. It is not a quick process. A future leader must get to know the politics of the gang and spend enough time to develop political support from various factions within the group. . . . He would need to have developed a power base within the organization (through making contacts) in order to gain office [p. 91].

Ironically, for all of Tone's strategizing, it was the action of the government that finally cleared the way for him to become the ultimate among New York City's street nations. But how should we read the moral development of King Tone's career? How did his values and goals change? How does he explain his transformation from being primarily a small-time player and later hustler in the street political economy to being a champion of social justice and a practitioner of liberation spirituality?

To answer these questions, we trace the life of King Tone, based on his own remembrances, from his early childhood in one of the toughest and most economically deprived neighborhoods of New York City, to the circumstances under which he became a King, until his coveted position as Inca of the New York State ALKQN. This life history approach, in the words of a noted anthropologist, allows us to see not only the contexts behind the choice and values of a human being but "the working out of a culture and a social system that is often obscured in a typified account" (Behar 1990:225, quoted in Escobar 1992:77). Above all, we get to understand a little more about what we might call "the dialectics of violence." By this we mean the relationship between the indirect violence of structured denial and want (Salmi 1993) and the direct violence associated with recurrent patterns of interpersonal conflict.

"Freaky" East New York, Religion, and a Female-Dominated Family

Rain is falling steadily as I emerge from the subway in East New York. The grayness in the sky matches the streets and the houses. Every other house in the area is vacant or burned-out and every other lot is empty but for rubble

FIGURE 6.1 King Tone is interviewed by Luis Barrios. (Photo by Steve Hart.)

and rusting cars, in which the kids play in the summer. Some streets are better: houses are adjoining and windows and doors are occasionally painted a bright red or blue. Behind the wire fences and gates huge 1960s cars sit with Doberman Pinschers or Great Danes sniffling around them and barking angrily as you walk by. Decals on the car windows testify to religious convictions: "Jesus—Say It Louder." The two corner stores at the end of Weeza's street are open for business, although it is not immediately obvious. They are covered in metal sheeting instead of windows, and the doors are entirely cased in metal grill. Inside one, it is dark but for the refrigerated cold-drinks cabinet. I buy a six-pack of Budweiser and some Hostess Twinkies for breakfast; they are not cheap. In the back of the store are two telephone booths which do a good business [Campbell, 1984:107].

Anne Campbell's rich, early-1980s, ethnographic description, above, is of virtually the same neighborhood where Tone was raised. It was an area that had been and continues to be one of the poorest in New York City, spanning almost a century (Burrows and Wallace 1999). Its public schools are almost all in the low-tier range of the educational system; its rates of infant mortality are as high as any in Harlem or the Bronx; for much of the 1980s, the area around the 73rd precinct was one of the "murder capitals of the United States" (*New York Times* 1992); and the income levels of its residents have been in the lowest quartile for city residents every year during the past two decades (Citizens Committee on Children of New York 1998, 2001). Despite this daunting environment, Tone, however, did not come from one of the stereotypical "broken" or "dysfunctional" homes that are usually associated with emergent street leaders.

> King T.: I got four sisters. I'm the second to youngest. And no brothers. Moda, María, Martha, and Lucy. The family was a tight-knit family, but it was basically a dominant woman ruled the house. Pops was the quiet type. I used to watch and I used to say: "Wow, man, this guy doesn't have no say in this joint." But they were a good family. They been married now about 37 years. They are Christian. Holy Ghost Christians, you know . . . they are into the Lord very much. So it was hard for me to communicate with them on that level because I didn't see God in the neighborhood, or the way the pastor saw it. I just saw it like it was all freaky. As far as my family, my two older sisters got pregnant at an early age: 14. And then the next one got pregnant at 15. In those days, when you got pregnant, usually the boyfriend moved into the house. So, the boyfriends came in and we also had two new little babies. My first niece was born very sick. She died three times on the table. She

had collapsed lung, no jaw bone, deformed face. So while they were going through that whole crisis I was in high school [Interview with King Tone, 3/31/1998].

In the above, Tone singles out four factors that shaped his early life: (1) the "freaky" environs of East New York, (2) the religiosity of his family, particularly his mother, (3) the preoccupation of his family with maintaining gender boundaries for the children, and (4) the prominent roles of women in the power structure of the family. Below, Tone elaborates more on the unintentional consequences of gender stereotyping.

King T.: My sisters wasn't happy that I was the only boy. Like if the housework had to be done, Tone had to leave. . . . My father was a strong man, he made it that I had to sleep alone. I had to have my own room. I did whatever I wanted. Just don't do what the girls did. You know? As long as I didn't act like a girl, he was happy. He didn't care what I did out in the street. Just don't be a faggot. You know that was his mentality, and I seen it. So, of course I said: "Well, if that's what they want. . . ." So the street became where I learned all of my tricks, all my trade. 'Cause Pop—my father's a bread delivery man . . .he started out at 4 and came home at 5:30 in the morning . . . when he was home, he was asleep. So I basically dealt with my mother and my four sisters. Those were, like I said, the dominant ruling in the house. So for me it was better to be in everybody else's but my house. So, I went through that . . . that stage. School became . . . just a place to say I was going to. To jet from the house. My mother was so busy checking the girls' grades, 'cause see—they would check the girls' homework, but not my homework . . . I guess that's the old Spanish ways [Interview, 3/31/1998].

This tremendous contradiction between the discipline and control of the women/girls versus the lack of sanctions and attention given to the men/boys provides the familial context in which Tone drifted (Matza 1964) into the streets. Making things worse were the extra bodies that seemed to invade the house as the pregnancies of his sisters brought both their children and their husbands all under one small roof. In this environment the leeway given Tone because of his manhood was used by him to escape from the family's domain at every opportunity.

I learned very early in life that nobody was checking up on me. So I could get away with actually anything as long as it didn't come into the house. That's when I started. I told my mom she can't support me. You got these kids in the house. You got these jerks in there. You always comparing me to Jesus, you comparing me to the brother-in-laws, I'm tired of this shit. So I left the house. And I started dealing [Interview, 3/31/1998].

Nonetheless, the lure of the streets did not have to be so irresistible nor its influences so complete if other avenues were there for this bright, if unsettled, young man. Unfortunately, as for so many working-class minority youth, the very institutions that could have provided the direction and encouragement he needed only fueled his flight into the interlocking worlds of hedonism, experimentation, and delinquency (Kelly 1978).

High School Dropout but I Ain't Dumb

King T.: The funny part is, I was in East New York and I made it to John Jay high school. I was in CJ-1, the Criminal Justice Program. I was specially picked. Because even as I fooled around when the ACTs used to come I used to bust them out . . . bop, bop, bop. It was just natural. The only thing I couldn't do was write? You understand? I could read, I could comprehend, I could do everything, but at the writing skills . . . I probably right now still have a Third Grade level writing skills because. . . .

D.B.: . . . it was never developed?

King T.: Never developed. Because when I was in Third Grade, I had a teacher, who was Mr. C., I remember. I remember it for the rest of my life. He would give spelling tests every Friday. So I wasn't good in spelling, so I used to not go on Fridays. So one Friday I had to go. I found myself having to take the test, but I didn't know the words. So I had a girlfriend next to me. I'm sweating and she's looking at me like, "I know you gonna fail . . . do your best." So when he caught me looking at her, he thought I was cheating. You know, he did the whole scene. He grabbed my paper, put a big red zero and said: "You stupid Spic." And you know he gave me the zero, he put the paper on the top of the board and I just remember I said, "I will never, ever do a spelling test again." And from the Third Grade on, I didn't spell. And if you would try to give me something, my brain cut off, you know. But, believe it or not, I made it to the Eleventh Grade without knowing how to write! [Interview, 3/31/1998]

Tone's account of his interaction with an established teacher is one of the few recollections he has of his high school years. For him, schooling was about "getting over," being humiliated and nonacademic social relationships. Education, in terms of cognitive development and scholarly progress, was a subject that was simply not remembered by him as relevant to his school experience, a finding that is prominent in so many studies of lower-class youth for whom schooling is an exercise in cultural devaluation, ritualized conformity, and tracked exclusion[3] (Hollingsworth 1948; Rist 1979; Kozol 1971; Macleod 1997; McLaren 1993; Fine 1991).

Not surprisingly, Tone, rather than linger in the hallways until the twelfth grade, concluded that he was not going to "make it" (Macleod 1997) and removed himself from the system entirely.[4] Such a choice for barrio youths during the 1970s and 1980s was not particularly unusual nor was it particularly stigmatizing. According to one of Tone's ex-girlfriends who attended the same local public institution, "dropping-out" was almost considered the norm:

> I knew very few people round here who made it through the twelfth grade. Most of us were gone by the tenth grade for one reason or another. In my family none of my sisters graduated; it's true, none of them. No one pushed us or took any interest in school and the teachers, well, what could they do? [Interview with Ms. M., 8/13/2000].

Tone's combined alienation from the expectations, values, and concerns of his family and of his school leaves him with few options but to make his own way in life in the alternative opportunity structure (Cloward and Ohlin 1960) beckoning him onto East New York's streets. There, at least, he could shed his old identity characterized by intellectual mediocrity and failure and adopt a new one in which he would be "somebody," complete with status, power, and money. What did it matter if his new career and his means to attain it would severely embarrass the good moral standing of his parents? In fact, that was part of the reason for doing it (see Katz, 1988):

> King T.: At the Eleventh Grade, the old, old teacher, I remember . . . she said, "You got a severe writing problem." And she caught me. That's when I decided I got to drop out. You know? I'm not going to make it any more. They found out my secret. I'm dumb, I can't write. At that time I was already, on the block, a strong individual within the community and, you know, my mother is a very outgoing person, she speaks a lot, she's very funny. So everybody knew I was Esther's son . . . So I was really settled in the community. I made the choice that I had to leave. I left home. It was funny because I opened my first drug spot two houses from my mother's house. I just wanted her to see that I could get the best sneakers, the best shoes, everything I wanted without her or

my father's help. And I grew dreads. I believed in, you know, the Rastifarians. I grew my dreads and used to use the chalice and meditate. And my mother used to see me: "That's not my son. Look at you with the dreadlocks!" She didn't really dig it. But I knew what I was doing. I was doing as much as I could to rebel and show her I was going to be who I want to be without you, because you ain't helping me out! [Interview with King Tone, 3/31/1998].

Leader of a Street Crew and "I'm the Man"

The environs of East New York, in this period, are as full of street dramas as any area in the city. A former resident who was born and raised in this neighborhood recounts her teenage years in the mid to late 1980s:

> Q.: I remember it well. My mother was a member of the Sex Boys and they was at war . . .They petrol bombed our house, we all had to evacuate and leave the area. Every day you expected something to happen. Every street had its gangs and every gang had its turf, you couldn't help be involved. You almost had to be involved in order to survive [Ms. Q., 7/11/2000].

But the mosaic of youth subcultures only reflected the increasingly diverse ethnic mix of the residents, as more new Caribbean-born immigrants made their way to this poverty-riddled area, attracted by the low rents, its access to the employment hubs of Manhattan, Queens, and JFK airport, and its proximity to other settled ghettos of the city. As the population shifted, so the youth and the young adults began their own battles for ethnic succession (Suttles 1968), much as previous generations had done throughout New York City, almost since the city's inception (Asbury 1927; Burroughs and Wallace 1999). The only difference was that drugs and their political economy and not just ethnocultural backgrounds were now a primary motivator which consequently upped the physical ante of the resulting battles:

> King T.: The biggest war broke out between the Dreads and us, you know the Latinos on the block. Even though I had dreads we were Dominican, Puerto Rican . . . We wanted to be like them, but we didn't want them taking over our neighborhood. It led to a cold war. It even made the center page of the *Daily News*. It was called "Dog Day Afternoon." Then they had the wax museum, if you remember in East New York, the whole family was shot once in the head and they put them in the spotlight. That was all dealing with the war going on in East New York. And I was very much part of the movement at that time, because I didn't want the Latinos to lose their ground [Interview with King Tone 3/31/1998].

Tone's criminal career, however, did not stop with his involvement in the competition for minor drug turfs, and soon he and his crew set their sights on other schemes that could provide him and his "boys" with quick and easy money. One of the first new ventures that came to mind was sticking up the cash-carrying "runners" of the local numbers rackets. This relatively lucrative means of "getting paid" (Sullivan 1989) contained some risks, however. First, of course, there was the possibility that the victims might resist, and since many of them carried guns, this reaction was not unlikely; and second, there was the knowledge that much of this illicit trade was controlled by different families of the Mafia.

> King T.: We used to also stick up the number spots. You know, the Italian number spots. And unfortunately, one of my friends killed one of the guys in the number spots. So we found ourselves not only running from the Dreads, now the guys from the number joints was after us. I had a friend who was tied to a front of a car and dragged. I had another friend that was on his motorbike, they rolled him over almost thirteen times. He had a closed casket. I had a friend that they held his head so they piped him 'til his nose went in his brain and bursted. So now I'm in hiding. I'm like, "Oh, boy, I did it now." My father had a strong influence working in the bread factory. He works for . . . La PG's, that's the name of it. They knew people who knew people who knew people, you know, they were Italians, and they loved my father because he worked for them all his life. So they made a deal. They got me to work in the bakery. I lived in the joint, but I wasn't hurt. And I made up. You know how Italians are [Interview, 3/31/1998].

Tone, given his history of running around the streets, could not remain in this state of confinement for long, even though his life depended on it. Age-wise, at least, he was his own man and his kind of driven personality thrived on the excitement, unpredictability, and tenuous freedom of urban street life. Further, he had grown used to the untaxed compensation that the underground economy could provide, and since he knew that he had a talent for this kind of entrepreneurialism, why quit now? Consequently, it was not long before he struck out once again in search of the barrio's version of Horatio Alger (see also Bourgois 1989):

> King T.: At that time, it started getting to a point where I didn't care no more, you know? I said: "Freak these guys. I don't want to be in this bread factory all day, every day." I jetted and I opened up a dope spot. It was called "COD"—"Cash On Delivery." And I remember I met this connection.

His name was B. and he was like: "You're a very smart kid and you got business smart." And he gave me two bundles. I remember he said: "Here's two bundles and if you make this move, don't worry." So, the first thing I did, I took the two bundles and I give them out to everybody for free to all the junkies and I said, "If you bring me customers, I give you a dollar every bag and I give you a morning bag and a night bag so you won't ever be sick." So Mr. B. comes back and says: "Where's the money for the two bundles?" I said: "It's gone." He says: "Good." And I said: "No I gave them for free." And he started flipping: "What do you mean?" I said: "Give me five bundles now and let's wait." And the guy was like: "Okay, I'm gonna trust you. . . ." He gave me five bundles. I called him in a half hour it was gone. I was known in a matter of two months I was counted thirty-five hundred dollars ever two days, you know. Things was starting. I was the man. I was the man. Although he was the man, in the neighborhood I'm the man! [Interview, 3/31/1998]

Lesson Number One: When You're the Man You Never Use Your Own Product!

King T.: Now I'm the real man, but I didn't know how to handle that money. I snorted so much coke for about three months that I had to go to the hospital because I burned my nose out to where I used to sleep and I used to just tear, because I thought my eyeballs were going to burn. I used to scream: "Ahhhhh . . ." So when I noticed I couldn't do no more through the nose, I started basing. That's when base wasn't crack, that's when only the drug dealers went and copped $100 pieces, $200 pieces and we used to sit with the little chalice. And that took me to where I never was before. The all-time low. I lost control. I tried to kill myself with crack. I smoked so much that my gall bladder and my kidney dehydrated and swelled. They had to rush me to the hospital. People say you don't kick crack. I kicked crack. Three days I went through convulsions, I went through sweats. I was just an addict. As a matter of fact, I remember when the machine—the heart machine—was on. The doctors, when they wasn't looking, I still had a capsule in my pocket. Lying on the heart machine, ready to take a blast. And my mother comes in: "Ahhhh! You crazy!" [Interview with King Tone, 3/31/1998].

Research studies abound in which interviewed drug dealers recount similar stories (Inciardi 1990; Johnson et al 1990). They, like Tone, warn of the dangers of not separating business from pleasure. Yet his involvement in the trade and his drug use paralleled the kind of drugs he was distributing—from marijuana to cocaine and finally to crack. As many studies have shown, the social decline of individuals who use crack regularly is more rapid than with almost any other drug, with its physical and psychological impact devastating to almost all regular users. In this regard, Tone was no exception to the rule, and when he transgressed the street dealer's code of personal survival, his descent into both a personal and a social abyss was assured. Without any exaggeration, he was barely able to make it out alive:

> King T.: 'Cause let me tell you, when I smoked crack, I hit the bottom. I even robbed from my mother. I stole from anybody who came around. Drug dealers in East New York already knew that I had fallen from grace. So that if at twelve o'clock, if your worker was out, I robbed him. I had a team of guys like Robin Hood: "we'll rob you, smoke your crack with the crack heads on the block and go back on your block and sell it." So I became really wanted in the neighborhood. But some drug dealers knew me for so long that they didn't want to harm me. They just wanted me out of the way. You get where I'm going? Out of their way. So then again I started seeing members of my team start dying . . . my crack team. Disappearing. I remember one day I got caught by this guy named "R." and they took me into a dark room, and I was smoked out. I couldn't even fight no more. The gun was there, I couldn't even draw it. They took me to a room, they tied me to a work bench. These guys tied me—they had machetes, they had syringes with rat poison, and they would run them on my vein. And they trying to make me beg for my life. And I'm like: "Do this. C'mon, let's do this. Kill me." And then things started racing through my mind. And that was my first time I ever pleaded for my life . . . and then out of nowhere I hear a voice in front of the pool room saying: "Where's Potchie [Tone's nickname], I know you got him in here." And I looked and it is A. And he came in and he said: "Look cabrón, they going to kill you. You see? 'Cause you are . . .blah, blah, blah." Like he owed me that favor. I don't know how he found me. How he got me, but they got me out. And I left and I made a decision and I said: "Wow, man, this ain't for me" [Interview with King Tone, 3/31/1998].

Doing Time and Joining the Kings

Tone, once again, survives, managing eventually to pull through with a little help from his neighborhood friends. Subsequently, Tone enters a temporary stage of stability during which he begins a process of "recovery," establishing a stable and meaningful relationship with a local woman and acquiring a full-time job in a Manhattan delivery room, earning clean money with a regular time structure that he enjoys. For a while, the combination of the job, the relationship, and crack-free daily life enables him to take more personal responsibility for his life while being increasingly accountable to others. Still, without undergoing any serious detoxification treatment and without moving away from the neighborhood influences that could encourage his relapse, he soon returned to his erstwhile state.

> King T.: I had a real strong relapse where even my job didn't find me. I was gone. And that's when I started getting arrested. Getting my little bullshit cases. Used to get caught with a stem. And the judge used to see me like four times in one week. I remember a judge actually said: "Mr. Fernández, you need a rest. I just seen you here two days ago." So they put me in Brooklyn House and that's where I got jail in me. I wasn't a King yet. I used to know Kings, but I was too wild, they used to say: "Ahhh, you no good because you not righteous. You fight for the phone, you fight for everything. But you going back to smoke crack." They used to tell me. So I did this for a while, to once I got a bid in Manhattan. I got caught in Manhattan with two capsules. And this judge did not give me no play. He was talking about a 3 to 6 and a 2-1/2 to 5 for another case I had. And he didn't want to run it concurrent. So now I was scared. I was really for the first time being detained and looking at a long time [Interview with King Tone, 3/31/1998].

Charged with the criminal possession of a controlled substance— possession of five narcotic drugs with intent to sell[5]—Tone is sentenced to four years but in the interim, he finds himself awaiting trial in Riker's Island. However, rather than calm down and reflect on his mixed blessings, Tone cannot remain uninvolved in the political economy of prison life for long and he is almost murdered by other inmates for stealing their sneakers. What will it take for Tone to accept that his penchant for impulsive and self-destructive behavior will inevitably make him one more statistic? In a sense, he cannot go anywhere else but up, although with his distorted sense of self, his rampant opportunism, and his tendency to lie pathologically, Tone finds escaping from his social, psychological, and legal morass extremely difficult.

At the same time, Tone has a number of skills that, if harnessed, could help him move in the right direction. For example, he has an abundance of charisma, he is unafraid of stressful situations, and he is confident enough of his interpersonal skills that he can move easily between different social circles. Moreover, as his schoolteachers recognized and his early supplier of cocaine was thankful for, he is extremely quick-witted and possesses boundless energy. On the other hand, as far as Tone sees it, while he plots and schemes endlessly his efforts are all to no avail. He always ends up back in the ghetto/barrio, only now he is back in its most repressive form (Jackson 1969): the state's correctional system. At this juncture his "deviant moral career" (Becker 1959) takes another turn.

> King T.: So I went into the dorm and that's the first time a King approach me. A real old-timer. His name is Mafia. He came up and he said: "Tone, you real. But you so real that you're fake." I said: "What you mean?" And he said: "Read this." So I read a page and I said: "Yo, I am not with this quiche. I know about you all. I don't want protection. I protect myself." He said, "It's not about that. Find yourself." So one day I just started reading them and I locked myself in my cell. Three days, no body seen me. I just studied and studied and studied. And it hit me. And it hit me full. "You're a Latin King. You are special. Blood has done this and. . . ." I was reading and I was saying: "Wow, man, this is me." You know? And in the cell, like I told people I made three promises, you know. I said: "I want to become the best leader that the Nation is ever going to have." You know there's me in my little old. . . . "I'm never gonna come back to jail and I'm never going to smoke crack ever again" [Interview with King Tone, 3/31/1998].

Thus, Tone joins the Latin Kings in jail during a period in which the group's membership was mushrooming throughout the correctional system (see chapter 4). This account gets repeated in numerous speeches at universal meetings in later years as he uses it to remind himself and his followers of how far he has come and to demonstrate the power of the Nation's spiritual and collective remedy for nihilism, alienation, and self-hatred. Below, Tone recounts this same experience, this time using the King's metaphorical language of the warrior and revealing much more about this epiphanous (Denzin 1994) moment in his life:

> King Tone was made in a cell and, you know, my personal experience with the crowning was bigger than any time they could give me. I was in that cell and He appeared and, in splendor, he told me, "Get up, Tone," and "Here." He gave me this sword and then He just gave me the shield. He gave me a breast plate and He armored me. He put the full armor for God

on me. In that cell, in C-95, I thought I was the craziest motherfucker in that building at that moment. Here I am, sittin' on the bed, with Latin King lessons, a bible, and weighing 90 pounds, because I was in the streets abusin' drugs. I was gettin' down in the jail and doin' all kinds of crazy shit. I remember that day I wanted the phone and I was gonna do what I had to do to get the phone and twelve low, and no matter what. People were lookin' at me, seeing I wasn't playin.' That day King Mafia comes up to me and says, "Lock in and here's some lessons. You get down but you're a real stupid fella." I remember that day and I took his advice. . . . Then I said, Let me read this shit. Everybody's talkin' about it in this buildin', about these Latin Kings and, "It's real and it's righteous." So, I took it and I went in that cell and I started readin.' Man, I wanted to be able to walk that buildin', say, "Look, man, I'm King Tone. I know who I am." I wanted to find myself in the midst of the confusion of life. I needed something. I needed something to put me back, to put me back on track. I needed somethin.' Not my mother and not my father. None of that shit. I need somethin' for me. I needed me to tell me somethin.' When he was readin' that, man I started talkin' to myself. I started tellin' myself realities that I wasn't lookin' at. I started instructin' myself in situations that I knew I had to solve, that I was runnin' from a hundred miles per hour. I kneeled down before the Almighty Crown and I told my God, I said, "God, I've found somethin' that'll make me somebody. I have found somethin' that I could go in and be a part of it and help change stuff for Latinos" [Oral diary by King Tone, 1998].

Back on the Streets

In the months that followed his initial recruitment, his commitment to the group grew in intensity, as the Nation's codes of interpersonal conduct and its myriad homespun philosophies resonated well with his own personal ordeals and those of his community. The longer he stayed in prison, the more time he had to dwell on his past and on his future, and he began to see the connection between the group's exhortations on self-renewal and community leadership and his own long-term aspirations. By the end of his sentence, he had emerged both psychologically and emotionally stronger and felt eager to take on the world, despite the stigmata of his two new identities: that of an ex-felon and that of a neophyte Latin King. On hitting the neighborhood streets again, however, he was thrust immediately back into a turbulent subterranean world in which the meaning of his gang membership would have many more connotations and interpretations than he had ever considered.

King T.: I became a King in '90 in jail. I came out in '92, so let's say three or
four years ago. So when I come home, I have my big bumble beads and
my hands, you know, walking down the block. And I remember this kid
grabs me and says: "Show me . . . why you flying your colors like that?"
I said: "What are you talking about? I am a King." He goes: "You gotta
watch it, there's a King named 'T.' out here and if you don't report, they'll
kill you." That was the first time I heard King T.'s name. "Kill me? Are
you crazy man?" I thought I was it. So I walk on and I meet a King
named C., who's also in the Feds now. And he pull me over and he say:
"You real?" I say: "Yeah, I'm real." He say, he tested me, he say: "Tomorrow we go to your first meeting. You better be here." I say: "I'll be here."
So I go home and I come the next day. Sure enough I go to downtown
Brooklyn. There's about 300 Kings there. Now I'm open, so as soon as I
come in they pull me to the side. Now the Fourth Crown checks me out:
"What's your name?" Break it down. And I'm breaking it down. It's so
funny because the Fourth Crown who tested me now is still the Fourth
Crown of the Second Division Arawak Tribe. But I always tell people:
"Tell him who tested me." He stands up: "I did." And here I am The
Inca, now, you know what I mean? But he tested me and I met T. that
day. What happened was T. crashed a member's car. I found it funny that
the Supreme Crown of New York State couldn't drive. So I laughed at
him. After I laughed, this man says: "Who the fuck you think you laugh-
in' at? Don't you know who I am? I'm T." So all of a sudden I have five
guys putting me on the wall in church and I say: "What the fuck is goin'
on?" So C. says: "Shut up . . . that's the. . . ." And he's whispering who
he is and la la la . . . so alright I shut up. And he pulls me and says: "Why
you laugh?" I said: "I thought it was funny. No harm. No bad intention."
So he looked at me and says: "You think you're real?" I said: "Yeah." And
he says: "Now you my BG [bodyguard] sucker [Interview with King
Tone, 3/31/1998].

The "Stripping" of King T.

In all of Tone's previous street roles, there is one characteristic common
throughout: he was never content to be simply a follower. Quite the contrary,
Tone had to be a leader, an organizer, and a shot-caller of all the respective
groups that he joined or formed. The same is true of his early days in the street
faction of the ALKQN, but as Thrasher (1927) found, to rise in a gang's ranks
to its leadership strata you have to know the strengths, weaknesses, and alliances of those around you, especially when you "make your plays." Just a few

months after being released from prison, Tone has already become a minor player in the Nation's internal leadership struggles. After demonstrating his ability to "take care of business" he is promoted to be one of the enforcers (of discipline). From this vantage point, he is perfectly positioned to acquire the kind of organizational knowledge that will later aid his ascent.

Needless to say, he is not impressed with the leadership as it is currently constituted, though he sees many strong men and women in the wings waiting for their chance "to shine in the sun." For Tone, the two major issues that continued to bother him were: the way dissent was being dealt with, and the culture of physical discipline that had become normalized. In Tone's eyes, the Nation in its present state could not legitimately claim to be a "righteous" organization (cf. Thrasher 1927:359) of the barrio, and his misgivings about the group's trajectory and his deepening knowledge of the tensions inevitably drew him to other malcontents. Unbeknownst to Tone, however, King Blood was also hearing complaints from the rank-and-file that King Blood's leading man on the "outside" was demoralizing the membership and abusing his personal power. Rumors began to circulate and it became evident that the founder of the ALKQN would soon send his all-important letter to remove and discipline the current leader.

> King T.: At this time, the Nation was in—what you could say—a Civil War. . . . Blood gave permission to take down T. So, now T. has to be brought in to be stripped. But E. and S. are too much of a coward to come to Brooklyn to get him. So T. is already preaching treason. You know: "If brothers ever strip me, I'll put them with me . . ." and everything. So again, I'm in front of his store, 'cause for T. to be secure he used to work in one of those Chinese little stores, you know, where they sell, you know, souvenirs. We used to go with him to open the store. Stand in front of the store at attention, two on the side of the store, all the way to seven thirty at night until he closed. We couldn't eat, we couldn't talk to people and we couldn't smile. So I remember that day, I seen A. he goes: "Tone, would you follow me?" And I said, "Yo, check this out, if the paperwork is right, you gotta go in." So that's when I called C. I say: "Yo, C. the paperwork came down. E. and them are waiting for this Nigger. I think we should bring him. He should face the music [Interview with King Tone, 3/31/1998].

When the final act came, though, it did not quite turn out as he and his confederates had expected. In the following account, Tone describes the tumultuous meeting where Kings and Queens from all over the city amassed in a Manhattan housing project to witness the "stripping," i.e., the demotion and deposition, of the city's most powerful Latin King:

> King T.: There is about 600–700 people. And one half has guns for King E. and the other half got it for King T. Now, I'm looking in there, I'm saying: "We all gonna die today!" You know, this is me and my mind. So they read the letter and they going to strip him. So Brooklyn agreed after a long speech, a long battle. We agreed that he had to be stepped down. Me and C., in our minds, always planned this, we had to get rid of this coward. But what we didn't realize was that instead of Brooklyn having the main manpower, the Bronx and Manhattan took it. So now we not only losing our main piece of power, we became the herbs of the Nation. We gave them T. They want to violate him. So me and C. stepped up in the circle and we went: "Nah, you strip him but you can't violate him . . ." they wanted to give him the five slap violation—it's something he created. Blood's frame of thinking was: "Give him what he gave out." So the five slaps were coming. Z. and me we started screaming, you know, the love speech: "Please, let's end it here." They settled, right? But then I seen a funny movement. Everyone left before Brooklyn left, it was storming and a cold day, I remember it clearly as we came out. I'm next to T. then all of the stuff from the roofs, like AKs, start going off. "Cluck, cluck, cluck . . ." Now here's Queen Z., she's got four daughters, and I'm stuck with protecting them. So of course, I'm like: "They shooting at me. I can't shoot. I'm not going to reach them." But all the security guards ran away from Z. So at that minute I have to think quick. Z. and C. knew how really I loved her . . . I took out my guns—I'm shooting at the roof to try to hold fire, then I take my other gat out—'cause I always carried two gats when I was out there, you know that was my frame of thinking from when I was young. And I start pointing at the rest of the Kings and I say: "If you don't come back and pick Z up, I'm going to kill youse." There's me screaming in the middle of the night. They get Z., they throw her in the car, I back up and we get away [Interview with King Tone, 3/31/1998].

The Big Sweep, Moving Up in Rank, and "Tone Is Down in Town"

Once again, Tone makes it through another life-threatening situation, and he is convinced that only divine intervention has been keeping him alive. However, he has little time to rest on his laurels for now he must act decisively to make good on his particularly strong situation in Brooklyn where the entire upper ranks are temporarily in disarray.

But what do we make of these "palace intrigues" among the elites of the street elites (Katz 1987)? Is there something unique in the way power gets played out among gang leaders in comparison to the rest of society? The competition in the upper strata of the group is not unlike the intrigues found among many mainstream bureaucratic organizations at the highest level. In politics, in business, and in academia, the factional in-fighting, the conspiracies, the purges, and the coups are all present in the ongoing struggle between personalities, visions, and ideologies within the same organization. The big difference, however, is the propensity for the Latin Kings to use violence to settle disputes—a carryover from the Chicago and the King Blood gang traditions. Fortunately, on this occasion of a mass showdown, there were no fatalities or even injuries and Tone began his move up the ranks.

With T., the First Crown, out of the way, Tone enters the Supreme Team of the city's power structure, which enables him to be more effectively proactive in restructuring the Nation, especially his own Brooklyn tribe. Nonetheless, because he is now increasingly visible and his influence on the Kings is more noticeable as the Brooklyn tribe becomes better organized, he is the subject of increasing police surveillance. As the events pan out, he is not one of those who are picked up or even officially wanted, at least for the time being:

> King T.: Mary Jo White[6] came and did the sweep. T. was taken, C. was taken
> from me. From right at my job. I hired C. from my job to try to keep
> him safe? And the sweep came. And when the sweep came, I remember
> it clearly, I was at work. I hung up the phone, they called me. I thought
> I was on the list. I jetted. I told my boys: "Give me my paycheck, I'm
> outta here." So then I called Blood's lawyer and he says: "You're not on
> the list. But there's a second one coming down, you better watch that"
> [Interview with King Tone, 3/31/1998].

The "Feds," in essence, do Tone a great service by clearing away many of those who could have obstructed his rise to the top. But he is not the unanimous choice of all the Kings, as he explains below.

> King T.: And sure enough, they took everybody that I would have had to
> fight—believe me when I tell you—to be what I wanted to be. So all of
> a sudden here I am—the slate is clean, Blood has got communication
> with me, already for a year. So the next Universal that was thrown, everybody was in chaos. I didn't even know a letter was going to be read, a letter that claimed me Inca of New York State. So you know, first off, I said:
> "No, I don't want it. I'm not going to take it." M. and them were like:
> "You got to do it, 'cause we got nobody else." And you could see every-

FIGURE 6.2 King Tone speaks to members in the circle of a "Universal." (Photo by Steve Hart.)

body in the circle say: "Tone, him? The little cripple dude." You know, everybody was surprised that Blood had chosen me. And when the letter came I hold it close to my heart and I made a promise to myself: "Blood would never ever make me do anything that I don't want to do." And if he tries, we'll fight [Interview with King Tone, 3/31/1998].

Sorting Out the Prisons

After this extraordinary series of events, Tone eventually wins control of the street-based Latin Kings and Queens, and he is officially ordained as Inca by King Blood himself in a letter to the entire Nation in the fall of 1996. There are, of course, other competitors for the position, but the reality is, there is no one else currently active in the leadership who has the experience, the charisma, the organizational abilities, and the street credibility to do the job. Below, Blood's lawyer reflected on the reasons for Tone's ascent:

> Lawyer: Even as bad as some of the members were back then, they still weren't dealing drugs, or if they were, they were too stupid and they weren't making any money because there was no drugs and no money found. So then Tone bridged the gap because Tone was a little bit of both. He had been in jail, he had been a crack addict, but he also related to the people on the street and, you know, at the time, he was preaching "no drugs" and the whole thing. So, he was perceived as somebody by Blood and Queen Z. And, basically, they were the ones who decided that he would become the next Inca.
>
> D.B.: So, Tone was perfect.
>
> Lawyer: Yeah, he was perfect because he had been on both sides and he was articulate with the media. He went the John Gotti route, he put himself into the media any chance he got and he got in their face, but even so, I don't think he had any authority over the people in prison. I think that he was upset with that, because the thing he heard from them, from what I understand, was that he had no authority. They wouldn't listen to him [Mr. L., King Blood's lawyer, 2/17/1999].

As Mr. L. points out, the prisons are a different category. "We are like two different Nations," Tone would often say. Tone at this point in time faces three major problems: (1) he must win widespread support from the entire street Nation and, in so doing, unify all the different tribes under one leadership; (2) he must reassure Blood that he will not pose a threat to the founder in his increasingly vulnerable state; and (3) he must find a way to gain respect from the prison membership, such that he is not constantly facing efforts to unseat him from the "inside." As for Blood, Tone knew that he had to communicate with him constantly in order to keep him involved and allay his fears of any further conspiracies.

But what to do about the prisons? It was one of the most pressing issues for Tone throughout his reign, as it always involved a highly complicated process of: (1) reaching an agreement with the prison leadership not to interfere in the Nation's business on the "outside," even if the inmate leaders were not in agreement with the street Kings and Queens' version of the organization, and (2) neutralizing all efforts to physically remove him without resorting to the internal bloodshed that had almost proven the Nation's downfall. The letter reprinted below, from a leader of the Latin King inmates to King Tone, is an example of his efforts to negotiate with the prison power brokers:

> *Beloved One,*
>
> *At times, I don't like the fact that when I do something that involves your name, you right away think that I am trying to make you look bad in our brothers' eyes or that I'm trying to take over. By now you should know that that's not my style. I don't have time for that specially when our nation needs our dedication the most. If I were after taking over, I would have had never accepted your offer to unite our nation. Brother's love me because they know I don't play games when it come to our nation. [M]y record speak for itself. I don't have, never had nor will I have a bad jacket placed on me. Whenever I had mentioned your name or anything I wrote, I had done so with the only intention of clearing your name. You should know that those interviews of yours in news papers, live t.v., and magazines make you look like a Rat specially for people's behind these walls's eyes. You can't imagine how many good bros and friends I lost since we united. I have been through hell explaining that you had your reasons to say what you said and that it was in order to look good in the Devil's eyes which is the only way possible to help K.B.*

As the letter suggests, there was no shortage of intrigue coming from rank-and-file inmates, and neither could the prison leadership be counted upon, despite their claims to the contrary. The trick was to keep communication open at all times between the street and prison leaderships, and never do anything to disrespect the power and authority of the inmate hierarchies within their own domains. But facing down the second type of inmate threat—the direct assaults on his life—was a different matter. How many ways are there of diffusing such high-risk situations? Using all the tactics at his disposal, Tone resorted to a mixture of physical intimidation, intelligence gathering, and the Kings' version of street pedagogy to save himself and his dream:

> King T.: Now the hard part is we can't be pacifist. I'm still in New York. And I'm still surrounded by another fifty states that don't believe in what I'm doing. And I got jail. So, if somebody comes out of jail, like last week, with four letters, Kuby[7] got the letters, one asking for my head and two asking for the position to be taken over, and all these by the man that Blood left in charge in jail, who's supposed to be my brother. You get

where I'm going. So they send the kid, and I tell you I slapped the fire out of this kid. This kid was about—real big. He went to the Tribe and he told them: "Look, I got these letters. Y'all gotta follow me. I'm risking my life doing this. We gotta take Tone down, and you're the Tribe to help me." My people being so innocent, "Of course, what's your name? Man, we've been waiting for you." They had this kid so suped up. This is where I see that the kids really don't want to go back. There goes a man with letters that any of them could use to take my position. . . . So they bring him into my house. Now the kid is walking in big, and he's like: "Who's that? Who's that Queen?" And then one of the tribe goes: "You know who's that, right?" The kid turns white. The brother from the tribe goes "That's King Tone. You thought that we were going to give you Tone? Well, here he is." This kid goes, "I'm just a messenger." Well, me having to be a leader, sometimes I have to strike. So I struck him like a little boy and he said: "Why you hitting me?" Now, there's a man who just did nine years in Attica, he's on work release, not even home a week, and some fool gives him an order to already go kill. So I'm slapping him to see if I can wake him up. After a couple of slaps, I say: "Don't you see what you're doing?" And I walk away and give him two minutes to think and then I come back and mush [hit] him. And then when I seen total fear take over his heart and he was ready to listen, I stopped. I told him, "What are you doing? Didn't you just come home?" He goes: "Yeah." I go, "Aren't you still on work release? . . . Don't you know that whoever sent you doesn't love you? You're set up. Don't you know that years ago you would have been chopped up, put in pieces in the Bay?" At the end, this man knelt down, kissed his Crown and said: "I didn't know." And this was the problem, he came to kill after another member told him that I was a snitch [Interview, 3/31/1998].

God, Kingism, and Community

No longer the cocky, self-made street dealer, the down-and-out "crackhead," or the dutiful soldier of the Latin Kings' leadership, Tone finally comes into his own as a charismatic movement leader who is convinced that history and God are calling him. There are three key characteristics in this stage of Tone's development: first is his embrace of religion as his main ideological resource and his "from-below" interpretation of its many messages; second is his radical vision of the group and its potential direction; and third is his growing insistence on the reciprocal interplay between the ALKQN and the community. Below, Tone discusses the role of God in his reform of the group:

FIGURE 6.3 King Tone and Father Luis Barrios (coauthor) jointly preside over a Baptism ceremony for Latin Kings' and Queens' children. (Photo by Steve Hart.)

King T.: So everything I learned in Kingism that would match a story from the Bible, I would preach it to the kids and break it down in knowledge . . . and it started working with them. They started getting a sense of spirituality, they got a sense of belonging. They got a sense that I didn't want them, like the pastor, to be Jesus. I just wanted them to try to walk like he did. So when the kids started hearing a message not condemning them, and not criticizing them for not being like the great Jew, but actually complementing them for trying just to be—even a little bit—close to his steps, was good enough for King Tone. They believe. They started looking to God again. And they went home and said: "Jesus prays like this . . ." It gave them a sense of belonging. And that's how I use religion to capture their minds . . . my scariest thing was that if I leave, they would believe in a man again. And the Bible says it clearly: "Damned is the man who puts all his trust in the next man, because man should always fall short of the glory of God." So then my main goal was to make sure that if I ever leave, that they know it wasn't King Tone, it wasn't Blood—it's God. Whatever God you choose [Interview with King Tone, 4/24/1998].

Tone embraces the symbols and parables of religion because he knows that they are effective in communicating to the group's diverse ranks the new personal and organizational politics of the movement and the new expectations of the leadership. Of course, he knows well that many of the Kings and Queens have been raised in the Catholic church and understand implicitly many of the references to which he refers. Further, as we read in an earlier chapter, the Latin Kings' manifestos are sprinkled with references to God and other religious themes; thus Tone is on safe ideological ground, which is a major consideration in this transitional period of reconstitution and consolidation.

Thus, Tone's brand of leadership is in stark contrast to his predecessor. For him, making long speeches at universals, setting up discussion points for the whole membership to debate, and constantly urging members to take their Kingism one step further is what true leadership requires. It is about making the personal political, seeking an alternative humanistic understanding of people's development, and living in perpetuity.

King T.: And then Peter became a different man because he had that personal experience with God. And that's what I'm saying. I've had my personal experience—life changing experience with God already. I've been with Peter. I've denied. I've stepped on him. I've questioned God. I've fought him. But he's given me the chance to say: "Tone, do you love me?" And all he said was: "Then go get the flock." And everybody makes this a difficult story. The whole story is Jesus made me a shepherd and I have to do my job. And if I love him—'cause the Kings remember something that is learned is not taught. A Kingsman's goal, you'll hear us say: "We don't die, we multiply. Cowards die many times before death, but a King takes death but once." So, I've got the trick that's eternal life, but to get eternal life you must be righteous [Interview, 4/28/1998].

Therefore, to be a King allows you to live forever but only if you reform your ways. This postulation, which comes straight out of Christianity and the notion of "good works," is extremely effective with both youth and adults who appear destined to live their entire lives in society's economic and political margins. Now, as Tone says, "They got hope" and all they have to do is bring their beliefs into line with their actions in order to find true happiness. But what are the actions that are called for? What is his vision of this new quasi-social movement and its many enthusiastic followers?

> King T.: I want to make the Kings—like the Muslims and the Jews. The Jews scream: "Give us a school!" They'll get it in five minutes, with the fence up, the windows new. And nobody can go in there but Jews. The Hasidics—it's there. It's a seen fact. I say: "How do they do it?" Because if one synagogue says: "You don't vote for somebody." The whole Jewish community won't vote for you. And the beautiful thing about it is that I learned that they—in the same district—their vote is powered in one. So what's happening with me, I'm learning the trick. First I got to unite the people abroad. But then I got to get financially stable so then I could buy a piece of land or any project. I'm looking big where I could fill it with my people—yes! Only my people. So when my people speak, they will be listened to [Interview, 4/28/1998].

Tone takes his cues from a number of other social movements and their base communities. Chief among them are the Black Muslims and the Orthodox Jews, both of which are well represented in New York City and with whom Tone has had numerous dealings. Consequently, Tone sees his "Nation" in a way that is similar to both of these communities that have built strong interdependent social, political, and economic networks from which they are able to demand more power and resources. Thus, this dream of his, to own a building and to construct a church where his organization can meet and worship away from the interference of the state, is straight out of the U.S. ethnic rule book. Almost every community that has come to the United States has done the same at one time and his beloved subgroup of the larger Latino community should be no exception. Therefore, for Tone, this conceptualization of the Kings and Queens' future is more than just wishful thinking or a vain hope; rather, it is a concrete goal that his members can relate to and a reachable aim that will eventually be realized. Morever, it is also a means to raise the sights and consciousness of the members and to focus their gaze on an elevated personal and collective ideal—an ideal which is, after all, mapped out in the three stages of Kingism, the unifying doctrine of the Nation.

Our interpretation of Tone's life history, above, shows the personal and historical context in which Tone made many of his major life choices as well as some of the consequences of those decisions. In revealing this interplay between Tone's environment, his thinking, and his action we have emphasized three aspects in his development.

First, we see many of the factors that influence his value system and, over the course of time, begin to shape a specific worldview that culminates in his version of Kingism. This personal and collective philosophy is, on the one hand, highly eclectic and utopian, drawing on street lore, religio-political resistance themes, and inter-generational gang codes; on the other hand it is clearly rooted in the traditional norms of barrio family life, with its idealized themes of masculinity and femininity, material and spiritual transcendence, and collective upliftment.

Second, we see the importance of Tone's personality on how he came to shape his life circumstances. In this, we want to highlight the constant tension between Tone's indefatigable will to control his fate in the world and a powerful, self-destructive urge that could easily have ended his life at any time. To some degree this reminds us of Jankowski's (1991) notion of the gang personality type, which he calls "defiant individualism." But as Tone matures what takes over his sense of self is his notion of a "calling"; he feels that, like Jesus, he is giving up his life so that the larger collective and its spiritual embodiment can survive.

Finally, the most critical feature of this analysis concerns Tone's pathway into the ALKQN's leadership. We have shown that Tone emerged out of a specific confluence of historical, social, political, and individual circumstances and that Tone was, at first, reluctant to assume the Inca position. However, once in power, Tone wasted little time making headway in developing his leadership skills and broadening the goals, practices, and outlook of the group (as we shall see in greater detail in the following chapter). Some have asked this question: Did he believe that he was simply leading another gang, or had he long been harboring other ideas about the group's potential development? The question is difficult to answer conclusively, but what we do know is that once he had summoned up the courage to give the group a new orientation, there was no turning back, and the specific intersection of internal and external forces propelled the group forward. This process is exactly what Touraine describes as a movement's historicity, by which he means the capacity of a group to act on itself and thereby to remake itself. Therefore, Tone's transformation from dope dealer, to gangbanger, to social movement leader is historicity working itself out at the level of the movement actor.

CHAPTER 7

NONGANG TRADITIONS II

Is not our main task now—as it always was—to resuscitate social relations, opposition, defiance, struggle and hope wherever they have been crushed, distorted or stifled by order, which is always the order of the state? It is not enough simply to denounce the order; one must show that it is not all-powerful, one must rediscover the spring hidden beneath the cement, the word beneath the silence, the questioning beneath the ideology. This is what is at stake, and if we are to lose we shall have to give up believing in social movements and even in what we call society; we shall have to admit that there are no longer any citizens, only subjects, no longer class actors, only victims.

Touraine 1981:55

Remembering these years is painful because many friends are dead, but I refuse to have researchers, politicians or journalists who weren't there ignore what we achieved, write off what we accomplished as a liberal experiment or diminish our success by remembering only the South Side gangs.

Dawley 1992:xv

Introduction

As the leading French sociologist Alain Touraine (1981, 1988) suggests (above), one of the most important questions that a sociologist can ask is: How do people who are not generally considered the makers of "history" become movement actors in the postindustrial epoch? We argue that the ALKQN, in its incarnation (i.e., during the 1996–1999 period of research) as a quasi-social movement provides a perfect case study through which to pursue this interrogation.

Nevertheless, as we excavate these movement "possibilities" in the data, it is clear that the gang literature alone cannot adequately guide our inquiry or our analysis. The prevailing tendency in the research, as we have seen, is to treat gangs and gang members as socially deviant phenomena devoid of both history and consciousness[1] and incapable of a prosocial transformation. As one would expect, scant attention has been paid to empowerment techniques and processes, except in terms of adopting and transmitting delinquent definitions of social reality (Sutherland and Cressey 1966). Consequently, the relationship between politics and the street gang has been largely occluded, although where it has merited attention the consensus has been that gang members remain overwhelmingly conservative in their political outlook (see chapter 3).

Moving Beyond Chicago and King Blood

With a new leadership, more or less, in control of the organization, and with the emphasis on improving the self-image of the group, two of the immediate tasks that lay ahead were to develop indigenous models of self-organization and sets of practices (Morris 1984; Oberschall 1977) that: (1) historically resided in the members' own communities, (2) would demonstrate to the public the new status of the group, and (3) once in place would be self-reinforcing. This feat of drawing on the community's "mentalities,"[2] or the members' "structures of feeling" (Williams 1965) for the ALKQN was not without its problems, however, and there was no shortage of members that preferred to restrict their oppositional behavior to delinquency and resentment rather than purposive social action (see Tarrow 1992:180 and the section in chapter 12 of this book on the "Ghost Tribes").

Nonetheless, despite the perceived interests of some hard-core members who clung tenaciously to their old gang lifestyles, the threats and intimidation of law enforcement, the social and political betrayals of both "insiders" and "outsiders," and the lapses in moral fortitude of the leadership, the good faith efforts that were made to elevate the organization from a street subculture to an anti-Establishment community force cannot be denied. Table 7.1 delineates the major models of "collective action" (Tarrow 1992) that influenced both the philosophy and the practices of the new Latin Kings and Queens during the 1996–1999 period.

TABLE 7.1   Empowerment Models Used in the ALKQN's Reform Phase

Radical Political Models	Spiritual Models	Self-help Models	Other Models
Black Panthers; Young Lords; Puerto Rican Socialist Party	Judaism; Christianism (Roman Catholics and Protestants); Africanism (Yorubas/Santería, and Paleros)	Alcoholics Anonymous; Alternatives to Violence Program	Orthodox Jewish Community; Black Civil Rights Movement

Radical Political Models

What lay behind King Tone's invocation of the traditions of the Young Lords and the radical politics of the 1960s? Is this simply the radical rhetoric of a street-savvy parvenue who wants to impress the "outsider"? Or does it come from a much deeper process of historical and ideological reconfiguration in which the group's leader is seeking to link contemporary subcultures of the street and the traditions of resistance that have been so key to New York City's past and present? To understand the context of King Tone's statement, we need to step back in time to a period when street gangs and street radicals were both socially and culturally intertwined,[3] and thereby trace the complex relationship that developed between them, only to be rekindled in the imagination and practices of the ALKQN some twenty years later.

Youth Resistance from Street Subcultures to Radical Nationalism

And I saw the discrimination and I saw the bullshit and then I heard Malcolm and I heard Don Pedro and the Panthers came out and then the Young Lords were destiny. This is why I believe in destiny. I walked out of my house one day. I said "good-bye, I'm going to join the Young Lords" [Mr. A., ex-leader of the Bronx Young Lords].

Mr. A., a South Bronx resident most of his life, describes his first entering the movement of radical Puerto Rican opposition to internal and external colonialism, recalling in the same sentence the presence and influence of the Black Panthers and Malcolm X. This was the late 1960s in New York City, where militant political resistance to the city's status quo, to the racism, the class oppression, and the lines of patriarchal domination were everywhere. The masses, especially the youth, were in revolt and it was not a white-led, middle-class movement (Muñoz 1989) that they were flocking to:

> As black activism moved North, it, too, played its part in educating and in-volving young blacks. From the mid-sixties on, Northern cities were the scene of direct group action concerned with the basic needs of the commu-nity—housing, education, employment, health. Rent strikes, picketing, chain-ins, sit-ins, all represented the community's attempt to deal effectively with its ills [Burns 1971:xv].

Consequently, The Black Panther Party, formed in New York City in 1968, having first originated in the ghettos of Oakland and Los Angeles in California before spreading to other heavily disenfranchised Black communi-ties in Chicago, Detroit, and Newark, emerged out of the ongoing struggle of Blacks for political self-determination. When the movement came to New York, it built on already existing traditions of community struggle and or-ganization. Similarly, the Young Lords arrived at around the same time, in 1969, having originated in Chicago's predominantly Puerto Rican barrios as a street gang before its call for a militant, socialist opposition to the contem-porary capitalist power relations was responded to by thousands of marginal-ized Latino/a youth throughout the barrios of the Midwest and Northeast.

While these radical groups emerged at a particular time of generalized un-rest in society, street gangs had been omnipresent in the barrios and the ghet-tos for many years though their numbers varied according to the natural his-tory cycle of street gang subcultural life that was typical of New York City (Brotherton 1999).

> The gangs of those times were number one, they were a means for the younger people to survive against, like, the Italians that used to be down on . . . Avenue X and down below 96th Street, and stuff like that. It also be-came totally within El Barrio, OK? And all that was destroyed by heroin. It was an influx of heroin that was directly related to Vietnam and the CIA's involvement and how they would gather intelligence and trade opium for intelligence. That's how this thing was happening . . . because of the urban unrest—heavy heroin came into Black and Latino communities, and El Bar-rio was no exception. And so the addiction of heroin in the young people destroyed the organizations [Interview with Mr. P., ex-Young Lord, 1/18/1997].

Mr. P., above, discusses the emergence of gangs in his South Bronx neighborhood during the late 1960s, relating this development to the ethnic competition in his district. He also alludes to the conspiratorial reasons for the systematic disappearance of these street collectives, particularly its leadership. In another account of the mid-1960s era,[4] ex-gang leaders recount many individual gang members who spontaneously participated in radical actions against the state.

> I can remember back then . . . yeah, we had a real radical with us . . . I remember when they put a Puerto Rican flag on the Statue of Liberty. That was 1977, do you remember that, during the Bicentennial? It was actually a protest and that was Ponce. He was a Savage Skull . . . and now he's one of L's professors [Interview with Black Benjy, the founder and president of the Savage Nomads, one of the two largest gangs in New York City, 5/20/1996].

Toward the mid-1970s a few gang collectives, most notably the Ghetto Brothers in New York City, shifted more consciously in a radical direction and rather than have members leave the gang to begin a political career on the organized radical left, some gang leaders decided to change their own organization into a radical movement.

> D.B.: Now go back and tell me a bit about the structure of the organization
>
> Y.B.: The organization [i.e, the Ghetto Brothers] began when I started seeing the political organizations coming up, like the Black Panthers, The Young Lords, and the Puerto Rican Independence movement. I started to look into their platforms and I started to think that the Ghetto Brothers could go in the direction of the Puerto Rican independence movement . . . that's cuz I was Nacionalista. I was a Nationalist, I wanted to go that way . . . I decided that we should start to shed our gang club. . . . We're an organization, we're a family, we're this and this. . . . What is the aim of the Ghetto Brothers? It's to bring all our brothers and sisters together. It's to do something for our community. To get rid of the drunks, to get rid of the pimps, to get rid of the prostitution, to get into education, to get into all of this. . . . We outstretched our hands. That's what Jesus was all about. We're about using these hands to hug you, to touch you, to build things, not to hurt you [Interview with Yellow Benjy, 5/20/1996].

Can it really be said that the gang members of the day only coined the phrases of the revolutionaries as a form of "justificatory vocabulary" as some criminologists argue (Jacobs 1977)? This explanation for the widespread use of antiestablishment language and tactics by gang members does not explain the deep-seated philosophical and cultural attachment that some gang leaders were developing for the "causa" of national self-determination and the goals of ghetto/barrio empowerment. It is as if only the middle classes can express such sophisticated thoughts as those below and mean them.

> We are being oppressed by the North American Yankees. We the Puerto Ricans should rise up and defend ourselves against these dogs who oppress us, and liberate our country from capitalism and imperialism. The North American is trying to steal our identity as Puerto Ricans, and call us Americans. We Puerto Ricans, are Puerto Ricans from the day we are born, until the day we die [Yellow Benjy, sixteen years old, cofounder of the Ghetto Brothers, interviewed in 1973; quoted in Chalfant and Fecher 1987].

We argue that, similar to what is going on today, there is ample evidence that street gangs and their members were not the one-dimensional, empty savages of the Conradian urban jungle (Gilbert 1984)[5] but that many gang members were deeply influenced by the communitarian philosophy and practices of the radical groups, who could show them the possibility of uniting a search for identity with militant, antiestablishment action (cf. Schneider 1999). Of course, while many of the gang youths undoubtedly remained apolitical (in a transformative sense), their worldview bound by the gang's limited focal concerns (Miller 1955) and/or saturated by the psychosocial themes of self-hatred (Burns 1972; Clarke 1972), others who came from the same setting struggled to find a way to organizationally, politically, and culturally thwart their lower-class "fates."

> Puerto Ricans had been psyched into believing this myth about being docile. A lot of Puerto Ricans really thought that the man in blue was the baddest thing going.
>
> Things were different in the gang days. Gang days, we owned the block, and nobody could tell us what to do with the street. Then dope came in and messed everything up messed our minds up and just broke our backs—dope and anti-poverty. Anti-poverty wiped out a whole generation of what could have been Puerto Rican leaders in New York City. . . .
>
> So we had no leadership, and we had no people—our people were dying from dope. But we knew that it was there, man, 'cause we knew that the fire was there. Those of us who got together to start the thing, we knew weren't freaks—we didn't feel that we were all that much different from the people.

There's a tendency to say, "the people," and put the people at arm's length. When we say "people," man, we're talking about ourselves. We're from these blocks, and we're from these schools, products of this whole thing. Some of us came back from college—it was like rediscovering where your parents had come from, rediscovering your childhood [Pablo Guzman, cofounder of the Young Lords Party, interviewed in 1971, quoted in Franklin 1971].

The Interpenetration of the Radical Past and the Accommodationist Present

The discussion above not only helps to locate the present study in some historical context, but it represents a way to understand how the ALKQN was able to even consider transforming itself during a period that, according to most observers, did not offer a supportive environment. In this decidedly nonradically progressive era, therefore, several questions need to be addressed: (1) How did the relationship between gangs and radical social movements of the past manifest itself in the ALKQN some twenty years later? (2) How were the political lessons of the earlier radical period learned? (3) Who were the carriers of these historical scripts?

Making Sense of the Present Through the Past

Interviewer: What would you say are the main goals of the organization?

King J.: Well, I would think it is the reason why I joined . . . to help our people. Like, I look back and I see Young Lords, Black Panthers, how they were. You could say they would fight for their rights, and as I was growing up I didn't see any of that, you know? And I strongly believe that this Nation uses all its efforts to uplift its people, our people, my people. And, as a King, it's my right, my duty, to make sure when I see something that I don't like, like a definite injustice, I just step to my business and take care of that. But most of the time it's hard. I mean it's hard to go to work 12 hours a day, get home, and go outside and make sure that my brothers are all right. Find out what's happening in the neighborhood, make sure there's no cops beating up Latinos, and all that. You know, like I don't believe that anybody should be picked on cuz he's smaller. I don't believe that anybody should get picked on because of their skin color, regardless of what color that is. And those are my beliefs. Those are my strong beliefs. I don't believe in abuse. That's what I'm here for. I need to do my part in getting rid of abuse [Interview with King J., 7/7/1997].

King J., above, discusses his membership in an unambiguous, combative language that meshes his self-image as a defender and leader of the Latino community with the exploits of past radical political movements. This combination of his righteous indignation at the ongoing social injustices to his community, his memorization (McDonald 1999) of past insurgencies, and the lack of legitimacy that he attributes to repressive authority is reminiscent of what McAdam has called the emergence of "cognitive liberation" in social-movement actors, a term that is rooted in the studies of poor peoples' movements by Piven and Cloward:

> The emergence of a protest movement entails a transformation of consciousness and of behavior. The change in consciousness has at least three distinct aspects. First, "the system"—or those aspects of the system that people experience and perceive—loses legitimacy. Large numbers of men and women who ordinarily accept the authority of their rulers and the legitimacy of institutional arrangements come to believe in some measure that these rulers and these arrangements are unjust and wrong. Second, people who are ordinarily fatalistic, who believe that existing arrangements are inevitable, begin to assert "rights" that imply demands for change. Third, there is a new sense of efficacy; people who ordinarily consider themselves helpless come to believe that they have some capacity to alter their lot [Piven and Cloward 1970:3–4; quoted in McAdam, 1982:50].

This description of the interlocking conditions under which the subjective state of movement actors proactively changes aptly applies to the thinking of King J., and it could equally apply to many other members who repeatedly described their experiences of direct and indirect violence (Salmi 1993) at the hands of the police, the schools, the prison system, and the political economy. In addition, there were many who would recall selective makers of history, however inaccurate, to situate their present struggle, and give it an air of common sense:

> If we don't get education there's nothing to fight. You know, a wise man will use his mind. A regular person who doesn't care will use his hands, you know? Years ago we thought that we had to get everything by force. It's kind of like Malcolm X and Martin Luther King . . . Malcolm X thought that we had to fight literally with his hands to get things accomplished, but Martin Luther King fought with his mind. We've learned, OK? We did our hands already. That didn't work. It brought more problems, we lost people. Now we're using our minds, we're getting ahead and it's making a difference [Interview with Queen J., 9/10/1998].

In general, we found that those Kings and Queens who were grappling with the more activist kinds of social and political questions were always searching for ways to frame themselves and their specific struggles. And, since there were so few living reference points that demonstrate successful challenges to the status quo, this quest inevitably took them back to the days when political and cultural resistance was the norm. In this process of searching for prior exemplars to vitiate the present, they also discovered that many of the issues that prompted the earlier radical movements were similar to those now filling the protest agenda of their own group: police brutality, police corruption, substandard schooling, dead-end jobs, cultural invisibility, institutional racism, redlining, attacks on welfare, and so on.

However, apart from the development of a radical subjectivity that was being promoted by the new Inca, King Tone, and other more class-conscious and intellectual leaders in the group, there were many practical reasons why these radical political models were so appealing. First, to consciously reject the normalization of everyday state repression and economic marginality and plan to effect social change at the street and community levels (like the Panthers and the Lords did before them) is an enormous step in terms of political and social empowerment. Few youth in the barrios and ghettos of the inner cities take their resistance this far (Schneider 1999), and so it is comforting for such social actors to at least feel that there has been some historical precedent. Second, at times when the group came under great pressure from law enforcement or when it was being featured negatively in the media, it was helpful to invoke the lessons from previous political struggles with authority which placed their own difficult situation in a much broader perspective.[6] Third, in a period when the ALKQN was systematically challenging its gang label, this strategy of members to liken themselves to former radicals was an excellent way to increase their legitimacy both as individuals and as a group in the eyes of the community. Finally, infusing their present struggles with the actions of radicals allowed them to win wider acceptance from a range of leftists and liberals who might normally keep a distance from gang members who, historically, have been seen as antisocial and lumpen.[7] Below, C.R. brings greetings from the Workers World Party at one of the ALKQN's universals:

C.R.: Brothers and sisters, I'd like to wish King Tone a happy birthday and also tell him that he's catchin' up to me. I feel proud to be here today bein' that this universal, this celebration, is being conducted on a weekend of the so-called Thanksgiving holiday. When our Native American brothers and sisters experienced one of the greatest horrors in all human history—the ripping off of their lands and the murder, the systematic murder that has taken place and is still goin' on till this day. Brothers and sisters, it is no wonder why the police is scared of you. This kind of unity is the unity we have to build at every corner of this country and finally rip our oppressor's throat one by one. Let us not forget. Let us not forget—that the same people that are shooting us in the back here in the city, the same people who keep us unemployed, the same people who are closing down our schools, are the same people who invaded Puerto Rico nearly 100 years ago.

Audience: Amor de Rey!

C.R.: Brothers and sisters, on behalf of The Workers World Party, whatever throwdown needs to be made we will be there next to you doin' it.

For all these reasons it was no coincidence that many members, in their public selves, made repeated references to the Young Lords Party, in particular. Perhaps the most demonstrative statements that the group as a whole made in this direction came in 1998. First, Lolita Lebrón, the Puerto Rican nationalist heroine who was a member of the Puerto Rican Nationalist Party and who had been in federal prisons for twenty-five years,[8] appointed the ALKQN to protect her during a demonstration in front of the United Nations. Second, Rafaél Cancel-Miranda, a nacionalista who had spent twenty-five years in federal prison, attended an ALKQN universal and received a rapturous applause from the ecstatic audience. Third, Ms. Adelfa Vera, a Puerto Rican activist at the age of eighty-five, attended an ALKQN universal and was given the group's sacred beads by the leadership. Barrios, the author, describes the event:

The experience with Doña Adelfa Vera, a parishioner in our church at St. Marys, was incredible. This 85-year-old woman, with a long history in Puerto Rico and New York City of struggle asked me what was going on in the park next to the church. I explained it was an ALKQN universal meeting. She told me that she wants to go there and bless them. I spoke to King Tone and he was happy to allow her to address the people. It was amazing when Doña Adelfa started talking to them. They were stunned, listening to this old woman saying the government always tells you that you can't change this political system. But I'm telling you, she said, "Fuck the government and believe in yourself, believe in your group and don't give me any excuses. Here I am, an 85-year-old lady and I have no excuses." The members starting applauding her and screaming ADR and she gave her blessing. Then the group created a special prayer for her, and with their black and gold necklace, proclaimed her a Mother Queen. At the end we hugged and she told me, "I'm a Queen, what a great honor. These kids are the hope for our liberation struggle. I can die in peace, because we found the continuation."

These living examples of anticolonial resistance to the greatest imperial power in the world were not only a tremendous inspiration to all those members so used to being either pilloried or dismissed by the dominant social and cultural order, but their presence at one of the group's gatherings was an unmistakable sign of the group's legitimacy among a revered generation. "The ALKQN has come a long way from meeting secretly in parking lots," King Tone often used to impress upon the youth who regularly attended the group's universals. Now they could see for themselves that icons of the community were coming and sitting at the same table. Therefore, they must be legitimate.

Intergenerational Radicalism

Few gang studies have seriously explored the influence of parents on members. What research has been carried out mainly focuses on the intergenerational deviant connection—for example, the numbers of gang members whose parents were in gangs or gang members who have had parents in prison. However, family members who have had a radical political history are rarely considered:

> King M.: Both my parents are Puerto Rican. My father was actually born in Lares, which is the place where the [1898] revolution in Puerto Rico took place. My mother is from Santurce, which is near San Juan. They were both very poor, very, very poor. My mother came to this country when she was 14, my father, I think a little bit before that, and still living in poverty, living with family that didn't want them. My mother remembers walkin' down the street one day and she saw a Puerto Rican flag, and that's how she met the Young Lords, cuz somebody came out and said, "Hola," and she was like, "Hola. Oh my God! That's Spanish!" and she went in there and she got involved with The Young Lords.

> D.B.: This was in the '60s?

> King M.: Yeah, my mother was really involved with them, and then she also got a little bit involved with The Black Panthers, also. My father basically had to raise himself, so he wasn't too politically involved. At the age of sixteen my father bought a birth certificate, said he was eighteen, and went to work in the post office [Interview with King M., 9/2/1998].

King M., above, provides an excellent example of such a relationship. His Puerto Rican-born mother had been an active member of the Young Lords Party in New York City and, as a child, he remembers her frequently taking him to demonstrations and protests. In the interview he describes the political and intellectual training that he received from her and the degree to which she shaped his radical outlook both as a teenager and as a young man. At the time of the interview, King M. was the 20 year-old leader of the Nation's youth section, the Pee Wee tribe, and an undergraduate at Hunter College. He had attended a prestigious public high school in the city, and by the time he graduated he had won a city-wide debating prize as part of the team sponsored by the Latino/a students organization.[9]

As with Dominican-born members of the Nation, we found several members whose parents had deep attachments to socialist and nationalist movements in the past and whose political experiences in the struggle against the dictatorships of both Rafaél Trujillo and Joaquín Balaguer were integrated into the worldviews of their children. Although we do not want to exaggerate the degree to which respondents traced their new-found political involvement to their parents, we do assert that there is a much stronger relationship between the radical political experiences of parents and the onset of different modes of resistance among gang-related and street-organization-related youths than has been generally supposed.

The Role of Organic Intellectuals

As the ALKQN increasingly organized around local and national social-justice issues, more "outsiders" whose experiences and reputations were rooted in the radical past gained access to the group's outer and inner circles. We have used the phrase "organic intellectuals"[10] to describe the kinds of social actors who involved themselves in the ALKQN's transition and who themselves became key factors in the reconstruction of the group. By this term we mean older radical activists who had developed sophisticated theories of oppositional action and who had stayed grounded in the daily life of the barrio.

J.E.: Why do you think the Latin Kings are different here [in New York City]?

King L.: New York has took the Nation to another level more beyond Chicago itself, which is the motherland. . . . Chicago, they still bangin' out there. You know, Tone, he turned us into somethin' positive because you would never see Latin Kings back in the days doin' meetings with political people such as Mr. Richie Pérez and Father Barrios and all those great leaders [King L., 2/23/1999].

The ALKQN's embrace of radical community leaders with long credentials in the radical movement was sharply different from anything that had transpired before with the group, except for a brief relationship with the local Democratic Party in Spanish Harlem that occurred during the State Assembly campaign of Nelson Denis in 1996. This relationship between the older, more radically political generation conflicts with the argument that the "old heads" (Anderson 1999) of poor communities no longer function as mentors for street youths, or have simply fled the impoverished scene (Wilson 1997). Below we describe four different types of organic intellectuals who played a leading role in the radicalizing process of the ALKQN. It is important to understand that while each of these social actors had their own distinct role within the ALKQN, their contributions to the growth of the movement were generally complementary to each other.

THE AUTHENTIC RADICAL

D.B.: So, when you first started talking to them, they were coming into meetings, you were meeting them on the street , how did it happen?

Mr. P.: We invited them [the ALKQN] to come, two years back, to the Mobilization and Racial Justice Day. And so they came to the rally, you know. I think the other thing that was helpful, and it's not that these young people are easily impressionable, but I think that one of the key components is that Richie P. and myself were ex- Young Lords and they respected that. The Young Lords, as far as they've struggled, are our ancestry. And, you know, it happens that of all the ex-Lords, I think Richie and I have the same basic commitment from 1969–70. And, you know, we happen to be—not that we're better than anybody else—but we happen to be up front people. You know, we stand up for ours, you know. Nobody questions anything about our personality. You can't question our integrity, man. You know what I'm sayin? My word is all I got. You know, I go with my face any motherfuckin' place, you know, and that's what they respect. And it's not to say that it's been a smooth ride all the way through. We've had differences and stuff like that, but we deal with differences as men. You know what I'm sayin'? And we respect and, you know. . . . I don't care how angry I get with somebody from the Kings or Netas. Nobody's gonna fuck with my children. Those are my younger blood, OK? And as far as I'm concerned . . . as long as they moving in the positive direction, yo, I'm gonna do, and we are gonna do anything within our ability to help them [Interview, 1/18/1997].

What Mr. P, above, brought to this relationship was a seasoned commitment to the Latino community that he took also to mean a commitment to the sons and daughters of his community whom the mainstream had systematically demonized, labeled and written off. For Mr. P., it was his authenticity as a highly respected barrio radical, and his outspokenness in the face of authority, that captured the imagination of both the ALKQN leaders and the rank-and-file. Frequently, at universal meetings, Mr. P. could be seen making rousing speeches in solidarity with the group's trajectory and challenging the organization to become involved in efforts to combat the prison-industrial complex, to remember the lessons of the Attica uprising, and to struggle on behalf of the Puerto Rican political prisoners.[11] Not only did he have the community credentials, however, he also had deep links to organized labor that could potentially provide work opportunities and social support in defense of the group's political actions.

THE THEORETICALLY INFORMED RADICAL   Mr. R, below, introduced another kind of influence. For him, it was important that the ALKQN and its leaders receive an education in political economy and in the substantive and theoretical reasons why they could not allow themselves to return to the days of the lumpen, anti-working-class gang:

> A couple of years ago I was invited to the universal and Tone was still inside, and, uh, so it's a great pleasure to be here because it really was the people's struggle that brought him out and it's gonna be your struggle that will keep him out because the government wants to put him back because they don't want the Almighty Latin King and Queen Nation to turn to the positive. They don't want it to happen that way. They want our young brothers and sisters to keep on killin' each other. That's what they want. It's nothin' different from the days of slavery when one of the ways the slave master would maintain control was to have the slaves fight each other. We need to turn our back on that part of history because there's a new part ahead and you're the makers of that history. When we were in the Young Lords we didn't know we were makin' history. We were just doin' what we thought needed to be done. Now years later, that is part of our people's history. So what you do today is gonna be part of our people's history that our people will be studying in the future [Speaking at a universal meeting, 11/29/1997].

Mr. R, a former leader of the Young Lords Party along with Mr. P., was not only instrumental in initiating contacts with the ALKQN, but helped to provide them with material and legal support during critical periods in their transformational history. As a leading mentor of the group, he was always on hand to discuss with members of the Supreme Team issues of strategy, tactics, and political history. What made Mr. R's influence so important was his insistence that the group develop a consistent political analysis of its own position and that the membership be thoroughly versed in an oppositional ideology and practice based on an eclectic socialism, which made sense to the Kings and Queens' particular subcultural history. In turn, both the leaders of the ALKQN and the rank-and-file members warmly accepted Mr. R's comradely advice and entreaties and saw in him a trustworthy leader from within their own community who would not turn his back on the group.

THE RADICAL AS TRAINER Mr. B., a former member of the Harlem Black Panthers in the late 1960s, lent the ALKQN a great deal of support in its early reform stages and was always on hand to give advice on strategy and problem-solving techniques from his position as head of a corporation specializing in leadership development at the community level.

> C.B.: They used to come in here and meet every week [Mr. B. points to a meeting room], thirty or forty of them, every week, rain or shine. We kind of adopted them and we used to talk about everything. They were very intense and totally committed to what they were doing.

> D.B.: How would you describe them?

> C.B.: To me, I saw them as a political movement trying to organize the community. Of course, they were full of contradictions as we all are but they were genuine. There was no doubt about it. They wanted change, they didn't want to put up with the oppression any more, they didn't want the pain of living under this system, they wanted something else and when they came to us they were basically asking, how do we go about getting this change? How do we go from where we are to somewhere else. But this is what makes me so angry. When they were out there on the streets, hanging out, gangbanging, doing whatever, the authorities would pick them up every now and again and go against them a little bit here a little bit there. But when they came out and said they want to seriously take on the status quo, to challenge the establishment, to be something other than oppressed Latinos and get organized, then suddenly they are the biggest danger in New York City. What's all that about? Why did they need to spend all those resources on ending this experiment? Why couldn't they support it and use it for the good of the community? So, when I saw all this happening it made me think of my Panther days. And

how the establishment were keen to brand us as thugs and terrorists when all we were doing was organizing the community to help them reach the things that we were promised in the Constitution [Interview, 5/16/1998].

According to Mr. B., the Kings and Queens who came were hungry for knowledge about how to build their organization and themselves. But there was nothing patronizing or paternalistic about the relationship he developed with them. On the contrary, they were there to learn from each other and to share the fruits of victory and the lessons of defeat. This kind of relationship, which is based on a shared commitment to the process of liberation, resonates well with the notion of the ALKQN as a social movement entering a dynamic and radical phase in its development but under the extreme pressure of the state.

THE SPIRITUAL RADICAL   Luis Barrios, one of the coauthors of this book, had an important influence on the development of the ALKQN in general and on the leadership in particular. Like Mr. P and Mr. R above, he was (and is) a radical activist with a reputation in the Latino community for defending the rights of the oppressed and for offering up an alternative vision (e.g., social and political dimensions of spirituality) of where the community should be going.

> L.B.: Let me tell you what I'm supporting in the Latin Kings/Queens Nation. They came out taking sides against police brutality and I came out saying, "That's good. I'm supporting you." They came out with this issue of organizing tutoring sessions for children after school, and I said, "I support that." They came out against Mayor Giuliani, and I said, "I support that." And every time they come out with one of these issues, I'm saying, "I support them. OK?" [Interview in the *New York Times*, 10/21/1997]

But more than his political solidarity and his role model example, Barrios offered the group both institutional support and spiritual guidance that were crucial interventions at a time when the group was grappling with all the difficulties of trying to shake its gangster past:

> L.B.: The phrase that we're using is "creating a sanctuary." A sanctuary, that's in the First Testament, it means protection for those that are marginalized by the system, so this is that kind of place. It's like a refuge.

> King T.: Very much! We got 700 youth in a park right across the street from the precinct and they don't even cross the street.

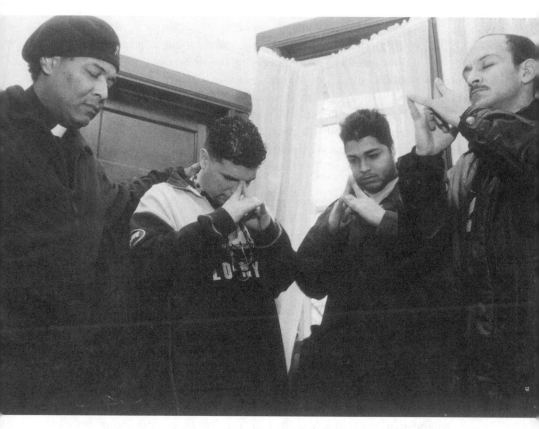

FIGURE 7.1 Luis Barrios (coauthor, left) leads a silent prayer with King Tone (center), King N., and King H. (far right) on May 10, 1999, the day that Tone was going to federal court to hear his final sentencing. (Photo by Steve Hart.)

L.B.: Never. Never. They don't dare to cross because they feel that it's like a prohibition.

Above, Luis Barrios is discussing with King Tone the next meeting of the ALKQN at St. Mary's Episcopal Church in West Harlem, which stands directly opposite the 23rd precinct house. During the time in which the ALKQN first met with Father Barrios, the group was being hounded by law enforcement wherever it attempted to meet in the open, and it was rarely able to gain permission for its members to meet in seclusion (except for a brief period in 1994 when the group managed to persuade the Board of Education to let it meet in a Brooklyn Middle School).

As Barrios saw it, the church was a space, a liberating zone (Barrios 1998a) where the socially and politically outcast could come and find a safe haven, just like many U.S. churches during the 1980s that were used to shield prodemocratic Central American refugees who were fleeing U.S.-backed dictatorships.[12] Barrios' position was in keeping with that of many liberation theologians in Latin America who saw religion as a means to demystify oppression, spiritually uplift the poor, and play a constructive role in personal and collective rehabilitation. In an interview with the *New York Times*, Barrios explained why he was going to visit King Blood:

> L.B.: I believe one hundred percent in reconnecting people with God and with responsibility. . . . You see, in the criminal justice system, the issue is you go for punishment. In the Christian foundation you don't do this. You have to condemn what the person did as wrong, you have to face the person with the consequences of the responsibility of whatever the person did, if it's a crime or whatever. You do not take away that responsibility, you do not take away the consequences of whatever the person did, and you do not turn your back on that person. You have to stay there with that person to support this person [10/21/1997].

Barrios' embrace of the ALKQN both collectively and individually grew out of his conviction that the church had legitimacy only if it could demonstrate, in practice and not just in theory, that it was an ally of the disempowered and that, on principle, it had to function as an institutional bulwark against the physical, economic, and ideological attacks of society's most privileged and powerful elites (Betto 1992; Barrios 1999, 2000). Therefore, quite logically, the teachings and the resources of the church had to be channeled into the struggle for social justice; in fact, he called (and still does) his congregation a "justice ministry." Consequently, both Barrios' private support for and public defense of the ALKQN was a natural extension of his religio-political praxis, and it even manifested itself in his weekly column for the city's leading Spanish language daily, *El Diario La Prensa* (see figure 7.2 and Barrios 1998c).

Finally, Barrios' joint roles as spiritual advisor and consultant on theological matters were critical influences on the ability of the group to combine different religions and belief systems, many of which originated in the cultures of other dominated peoples. Below, Barrios is discussing with King Tone different ways to interpret and practice religion in response (see chapter 9) to Tone's decision to integrate both Native American and Santería (Yoruba-African) traditions into Kingism:

el diario
Fundado en 1913

Decano de la prensa hispana en los EE UU
The Oldest Spanish Language Newspaper in the U.S.A.

Carlos D. Ramírez *Gerente General/Publisher*
Peter W. Davidson *Presidente/President*
Rossana Rosado *Directora/Editor in Chief*

OPINION

el diario/LA PRENSA

el diario/LA PRENSA is published by Latin Communications Group, Inc. daily, doing business at 143 Varick St. NY, NY 10013 (212) 807-4600.
Latin Communications Group, Inc. no es responsable por las opiniones expresadas por los columnistas.
The opinions expressed by the columnists are their own and do not necessarily reflect the opinions of Latin Communications Group, Inc.

el diario/LA PRENSA JUEVES 12 DE FEBRERO DE 1998/16

'Amor de rey, amor de reina'

Esta es la expresión de saludo, o el grito de victoria de quienes son miembros de la Nación de los "Latin Kings/Queens" en la ciudad de Nueva York, con quienes en los últimos dos años hemos estado trabajando como parte de nuestro ministerio.

En una conversación que tuve esta semana con la pastora de la Iglesia Metodista de Broadway Temple, Revda. Magali Beltre, ésta me contaba cómo policías del cuartel 33 del Alto Manhattan estaban muy "enojados" o "desilusionados" porque la iglesia nos había prestado el local, en dos ocasiones, para llevar a cabo este ministerio. Yo no sé si ella entendió el proceso, pero a mí me parece que trataron de atemorizarla para que de esta manera su iglesia no sea parte de este ministerio.

La última reunión en la iglesia fue de maravilla. Como a las 2:00 p.m., llegaron como doce policías diciendo que a la comunidad había llamado porque "los Latin Kings/Queens estaban en una pelea". Todo era falso. Como a las dos horas regresan otro grupo de policías, esta vez como unos quince, diciendo que alguien llamó porque "los Latin Kings/Queens estaban vendiendo drogas". Todo era falso.

No pasó una hora, ya son como las cinco, regresan como diez policías con pistolas en mano alegando que la comunidad decía que los "Latin Kings/ Queens" los estaban hostigando. Todo era falso. Como a las 6:00 de la tarde llegaron como ocho camiones de bomberos que querían saber cuántas personas estaban reunidas en el local de la iglesia. Nada pasó, porque la información era falsa.

En resumidas cuentas, el pánico y la histeria por parte de la policía creó una reacción de mal gusto en la comunidad. No hacia "Los Latin Kings/Queens" sino hacia la policía, que ese día demostró de una manera brillante dos manifesta-ciones de lo que ellos saben hacer bien: "brutalidad policiaca", "hostigamiento" y "violaciones a los derechos civiles".

Es increíble la manera en que la Policía de Nueva York ha tratado por todos los medios, de proyectar a esta organización como una pandilla de criminales.

Mi experiencia y ministerio por los últimos dos años con este grupo de jóvenes es que, sin negar de dónde pueden haber venido, han demostrado que el ser humano tiene la capacidad de cambiar en cualquier dirección, para bien o para mal. Ellos lo han hecho para bien y se siguen convirtiendo en una "organización política de la calle".

PADRE LUIS BARRIOS

Partiendo de esta realidad tendríamos entonces que buscar las respuestas a tres preguntas básicas. Primero, ¿qué es una pandilla? Quienes claman ser los expertos en esta materia no tienen claro el cómo definir este fenómeno, por lo tanto las definiciones, que nunca dejan de ser arbitrarias, no ayudan mucho en este asunto sino más bien nos demuestran una ideología de la clase dominante por tratar de establecer un control social.

El Alcalde y el Comisionado de Policía definen una pandilla como "un grupo de personas que cometen crímenes". A mí me parece que ésta es una de las mejores definiciones para describir al Departamento de Policía, mejor conocido como "La Pandilla de los Azules".

La segunda pregunta se articula de la siguiente manera, ¿por qué surgen las pandillas? Las pandillas surgen como un fenómeno social en un momento determinado como manera de responder a unas realidades políticas y económicas; ejem plo, la pobreza, el racismo, la explotación, el desempleo, la falta de recreación, la marginalización, la preservación de la identidad, y la colonización. Por lo tanto, si alguien tiene intenciones serias de combatir las pandillas, lo cual es un síntoma de las desigualdades políticas y económicas, tendría que comenzar con eliminar las raíces del problema y no los síntomas.

La tercera pregunta que nos corresponde contestar es, ¿qué porciento del crimen cometido en la ciudad de Nueva York está relacionado con las pandillas? Ninguno de los expertos quieren contestar esta pregunta la cual es básica antes de declarar un estado de emergencia. Digo que no quieren porque ellos saben muy bien que el porcentaje es sumamente bajo y no justifica todo el circo político que han organizado, ni mucho menos el crear el "Gang Intelligence Unit", que de inteligencia le falta mucho.

Yo me pregunto, ¿por qué no crean una unidad de inteligencia para combatir la violencia doméstica y el abuso policiaco, dos crímenes que están fuera de control? Que resuciten el informe de Amnistía Internacional (1996) que declara los crímenes de la Policía en la ciudad de Nueva York. O tal vez, ¿por qué no crean una unidad de inteligencia para combatir la pobreza, que destruye diariamente a nuestras comunidades latinas?

Por otro lado yo reconozco que la policía tiene que justificar su salario y su existencia. De esta manera muchas veces se ven obligados a crear crisis y temores en donde no existen. En otras palabras, tú me necesitas y yo te protejo. Si de alguien tenemos que cuidarnos en esta ciudad no es de "los Latin Kings/Queens", sino de no caer en las manos de policías corruptos de la ciudad de Nueva York. Dios nos proteja de la Pandilla de los Azules. Amor de Rey y Amor de Reina.

El Padre Luis Barrios es un sacerdote puertorriqueño de la Iglesia Episcopal de Santa María.

FIGURE 7.2 One of Father Luis Barrios's weekly columns in *El Diario La Prensa*.

L.B.: I was listening to you and you are getting more and more into reflection and meditation. You see, Western religion was putting out graphics and ideas about God based on concepts that God is a man, God is white, or God is in this particular place, or looks like this, and you talk to God. Eastern religion went into another direction, into meditation. You find God wherever . . . it's found in the moon, the trees, the sun, the birds . . . but then you can't only talk to God, you need to let God talk to you. God is talking through all these things that we have and that's the big decision . . . how we communicate with God. Most of the time when we use this kind of prayer we are the ones who are talking and we never allow God to talk. That's the reason we never know what the hell God is saying! [Conversation recorded 8/19/1998].

The Nation Claims the Past as Its Own

To further understand this relationship between ALKQN and the radical past is to grasp the nature of the struggle in the present. Who currently could inherit the mantle of the former radicals? Where is the Young Lords Party today or anything that resembles this militant and forward-looking group?

Before the activists would make the movement in New York, we are saving a movement. This is different. I think our brothers have lived it and we are rejuvenating a movement that was dormant, and I think we have shamed a lot of the old activists into action now . . . and some of the pretend activists have stepped up their rhetoric but in direct response to what we're doing. It wasn't the activists that were doing anything. I had to infiltrate the activists! I think it was us who said that we have to make change. For me, I recognized the strong leadership and the righteous leadership that exist in these organizations in this time and space. I was able to recognize the spirituality and the true love that these brothers had and that's what keeps it together [King H., 7/4/1997].

King H., above, is making the crucial point that the ALKQN saw itself as the legitimate continuator of the radical past and often felt that it was alone on the proverbial barricades. To outsiders, this might seem strange for an ex-gang to have such radical pretensions, but it should be remembered that this organization could bring together 500–600 members with little effort and regularly had local branch meetings with 100–200 members present. Thus, when its leaders did not see similar responses to other radical groups' organizing efforts, it concluded that it was in the vanguard of the popular resistance.

Using the Rules of the Past to Shape the Present

Thus far we have discussed the links between the past and the present in terms of social actors, phenomenology, and transferred cultural traditions, but we have neglected to mention a connection that is rarely discussed in either the gang or the social-movement literature: the organizational and disciplinary norms of radical political movements and their parallels to groups such as the ALKQN. To grasp this point, let us consider some of the thirty rules of the Young Lords Party (Franklin 1971:124–125):

(1) You are a YOUNG LORD 25 hours a day.

(3) Any member found shooting drugs will be expelled.

(5) No member will violate rules relating to office work or general meetings of the PARTY ANYWHERE.

(8) No PARTY member will commit crimes against the people.

(11) The 13 Point Program must be memorized and the Platform must be understood by each member.

(14) All PARTY business is to be kept within the PARTY.

(15) All contradictions between members must be resolved at once.

(28) All Traitors, Provocateurs, and Agents will be subject to Revolutionary Justice.

(29) At all times we keep a united front before all forms of the man. This is true not only among LORDS, but all Revolutionary Compañeros.

Now compare these disciplinary codes with some examples from the ALKQN's bible:

(49) Every Member must become familiar with the entire history and philosophy of the ALKQN.

(54) Every member must read and become familiar with the ever changing literature that they receive in order to stay knowledgeable of updated news.

(57) A member must speak the truth at all times. You must never become involved in a physical relationship with another member's spouse. A member must not consume any type of drug that is unhealthy to the mind, body or character of oneself.

(58) A member must not discuss any details of their affiliation with the ALKQN with anyone that is not a member. You must report any violations by another member witnessed directly by any member to one of the five crowns.

(4) A member must not inject illegal drugs into their body.

(8) A member must not steal.

There are similarities between the two organizations on many levels. They both enforce a strict code of discipline, they call on their members to engage in self-sacrifice for the greater good of the organization, and they punish those who put the organization at risk. Of course, there are many differences also, especially since so many rules of the ALKQN were formulated in the prison system and they reflect the all-male, highly structured, and racially competitive environments that are common in such institutions. Nonetheless, the notions of self-discipline, conduct rules, guidelines for organizational structure, and self-empowerment obligations are directly taken from the history of social movements and organized resistance in oppressed communities. King A., below, explains how he integrates the Nation's rules and principles into an idealized behavior. The passage is taken from a speech he had written in advance and later made to a universal (undated) during 1998.

I wrote this to express my feelings and in hopes to open the minds of some of you brothers and sisters and make you's who have not yet realize who we are realize what we are:

Love is everything without love you have nothing. You are alone, you have no sense of being. This Nation consists of Love that is why you have to abide by the true meaning of the word in your heart & soul. To be a true King and Queen. To be a true King & Queen you have to live your lessons not memorize them so you can be down and throw a crown. This is who you are. Your Roots. We are Royalty! This is the way we are suppose to be living since the very begining of the existance of this Latin Race.

A King's Roots of Character are those who preserve there integrity, remain unshaken by the trails and tribulations of Daily life. They do not stir like leaves on a tree or follow the herd where it runs. In their mind remains the ideal attitude and conduct of living. This is not something given to us by others. It is our roots . . . it is a strength that exists Deep within us. Cause a King without the Knowledge of his Nation is like a tree without it's Roots. Live Black & Gold Maintain 360E Cause the soul is dyed the color of its thoughts. Think only on those things that are in line with your principles and can bear the full Light of the Crown.

The content of your character is your choice. Day by Day what you choose, what you think, and what you do is who you become. Your integrity is your destiny. It is the light that guides your way. Be humble in your manner of being and strike like the Almighty Lion who you are when its called upon. There is no room for error in this society now. Analize everything you do. And exicute with persisness.

You Live with your Crown inbedded in your mind & heart as a symbol of knowledge honor & victory. If you do not use your mind to attain the knowledge of this Nation we will never reach the goals this Nation is trying to achieve. It is an honor to belong to this Almighty Nation of ours. And it is victory what we achieve when we teach our children our brothers and sisters and they live the true meaning of King and Queenizm.

These young brothers and sisters our children & our children to be are this Nation's future and we must guide & teach them to achieve what we were not able to achieve. To bring this Nation to new heights. And fulfill the Dream of our fore fathers. We have come a long way but we still have a ways to go. But that does not matter this Nation will never cease to exist. We don't Die we multiply. Amor de Rey.

Spiritualist Models

We have our own prayers, we don't pray to our own God, though. It's like—this is my belief—you can believe in whatever God you want to—God, Jehovah, Allah, Buddah, Changó—it just uplifts whatever religion you believe in, but I think religion plays a big role 'coz how could we be God's children and kill? That's one thing that was said by one of our leaders—how we supposed to be reaching our goal of being with the King of Kings if we're out here destroying each other—destroying ourselves? So if there was no religion's influence on us, I guess we'd be out there sellin' drugs and killing and doing all the stupid things in life.

King S., 4/2/1998

We have seen in the prayers of the organization, in the efforts by King Tone to connect God and Kingism, and in the role of Father Barrios as mentor and confidante that spirituality would always be a key aspect of individual membership and collective group life, and that this practice was tied to members' quest for a new collective and individual identity. In essence, ALKQN's interpretation of spirituality was a key component of its resistance repertoire and was tantamount to what might be called its spiritualty of liberation (Barrios, 2000, 2003). By this we mean that through its spiritual practices the ALKQN resisted all attempts to become dehumanized, objectified, and/or criminalized by the dominant culture. But how did this occur? What are the spiritual underpinnings of the group and whence do they derive?

The ALKQN historically had drawn on a range of spiritual traditions in the Latino/a culture to create a coherent if unwieldy belief system called Kingism. Of course, while great importance was placed on the notion of a Supreme Being, i.e., God, it is important to note that this creation came out of references to the Judaic tradition found in the Chicago Manifesto, where the group refers to itself as the Latin American Tribe of Yahweh.[13] Nonetheless, in line with the group's democratic impulse, it is also specifically written (see King S.'s statement above) that members may have different gods and that there is no obligation to believe in a single deity. In fact, in different texts of the ALKQN there are references to Yahweh (the name of God in the Jewish tradition), to Allah (the name of God in the Islamic tradition), and to Jesus Christ (the name of the son of God in the Christian tradition). Hence,

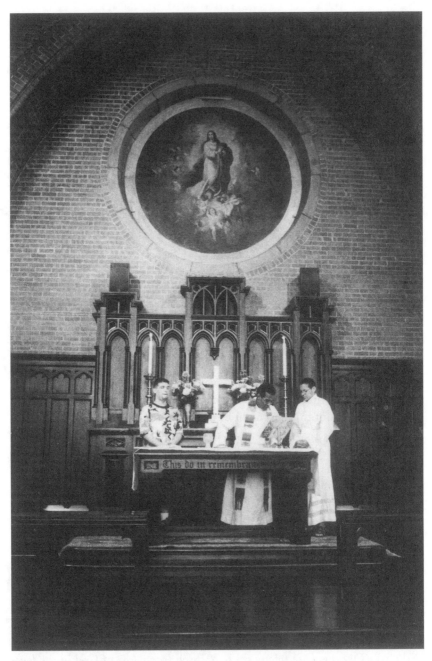

FIGURE 7.3 King Tone stands to the right of Father Luis Barrios
(coauthor) during a Sunday mass at St. Mary's Church.

both the spiritual belief system and the practices of the ALKQN, like so many of its other cultural characteristics, are steeped in an eclecticism (e.g., Santería) that freely draws on a range of traditions, themes, and frameworks from both mainstream and alternative theologies. This is a conscious attempt to create a form of religious autonomy[14] that is common in resistance movements across the globe. Below, we see further evidence of the Kings' complexly layered, religio-philosophical belief system that is constantly being reconstructed in the face of different forms of domination.

> ALKQN though not a religion is essentially religious, most of its struggle and goals are of a sacred nature, much of it is woven into the structure of Christianity. We have learned to consider our own religious [sic] as the only inspired one, and this probably accounts for much of the misunderstanding in the system of Correctional Facilities [prison, jails, etc.]. Today concerning the place occupied by the ALKQN in the culture heritage, and spiritual ethics of our race ["Latinos"], a religion is a divinely inspired code of morals. A religious person is one inspired to nobler living by this code, he is identified by the code which is his source of illumination. Thus we may say that a Christian is one who receives his spiritual ideals of right and wrong from the message of the Christ, while a buddhist is one who molds his life into the archetype of morality given by the Great Gautama or one of the other buddhas. All doctrines which seek to unfold and preserve that invisible spark in man named "Spirit" are said to be spiritual, those which ignore this invisible element and concentrate entirely upon the visible, are said to be material. There is in Religion a wonderful point of balance, where the Science and theology are two ends of a single truth, but the nation will never receive the full benefit of their investigations until they have made peace with each other and labor hand in hand for the accomplishment of the great work, the liberation of the spirit and intelligence from the three dimensional prison house of ignorance, superstition, and fear [ALKQN Manifesto].

Self-help Models

A primary tenet of the ALKQN's philosophy is to rebuild the community by rejuvenating and reconstructing the individual, which is part of the overall premise that the Latino community is an injured community and is in need of healing. Thus, many of the Nation's members (1) have spent time in prison, although by no means all of them; (2) were "in recovery" from drugs (including alcohol) use/abuse; and (3) had been the victims or the perpetrators of domestic violence. Consequently, participation in therapeutic counseling, twelve-step programs, and aggression-management training-was extremely common.

> King T.: Some of the members, the kids especially, need special help. Some are very depressed and they don't have the support to get outta their situation. In another year I believe we will have that . . . we have AA, AIDS Awareness and we tried NA but they were coming high (he laughs), so we had to put a stop to it. Another thing is we can write about it. You know, we can put it in the Grito [the ALKQN newsletter]. You know in the last issue this Queen wrote about having AIDS and the response was amazing. [Interview, 9/23/1997].

> Queen S.: Hostility classes is a chance for the sisters to be able to have a safe setting to let their anger out, you know. That's one example, if you like, of trying to reach our goals [Interview, 4/18/1998].

What is the difference, however, between the models of self-help in the prison system or in the larger society and those of the ALKQN? This question is crucial to analyze if we are to understand the positive roles that self-help philosophy and practice played in the radicalization of the group.

The first major difference is that self-help in the Nation was used as a form of collective empowerment and not just as a solution for the individual. Hence, while the ALKQN urges self-help techniques to aid the individual in overcoming his/her pathology, it does so in order for the individual to become a highly functioning member of the organization. Furthermore, in many self-help ideologies the individual is powerless, whereas for the ALKQN, power is returned to the individual.[15]

The second difference is that, often, self-help therapy or programs take place in a vacuum, and unless one is living in a "therapeutic community" there may be little support in a person's everyday environment to ensure that the empowerment process is maintained. With the ALKQN, self-help messages are an integral part of the overall culture of the group, which ensures that members can experience a high degree of consonance between the philosophy and the practice:

> King T.: When I was a Christian and I used to serve Jesus, I still used to end up in relapse on crack. I joined The Nation and I'm 6 years clean. So you get what I'm sayin? I found somethin in his (King Blood's) literature that I actually didn't find even through my pastor and all his hard work. "Oh,

you're saved if you just give all your problems to Jesus." That didn't work for me. What worked is what I found in his [King Blood's] literature that says, "No, you believe in the Higher Power, but you still gotta fix your own damn problems, and this is how you start off—one, by believin' in yourself" [Interview, 2/4/1998].

Finally, it is extremely rewarding for Kings and Queens to take the self-help programs that are utilized in prison as a technique of social control and transform them into a vehicle of collective empowerment. Inmates today have less and less access to higher or lower educational opportunities, they are denied almost all contact with radical political organizations that were mobilizing in the 1960s and 1970s around prisoners' rights issues, and they are faced everywhere with a management culture that views rehabilitation as an ideological relic (Parenti 1999). In this return to neoclassical forms of penitentiary punishment and discipline, the inmate population is characterized by horrific levels of psychosis and depression, institutionalized trauma, and intergroup violence that the authorities mainly respond to by way of containment and the building of ever more "sophisticated" designs of incarceration. The only "soft" approach to control that is allowed is in the form of self-help programs and the outside groups that are frequently associated with them, a development that most inmates are all too often unaware of.

Other Community Organizing Models

As we saw in the chapter 6, King Tone was convinced that the community models of the Black Muslims and the Hasidic Jews were appropriate models of self-empowerment for the ALKQN to adopt. He had seen them work with his own eyes and many of his most trusted leaders had endorsed them:

Look at the Jews in Williamsburg and round there. They have their own community centers, their own churches, their own hospitals, their own transport and even their own police. You never hear of no crime there. People are not afraid to go out and they do it all within their own community [King P., a leader of the Brooklyn tribe; interview, 5/3/1998].

Tone, meanwhile, had worked for orthodox Jews, from whom he had learned to respect (1) their ability to organize on social, political, and economic fronts; (2) their consistently high commitment to internal ethnic solidarity; and (3) their disciplined spirituality. Similarly, the Black Muslims represented to him an effective means of organizing and emboldening the equally marginalized African-American community in the city. He had witnessed this in prison and in the declaration of solidarity that he received from Minister Diógenes Mohammad, the Latino leader of the Nation of Islam who was one of the first community radicals to openly declare his support for the newly politicized Latin Kings and Queens.

By contrast, when Tone looked at the Puerto Rican community, he found it wanting in terms of regulating its own social and economic institutions (i.e., schools, universities, banks, hospitals, etc.), and he concluded that the absence of internally developed networks of financial and human capital served to fragment the community over time and made it vulnerable to manipulation by insiders and outsiders alike. Therefore, he reasoned that without such institutions Puerto Ricans and more generally Latinos/as would always see their independent political power limited in the city and beyond, and thus the community's great potential for mobilized resistance would always be shackled to the self-interested agendas of careerists and opportunists who episodically emerged to solicit their vote.

Consequently, Tone and other ALKQN leaders argued that it was only through a blueprint of renewal, however utopian, that the community could begin to "imagine" an end to its dependency and subordination. Such talk, of course, coming from the mouths of street leaders sounds grandiose and wildly out of touch with its relationship to the distribution of political power in the city, yet it was perfectly in line with the group's new radical orientation and its growing self-confidence. Moreover, on a more pragmatic level, there was a constant need for the leadership to espouse such radical plans for the group in order to help negate the parochial, street-level consciousness that still dominated many members' thinking. Thus, what better way to do this than to show the idealistic future in store for the Nation's members, if they would only stay the course:

King Tone: Ain't you tired of borrowin' places? Ain't you tired of people tellin' us we can't be there to pass the time? It's time to take our land and to buy it and to take it so when these cops wanna come in we don't need somebody to go to the front door for us. We go to the front door. "This is our house. What you want? What do you want?" You understand me? But we're still thinkin' about, "Oh, this brother said this about me and I gotta make a big case." We fightin' to get youse education, get you jobs, get you on the next level so the Bloods, the Netas, the Zulu—whoever wants the jail system, they can have it! I don't want people to be confused. They go say, "Oh, Tone say he don't love the people in jail." That's a damn lie! Today, after this, I'm not goin' to jail because I'm here with you.

M.: Amor de Rey!

King Tone: I'm not sayin' I wouldn't do it. But I love those brothers in jail, but what I'm tellin' them is, "They feed you three times a day, they give you TV, they takin' care of you right now, and if you do the right thing you come home, but you let me take care of the other side of the business, which is to get a place for you to come home to." You know how many letters come to me sayin', "I ain't got an address. Tone, I gotta go to a shelter. Yo, Tone, could you find me an address for me? Tell my hermanitos I'm all right?" You know how many letters I get? Do you get 'em? How many of yous write? How many of youse care? You understand me? Look at it, two people raise their crown out of about 900. So I didn't forget about the prisoners. But what I'm telling you is I don't wanna run the jails, I'm tired of the Kings being the toughest gang in jail, I want us to be in the street! I want the population in jail to decrease and the population in New York to increase. I want the mothers that are waitin' on a visit for hours gettin' dissed by CO's to have their husbands at damn home where he's supposed to be, eating the real food—Arroz con Habichuelas [King Tone addressing a universal on his birthday, 11/29/1997].

We have highlighted above the many different ways in which the ALKQN interacted with empowerment models and traditions, some of which predated the group's existence, but all of which played very specific and observable roles in its sociopolitical development. The ALKQN unabashedly drew from other traditions—those of the Young Lords Party and the Black Panthers, those of long-time community activists and intellectuals, and those of Jewish and Muslim empowerment projects—to create a new self-image and orientation to the world. Many gang researchers and law enforcement "experts" prefer to see such groups as emerging from within their own deviant traditions or being mechanically shaped by pathological currents in the community. But we clearly show that this group could trace its history to myriad influences in its own community, which is a primary reason why the organization was able to assert itself politically and to take on a whole new identity.

PART III

THE FORM AND CONTENT OF A
STREET ORGANIZATION

CHAPTER 8

THE LEVEL OF ORGANIZATION AND STRUCTURE
OF THE LATIN KINGS

Roughly 400 Latin Kings and Queens are in attendance. They pack the inside of the church, covering all the pews, and then more line up along both sides and across the back of the church. Most of those in attendance are young men between the ages of 16 and 20 years old, along with significant numbers in their late 20's and early 30's. Some of the older male members have their children in their arms. About 50 Latin Queens are also present. They sit together on the left side of the church, many with their children sitting beside them. The leadership which comprise the Inca [the President] and his Supreme Crowns are positioned at the front of the church, high on the steps in front of the altar. 10 Latin Kings stand in front of them acting as security detail. . . .

After several speakers, including the Cacique, or Vice-President, and one of the leaders of the Latin Queens, the Inca rises to speak. He has a few notes in his hand as he strides confidently to the rostrum.

"The truth is that we are a true and great nation. Yet we seem to feel that we have to walk with our heads down because that's the way we have been treated as Latins all our lives. But we don't have to. King N. touched on a very sensitive point there, we are in a war at the moment and this goes back to 1940 and not just 1986. The struggle goes on, it's like a roller coaster, it's full of ups and downs."

DB, Field notes, 10/27/1997

Introduction

Jankowski is largely correct when he claims that "although researchers have an intuitive understanding that the gang has organization traits, for the most part, studies of gangs have not closely examined the nature, dynamic, and impact of the gang's organizational qualities. I believe that one of the reasons that society does not understand gangs or the gang phenom-enon very well is that there have not been enough systematic studies under-taken as to how the gang works as an organization" (1991:5).

Jankowski explains that this deficiency is a consequence of the dangers as-sociated with doing gang research and that few investigators have gotten suf-ficiently inside a gang to write about its internal workings and relationships. There is some truth to this claim, and certainly many if not most accounts of gangs are based on "one-shot" interviews carried out by hired interviewers or what Hagedorn (1988) calls "jail house criminology," which refers to the ten-dency to base findings on police reports and other secondary data that origi-nate from criminal justice and/or law-enforcement bureaucracies. In other words, few gang studies are the work of researchers with sufficient access to study the gang up close as a multi-layered organization with varying levels of complexity.

Nonetheless, the generalized absence of a focus on organization cannot totally be explained by the distance kept by researchers and their assistants. First, there are some notable researchers (e.g., Moore 1978, 1991; Hagedorn 1988; Suttles 1968; Vigil 1988; Campbell 1984; Conquergood 1992, 1993; and others) who, after becoming trusted archivists of gang life, have chosen to interpret the gang as a dynamic form of social and cultural process (rather than as an example of rationally organized responses to marginalization).[1] Second, many gang researchers have found that the gangs they have studied are not particularly concerned with being organized in any formal sense, and that the notion of highly organized gangs resonates more with the social con-structions of police departments (see Hagedorn 1988: 85–86) than with the gang members themselves. Third, the lack of discussion on the internal orga-nizational properties of gangs has a great deal to do with the focus and train-ing of the individual researcher. Hence it is contingent on whether (1) he or she is setting out to look at this question, and (2) the concept of organization is subsumed by the abstract notion of structure.[2]

In this study of the Latin Kings and Queens, we have found that this ques-tion is not an abstract one but is the nature of the group itself and its consis-tent pattern of practices over time. Quite simply, the ALKQN has always em-phasized its ability to organize on a number of different though related fronts. First, it has consistently demonstrated that it can emerge and develop in high-ly restrictive settings, such as prisons. Second, it has shown that it can effec-tively mobilize, both politically and socially, some of the most marginalized youth and adults in poor barrio communities. Third, it has been openly proud of its ability to invent and reinvent a range of role definitions for its members. Fourth, a key to the group's ranking system is the acquisition of knowledge, part of which is measured by the ability to learn from written texts which have been amassed from generations of members. Hence, all these properties of the group point to the degree to which organization is a core, conscious activity that is specifically situated in an historical time and space.

The Literature on the Latin Kings/Queens As an Organization

Not a great deal has been written about the Latin Kings as an organization, even though it is recognized to be one of the most structured and largest "gangs" in the United States (Decker, Bynum, and Weisel 1996; Knox 1997). What has been written, however, offers some revealing insights about the group in its Chicago domain.

In the group's early years, Jacobs (1971) found it to be highly organized in the Illinois prison system, where it functioned as an assertive self-defense organization, providing its Latino/a members with a collective identity in an increasingly racialized inmate population and with access to the prison economy. He argued that the group had mushroomed (along with other Black prison gangs such as the Black Peace Stone Nation and the Gangster Disciples), occupying a new political space provided by judicial reforms aimed at "humanizing" the system of corrections nationwide. In comparing the group's members to those of other prison gangs he saw them as tightly disciplined and not given to acts of reckless bravado either against other inmate groups or the prison administration. Much later, in the 1980s and 1990s, Knox (2000) describes the organization as a criminally involved gang that uses its pro-community rhetoric and its ability to self-organize to effectively distribute drugs, engage in the weapons trade, and practice extortion on a city-wide scale. He argues that the group has two guises: to the youth it is a group practicing "defensive localism" and has a number of rituals that are both normative and appealing to poor, alienated young residents of the gang-riddled inner city. But for the older members, the group is nothing more than a social hub of illicit activity where youth can be easily recruited and trained for careers in the illicit economy.

The Chicago street ethnographer, Conquergood (1993), meanwhile sees the group's members as "bonded communitarians" meaningfully coming together in search of respect, identity, and comradery in the marginalizing contexts of an inner city where "enforced leisure" time is the norm and the insidious, interlocking systems of surveillance and social control have successfully labeled gang memberships as primitive, pathological, and diseased. Consequently, the group's organizational properties should be approached on multiple levels, taking care to consider their communication system, their performative rituals, and the larger subcultural gang universe in which they are embedded. In terms of their organizational type, Conquergood has found them to be neither an organization nor a group process, for "gangs are both. Gangs are complex border-cultures that at any given moment in time slide between the categories of organization and a small group, and it is that slide along this continuum that distinguishes the gang experience"(1993:3).

Thus, the Latin Kings and Queens, at least in Chicago, have already inspired several efforts at organizational analysis, providing a small, diverse, though valuable literature against which we can compare our data. What follows, therefore, is our own attempt to offer a cogent analysis of some of the organizational aspects of the ALKQN, drawing on the knowledge of the group in other sites as well as on the history of street subcultures in general. To this end, we have subdivided the chapter into the following areas: (1) the group's structure, including an organizational comparison of the Queens and Kings, the flows of membership, and the group at the local and national levels; (2) the performance and acquisition of members' defined roles; and (3) organizational changes during the reform period.

The Structure of the ALKQN

In Jankowski's work (1991), the author argues that gangs in New York have tended to develop a vertical-hierarchical structure due to: (1) the organizational, competitive culture of New York, (2) the tendency of gangs to mimic the institutional traits of the outlawed Mafia, and (3) their entrepreneurial and social goals, which necessitate a rationally efficient organization. Certainly, the ALKQN was formally a hierarchical structure with layers of leadership that stretched across both the city and the state, but it was also a highly contradictory organization, and the means-goals relationship within the group often defied the Weberian logic of analysis.

Below is an outline of how the organization looked as a vertical network made up of different leadership councils flowing down to the rank-and-file. However, it is extremely difficult to ascertain how the decision-making process functioned between the individual parts of the organization other than to say that most of the edicts came from the Supreme Team and were then passed on to the subordinate councils for implementation. At the same time, we were told that members on any of the bodies below the Supreme Team could originate their own proposals, which would be submitted to the council directly above them via the Cacique of that council. The council would then consult the constitution of the group to check on the proposal's validity. Finally, if the proposal has merit after being discussed among the various crowns it gets passed on to the Supreme Team for further deliberation before being adopted or rejected based on a simple majority of votes.

Regarding the flow of decisions within the group, this is as much as we are able to surmise from the interviews. Clearly this leaves a great deal of the process clouded in ambiguity and there is much more that needs to be said about the various microrelations on and between the committees as well as between the rank-and-file and the different levels of leadership. Despite the paucity of knowledge in this area, we can discuss the specific bodies of the organization with more certainty.

The Supreme Team

Table 8.1 shows an outline of the pyramidal structure of the Supreme Team of the ALKQN, which was the highest organizational body of the group during most of the research and these same five[3] titles are replicated, more or less, throughout every other leading organ. The Supreme Team consisted of the

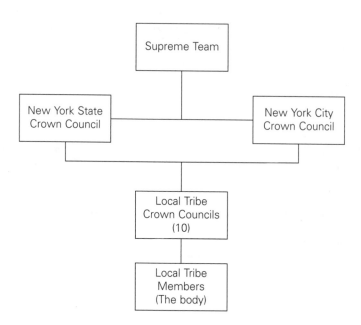

FIGURE 8.1 Vertical structuring of the ALKQN membership bodies.

core office-holders (Table 8.1), who would wear their symbolic stone color among their beads. This leadership structure was established in 1997 by King Tone and was the most powerful organizational body of the ALKQN, essentially replacing what was previously called the Supreme Chapter established by King Blood in the early 1990s. Although the constitution states that only five members are nominated for this supreme body, based on discussions with the leadership, the actual numbers fluctuated and there were frequently more than five members of this decision-making apparatus.

In terms of organizational policy, this body acted as a legitimator of the Inca and it became his team of personally chosen advisors and organizers whose job it was to ensure that his conception of the ALKQN was being adhered to by the rank-and-file, and no cliques were emerging that might threaten his hold on the organization. In other words, like the organizational traditions that Blood had established, they were ostensibly King Tone's band of loyal followers who would defend his leadership at all costs, something akin to an inner cabinet in orthodox political circles.

Despite the obvious role of patronage in developing such a structure, it should not be construed that consensus was easily reached among the members or that individual members were particularly quiescent before the Inca. In fact, there seemed to be a lot of room for disagreements on this body and frequently Tone would mention that he was unable to get a certain policy through the Supreme Team, which suggested that on certain issues he did not have enough votes to gain a majority. This is important because it demonstrates that even though the organization had many hierarchical traits there was still room for disagreement and contestation, and though consensus was the desired outcome at most leadership meetings there is some evidence that this was often a difficult outcome to achieve.

We then talk about the privileges and responsibilities of his [King Tone's] position, how he became Inca, and how someone else might legitimately chal-

TABLE 8.1 **The Positions, Titles, and Stones of the Supreme Team**

Crown Position	Title	Symbolic Stone
1st Supreme	Inca or President	Black stone or onyx
2nd	Cacique, Vice President, or the Prince	White stone or pearl
3rd	Peacemaker or Enforcer	Green stone or emerald
4th	Treasurer	Red stone or ruby
5th	Advisor	Gold stone or amber

lenge him for that position. He says that prior to his joining the only way would be force. Now, he claims, the process is democratic. There is a "supreme council" that decides, while ordinary members decide on the supreme council. He also says that anyone can propose a "law" for the organization by taking it first to the leader of their "tribe" and then it goes to the "supreme team." "That's more democratic than the United States. Here you gotta have money to be heard" [L.K., Field notes, based on a conversation with King Tone, 1998].

In terms of the Kings and Queens' legal structure, the Supreme Team's function was to hear all felonious charges brought against a member, while misdemeanor cases were heard primarily at the tribal level. What constituted a felony we are not sure but we surmise it was a very similar definition to what exists in civil society. For example, attempts at assault, murder, rape, personal robbery, these would all be considered felonies. In such cases, the member is assigned a lawyer from within the group who would represent him or her at a trial. During the reform period, since the death penalty was abolished, the worst form of punishment was "vanishing" which meant that the member was ejected from the movement, never to return. The only exception to this was if the Inca granted a pardon, which he was allowed to do three times a year. This power to give people a second chance was an important means of social control: "I dismissed King H. last year, I made him sign himself out. Recently, we did baptisms at Coney Island and I told King A. to call King H. and get him to come to the beach. I was gonna pardon him . . . I always know these have support despite my power" (King T.).

The characteristics of the Supreme Team are also worth describing. For the most part, there were no women on the Supreme Team except for during the early part of 1998, when King Tone announced that the head of the Queens, Queen R., would become the Secretary of State for the Nation and that she could attend Supreme Team meetings, take part in discussions and have a vote on the ruling body. However, after a short while, tensions began to emerge between Queen R.'s more feminist position on a number of internal issues and the overwhelmingly male-centered perspectives and presence in the rest of the body. In late 1998, Queen R. suddenly left the Nation following an internal dispute, and a new First Crown of the Latin Queens was brought onto the Supreme Team to replace her. The other restrictions on entry into the Supreme Team involved the Pee Wees. In the original constitution of King Blood, it explicitly stated that no Pee Wees could sit on the Supreme Chapter and we believe that this policy was maintained when the Supreme Team was created. Further, although there was no explicit function on the Supreme Team for a spiritual advisor, according to the constitution the Inca could appoint two Santos (spiritual advisors) to the entire Nation and, at least according to our observations, it appeared that these two figures were always part of the Supreme Team's activities.

The State Leadership

We can only assume that the core membership of the committee that organized the state was also made up of five members, since we have no documentary evidence to the contrary. Based on our sources, the State Supremas were drawn from across the region, with some members coming from upstate New York, located around the Albany area, and others drawn from branches much closer to New York City, such as Yonkers. We saw the State Supremas attend the monthly universals and based on informal interviews with them we can only ascertain that their role was to organize and build branches in the upstate areas where pockets of Puerto Ricans and other Latinos/as had made their home. From these discussions we deduce that most members upstate were recruited in the prison system, although certainly the conditions of economic and social marginalization that were the context for the growth of the ALKQN in New York City were equally if not more present in deindustrialized cities such as Buffalo, Albany, and Poughkeepsie.

> A.: My name is King X. of Chicago. I'm from the original Motherland, but I represent Rochester cuz that's where I lost my legs and I keep it funky. I wanna tell you one thing, everybody that wear black and gold has to be true. But I'm gonna tell you one thing, my King of Kings is Lord G. I don't know this brother King Blood, but I heard a lot of things about that brother. You know what I'm sayin? If I can take 12 more bullets, I'll do it, you know what I'm sayin? But I'm gonna tell you one thing, I came to Rochester, I didn't know there was Kings out here in New York. I started in the system. That's when I started learning about Kings all over the system. You know, um, I would like to say that for the young brothers out there if you're out there bullshittin' this is what you're gonna get (looks down at his paralyzed legs) . . . reality. OK? Cuz if you're not true you will not be here. Some way through somehow I got hit 12 times, I'm here for some reason. OK? Amor de Rey! [The audience screams back, "Amor de Rey?"; recorded at a univeral, October 1998].

The Local Tribes

> C.: Five structures in each borough?

N.: In each borough. Brooklyn would have a first, second, third, fourth, and fifth. The Bronx has a first, second, third, fourth, and fifth. If they go over 35 it's 1, 2—2, 2—1, 2, you know what I'm sayin? It's two threes, you know? Like Brooklyn. Brooklyn is gettin large so they got a first crown, second crown, third crown, third crown pearl—then they got fourth crown, fifth crown, and we gotta make sure all them people in check. You know, we do what we gotta do. If there's a situation that sometimes we get too much of a bigger problem that the structures themselves can't handle it, that's when we step in, you know? (Queen N., 10/10/98)

The tribes of the Nation are akin to the branches of a political movement and they have a similar structure to the Supreme Team, with the fifth crown referred to as the "body" or "soldier," which is the rank-and-file of the organization. Although the Supreme Team members have the highest status and perhaps greatest power in the organization, they cannot overrule a first crown of a tribe but they can bring him/her up on charges. The tribes of the ALKQN are very powerful and each of them has its own character based on the traditions of leadership in the area, with each tribe given a name that is a signifier of their indigenous heritage or is a metaphor for pride and courage. For example, the Brooklyn branch was called the Lion tribe, the Washington Heights branch was called the Caribe tribe and the Manhattan branch was called the Arawak tribe. Each tribe was based on a geographic area except the Latin Queens tribe which was based on their gender and the Pee Wee tribe which was based on the members' age.

The role of all these tribes is to give every member, new and old, a common relationship to the organization; to support the growth and training of members in their local communities; and to socialize members into their new roles as members and as leaders. Furthermore, the general health of the organization is contingent on the efficient running of each local branch, which means that dues are being collected regularly, youth members are attending school, local disputes with other groups are not spiraling out of control, and all members are keeping it "real," i.e., representing the Nation by defending the organization's name and integrity while not becoming involved in incidents likely to embarrass the group within a given community.

Meetings

According to the research, only a small number of mostly hierarchical gangs develop any type of sophisticated meeting structure. Jankowski (1991) notes that the East Coast gangs tended to develop an organizational culture, which included meetings and hierarchical leadership roles, as part of the area's tradition

TABLE 8.2 Tribes, Geographic Locations, and Membership Totals

Geographical Location	Name of Tribe	Approximate Number of Members
Upper Manhattan (Washington Heights)	Caribe	150
Lower Manhattan (Upper West Side, Spanish Harlem and Lower East Side)	Arawak	250
Brooklyn	Lion (East New York), Aztec (Sunset Park)	200, 100
Staten Island	Not available	50
Queens	Aztec	100
Bronx	Taíno	200
Latin Queens	Maya	50–100
Pee Wees (Youth Section)	Cacique	100
Long Island	Toltec	200–300
Upstate	Not available	75

of social organization. In comparison, the West Coast gangs were much more informally organized and meetings tended to be ad hoc, with little structure, as befitted their horizontal typology. Certainly, among the Latin Kings and Queens, there was a tremendous emphasis on being present at the various assemblies. The range of functions of ALKQN meetings is provided by the following field note:

> At these meetings, members have the opportunity to address important issues considered to be of interest to the entire organization. In addition, stories are related that illustrate how members deal with authority figures who test their loyalty and devotion to the group. Stories often involve ways in which Kings/Queens can most effectively deal with the Nation's critics. During these meetings, updates are provided on changes in the organization's power structure, meeting places, or any other dynamic that affects the entire group. Symbolic rituals are performed, for example: new members are crowned, members completing a term of probation are reinstated by retaining their

crowns, children are baptized, prayers and poetry are read, and perhaps most important, their leader, King Tone, speaks to them on issues of cultural reaffirmation. His speeches were nearly always constructed to promote Kingism, and he often discussed why members chose to be a King or a Queen. The leader is seen as a source of strength to members in the struggle for their rights that are under constant attack by more powerful forces. The Nation believes that its main threats are: Mayor Giuliani, the NYPD, and the under funding of local public schools [C.S., Field notes, 11/9/1997].

The Supreme Team meets weekly, as do all chapters, but Supreme Team members go to both meetings (i.e., the Supreme Team meeting and the meeting of their own chapter). The Supreme Team members are often different from the First Crowns of the chapters since their task is to lead the growth of the organization over the entire area and not just in one locale. The members of the Supreme Team, therefore, are those who are closest to the Inca, and they cannot be chosen unless the Inca has designated them for this position. In the third week of each month there is a universal crowns meeting and this is followed a week later by a city and state universal meeting of all the members. Issues that come out of the tribal and universal crown meetings get put on the agenda for the monthly universal meeting, but they first have to go through a filtering process—from the Prince of the local tribe and finally to the Cacique of the Supreme Team. Attending local meetings is an important sign of one's loyalty to the group, and it is also taken as a strong test of leadership:

> Queen D., Queen F., and Queen H. arrive. We greet one another and Queen D. excuses herself for being late. She tells me that her sisters can tell me the reason for her delay. I turn to them as Queen H. explains that they have been at the hospital all morning because Queen D. is sick. Queen D. continues by explaining that she has bronchitis and a fever which is very bad for her as she has the HIV virus. I ask her if she should not have stayed home. Her answer comes very fast, "These are my meetings. I would have to be dying to miss one" [C.S., Field notes, 11/9/1997].

Dues

There has been a long tradition of gangs in New York requiring their members to pay small weekly sums of $5.00 to the central treasury of the group. This tradition goes back to the old ethnic social clubs of the city in which working-class migrants and immigrants bonded to face a host of economic, social, and cultural problems through their own organizations. As they did so, they showed their capacity to achieve a certain level of autonomy within New York's ethnically mixed civil society. The payment of dues, therefore, is both a symbolic gesture of ethnic organizational resilience and a material necessity to enable the group to fulfill its basic administrative tasks in the service of its members.[4] Below, King Tone talks about the treasury of the group, known as "the box," and scoffs at the idea that the small pittance collected from its members could be used for illicit purposes:

> Turning to me, he asks "you see what I gotta go through" and then mimics a question and answer session in which fictive people are asking questions like "how many people have you killed," and "we're not interested in that political stuff, tell us about the box." The box refers to a collection of dues from members. According to Tone this is minimal, only a thousand dollars or so a month, sometimes two, which helps cover the expenses of the organization such as "printing" and is also used to help members who are down on their luck. Apparently, the police have claimed that the box refers to money from extortion and drug dealing. Tone says that there is controversy in the organization too over the box, because some members have accused him of taking dues for himself [L.K., Field notes, 8/26/1998].

The Organizational Condition of the Queens

The ALKQN liked to say that males and females shared a common status in the organization and that questions of gender were subordinate to group solidarity and "Nationhood." However, on a range of issues there were deep schisms between the two subgroups, even though at mass meetings outsiders could be forgiven for believing that a group consensus was alive and well in the organization and that the ALKQN had achieved a remarkable level of gendered integration. But before we discuss some of the comparative characteristics of the group, let us briefly highlight some findings in the literature.

Unfortunately, there are few serious accounts of the comparative organizational worlds of females versus males in street gangs or in street subcultures generally. Certainly, there are hardly any studies on the Latin Queens, either in New York or Chicago, other than media reports during the King Blood trial that focused on the sociopathic leadership of one leading Latin Queen, who was interesting because she became the only female member of the group to receive a serious prison sentence (see chapter 2). What the literature does show is that "gang girls are: (1) "horizontally" organized with few formal leadership structures (Campbell 1984; Miller 2001; Quicker 1983), although some groups may have informal "opinion leaders" who partake in ritualized meetings with voting procedures; (2) bereft of collective goals that are openly articulated,[5] although they might have informal goals of personal betterment, ethnic solidarity, and class allegiance; and (3) seeking some form of personal and/or group autonomy from males (Moore and Hagedorn 2001), although this varies widely depending on ethnic and geographic circumstances.

We have found that organizationally the Queens represented a strong contrast to most of the reports in the literature, and only at the levels of group loyalty and autonomy did they share characteristics with other research subjects. Further, we found that the Queens, like their male brethren,[6] are formally organized, highly motivated by both personal and collective goals and they have well-defined group roles with a deep sense of commitment to group solidarity and to their own relative autonomy within the organization (see Brotherton and Salazar 2002). But for all the talk of shared nationhood and common agendas within the group, there were clear differences between the Kings and Queens at the organizational level, which, as one might expect, could be clearly traced to the contradictions of gender.

Discriminatory Power Relations[7]

For the most part, as the Queens increased their influence in the organization, they were supported by the Kings, who saw the change in the balance of power between the sexes as a necessary outcome of the internal reforms. King D., below, articulates a fairly common position among male members who referred to women in the movement as the "backbone" of the organization:

Interviewer: Has the position of women in your organization changed over the years?

King D.: Yes, it has. . . . When I first came into this Nation I was incarcerated, the women's position didn't mean nothin' important to us whatsoever, and now, what they say, it's very important to us and we listen to them more than we would listen to a man.

Interviewer: Would you like to see more women in the organization?

King D.: Of course I would because I feel like without the women, the women are our backbones, that's how I consider it. They are our backbones, you know? Without a woman a man could go free and do a lot of stupid things, but when you have a woman telling you, "Listen, do not do things like that, try to do it like that," it's beautiful. I mean, they do help you out a lot and how would I love to see more? I would love for a lot of women to really get involved with our Nation and see what we're all about. We're not all about violence the way they portray us, we're not. As far as we . . . look, I have three daughters myself. . . . I've been with my wife 12 years and I have my three daughters and I give them their choice. When they're old enough they could make their own decision if they wanna become a Queen or if not, you know? It's just like my wife, I've been with her 12 years. She makes her own decisions, but I would love for a lot of Latin women or Black women or anybody just to get involved with us and see what we're talkin' about [Interview, 3/6/1998].

However, the notion of a backbone is not the same as the notion of a leadership, and in many respects this position vis-à-vis the Queens is not so dissimilar from the role attributed to women in traditional Latino culture (often referred to as *Marianismo*), where she is expected to be strong, stoic, and the loyal anchor of the family (Campbell 1984). In a field note summarizing almost two years of interviews and "hanging out" with the Queens, one of the female researchers wrote the following:

At most, the Queens represented ten percent of the Nation's total membership. During the study, the Queens' ranks in the ALKQN fluctuated from 40 to 70 active members while the numbers of Kings who attended Universal Nation meetings were between 500 and 700. Although the Queens felt frustrated by their lack of power within the organization, they faced a problem: remain outside the group and face ethnic discrimination or join the group and face gender discrimination [C.S., Field notes, 10/9/1999].

Therefore, at the organizational level, how did this "gender discrimination" manifest itself? Below we discuss two areas of discriminatory relations that were consistently observable and which members, both males and female, discussed at some length: (1) sexual relations, and (2) division of labor.[8]

Sexual Relations and Sexist Behavior

Queen N.: We clashed with some of the Kings because they're so old school . . . but even some of the old school, they like the change. Some of them feel that it should be no Queens in the Nation but they contradict themselves. One'll say, "Yeah, they're the backbone of the Nation," but then they'll say, "The Kings' worstest enemy is a woman." This is the way they put it, not to be nasty or whatever, or, "The Kings' deadliest enemy is a woman's pussy." I actually heard it come out of a brother's mouth, you know, and we try to explain to them, "It's not their pussy that's deadly, it's their minds. Who knows how to control their pussy and to know how to use it to get what they want or to do what they wanna do" [Interview, 5/6/1998].

Queen N.'s example of a sexist script used by male members against female members is based on the widely held myth that certain "loose" women are evil seductresses whose actions, whether intentional or not, serve to undermine male solidarity. This very common sexist trope in the popular culture, as many feminist commentators have written, emerges from the unequal power relations between the sexes and the need of certain males to maintain them. Essentially, it masks the double standards of males, who feel it is their gendered right to be sexually promiscuous, while females, who may practice slightly similar behavior, represent immorality, depravity, and danger. This tension between males and females in the group, while it is learned from and reproduced by the patriarchal culture and its specific ethnic articulations, was rationalized by the group's residue of sexist rules and practices that were only partially challenged during the reform period. Hence, prior to the reform, the Manifesto allowed Kings to have wives and mistresses, while Queens had to be loyal to their King or face the punishment of expulsion (and probably worse). Currently, the Manifesto states that Kings have to be loyal to their Queens and vice versa, the only exception being in times of long-term incarceration and separation, when both parties mutually agree to start new lives. However, based on observations and interviews, several (leading) females were expelled from the group for committing so-called adultery with another King while a similar punishment was never meted out to the male involved in the relationship. In fact, it was clear to us that a number of leaders went outside their monogamous relationships in search of other sexual partners without facing any consequences. Further, the attire of women was strictly controlled, while that of the men merited little attention. Below, a field researcher notes the obvious discrepancies:

The ALKQN sets out specific rules about the manner in which female members are to dress during the meetings. They are told to dress respectably, and are specifically forbidden to wear tight clothes or short skirts, and are instructed not to reveal cleavage or bare stomachs. Not following the

Queens' dress code runs the risk of being put on probation. This is a clear punishment that is demonstrated to all members through the stripping of the violator's crown. During a designated period of time, usually two months, probationers are not allowed to put their regular crown up. Instead, they must use the probation crown. This is an effective method of social control since it brings visual shame and degradation to the deviant member every time she greets another member, a constant reminder of her wrong-doings. I did not observe that the male members had any given dress codes [C.S., field notes, 10/15/1999].

Another factor compounding the sexist behavior among males was the Nation's view of abortion. In the Manifesto it states that female members are not allowed to have abortions in line with the Kings and Queens' credo that women are needed to breed more members. Such a ruling, of course, only de-nies the right of women to choose and act in defense of their own interests and seemed to contradict the rhetoric of the organization, which claimed to empower and to give equal respect to all its members while demanding that increased civil liberties be granted to Latinos/as in general. This conflict be-tween a traditional view of gender roles and the more modernist approach of entering females produced endless tensions as the Queens grew more organ-ized and self-confident:

> Queen M.: You have one person up there who writes the lessons and then you have another person who writes the lessons, you know? That's just like now . . . the biggest . . . fight right now is to get the lessons changed or to have new constitution lessons written for us because it states in our lessons we have to reproduce. Our main concern to this Nation is to re-produce. Don't tell me I'm gonna be here just to reproduce, cuz then that's the way they put it, you know, the way the Kings say it. It's like, "No, no, no," and then that King could have a mistress and this, this, da, da, da. No, no, no, no, no. See, that shit don't fly with me and it don't fly with a lot of the Queens, let me tell you [Interview, 4/6/98].

Nonetheless, a number of female members did opt to have abortions de-spite the group's ideology and thereby, at the individual level, chose to exert their independence (which, after all, was constantly championed by the group). Thus, the issues of having children and child-rearing should not be seen in purely black and white terms, since there are both historical and contextual fac-tors that need to be appreciated regarding the seeming clash of cultures. The following field notes provide a glimpse of the complexity of this issue:

The lack of organization and structure in their lives prior to joining the group serves as a major obstacle to a secure future for the girls. They recognize that membership in the A.L.K.Q.N. provides them with feelings of empowerment and hope for the future. The women feel that they are no longer struggling alone; rather, they come to see themselves as part of a social movement that cannot be ignored, as they so often felt prior to induction into the group. In this micro society, everything that they represent and that was seen as negative and to their disadvantage in the mainstream society, such as their culture, is valued and glorified. As Queen D. says, "A Queen always holds her head up high."

However, as previously mentioned, maintenance of their ethnic culture in the group includes the continuance of traditional Latin gender roles that the women want to shed in modern times. Because of the history of colonization experienced by most of the ethnic groups represented in the Nation, members are in a constant search for cultural identity and reaffirmation in an environment that will praise Latino tradition. Going back to their roots, even if they are ironically enough going back to an earlier oppressor (i.e., the Spaniards), gives them a feeling of control and pride. They feel part of something powerful, an ancient and rich cultural tradition. Unfortunately, engaging in this culture compromises the females' freedom, alienating her and relegating her to positions involving caretaking and home-related duties [C.S., field notes, 2/20/2000].

Sexual Division of Labor

Just as sexual relations within the group reflected ongoing discriminatory thinking and practices between male and female members, so too did the multiple ways in which the group organized its division of labor. We have already cited the absence of females from certain powerful committees of the Nation, an omission that was partially addressed as the reforms got underway, but just as important were the everyday organizational practices of the group that tended to mirror the traditional, gender-based divisions of the family. For example, at large meetings when many members brought their children, and food and drinks were served, it was the Queens who virtually always took care of the children while the Kings were allowed to participate fully in the meetings. Further, it was the Queens again who prepared the food in advance and served it while the males were free to socialize and go about their organizational duties unhindered. Certainly, it was observed that there were occasions when King Tone would demonstratively remove himself from meeting proceedings and spend time in the day care area, but his example, while followed by some other leading Kings, never became a group practice.

Such examples of organizational differences between the Kings and Queens not only paint a more complex picture of the group's unity, they also provide a context for the tensions around the presiding male hierarchy. When the leadership was asked why more was not done to address some of these sexist practices, the response was usually twofold: (1) the sexism by the members is simply reflective of sexism in the public at large, and therefore outsiders should not hold the group to a standard that society itself could not attain; and (2) the group was 90 percent male and 10 percent female, and to give more power to females before they had a greater share of the membership would be inappropriate.

Although both arguments have their strengths, the former avoids the central issue of progressive leadership that the ALKQN was supposed to be providing, and the latter simply rationalizes the status quo (for one of the best ways to recruit more females is to show them in more prominent positions of power). Arising from these gender-based tensions were two important consequences for the organization. First, the uneven application of sexual mores between male members and female members distracted the group from its central goals because members became embroiled in petty, internal sexual politics. Second, the more committed and radical female members were left feeling frustrated and resentful at the double standard, which seemed to be institutionalized.

The Local and National Picture

In an earlier chapter we discussed the Chicago chapter and its connection to the manifesto found in the New York branch. Based on this and the numerous references made to the Motherland and to the Kings in Chicago by the ALKQN leadership, it was obvious that the New York Kings were always very respectful of Chicago's authority and legitimacy, but there were some significant contrasts between the two subgroups. First, the ALKQN was significantly smaller than the various branches making up the Chicago homeland, perhaps amounting to a fifth of the total membership. Second, Chicago was very much tied to local street networks and microcommunities whereas the branches in New York cover much larger areas, a fact that contributes to the lower number of local conflicts.

In addition to New York, other franchises of the organization were Pennsylvania, New Jersey, Connecticut, Boston, and Florida, all of whom sent delegations to important large gatherings such as Kings' Day, the last universal before King Tone was sent away to prison, and the anniversary of the New

York chapter's founding. On such occasions, twenty or more members from these other branches attended, demonstrating a significant level of nation-wide organization considering the distances involved. But what was the organizational relationship between these entities?

Essentially, each organization appeared to enjoy a great deal of autonomy as long as it practiced the basic principles of the Motherland's manifesto. For example, both Connecticut and New York created their own manifestos based on both the Chicago text and the particular interpretation of their respective leaderships. Of course, the Motherland got to see each rendition and it can be assumed that it possessed some form of sanctioning power. But talk of conflicts between the different franchises and Chicago was seldom heard, and what conflicts did take place appeared to be resolved through negotiation rather than violence. In fact, at one point in the mid-1990s, New York was overseeing both Pennsylvania and New Jersey,[9] which seemed to indicate that certain dynamic franchises were being allowed to organize across large geographical domains with considerable memberships. We estimate that at the peak of its operations, New York had more than 3,000 members, spread throughout the five boroughs and upstate New York.[10] In addition, although under a different leadership, a further 5,000 members were found in every institution of the state's prison system.

Membership Flows and Configurations of the Organization

Researchers have long discussed the different configurations that emerge in gangs that fall somewhere along the continuum of formal and informal group organizations. For example, some researchers have written about the core and the periphery of gangs (Hagedorn 1988; Klein 1971; Short and Strodtbeck 1965; Yablonsky 1963), others have discussed the strong presence of cliques within gangs (Moore 1991; Conquergood 1993), and a wide variety of studies has been done on gang expansions and recruitment (Taylor 1990).

Core and Periphery

Those who have studied the phenomenon of gang nuclei argue, quite logically, that the larger the core of the organization, the greater the stability of the group. In the ALKQN, the concept of the core was both theoretically and practically very important since it was the leadership nucleus that was responsible for managing a whole array of problems and opportunities as the group grew and became increasingly involved in community life. Over the three years of research, we encountered more than a hundred members who held various leadership positions and who we saw repeatedly at most major events. For new members coming into the group, it was impressive to witness such a large, relatively stable leadership structure made up of mature men and women. It verified to them two properties of the organization that serve to reinforce their affiliation to the group: (1) Kingism was a life-long commitment, and (2) leaders were not necessarily going to prison or getting killed, so that membership did not necessarily compromise one's life.

Cliques

A second area of fruitful discussion has focused on the emergence of gang cliques. Certainly in the ALKQN there was substantial evidence of cliques that formed around life-long friendships and family ties in different tribes. Similarly, within these cliques there was also a series of dyads and triads in which members stayed close to one or two trusted colleagues, often moving up or down in the ranks of the organization with their "compadre(s)." The ideology of the organization further cemented these bonds with its emphasis on loyalty, group solidarity, and vigilance. As in other studies, we found that many cliques developed out of childhood relationships within certain, often impoverished, neighborhoods over time. Thus, members talked of attending the same schools with their closest *manito*, of being involved in the same or similar street conflicts, and usually of sharing the same ethnicity.

Expansion and Attrition

The organization grew repeatedly as potential Kings and Queens inquired about the organization and desired to join. In the popular press, there is a wide belief that such "gangs" are constantly luring youth into their deviant midst and that the most desperate and/or ruthless of groups resort to almost "coercive ganging." Our observations of the ALKQN saw very few attempts to pressurize nonmembers into joining, and, in fact, due to the complicated and arduous process of the initiation (see next section) and the need to maintain a tight discipline in the ranks, there was little motivation to engage in any mass recruiting. In other words, the organization was only able to manage a certain number of members at any one time and it was constrained, above all, by the number of local leaders it was producing. "We are not into recruiting anymore. We don't have to recruit, people are coming to us continuously and asking if they can join" (Ms. R., Latin Queen).

At the same time, this is not to argue that members did not ask friends and acquaintances if they wanted to be involved. For example, one of our field researchers who is Mexican was asked by a relatively unknown Mexican acquaintance if he was interested in joining the Latin Kings since "Latinos have to stick together." The incident took place in an upstate city where few

Latinos/as are visible and where the white power structure goes relatively un-challenged. Another field researcher reported that certain respected members of the Long Island tribe, while hanging out in certain street locales, would approach other street Latinos/as about their organization. On the other hand, in numerous schools we visited, where the Latin Kings and Queens had sub-stantial memberships, few non-ALKQN students reported being harassed or pressured to join the organization. In fact, in many schools it was noticeable that members and nonmembers of the group would "hang out" together, al-though in certain schools where the population was split along racial and eth-nic lines it was more common to see Latin Kings and Queens forming visi-ble bonds and discretely representing their nation. In the following interview, the respondent is describing a very common process of entree into the group:

L.B.: OK, so why do you think they got involved with this group?

King P.: Well, to tell you the truth, I didn't wanna be a King because I was like, "That's WAK." You know? but then, my cousin knew a few of them cuz he used to go to school with them and I was always with my cousin. So, me and my cousin, we started chillin. And it wasn't that we just got down just to be down, it was that they was lots of love in the family, you under-stand? When I was small, I had did somethin, you know, and the cops was lookin' for me . . . I ran to where my cousin was at. And I was tellin' my cousin what happened and he comes out like, "Yo, come up to my place. You can stay in my place for as long as you want." And I'm like, I don't even know the guy, you know?, and he's tryin' to offer me to stay in his crib. So I stood there for a couple of days and then . . . he talks to me about bein' a King, you know? And it's like, "Why not? I don't know this guy and he offered me to stay in his crib. That's mad love." I figure that's love. And plus, it was good, you know, hangin' out all the time like I just come out of school or, I come from work or somethin' and I just chill. And then one day when brothers was fightin' and me and my cousin was there and we ended up fightin' too. We was a couple of times there that we was fightin' and the brothers seen that and they was like, "Why you don't get Kinged?" So one day they was like, "You're all just on probation." And I guess we be-come Kings since that day [Interview, 9/8/1997].

Whereas a great deal has been written about street groups and their mem-bership growth, little attention has been given to the issue of attrition. In the ALKQN, this issue is quite salient for a number of organizational reasons. First, during the early reform period a number of drug dealers were purged from the group, many of whom had long histories of organizational responsibility. This action, on the one hand, left holes in the leadership structure but on the other it rid the organization of the threat of internal spheres of influence that could potentially undermine group unity and the group's newly adopted social and political goals. Second, the ousted members, many of whom identified with the group's "gangsta" past, went on to form their own underground cliques, sometimes referred to as "ghost tribes" (see chapter 12), that became enemies of the official ALKQN, leading to a range of physical and nonphysical conflicts.

The Acquisition and Maintenance of Organizational Roles

So far, we have described some of the basic structures of the group and the minimum obligations of membership, such as attendance at meetings and the payment of dues. But how does someone become a member? What are the organizational rites of passage that everyone has to pass through in order to be accepted? Finally, how are members held accountable? In the following, we discuss each of these questions and show how they are built into the day-to-day structure of the group.

Unlike almost all street gangs, the Kings and Queens are not subjected to violent initiation rites. Instead, they go through a long and complicated set of procedures or "stages" that constitutes their entree into the group. Each stage is carefully administered by the respective leadership of the tribes, and finally, when members have passed all the different trials, they are welcomed into the organization. Below, we explain the various stages before men and women attain their rightful place in the organization.

The first stage in crown attainment is carried out under the watchful eyes of one or more superiors (i.e., tribal leaders) and is the most supervised aspect of membership. This critical stage of gaining acceptance by the group, called "five alive," is when members must show their intrinsic and extrinsic worth and their commitment to the cause. Substantively it means that members must (1) regularly attend meetings, (2) constantly broaden and deepen their knowledge of the group through reading, verbalizing, and interpreting its lessons, and (3) outwardly demonstrate a level of self-worth that is commensurate with the ALKQN's notion of self-respect. Members signify this stage of their career to others by slapping their heart with all five fingers and then throwing their hand into the air, thus representing a five-point crown. The "five alive" stage can last several months and is followed by a second stage called a probationary stage.

Prospective members remain on probation until they have adequately demonstrated knowledge of the Nation's rules, regulations, and "lessons," their grasp of which is tested at different intervals by the leadership:

C.S.: In what way are you tested? Do they [the leaders] ask you questions?

Queen G.: They ask us questions, like for culture, we get a sheet of paper and we write down what we learned and then we get scored on it, you know? But we never get an "F" because the more you try, that's an "A" right there, you know? That's how we feel. As long as you try, you make it.

At this second stage of membership candidacy, members may throw a probation crown (place their hands in the air in the shape of a crown), which is represented by a double-handed version of a crown. On passing the probationary stage, they attain their full crown from the group's leader, King Tone, who presides over a celebratory ritual in which he blesses all the inductees individually at the end of a general meeting and gives them their new membership beads. At the end of the blessing, everyone has to repeat the oath of membership, which is followed by an ear-deafening series of *Amor de Reyes* from the enthusiastic audience.

Receiving the crown is a very prestigious and emotional moment, and if members misbehave or do not obey the rules, they are subject to the loss of their crown for two months, after which they are required to go back to the probationary stage, or even further back to the "five alive" stage. The loss of the crown is degrading, and serves as a common form of punishment and social control within the Nation (see chapter 4).

Obligations

Once one has been accepted into the group, it is time to embark on a full membership career and begin to eke out a place within the broader organization. This is done through consistently meeting the basic *obligations* of membership and coming to terms with leadership, since the longer one remains a member the pressure to rise in the ranks becomes almost irresistible. This is not to say that everybody who joins wants to become a leader. There were certainly members who seemed quite content to remain a member of the "body" without seeking any higher office. However, the everyday needs of the group and the various situations that the group encountered, in which members are called upon to perform and sacrifice on its behalf, make it difficult to stay forever in the rank-and-file. Below, Queen N., who had been a member of the

FIGURE 8.2 At the end of a meeting, both inductees and more established members pose for a photo.

"body" for several years, had recently become a leader of a fairly large tribe and is listing the different obligations that leaders' roles entail:

> N.: My position . . . is difficult because it's like it's two people and we hold down all the brothers in New York State. So we gotta make sure that the structure in that one borough is doing they job, you know? That their paperwork is correct. That everybody's doin' good, their Pee Wees are doin' good in school, you see their report cards, you got permission slips, if they stayed out late, if they got in trouble—all of that—up to date, up to par, and that's in everywhere and every one of the structures [Interview, 10/1/1998].

Clearly, the Kings and Queens who had real power in the organization took their positions seriously and saw it as a privilege to become a leader and to have evolved and grown through the organization. As we glean from Queen N., above, she is receiving training and a set of responsibilities that give her an important purpose in life. As long as she meets these obligations she is a crucial part of the group, helping to maintain discipline and morale while providing an example to the younger members who are looking to her for guidance and strength. Active membership in the organization is therefore about passing a continuous series of tests, many of which involve a display of vision and intitiative, but perhaps the most important test of all is loyalty.

Accountability and Monitoring

Unlike the former jacket gangs of New York, which were the main type of street-collective subculture other than entrepreneurial drug gangs (see Brotherton 1999) that preceded the street organizations, the ALKQN members were more accountable for their actions and group responsibilities within the organization. In fact, a critical aspect of the group's reform was to increase the accountability of the membership, particularly the leadership, in order to avert the disastrous dictatorial trajectory of the past and to reinforce the social movement momentum in which the group was heading. Below, we discuss three aspects of the accountability dynamic within the group.

Checking in on Yourself

We discussed earlier how much the group's ideology emphasized the need for members to be responsible for their own actions and to negate the years of fatalism that often imbues the worldviews of members from poor and working-class cultures. One way of achieving this is for members to be conscious of the degree to which other members are depending on their task accomplishment to carry the Nation forward, regardless of their position in the group. Queen N. offers a good example of what might be called an organizational consciousness, which was quite prevalent among both high- and low-standing members:

> N.: Oh, yeah. To me positions don't mean nothin' cuz regardless, it gets down to we're still brother and sister. I'm still a part of the Almighty Latin King and Queen Nation. I don't need my position to do what I'm doin'. My title don't make me, I make my title, so that's just the way I see it. But, you know, it is like a task for me, knowing that I got people actually lookin' up to me and I gotta guide 'em in the right way. I fuck up, they fuck up . . . it keeps me on my toes! [laughs] [Interview, 10/1/1998].

Listening to the Rank-and-File and Checking on the Leadership
A number of the Nation's leaders recognized that the tribes had different levels of leadership and that while some local leaders were quite experienced, others had only recently risen in the ranks and were facing many challenges in establishing a disciplined, loyal, and dynamic membership. Below, Queen N. describes one of her many duties as a leading crown in the New York area:

> My main focus is to keep on top of the structure and the structure keep on top of their body, you know? I don't go to all their meetings, they hardly see me, you know what I'm saying? Like this weekend past in Brooklyn, I popped up in Brooklyn because it was only Brooklyn's second meeting and I wanted to see how they was doing, how the structure ran their meetings, da, da, da, this and this and that. Now they won't see me again till maybe a month, two months later, you know, and that's for everything [Interview, 10/1/1998].

This role of checking and counterchecking among the leaders was an important way for them to gauge what was happening at the lower levels of the organization. One of the leaders most constantly eyeing rank-and-file developments was King Tone. In fact, one of his great strengths was his ability to move quickly among the various tribes and pick up on moods, tensions, flagging morale, and disrespectful behavior exhibited by leaders toward their members. He referred to this system of monitoring as "keeping the leaders and brothers on point."

D.B.: Is that what you used to do? Go round and check?

King Tone: Yeah. My trick was—is—that I was always in everybody's meeting, and if I missed your meeting one week, you would sure as hell know you're gonna see me next week. So leaders and the body knew I was gonna come see you. It's like a PO [prison officer], he's gonna check my urine, you don't know when he's gonna check it. I had them very much like that. Every Tuesday New York had crown meetings. So on Tuesday, when I wanted to talk to anybody that have problems, I knew each house. Then we had the weekly meetings. We start on Friday night with two tribes, let's say, Brooklyn, they break it down to two districts. I go to one meeting like 8 o'clock, I stay for the first half hour, I get in the car, and by the time the next meeting ends, I come to Bushwick, "Hi. I'm here," you understand? So I get in the middle of the meeting, I do my part til Friday's over. I wake up Saturday morning, I know I got a 12 o'-clock meeting in Queens. Then after Queens I know in Manhattan I got the four o'clock meeting. Then I know Sunday is the Bronx and Long Island, but everybody's seen me. I cared. You understand? I would actually go in and listen to them [Interview, 4/1/98].

Keeping the Enthusiasm Going, Putting the Finger on the Pulse of the Nation

Thus, a major concern to the leadership was the behavior of other leaders, particularly as newer members joined who had a rising set of expectations about the organization. Therefore, an equally critical issue to address was the need of the group to constantly mobilize the membership in order to keep them active and engaged. This means that social events had to be organized, political campaigns had to be waged, fund-raising activities had to be executed, and a dynamic sense of community needed to be felt by all those making the commitment.

> King Tone: I made my own little survey and I asked each of them, "When is the last time you seen the Suprema?" but then I got locked up. I'm callin' on my Supremas and they takin' care of business here but nobody in New York State has seen one of my leaders in over four weeks. So when I seen that I know I gotta get the bracelet off, you understand? I know they gonna take pictures of me in the circles again, because that's where I'm goin'. I have no doubt that I know what's needed now. All they need is a leader to say, "Hey! Everything's all right! Snap out of it! These guys are bad, they're no good [the present leaders], keep up the faith." Brooklyn is strong. From when I got home four weeks ago everybody's working, from Brook Point to Knickerbocker . . . they're working, but they not reporting, you understand? So now, last week they had 40 in their meeting. They went to the beach, they go there to party. I look for ways to show these leaders this is how you bring 'em back. "They're tired." "It's summer." "You're borin' them." "They wanna be with their wife." So bring their wives! So it was successful [Interview, 6/1/1998].

How Did the Organization Structurally Change?

Given what we have seen and heard over the years, it is clear that the group managed to reach a level of sophistication in its organization and dedication among its membership that can find few parallels in the history of street gang subcultures. But, of course, it was not always like this and for many years prior to the reform the group was treading a very different path of development and might not have lasted too much longer if the series of structural changes briefly described in Table 8.3 had not taken place.

Death Penalty Abolished

> When I became Inca the number one rule I made was a brother could never, ever kill another brother again. No matter what we find them guilty of. Because we contradict everything we stand for. . . . The death penalty was abolished, never to be brought back. And I think the Nation loves that about the movement now. (King Tone)

The abolition of the death penalty, which had been used against several Kings who had been accused and found guilty of treason, ended a notorious chapter in the group's existence. No longer would the group's leaders be able to issue TOS ("terminate on sight") instructions to subordinates—instructions that could literally mean the ending of a person's life for reasons that may only be clear to a few in the inner circle of the hierarchy. This reform, the first undertaken by King Tone, removed from the organization one of the principle foundations of a regime of fear, allowing a much freer atmosphere of reasoned debate, discussion, and innovative strategy development to become the chief characteristics of the new ALKQN.

Initiation Through Prayer and Probation

To get initiated nowadays you have to first go through a period of probation until we know that you really want to be a King or Queen. Then we ask you to do some form of community service such as work in one of the soup kitchens or help with the distribution of clothes to the poor [King F., interview, 3/2/1998].

Along with the ending of executions went also the curtailment of physical initiations in which men and women are supposed to prove their physical mettle and courage before joining the organization. The replacement by a long period of probation and a series of good deeds carried out on behalf of the community gave prospective members a very different idea of what constituted membership and encouraged them from the outset to develop their spiritual leanings, if they had them. Organizationally, it can be argued that such an initiation process produces a much more stable membership, because

TABLE 8.3 **Comparative Organizational Characteristics of the ALKQN, Before and After Reform**

Before Reform (Prior to 1996)	Reform and Postreform (1996–1999)
Death penalty enforced	Death penalty abolished
Initiation could include physical violence	Initiation through prayer and probation
Forbidden to talk to "outsiders" about the group's business, especially the media	"Outsiders" welcome to inquire about the group and many interviews given to the media
Physical intimidation used to control members	Physical threats ended against members
Few formal rights of representation for member accused of wrongdoing	The notion of a "fair hearing" incorporated into trials
Females largely subordinate to males	Efforts made to reduce gendered power hierarchies
Little emphasis on developing youth sections	Great emphasis on developing a disciplined and committed youth cadre
Limited engagement in political/community matters	High level of involvement in city and community politics
Little emphasis on educational attainment among members	Great emphasis on both educational and occupational attainments by members
Tolerance and discrete promotion of illicit activities (e.g., drug dealing through the group)	Rhetorical and demonstrative intolerance of illicit activities by group members

the organization and the prospective member take their time to experience each other before cementing the relationship.

"Outsiders" Welcome

The accessibility to the organization by "outsiders," be they community leaders, academics, or media personnel, meant that the actions of the group were much more permeable and subject to both positive and negative judgments. The impact on the organization was dramatic, for now the group could call on outside "experts" for consultation in such areas as leadership development, conflict resolution, fund-raising, legal advice, and political strategy, all of which influenced the way the organization saw itself in terms of both its public and private face. Thus, as the group's confidence grew in its dealings with outside elements and gained greater visibility, its own organizational practices were affected. For example, the group was constantly criticized by outsiders for its treatment of female members, which helped to promote and reinforce numerous debates on equality within the group.

> The Nation, well, basically . . . it's like we work with other organizations, like Mothers Against Police Brutality. I go to meetings on Tuesday nights on 22nd Street and I sit with them there for like three, four hours, and we're on a committee and we vote things in and we go to rallies, marches. We work with so many other people, like last year we was in an art gallery. They sold pictures of members, and we was there, like at the opening. There's so many other things we do [Interview with Queen N., 10/1/1998].

Physical Threats Ended Against Members

As physical threats declined or disappeared against members as forms of discipline, a much greater emphasis had to be placed on formal nonphysical sanctions to keep members focused and within the boundaries of their membership obligations. The result was a series of innovative measures that mimicked the mainstream society's apparatuses of judicial control, such as due process trials, group-based representation, written charges (although these were also in place before the reform), and a range of penalties, such as community service, push-ups, curfews, and fines.

"A Fair Hearing"

Although we have referred to this above, the notion of a fair hearing is particularly important, since it took away the fear of constant intrigue "from above" that was bedeviling the organization in its earlier incarnation. Moreover, the practice of such a liberal democratic tenet was an empowering mechanism, signaling to members that the group had reached such a level of maturity that it could experiment with the legal process.

Reducing Gendered Power Hierarchies

> In the summer of 1998, I began interviewing the Pee Wee Queens. By this time, the Queens had divided into different tribes. Young members under eighteen were now part of a new tribe, the Pee Wees, the only one where males and females were mixed. Leadership had decided that youth attending school and who did not have children had different priorities and issues to discuss [C.S., field notes, 9/1/1998].

One very important mark of the group's efforts to address the foundational issues of male power in the organization was the establishment of a coeducational tribe, the first ever (to our knowledge) of any group of Latin Kings or Queens across the country. As we have stated earlier, although the struggle against gendered hierarchies could have been taken much further—for example, homosexuals were still banned from joining and females still struggled to be treated equally—the capacity of the group to put into practice such a progressive structure could have produced a far-reaching effect on the overall organization if allowed to continue. Unfortunately, the new tribe had little time to prove itself, for soon after its establishment the criminal justice system effectively beheaded the movement.

Developing a Disciplined and Committed Youth Cadre

As more youth came into the Nation, producing their own cadres of leaders, an enormous dynamism was unleashed within the group that helped to inspire the older members and keep the group firmly wedded to the issues of the day. This emphasis on the youth ensured a continuous stream of dynamic, enthusiastic, and optimistic recruits who could provide a powerful bulwark against the tendency toward conservativism and cynicism that might be found among older, more established members. The role of youth was especially important when the group wanted to show and perhaps celebrate its presence at solidarity marches:

> One time the three mothers [Mothers against Police Brutality] each called a rally on the same day to protest their sons' deaths and I had a universal. I sent the Queens to Queens [the borough], 300 people. I sent the Brooklyn tribe to the Brooklyn rally, 200 people. I sent a church full of a thousand kids who waited and then went to the Manhattan rally with Mr. R. They all got in, finished the rally, then took the train to 126th street and at my meeting I still had 1,200. There ain't an organization right now in New York that could do that. You go find it for me! [Interview with King Tone by L.K., 1/18/1997].

Heightened Level of Involvement in City and Community Politics

As the ALKQN matured, it developed even more aspirations and illusions about playing a role in the allocation and distribution of social and cultural power in the city. Although different passages in the manifesto had always articulated that the group would eventually be a community power broker, it was only when the ALKQN started to look increasingly like a legitimate grass-roots organization that numerous city politicians, who had earned their reputations by championing the concerns of the disenchanted and disempowered, began to embrace them in earnest. This entree into a higher level of community politics exposed the group to a broad range of audiences, i.e., students, different ethnic groups, and civic organizations, which helped them to cultivate their message and their members. It also showed them (1) the possibilities for developing resource networks and (2) the need to consider long-range strategies if they were to evolve into a political force.

Emphasis on Both Educational and Occupational Attainments by Members

Encouraging members to develop their education and improve their careers ensured that members entering the organization were more motivated to build a social movement and were easier to organize. Such members were already used to a certain level of discipline and responsibility through their school and/or work activities and they exhibited less of a tendency toward individualism and antiauthoritarianism than would probably be the case in more stereotypical street gangs.

Intolerance of Illicit Activities by Group Members

For the most part, the group followed through on its determination to end drug dealing and other related activities. We have already argued that expelling certain people who had refused to compromise was a bold if necessary move. It helped the organization to reach and maintain a higher level of unity than would otherwise have been possible as entrepreneurial cliques developed into fiercely independent and competitive factions. Not all culprits were expelled, however, and some leaders were simply disciplined and removed from their position in the group if they pledged to change their ways. In such cases, the loss of leadership status might affect the members' commitment to the group as well as their enthusiasm for movement building. Leaving such members to wallow in their resentment was a dangerous practice, since their negativity could infect others less inexperienced and lead to factionalizing and morale problems:

> King Tone: Where are all the brothers that started with us in this church? Remember when they had positions? Where they at? The Supreme Team with the big titles, where they at? Huh? I said they wasn't leaders no more, now where everybody at? They too busy or there's an excuse just because they don't got a title no more they can't serve the Nation. Well I'm just telling you

that I wanna serve Blood with or without you, with the Nation, with your money, without your money [Recorded at universal, 4/4/1998].

In this chapter we have tried to show how the ALKQN came together to form a relatively stable nucleus of core leaders and rank-and-file members in a hierarchically ordered organization. We have found that the notions of unity and loyalty, which are key tenets of the group's ideology, are concretized by members' organizational roles and especially by the complementary notions of obligation and sacrifice. It would be easy to see the group as overly dominated by members at the top of the hierarchy—however, it is noteworthy that many leaders constantly reminded us that they were committed to the organization irrespective of their status and that they were loath to take the rank-and-file for granted. In other words, there seemed to us to be a healthy and respectful relationship between the various strata of the organization and it seemed that the group was well on its way to developing a system of decision-making and discipline-maintenance that in time could prove to be a novel form of street movement. This is not to say that there were not organizational problems—and that the typical issues of power abuse, inertia, morale, and gender inequality were not present to various degrees throughout the study period. However, it was impressive to see that such issues were openly discussed and that there were genuine attempts to come to grips with the kinds of organizational flaws that in time could surely corrode the most sophisticated of political apparatuses.

CHAPTER 9

MEMBERSHIP

They are all going to introduce themselves just as they did last week. There are some Queens present today who were not here last week and some that are absent. During their introduction, this is what I managed to get down:

Jacky wants to be a social worker. Queen H. is going to be twenty-one years old on Friday. She has been a Queen for four months and likes the Nation because it gives her knowledge of her history. Queen D. is in her forties, she has six kids and lives with Queen G. who is twenty-five years old. Queen G. has no "babies" but wants to have one as soon as her King comes back from being "locked up" in Florida. She talks about how members of the Nation will reach influential positions and how the Latino community has to get together to one day "reach the White House." Queen M. has three kids with her King. Their children are all Kings and Queens. Queen B. has kids with a King and wants to go back to high school eventually. Queen A. is twenty-one years old and comes from a family of eleven brothers and sisters. She wants to go to a technical college and is saving by working two jobs. In the future she wants to become a doctor. She talks about her deceased father who is her hero; a picture of his face is tattooed on her calf. Her mother is a white "Spaniard." Her mother's family has always looked down on her because she is dark-skinned, just like her father. Queen F. is fifteen years old, a Pee Wee. She goes to G. W. High school and has been a proud Queen for four months. She is not "totally Latina," still she feels that she has been "brought to the light." Queen M. is twenty- four years old and has two "babies." She went to college for two years, receiving an associates degree in business and now works on Wall Street at the Stock Exchange. She is not crowned yet and is still on probation. Her brother, who has been a King for two years, was the one who told her that the Nation was not a gang, which convinced her to join. Queen M. emphasizes that the media do not portray the good things that the Nation does. Queen J. is a twenty-year-old housewife with three kids. She has been a Queen for four years. At the time she joined, the Nation was not doing community work, even though it was already like "a big fam-

ily." Queen S. is eighteen years old. Her mother passed away eleven years ago. She maintains that most of the Queens come from broken homes and that they find a new family here.

CS, field notes, 11/1/1997

Introduction

In the ensuing chapter, we will describe some of the primary background characteristics of those who joined the ALKQN during its reform period as well as those members who stayed loyal to the group during this tumultuous time. The data are drawn from sixty-seven life history interviews carried out with thirty-nine Kings and twenty-eight Queens. In previous studies of mostly black and Latino/a gangs there have been attempts to chart gang members' family histories, occupational experiences, educational backgrounds, and criminal orientations. What we have mostly learned from these studies is that gang members are generally isolated from the kinds of mainstream, socializing institutions (i.e., schools, family, church, legal work) that make stability and social mobility feasible and provide the interlocking mechanisms for social control in their local neighborhoods. Consequently, the argument goes, youth who fail to bond with or who are rejected by these institutions are particularly susceptible to being socialized by their peer groups, which explains why they become wedded to the practices, lores, rituals, and norms that constitute the gang subculture (Thrasher 1927). This basic finding in the literature is certainly present in many Kings and Queens, but it is also strongly contradicted in a number of cases, as we note below. To provide as complete a picture as possible of the membership sample (see chapter 1), we have devoted this chapter to an analysis and interpretation of four spheres of respondents' socialization[1] process: (1) family life, (2) school life, (3) street life, and (4) prison life.

Family Life

In the literature on gang delinquency, descriptions of the family life of gang members has often highlighted the dysfunctional and stressful backgrounds of youth (Moore 1991; Vigil 1988), the lower-class cultural values of the parent class (Miller 1958), and the preponderance of female-headed households, particularly for male gang members (Miller 1958). As Spergel (1995:170) has summarized:

> Family disorganization is a key factor in the development of pressures that contribute to the development of alternate structures, such as youth gangs, to meet socialization needs of youth. A strong sense of youthful isolation and personal distress begins with insufficient social support and control relationships developed in the context of the family.

In our sample, while many respondents revealed extremely troubled pasts in terms of their family life, there were others who heralded from mainstream, high-functioning family backgrounds where there was quite adequate bonding and attachment to conventional social processes. Part of the problem with trying to analyze the role of the family in members' lives lies in the terms of the discourse, particularly in such concepts as "dysfunctional" and "conformity." For children born into a world that is being rent asunder by neo-colonial strains and stresses, as has happened to several generations of Puerto Ricans and Dominicans, maintaining a "functional" family is extremely difficult. Therefore, the concept of dysfunctionalism must be placed in this broader sociopolitical context to retain much meaning. In a similar vein, one dynamic of conformity is that it also produces deviance as people resist the moral constraints and social scripts of cultural systems that reproduce the status quo. This tension is nowhere more apparent than in girls who reject their gender-role expectations or in youth who question adult paths to corporatized social mobility and materialism.

In the following, we have divided the analysis into primary themes along gender lines, although there are clear commonalities among both sets of members. We found that the Queens, not surprisingly, tended to be more forthcoming than the Kings; they spoke the most about incidents of family abuse, which accounts for why so much of the data deal with the females.

Kings: Weak or Conflicting Social Controls ("I Wish I'd Had More Discipline")

A number of Kings spoke at length about the lack of comprehensive authority that their parents exercised over them. Sometimes this arose because of the absence of their fathers and the presence of mothers who were left to provide social order while managing meager resources to help the family survive.

D.B.: What kind of discipline did you have when you lived with your mother and father?

King L.: It was the same, you know, my mother was always the stronger one in the discipline area because my father was always working at the post office when they was together, so I didn't really see my father there to discipline [Interview, 10/10/1997].

In such cases, the mother could sometimes succeed, but often the burden was too much and the youth was raised as much by the streets as by the parents.[2] At other times, the respondent talked about conflicting regimes of control and the resulting confusion.

D.B.: Now, when you were growing up, can you tell me a little bit about your economic standing? I mean were you poor, did you get enough to eat, was your father working?

King R.: Well, my father worked all his life. The problem was that I was always in the streets. I mean, to this day I live with my mother and my father. They still in my life, they still together. My father, when I was younger my father was a very strict person. He was the type that if I wanted something I would have to earn it. He was very strict. My mother was different. My mother used to spoil me, so I had two parents that had two different ways of treating me. My mother spoiled me, she gave me whatever I wanted, and my father was very strict with me, so that tore me apart . . . where it came to a point where I was always in the streets cuz me and my father, we just really didn't get along. I felt like, because my mother gave me everything and he never gave me nothin'. I felt like he really didn't want me or somethin', you know? I wonder why he gave me his first and last name [Interview, 3/2/1998].

Kings: Unlimited Boundaries for Boys, Strict Rules for Girls

As King Tone recounted in chapter 6, boys and girls in traditional Latino families are raised within very different social and sexual boundaries, with the formation of their male/female identities and sensibilities predicated on stereotypical male/female qualities. For boys, therefore, the promotion of a male self denies personality characteristics and social skills that are deemed too feminine, and vice versa. Tone refers to the freedom that he was given to roam the streets and, in effect, explore and affirm his sexuality, as a direct result of his father's and mother's effort to make him a man.

In contrast, the girls in his household were expected to remain at home, occupying themselves with child care, housework, and homework, in effect becoming socialized for somewhat contradictory future roles—as mothers, housewives, and wage/salary earners. In Tone's eyes, and this was also apparent in several other insightful comments from male members, this form of family gendering was not only seen as responsible for his failure in school, but it began his embrace of the streets, leading eventually to his pathway to prison.

Kings: Abuse, Group Homes, and Tragedies

While most of the narratives of abuse centered on female experiences, there were several examples among the males who had personal histories in which they sustained extreme forms of emotional and physical harm from one or both parents, and even from their legal guardians. Below, King H. recalls this period of his life, in which he tells of being victimized by his mother's drug abuse:

Interviewer: OK. Was there a lot of violence in these places?

King H.: Yeah. My mom used to abuse me when I was like 8, 7. You know, my mom was a real creep, you know?, cuz she had me when she was 15 years old. My father was 30 years old and my mom used to abuse me for no reason, she used to use drugs, and, you know, she never give me no love, so I had a lot of struggle. But my life now is like it's all right. I just maintain it [Interview, 6/2/1998].

King P., on the other hand, just remembers the "beatings" by his father for reasons he had difficulty discerning:

L.B.: Let's talk a little more about your relationship with your parents. What kind of relationship did you have with your father?

King P.: My father, I don't have a relationship with him. Uh, we can get along for one day, the second day I wanna put a knife in his throat. It's that serious.

L.B.: So what does he do that gets you into . . .?

King P.: I used to get my ass kicked every day. Every single day that I remember being with him I used to get hit.

L.B.: So he was abusing you?

King P.: Yeah, a lot of physical abuse.

L.B.: Why do you think he was abusing you?

King P.: The abuse always stemmed around school until I was like 12 years old. I was doing fine in school. I passed all my classes and I still used to get my ass kicked. That time that I went back to Pennsylvania, that short time, that's when my mother passed away and he didn't even inform me [Interview, 6/2/1998].

But abuse can also come in the form of bureaucratic social service agencies designed to protect children and keep their families together. King S. and his siblings had already gone through a series of traumatic and damaging experiences with the sudden incapacitation of his mother caused by an auto accident (she was a pedestrian) and his father's conviction on drug charges, when the state intervened:

King S.: They took me away cuz my dad couldn't take care of us and my mom couldn't take care of us. So it was very bad. It was a bad time. It was like in the late '70s. It was very bad.

D.B.: Did you stay together with your brother and sister?

King S.: Well, that's how the judge put it on paper, not for us to be separated, but everything doesn't work out like they put it out to be, you know?

D.B.: What happened?

King S.: We went to a group home and the group home was gonna be turned into a place for the state, for rich people who have money and are invalids, so they started transferring people out and they put us in foster care. They put all of us in foster care. But I had a temporary father that he works for the Supreme Court in the Bronx. A Puerto Rican, one of these Puerto Ricans, one of these, you know, and then the mother was from England. He wanted me to call his wife "mother" and stuff, and then her sons . . . one guy was a bounty hunter in Fishkill, another one was a state trooper in Newburgh, and all this. So they was big-shots to the law. . . . They used to abuse me. They used to like beat me up, I mean, handcuffed to a radiator, I mean, tortured, you know. When I was a kid, I mean, I've been through a lot [Interview, 10/1/1998].

Queens: In Search of Security, Safety, and Support

In concurrence with much of the literature (see Brotherton and Salazar 2003; Hunt, McKenzie, and Laidler-Joe 2000; Miller 2001), many of the females joined the ALKQN after experiences related to their past and present immediate family, which often included different forms of intrafamily physical and psychological abuse. However, unlike what is reported in almost all the gang literature, most of the respondents found they could not escape their involvement in this cycle of violence (Widom 1998) until they encountered the Nation, which for them became the only social mechanism and strategy for ending years of victimization. Below, beginning with the search for security, safety, and support, we describe five themes that ran through the female respondents' motives for membership.

Many of the respondents spoke of suffering violence from either one or both parents, uncles, brothers, foster parents, guardians, spouses, and/or boyfriends. A number of the parents who beat their children were drug and/or alcohol addicted, and the beatings would come when the parent was mostly "high." Sometimes the beatings from the men would be part of a pattern of sexual abuse. The women reported that they had few options to stop these assaults unless a state agency intervened and at least six of the respondents talked of being removed from the parental home as a child or as an adolescent. In the following, Queen F. describes being physically abused by both her guardians:

C.S.: How about your uncle? You don't have any conflicts with him any more?

Queen F.: No, because, see, my little sister ran away. She's a runaway. They're lookin for her. We don't have contact cuz the last time I seen him he tried to hit me cuz he was running after my sister tryin to get my sister and the reason why we don't have contact with each other is because I went and I told the social worker that he used to hit me, his boyfriend used to hit me, and the boyfriend used to try to get fresh with me, so I told her and that's why we don't have contact with each other [Interview, 7/1/1998].

In many cases, the beatings only stopped when the subject encountered members of the Nation who assured her that the organization could be relied upon for support in the form of a refuge and sometimes physical intervention. Below, Queen R. remembers how she first crossed paths with the Latin Kings in California:

Interviewer: I wanna talk to you about the organization that you're currently a member of. How did you learn about it?

Queen R.: The Nation? I didn't really learn about it, the Nation saved my life
. . . almost 12 years ago. I was married at the age of 12, OK? And my
husband was chosen for me so it wasn't the right choice. For 10 years I
took abuse, beatings, insults, and I had 4 kids. One day on the beach, my
husband came back because his mistress had left him and that's the only
time I was ever happy, when he had a mistress, he wouldn't hit me. He
came by, he took an aluminum baseball bat, broke all my ribs, both my
legs, my arm, and he was ready to strike on my head when a Latin King
stepped in and said, "You hit her again and we're gonna give it to you to
see how you like it." You know? A while after that, my husband passed
away. He had a truck accident and uh, I was a mass of nothing. I don't
even consider myself at that time a human, you know? Cuz if you would
speak a little loud to me, I was already ducking and covering myself cuz
I thought you were gonna hit me. You know? They made me what I am
today. I could withstand everything and anything God dishes up to me
today. That was when I came to my Nation [Interview, 5/2/1998].

Queens: An Alternative to Rejection and Abandonment

So many parents not only beat their children, they rejected and abandoned
them as well. The act of abandonment seemed to come mainly from mothers who were going through the traumas of addiction to crack and/or heroin.

C.S.: Who took you away?

Queen B.: BCW [the Bureau of Child Welfare]. I didn't really see my mom
a lot. I wouldn't see my mom for like periods of two years each. Um . . .
then she came around when I was about eleven. She had my other little
sister. They took her away from her and she still hasn't lived with my
mom, my little sister. She stays with my aunt. Then my mom got drugs
four years ago and from drugs she jumped a guy and it's like guys are just
like drugs. I was always second, left home alone to take care of the kids
again, you know, and she basically did this till about January when I got
fed up of it. I'm basically the mother and she's the child and I don't feel
like bein a mother to nobody cuz I don't have to be and I gave her hell.
I gave her a little bit taste of her medicine, how she felt. She couldn't handle it so she moved out the house and left me for like three or four
months without paying rent. She didn't give me money for food, she

didn't give me money for clothes. The last time I went clothes shopping was two years ago and her ex-boyfriend bought me clothes. She never gave me money for anything [Interview, 7/3/1998].

If the mothers were often guilty of abandoning or neglecting their children, then the fathers were primarily responsible for rejecting their offspring, sometimes simply because they were girls and not boys. Queen F., below, is one of five respondents who spoke of fathers who openly denied their parenthood:

C.S.: How about, like you say, you have no contact with your dad, but you know who he is. How come? Is he the dad to all the other sisters, too?

Queen F.: No. Because my mother told me he just didn't want me cuz I was a girl, I heard, and then I heard that he didn't want me, he told my mother that if she had me he was gonna kick her stomach and not have me and she gave birth to me and ever since then, like when I was 12, he told me, "You're not my daughter," and I was like, "I know," and I just kept on walking. I mean, I know that's my father, but he's denied me [Interview, 7/1/1998].

Queens: Seeking Independence

All the females wanted some form of increased autonomy in their lives, as noted in the literature (Brotherton 1996a; Joe and Chesney-Lind 1995). They wanted to be (1) rid of their family's restrictive ties on their social lives and on their sexuality; (2) free of abusive relationships and of disrespectful men in general; and (3) "somebody" through continuing their education and eventually choosing a career beyond the options normally reserved for children of the barrio. Queen A. and Queen F., below, respond to questions on their home life and leave no doubt about the clash between parents who tried to enforce the gendered family traditions of the "island" and the more liberal approaches to the urban family in New York:

Queen A.: I was always home. Always home. I guess, the way my mother brought me up, it was the women who have to stay in the house. . . . Most of the time always home, home, home, helping my mom. . . . I didn't have many friends, girlfriends no. . . . Then I met the Nation I got involved by my ex-husband, he mainly got me involved first [Interview, 11/1/1998].

Queen F.: I had a lot of rules and regulations. I could never go outside, I could never have a boyfriend, I could never be with my friends, or noth-in'. I would just have to come home, do my homework, eat, take a shower, and then go to bed and then go to school the next day [Interview, 1/15/1998].

Queens: The Surrogate Family

The literature notes that in certain cases, females, particularly at the beginning of their gang tenure, can view the group as a replacement family. Certainly, the Nation in its manifesto and prayers constantly refers to itself as a greater Latino family that provides unconditional love and acceptance to those who are privileged to become members, and this same sentiment was reflected in many of the respondents' retorts:

C.S.: What does family mean to you?

Queen S.: All my Latin King/Queen Nation.

C.S.: And how do you define that?

Queen S.: Beautiful. Love, respect, I'm treated like gold, you know, like I should've been treated, you know? That's my life. You know, if I fall they're there to pick me up. They raised me, you know? I grew up in it [Interview, 6/3/1998].

There are few reports in the literature of cases where older members of a group both formally and informally adopt young females who have been victimized or abandoned by their kin. Yet this practice was not at all uncommon in the ALKQN (we should also add that some older females also adopted younger males).

C.S.: Are you closer to your mother or your father?

Queen B.: Um, see, I'm a daddy's little girl cuz I have so much hate for my mom. Not hate, but she put me through so much shit it's like everybody want me to swallow it and I just can't. I've been swallowin' it for too many years, and I'm a daddy's little girl, but I never had a daddy. That's where King Step comes in. Now I'm a daddy's little girl cuz that's my daddy.

Queen S.: I have a father through the Nation, you know? He adopted me through the court system. That's when I first joined the Nation and I was in trouble with the law and they helped me out big time, you know? They would always help me when I had a problem with my boyfriend. They was always there for me. It was just a family to me before I came in [Interview, 3/10/1998].

Queens: The Complementary Family

Much of the gang-intervention literature paints the gang-family connection in highly simplistic and alarmist terms (Hunt, McKenzie, and Laidler-Joe 2000), portraying persons who join gangs as virtually severing their bonds to anything approaching a normative family life. This was not at all the case with most of the respondents, however, who emphasized repeatedly that the Nation-family nexus was complex, flexible, and subject to change over time. Certainly, as we have noted, when the member came from a particularly destructive family background the Nation played a surrogate family role, but for those members who came into the Nation from high-functioning and cohesive family backgrounds it was a different picture.

C.S.: What does family mean to you?

Queen F.: Now? I mean, since I've been in the Nation family means a lot to me, but my mother and my sisters they mean the world. They mean the world. My mother and my sister, but the Nation, they mean the world to me, too. I mean, I love the Nation to death [Interview, 6/1/1998].

In other words, often the family-Nation relationship was quite complementary for female members, and several leaders reported working diligently with parents to get their children back into school and/or to bring more discipline and social control into their lives (e.g., imposing 10 p.m. curfews on young female members during weekdays). Since Nation members under eighteen had to get their parents' permission to join the group, it can be understood why the organization could have had a much more open, reciprocal, and supportive relationship with a member's family than is assumed by many outside the group.

School Life

In most studies of gangs, the role of school is described as peripheral (Monti 1994; Decker and Van Winkle 1996) even though it is one of the few social institutions (along with the criminal justice system) that gang members continue to be involved in. Reasons for the lack of involvement by gang students vary, but most criminologists agree that life in a gang competes directly with the time, energy, focus, and commitment needed for a successful school career. There are few exceptions to this line of reasoning, and most orthodox criminological findings, based on inquiries into gang members' "attitudes" and "orientations," continue to draw this conclusion. At the same time, more theoretical and critical approaches to the gang-school relationship have pointed to other explanations inherent in the institution itself, e.g., its "whiteness" (Fordham 1996); the middle-class nature of its dominant value system; its restrictive and conformist rules and norms (Cohen 1955); and the bureaucratic practice of excluding youth because of their potential for contestation (Fine 1991). Based on our data, however, subjects described their relationships to school along a broad continuum of experiences, ranging from high levels of engagement with teachers, fellow students, and the institution to deep feelings of estrangement and alienation from the educational process. Such a variation underscores: (1) that the worlds of school and of the street are not necessarily mutually exclusive and that there is often a subtle dialectical interplay between them, and (2) the "habitus" (Bourdieu and Passeron 1977) of street youth is often a complexly constituted set of dispositions that is masked by performances and rituals required of the street environment. In the following, subjects discuss their educational history, shedding light on a range of institutional, social, and pedagogical processes, many of which were experienced as obstacles to a satisfactory and successful school career.

"There's Only a Handful of Teachers Who Really Care"

A frequent complaint of respondents, both those currently attending school and those who were simply remembering their school years, was that positive, long-term relationships with teachers rarely occurred. In fact, when respondents (six of them) could recall such relationships, the role of the teacher was almost always as a pillar of social support rather than as an intellectual mentor. When respondents were asked if they felt that the school "cared" about them and their education, the response was mixed, with some saying that the schools did their best given the difficulties of teaching in the ghetto or barrio, while others blamed the schools for a variety of ills, including bureaucratic tyranny, mismanagement, and racial discrimination. One respondent, Queen J., who was considered a high achiever before the pressures of her family and her peers derailed her school career, offered the following carefully formulated response that summed up a number of similar views.

C.S.: Do you think the school cared if you did well or not?

Queen J.: You know, I don't really know. It's sometimes you think that they do, but then some of the things they do, like they don't take enough time, I know that it's not their fault. There's no money in the budget for them to take more time out for all the students, but I think that when you're teaching kids it shouldn't be about money, it should be about teaching them. So what if you work three extra hours and you don't get paid for it, I know that money makes the world go around, but they're kids and they have to grow up in this society and I believe if more people just took time out of their time and they showed these kids, "Look, I don't get paid to do this," the kids would think they actually care and they would be more inclined to stay in school [Interview, 11/6/1998].

"I Was a Well-Rounded Student"

There was a sizable number of respondents (ten) who reported that they had been diligent, mainstream students and participated in a variety of student activities.

C.S.: What kind of student were you?

Queen M.: A well-rounded student to a point where I went to school, I did sports, cheer-leading, rallies, to school spirit, to goin' on trips, to doin' community service, to workin', to goin' home, takin' care of business at home. I was very well-rounded. I mean, things changed now, because it wasn't the same as it was before, cuz I wanna finish school [Interview, 8/2/1998].

But of these, only three stated that they continued to do well through their high school years. The other seven admitted that in their teenage years their student careers declined abruptly and that this was partly due to: the influence of their peers (e.g., street gangs); myriad family pressures and crises, such as caring for sick or dying parents; personal crises, such as early pregnancy and/or entering the criminal justice system; and a general disillusionment with schooling itself. However, it is worth noting that none of these subjects made any connection between their present-day membership in the ALKQN and their deteriorating school performance, a sharp contrast to other studies in which gang members are usually quite frank about this clash of commitments (see, for example, Monti 1994; Decker and Van Winkle 1996). Rather, most interviewees reported that their membership in the group made them reappraise their past behavior and forced them to reconsider the factors that led to their "lost opportunities."

"You Go to All-Minority Schools and Then You Go Upstate"

A number of respondents described racist experiences during their school careers. Some spoke of demeaning remarks uttered by teachers—for example, being called a "spic" and/or "a dumb Puerto Rican" was remembered by seven respondents, while others openly wondered why all the schools they attended were populated almost exclusively by blacks and Latinos/as. A number of respondents, however, had experienced education in a range of settings, including inner-city and suburban school districts—what some respondents referred to as "upstate"—and could see the vast differences in expectations both academically and socially.

> C.S.: Did you ever encounter racism in school?
>
> Queen M.: No. Well, the school I went to was basically made up of Dominicans and Puerto Ricans and if you was half of somethin', either half black, half Dominican, half of somethin' so we all understood even though we was half and half, we understood that we were all Latinos. We were there for one thing, so we really didn't have any racism in the school.
>
> C.S.: How about upstate?
>
> Queen M.: Upstate? Yeah! Woooo! Yeah! To a point where the white people and that used to be like, "Oh, you spic," or "Oh, you yanjito," or "Oh, you Mexican," you know, it used to come to that point, or "You nigger," things like that, but it was to a point where it just flow over our heads like, "Whatever. I might be a spic, but you're a honky," you know what I'm sayin'? It was like that, but that's just the way it is upstate. People stick with this, people stick with that, but it's not like everybody's like that. . . . Other than that, a lot of the Spanish guys wouldn't go out with black girls. Why? Because they were black and a lot of the white guys, they didn't want the black girls . . . it was just preference up there. That's what it was, but not everybody was like that, but it is a big difference between up there and down here [Interview with Queen M., 5/2/1998].

"When Is Our Culture Going to Matter?"

Many respondents complained about the ethnocentrism of the curriculum and the lack of teachers to whom they could socially and culturally relate. More than thirty years after the upheavals of the civil rights movement, it is startling to hear respondents complain about the class and cultural divide as if we were living under some invisible form of the Jim Crow syndrome.

> C.S.: When you went to school you felt like you came from a different culture than the one they were teaching at school in history?
>
> Queen G.: Yeah.
>
> C.S.: In what way?
>
> Queen G.: It's hard to explain because my first teacher, like my kindergarten teacher, she's Puerto Rican. She would teach me a lot of things. We would do like Bachatas [a form of popular Dominican dance music] . . . we had dance classes and all that and she would teach us about Spanish heritage and our heritage, so I liked that class. But once I started going into the first grade and all that, it was OK with the students because I had students that were like me, Spanish or black with minorities, but the teacher was white, so she wouldn't teach us, you know what I'm sayin'? She wouldn't understand where we came from, you know, like talking about homes or projects. See, she came from a rich neighborhood like Long Island or something like that, you know, so sometimes it was difficult to communicate with that teacher [Interview, 3/2/1998].
>
> Interviewer: What subjects in school do you like?
>
> King P. (a Pee Wee): Basically, science and history. But really, I don't like history because all they teach is about white culture. I like to know about my own culture and that's why I came here [to the Pee Wees] [Interview, 4/1/1997].[3]

Like King P., above, Queen G. also went on to describe her frustration with the omission of her cultural heritage from the curriculum. It is noteworthy that so many Kings and Queens saw history as their favorite subject and considered it incumbent upon them to resist the official version, contesting what many of them saw as the Achilles heel of the dominant culture:

> C.S.: It's interesting because you say you like history, but still it wasn't the history you wanted.

Queen G.: Right. No, I liked history, but it wasn't the history I wanted to learn, only because I didn't know about history till I got here to the Nation, you know what I'm sayin'? We got culture classes and I learned a lot. You know, I learned things in Puerto Rico, but I learned a lot here, you understand? So now that I know what our history is about, I think about it, because before that I liked that history, you know? I liked to learn about the Revolution, the wars, and all that. It's good to know about our history in America, cuz I'm still an American, you understand? But I'm also Latina, so I have to learn about my culture. At that time I loved history. To this day I still love history, you understand? But it wasn't our history, what I wanted to learn, you know? It was what they wanted to teach us. You never see a social studies book right there that says about Spanish or Latino history, you know, all it says is about the Revolutionary War, black slaves, and, you know, things like that. That's all you learn [Interview, 6/2/1998].

"How Do You Focus on School and Block Out the Pain?"

We have already discussed the deep levels of psychic and emotional pain that came as a result of physical and sexual abuse, premature deaths of close family members, parental neglect and abandonment, and the trauma of living in high-risk environments. Yet the resiliency of youth who come from highly marginalized subpopulations is rarely appreciated in the "delinquency" literature, even though one of the first things that teachers working "on the front lines" explain to outsiders is the context of their students' lives. Queen S., below, puts a stage of her learning experience in this context:

D.B.: Now what was going on in school all this time? I mean, how were you getting on in school? Was it affecting you?

Queen S.: In school it was affecting me very much because I was lied to saying my family was my biological family, my father and mother would never be able to get me back, um, we would never see my father again. I mean, what's a kid supposed to do at this kind of an age. I mean, how can you study and, um, focus on what's the future gonna be? [Interview, 12/1/1997]

"School Was Somewhere to Hang Out or Run Away From"

A good number of the respondents are like many other youths from fractured working-class backgrounds where low levels of social and cultural capital are the norm and failure or refusal to see oneself as a stake-holder in low-tier, tracked institutions is inevitable and rather rational (Willis 1977; McLeod 1995; Oakes 1985). Consequently, since the state has long made school attendance compulsory, this institutional site often becomes used purely for socializing with peers, drug experimentation, and flouting the adults' rules. King S., below, describes the inconsequential role of school during his teenage years, a time during which his mother had abandoned the family, his single-parent father was imprisoned for two years, and he and his two siblings were placed in a group home:

> D.B.: When you think back on school, was it good times, was it bad times, or was it times you don't wanna think about?

> King S.: School, well, school, to me, like when I was a teenager and goin' to East Side High School in Patterson, school was to me like a hangout. It was like to get dusted. At that time dust [PCP] was the thing, so I was introduced to dust and then glue, you know. I didn't really get into the crack and the dope cuz I didn't go that route . . . I did my share of drugs in the past, you know, whichever was the drugs that was movin' at that time [Interview, 8/2/1998].

Sometimes, however, the school is simply a part of the "system," a place to avoid and escape from along with the panoply of social control agents and family members who try to stop those who are "always running" (Rodríguez 1994):

> D.B.: How old were you when you stopped going to school?

> King V.: Thirteen.

> D.B.: So you dropped out completely?

> King V.: In high school.

> D.B.: Did they try to bring you back?

> King V.: Basically I used to go to school [leave the house] and I never went, so my mother never knew if I went to school or not. . . . I was claiming I go to school [near his home in Brooklyn] but I was livin' in the Bronx [Interview, 2/3/1998].

Street Life

Since street adolescents often drift from one subculture to another as neighborhood styles and collective youth behaviors change over time, then we would expect a sizable percentage of the respondents, particularly the males, to have had prior membership in street gangs, cliques, and posses during the 1990s, 1980s, and, for the older ones, the 1970s. Of the sixty-seven interviewed, fifteen males and ten females described quite extensive histories with other groups, sixteen males and fourteen females categorically stated that they had not been associated with any other street subculture in the past, and the rest spoke of some vague associations where they were peripherally involved.

Similarly, with drugs and crime, some respondents described having substantial rap sheets while others had no history of contact with the criminal justice system at all. The issue with drugs was a little more complex. Among male respondents, eighteen reported having been involved in the use of hard drugs on a regular basis (six with crack cocaine, four with heroin, two with alcohol, and six with multiple drugs including alcohol), while the rest (twenty-one) stated that they had relatively little experience with drugs except for some experimentation with marijuana and the occasional beer. For females, the picture was quite similar: ten reported sustained use of hard drugs in the past, six revealed addictions to crack cocaine, and two each had problems with heroin and with alcohol. At the same time, nineteen reported little drug use in the past or present, although smoking marijuana was not considered a particularly deviant practice, and at least half of this number of "abstainers" imbibed in this "soft" drug on social occasions.

Gangs

Gangs served as peer groups in the teenage lives of almost all the respondents. That is not to say that they all joined a gang as a youth, even though most of them did, but gangs were present in their neighborhoods, their families, their schools, and, of course, during their time spent in juvenile detention and/or prison. But what form did the gangs take? And how did they experience them? Below, we divide the subtheme of gangs into the various distinctions that the respondents themselves made.

Turf Gangs

The Bachelors were a force to be reckoned with. Basically they ran the South Bronx. We always respected the Bronx as far as boundaries go, you wouldn't step into their territory but when they would try coming over the bridge it was on, you know. We had to do what we had to do to defend ourselves. What they were trying to do was to come in and take over. You know, eliminate the Kings, the Aces, and the Saints, to make them Bachelors, Savage Skulls, or Nomads because they were all cliqued together up there in the Bronx [Interview with King H., 9/2/1997].

Older respondents—in their late thirties—were almost alone in telling about gangs whose primary raison d'etre was to demarcate and defend symbolic territories in the ghettos and barrios of New York City.[4] By the mid-1980s such gangs largely ceased to exist and many of the veterans from this era either matured out of the subculture, entered mainstream life, spent many years incarcerated, and/or led stunted lives due to the impact of drug abuse, primarily heroin addiction.

Cliques

D.B.: Remember the names?

King F.: You had Atom Boys, Hit Men, um, Rough Kids, Smith Boys, you had The Wild Boys, you had MMC, Money Making Crew, CBS, Can't Be Stopped, you know, you had a lot of crews. And it's like everybody had their own blocks, so if I lived on 7th Street, I couldn't walk to 8th Street, I couldn't walk to 6th Street, I couldn't walk anywhere. I had to walk straight towards the Village to try to get away from my own neighborhood, you know? It was bad.

D.B.: Were you in the crew at that point?

King F.: At that time I was in 2 little gangs, you know what I mean? One was PHO, Puttin Heads Out. You know, I think about it now, and it makes me laugh, you know? The other one was SBD, which was a pretty big crew, Silent But Deadly, you know?

D.B.: How old were you back then?

King F.: How old was I? I was like 11 or 12 [Interview, 7/2/1998].

The respondents who spoke of their experience of cliques were mainly in their mid- to late twenties, and they are referring to their teenage years during the 1980s. As King F., above, articulates, they grew up in areas of New York City such as the Lower East Side, the South Bronx, Washington Heights, Spanish Harlem, and East New York, where gangs had been active since World War II, changing in form, ethnicity, and style with each new generation. The cliques were simply the more youthful, ephemeral, and spontaneous versions of the older gangs that many of these youths would normally later join. However, in the late 1980s, the crack epidemic had an extraordinary impact on these already poor, working-class neighborhoods where gangs had long been a symptom of collective marginality. Crack effectively helped to dismantle the social cohesion of a whole generation through its promotion of violently competitive illicit drug markets, its dramatic and debilitating effects on those who used, and its contribution to the criminalization of an entire social class (Bourgois 1995; Fagan 1996; Lausanne 1994; Reinarman and Levine 1995). In other words, many respondents who were members of cliques later became heavily involved in both the sale and use of drugs (primarily crack but also heroin) at a time when traditional, turf-bound street gangs barely existed (in contrast to the rest of the country). Thus, the next time these respondents joined a collectively organized street subculture was when they encountered the Nation.

Mixed-gender Gangs

Several of the Queens revealed that they too had previous careers in street gangs and cliques, and a number had participated in gender-integrated gangs at the same level as their male counterparts. While relatively little has been written about the involvement of New York City females in the street gang culture (see Campbell 1984; Brotherton and Salazar 2003; Fishman 1995), we found in the testimonies of these gang-involved female respondents a remarkably high level of participation in all aspects of gang life—to the extent that it was often life-threatening.

> C.S.: So that was when you were in La Familia, too?
>
> Queen J.: Yeah. I did a lot. Most of my criminal activity I did with La Familia. I used to beat people up, I sold drugs, I stabbed people, I would stay out late, I mean, I did everything possible to defy society just to say I wasn't gonna if they wouldn't accept me the way I thought I should be, then I wouldn't accept them the way they were [Interview, 4/3/1998].

From Social Control Gangs to Hip-Hop Street Cultures

In the late 1980s, street performance groups based on early rap music, break-dancing, and street vigilante patrols began to proliferate. The most famous of these was the Zulu Nation, founded by Afrika Bambaataa, whose influence in the Bronx soon spread throughout the city, becoming a movement to be emulated nationally and internationally. A number of the older male respondents spoke of their involvement in this explosive era of interconnected street subcultures and street scenes.[5] King S., below, vividly recalls this period of his life before he entered the prison system in the early 1990s to become an enforcer of the early Latin Kings.

> D.B.: So you left the Angels to join the Bishops. Did you have a lot of jackets with the name of the group?

King S.: Young Bishops, yeah. sometimes we had shirts with the *Playboy* rabbit, and then, later on after that, um, I left that gang. I wasn't with that.
Gang leaders was goin' to jail, dyin' and stuff, I started seeing that it was-
n't goin' nowhere, so then when Bambaataa introduced the Zulu Nation,
the founder in New York City of the Zulus (he came out of a gang called
The Black Spades in the Bronx), I was a Zulu member. I was a Shaka
Zulu and that's when we used to go to The Roxy and break-dance and
stuff like that. We used to break-dance for our problems, you know. All
our problems with the groups and gangs, so we used to break-dance and
I was a break-dancer [Interview, 8/2/1998].

Drugs

Of the male respondents, eighteen reported heavy use of hard drugs (including crack, cocaine, heroin, PCP, and glue) in the past and five reported moderate use, with the rest of the sample, roughly 40 percent, reporting little or
no use of drugs either in the past or the present. In contrast, eight of the females revealed they were heavy drug users in the past and two described their
drug habits as "moderate." Therefore, while the majority of the Kings in the
sample described themselves as heavy-to-moderate users, a minority of the
Queens placed themselves in the same categories. Consequently, many members alluded to the fact that they were "in recovery," although they would
never use such professional, therapeutic terminology.

In the interviews, however, the Kings were much more revealing about
their drug experiences than the Queens, almost a reversal of what we found
in pursuing questions about the family. The discussions focused on the path-
ways into hard drug use, the reasons for continuing to use and abuse drugs,
and the experience of addiction.

Getting High and Peer Culture

Many of the subjects, primarily the males, talked about their drug experiences
as teenagers, and eight of them revealed that they had started to use drugs as
early as ten years old (mainly marijuana and alcohol). One respondent tried
marijuana at the age of five, stealing "roaches" from her mother's drug inven-
tory! So how did respondents get introduced to drugs? Despite about fifteen
respondents describing their parents as moderate-to-heavy users of hard
drugs, and despite many respondents reporting a range of family members involved in consistent alcohol and hard-drug use, the majority were introduced
to drugs through their peer culture.

D.B.: Now, when you talk about doing drugs as a teenager, getting dusted, who was introducing you to the drugs?

King S.: Who introduced me to drugs? Um, other kids.

D.B.: Other kids.

King S.: Like teenage. You know, you hang out and, "Hey, go and get high, you forget about your problems."

D.B.: And that's. . . .

King S.: Peer pressure introduced me to drugs.

D.B.: Right, and PCP was the thing at that time, or . . .?

King S.: PCP, um, dust in the time that the Vietnamese, Vietnam people was comin' back from war so they was, there was just drugs all over the place. It was all types of drugs [Interview, 8/2/1998].

Escapism and Self-Medication

Throughout the self-reports about hard-drug use, both Kings and Queens often placed their drug habit in the context of coping with extreme levels of anguish and psychological turmoil. Thus, while hedonism and experimentation were one reason to first experiment with drugs, it was depression and other psychological distress that compounded their use and led them into cycles of abuse.

D.B.: You were escaping, really, from life and numbing yourself, right?

King F.: Well, it was like back then I was a very depressed person, you know? The first time, losing my father, depressed me. I didn't even know how to deal with it. I was young, I had nobody to talk to . . . it was depressive, you know? The drugs was to numb the pain, you know? The second time, basically the same thing, depression. I needed somethin' to numb the mind, to forget about my problems, which never works, but that's the way I thought. Now I'm back again on the streets and I know that's not gonna work no more. Ain't nothing gonna numb the pain. I have to deal with it in the surface or something, you know, something gotta give. So I know that now. I know now what I didn't know back then and it took prison to learn that. Somethin' that I knew school wasn't gonna teach me. I mean, I can read a lot of textbooks, cuz I was in college for a year and a half when I was young. You know what I mean? And I didn't learn in college or in high school what I've learned in jail. You know, because you're learning it first-hand, you know, from the guys who've been doin' it for 25, 30 years, or from just reading, taking that time to actually read [Interview, 10/1/1998].

Rarely did respondents speak of receiving any form of professional psychological therapy or counseling in civilian life (although several Queens reported being engaged in family therapy through their mothers), despite the obvious need in many respondents' lives[6] for some kind of mental health intervention. This leaves prison, ironically, as the primary institution where resource-poor individuals such as those in the sample received a modicum of help through the underfunded detox programs of the correctional system. In addition, "treatment" came in the form of advice from other knowledgeable inmates and the "cold turkey" of enforced isolation.

L.B.: And you started using drugs in . . .?

King J.: I started usin' drugs at 22 and then I started using drugs so bad that I was livin' in the street, I ate off the street, I took a shower in the street, I did everything in the street. It was like I wasn't home no more and it was like that for almost like a year until I got busted, really. When I got busted it's like you know how they say, " . . .at least they took you off the street. Now you could survive again." Well, yeah, that's what happened.

Fighting Addiction

King J., above, like King Tone (chapter 6) expresses what it was like to sink to the depths of addiction. It is difficult to arrive at an accurate number, but we estimate that almost a third of the sample had engaged in some form of prolonged substance abuse. As mentioned earlier, it was mainly the Kings who spoke at any length about this period in their lives, and usually they recounted: (1) the way the drug worked to destroy them economically, emotionally, socially, and physically; (2) the extreme difficulty of kicking the habit and leaving the drug subculture; and (3) how membership in the ALKQN was instrumental in helping their "recovery." Below, King H. describes another aspect of addiction: the contradictory highs and lows that characterize mood-enhancing and mind-altering substances and the complete loss of sequential time.

King H.: Yeah, it was heroin, heroin at that late age. I managed to avoid it all those years and then I started and I kid you not I loved that hit, till this day. I'm not gonna be like one of these ex-addicts that says I hate it when

I think about it. Nah, I loved it, it was warm, it enhanced my sex life. I don't care what they say, it enhanced my sex life cause I was numb. I couldn't feel nothing. I had maximum control, I be there for eight hours. Sometimes I even come. So, it gave me a sense of power and I just didn't care about the world. I thought that nobody could notice that I was nodding out and vomiting and my eyes are like this, and then I woke up.

D.B.: How long did it take you?

King H.: Ten years [Interview, 9/2/1997].

Crime

Nearly all the respondents discussed their first-hand experience of crime even if they had never entered the criminal justice system. For most, therefore, crime was a cultural property of the community (Shaw and McKay 1969; Sullivan 1989), i.e., an informal economic practice and "way of life" encountered in the "numbers" rackets on the street corner, in the money-laundering practices at the local bodega, in the drug-dealing interactions in front of (and sometimes in) their homes, and in the shifting life circumstances of myriad family members who always seemed to be somewhere between home and "the joint."

Those that had been heavily involved in "the system" had spent a good portion of their lives as "career criminals," engaged for the most part in the sale and distribution of drugs (primarily crack and heroin), but also in such pursuits as "stick-ups," receiving and selling stolen goods, car-jacking, bank-robbery, extortion, and fraud. For all the time the ex-felons had spent in prison and for all the various psychological and physical wounds they had suffered and/or meted out, none of them could claim that their criminal endeavors had left them with much of a profit. In fact, the lament from nearly all such respondents was that they had squandered their educational and legitimate work opportunities in the pursuit of "fast money" and instant gratification. Further, they would have to spend the rest of their lives repairing the damage both to themselves and to others. In the following, we have highlighted just a few of the most popular themes disclosed through our interviews.

"Taking What's Ours"

Not all the respondents who grew up around criminal activity actually engaged in it. More than a third of the sample had no criminal record, and by most accounts they did not have a deviant past. Their attraction to the group was based more on identity issues and the search for a dynamic collectivity. Nonetheless, for those who had grown up in extreme poverty and who had spent significant periods of their youth on the streets, the criminal life was a way to survive and to acquire the goods and money that spell success (or normalcy) in contemporary capitalist culture, even though this criminal lifestyle directly contradicted the moral value system of their parents, particularly their mothers.

> Interviewer: Who were you hooking up with back then?

> King R.: OK, back then, in the late '70s, in '77 was when I started. I was a good 11, 10 years old. I hooked up with this gang called The Little Wild Boys. The Little Wild Boys come from the Lower East Side and they used to hang out right there in 8th Street and Avenue D and it was a street gang, a hoodlum gang. I mean, we did everything, we robbed, we stole, we did whatever we had to do to survive out there . . . but . . . I was always raised to respect people . . . I'm like my mother. I always look out for those before I look out for myself, but when I started getting into the streets it's like I forgot about that. I forgot about what my parents and my mother taught me when I was younger. All I knew how to do is survive on the streets and move on for the next day and the next day. At that time my mother couldn't buy me a pair of sneakers so I would go out there and sell drugs and buy my own sneakers. I learned how to depend on myself at a young age, but I just did it the negative way, instead of doing it the positive way, the way my father did it [King R., 7/28/1998].

"What Else Was I Supposed to Do?"

While many respondents came from quite mainstream families, others were born into a criminal culture and faced great difficulties in reconciling the values and activities of school life with the environment of their home. King D., below, describes having to make sense of these oppositional worlds before he eventually succumbed to criminal deviance rather than accepting the school environment. Prior to his high school years (he dropped out in the tenth grade) he had been a very capable student, excelling in reading and writing; in his words, he "loved" the institution.

> J.E.: While growing up did you think that the values you learned in school conflicted with those you learned at home?

> King D.B.: Yeah, very much. Like I tell you, when I already turned 12 years old and we was livin' with my stepfather they contradicted a lot cuz

school told me to get educated so I could uplift myself, but when I used to get home I had to go cut drugs and I had to bag up dope and stuff like that. I would get a different perspective. It was like, "You should become a good drug dealer. You don't have to learn nothin' in school." So, yes, it did contradict itself.

"And the Females Could Muscle in Too"

While most of the female members were not involved in criminal activities at any time in their lives, a minority had participated significantly in different criminal subcultures. Queen J., below, was a very bright and resourceful young (eighteen-year-old) leader of the organization, and she had ambitions to become a public interest lawyer to fight for social justice issues on behalf of her community, even though she had dropped out of school in the tenth grade. However, as a teenager, this same drive and vision were put to another use on the streets as she told us of her exploits with the male-dominated drugs trade.

C.S.: And how do you own a spot?

Queen J.: Um, basically if the drug dealer's around the area you ask for their permission to stay. "OK, this is what I wanna sell here, this is how much I expect to come in. Can I?" If somebody else already owns a part of that area you probably have to pay them money to work there as well or you could just do like what a lot of drug dealers do, just fight about it. You shoot each other and kill, whatever head dies, the other one owns the spot, plus the other spot. But I never went through that. The guys who I was selling like around, knew that. . . . They really didn't think that at fourteen I could really own a spot, you know? So they let me. They were like, "Oh, yeah, go ahead," whatever, and they didn't realize how much money I pulled in until I started pulling it in and they were like, "OK, this little girl really knows what she is doing," you know? [Interview, 11/4/1998]

Violence

As we have already pointed out, violence for many of the respondents was endemic in their neighborhoods, schools, and families. Few could remember being raised in a violence-free environment—rather, the spectacle and drama of beatings, injuries, and even death were a normal part of everyday life, leaving deep psychological scars. Certainly, we felt that we were the first to ask most of the respondents about this aspect of their lives, and it was therefore not surprising that a number responded readily to our questions, talking graphically and freely about these repressed yet ever-present memories. At the same time, while most criminological and public health discourses focus on interpersonal violence, Salmi (1993) reminds us that the bulk of the violence we experience is structural and extremely impersonal, which he calls "indirect violence." This kind of violence, caused by the uneven distribution of wealth and power in society and leading to the denial of basic resources to masses of people, was cited by a range of respondents as the context for the violent culture that they had been exposed to.

"I Grew Up in a War Zone"

Ten respondents used the term "war zone" to describe the neighborhoods where they resided as children. When asked to picture these environments, they provided images of crowded tenements, day-to-day hardship, race-based conflicts among local youth (usually between Italians and Puerto Ricans or Puerto Ricans and African-Americans), and the constant exposure to drug dealing and other criminal activities. King I., below, gives a graphic example of how youth become inured to what should be one of the most sacrilegious of crimes, the taking of another person's life.

> King I.: It was like, you know, I'm 8 years old, and I'm seein' a lady get her head splattered all over the place and I'm like, "What's goin' on?" You know, I didn't even know how to react to that, but after that it became so common that I was like, "OK. Natural." You could actually go up to the guy, see him bleeding, he's dyin' or dead, and like, "Wow." You could just look at him and just like, just stare at him for hours like it's so interesting. You know what I mean? It's nothing new. It doesn't faze me to see somebody get killed because it's like you see it all your life, you know, living in a neighborhood like that [Interview, 12/6/1998].

"I Don't Like Fighting but . . ."

Naturally, growing up in such a risk-filled environment makes learning to fight a necessity. From their very earliest years, males learn how to throw a punch, duck and weave, "stick up for themselves," "not back down," and so forth, all strategies used to meet interpersonal conflict head on. This culture of fighting among boys from poor and working-class communities gets so ingrained into the everyday activities of the street that the best "fighters" among the males by the time they are in their teens have been in combat literally dozens of times and already have a reputation for "toughness." Sometimes, youths go beyond the culture of street fighting and get formally trained at a local gym—six of the males in the sample had been trained as boxers. But what about the females? Did they eschew fighting in favor of more "feminine" pursuits? Quite the contrary, most of the females had also grown up around and been inculcated with the values of the "fighting" culture, even if they expressed a dislike for it as an activity unto itself.

> C.S.: Why do you think you get into fights?

> Queen T.: I don't like fighting. I hate fighting, but when it comes down to me gonna fight, I'm gonna fight, you know what I'm saying? I don't like fighting. I'll be like I see a girl, I'll be like, "Bitch. What? You wanna fight?" like that. I don't like that. If a girl go up to me and hit me, I'm gonna beat the shit out of you, but if you calling me anything or "bitch" I'll be like, "Fuck you, too," you know? I ain't gonna go up to you and hit you. Once you comin' up to me that's different. . . . So I don't like fighting.

> C.: Did you learn how to fight on the street or did you go like to classes?

> Queen T.: I watched them by my sister beatin' the shit out of me. My sister used to beat the shit out of me [Interview, 9/1/1997].

What About Economic Violence?

Hand-in-hand with fighting went poverty as a characteristic that was powerfully present in the respondents' memories of neighborhood and family life, and a number had thought long and hard about this relationship. King D., below, takes on this issue at the beginning of the interview, as if he were trying to frame everything he would later disclose in the context of the political economy.

> J.E.: Is there a lot of violence in this neighborhood?

> King D.B.: Well, I could say this, as far as the violence it has slowed down a lot, yes, it has. . . . I've lived here ever since I was small and it has slowed down, but there's always violence. Either way you put it, when you have a place where the majority is not making that much money you're always gonna have violence. You got fathers that need to feed their kids and they

gonna feed them either which way they can and around here . . . this is a drug area and like I'm gonna tell you, as far as the violence, wherever there's drugs, there's violence.

J.E.: Has it affected your neighborhood or your immediate or extended family?

King D.B.: It affected me. It affected me ever since, wow! I could tell you ever since I was 12 years old. I started usin' drugs, you know, I was a heroin addict, I sell drugs, I got locked up for drugs . . . it affected my whole life. This whole community has affected my whole life, yes. If we're gonna come down to that simple question, it has affected my life, yes [Interview, 11/1/1998].

Prison Life

L.B.: Have you ever been in Rikers Island?

King J.: Many times. Forget it! I think I've been through the whole building. I was there when there was like three buildings. There was three buildings. Now it's like Fort Knox, right? Anywhere you go, man, it's like I've been all over Rikers Island.

L.B.: So what other prisons have you been in?

King J.: I think I've been all over upstate. Um, I've been to Armensborough[?],Washington, South Polk[?], Collins, Misty[?], MacGregor, um, Franklin, Sing Sing, Comstock, Clinton, Attica, Eastern Annex.

L.B.: How many years?

King J.: All together I did like 13 years. Yeah, I been through the whole building! [Interview, 5/16/1998]

As we have documented earlier, the links between prison and the ALKQN were evident on many different levels. The group was, after all, founded in the Collins Correctional Facility in 1986, and until the early 1990s most of its members were behind bars. Nonetheless, in the new Latin Kings and Queens, many if not most members had not been incarcerated, thus prison to them meant quite different things. For those who had experienced incarceration firsthand—which usually meant spending several years in a state and/or federal institution, often preceded by several months in New York City's pretrial facility, Rikers Island—it was often remembered as a life-changing event, one that they were still struggling to contend with and recover from. Quite understandably, none of these respondents wanted to repeat their prison experience, and one of the reasons for their present membership in the group was, contrary to the presumptions of most "outsiders," to keep them out of the system.

On the other hand, for those members who had never been incarcerated, prison was an institution they had visited to see friends or family members, and "ex-cons" deserved "respect" rather than scorn. At the same time, it was not a place that they treated lightly. We found few Pee Wees, for example, who relished the thought of doing time at "the rock" (as Rikers Island is known) as a way to attain more street status—an argument commonly found in texts on delinquents.

Experiencing Shame

A number of criminologists and sociologists have discussed the stigmatizing effect on human beings after they have been categorized and labeled by the system (e.g., Goffman 1963). There is no better example of this process than in publicly branding someone a criminal and ritualistically sending him or her to prison. In this vein, a number of ex-inmates talked about their prison experience and about the shame they had brought on their families. Moreover, they were at pains to emphasize that this criminal identity was not their true identity and that it was usually a combination of drugs, peer pressure, and a yen for the "fast life" that propelled their "drift" (Matza 1964).

D.B.: When did you get first sent away? What happened?

King F.: Uh, I got sent away in 1993 for a robbery.

D.B.: How old were you?

King F.: I was 22 at the time. It was kind of like a lot of shame involved because robbery is not somethin' I do, you know. Before that, you know, I admit I used to like to sell drugs, you know what I mean? That's what I did. The fast money was so enticing that I wanted it, you know, of course, like anybody [Interview, 5/25/1998].

Joining the Kings to Survive, Do Time, and Rehabilitate

Whether it was during their first or their seventh prison sentence, all the ex-inmate respondents declared that while incarcerated they had decided that a change was in order and that it was time to take responsibility for their lives. Most of them did not blame society for putting them behind bars since they knew that they had been breaking the law for some time before being caught. They also knew that when they were apprehended their lives were spinning out of control and that prison, paradoxically, had brought a certain amount of order to their fragmented selves. But surviving prison is an enormously taxing ordeal both psychologically and physically, and social solidarity in an institution where inmates are frequently competing for scarce resources is extremely important. Furthermore, how does one prepare oneself for release? Have all the demons been vanquished? Will the streets beckon to this fragile, diffident ex-con once more? King F., below, discusses how the Nation entered his life during his prison stay, an account that repeated itself in many different forms with most ex-inmate respondents.

> King F.: I seen the way their Nation with the Latin Kings was running the prison, and I liked it. You know, it was no fascination about . . . you know, "Oh, I see this as, you know, protection." I didn't see it as that because I didn't need none of that. You know, what I saw was somethin' that sometimes everybody seeks for, you know? That love, that attention, and, how you call it . . . what I needed the Nation to do for me was help me change my life. You know, to get out of this negative thing of thinking and get into something more positive, you know, get into my culture. And that's where I really learned everything I know now was in prison. You know, just bein' in prison and being a king, it helped me completely. It helped me learn my culture, it helped me be a man, it helped me accept reality, you know, and it also helped me get out of my drug addiction. You know? Completely out of it. And to this day, I've been home for what? About 10 months now, and I gotta thank the Nation for that because if it wasn't for the Nation, I'd probably be right back in jail, you know, for a long time this time because I already got these strengths, you know? And being out on the street, being involved with the Nation, I have no free time, I'm always busy, and I like that. You know, I don't have time to think about doing wrong. My mind is always filled with positive affirmation, and I like that, you know? And it's been good for me [Interview, 10/3/1998].

Enduring Punishment

It is one thing to be sentenced to a certain number of years, hoping to stay out of trouble and doing one's time, but it is another to enter a social organization as complex and as stressful as prison, where the primary means of social control is graduated forms of punishment, intelligence gathering, administration-inmate alliances, and institutional privileges. Inmates who join prison gangs, perhaps 20 percent of the population, become a target of the administration, since they openly contest the authority of the institution. Further, gang inmates are likely, at some point in their career, to come into conflict with other gang-related inmates, since prison is as much about the power of competing groups as it is about the rituals of containment and the enlightened devices of control.

D.B.: Where did they send you upstate?

King F.: They sent me from Livingstone to Attica. From Attica I went to Orleans. Orleans I come home.

D.B.: And how are they different?

King F.: In Livingstone I learned everything there was to learn about drugs and group therapy. In Attica, I mean I saw hell and back, you know what I mean? You saw, all the war stories they told you about, you saw it. There was no lies. Everything was true. You saw it right in front of your face, there was no gettin' around it. Survival. That's what that bid was all about, survival [Interview, 10/3/1998].

Although not all ex-inmates had experienced solitary confinement, at least half of them spoke of having endured this most extreme form of punishment for extended periods of time. Below, Queen I. recalls this phenomenon several years after the fact, and it was still painful to remember.

C.S.: So when they found out that you were. . . .

Queen I.: Latin Queens. They send me to Albion Correctional. That's where it started.

C.S.: And how long did you have to stay there?

Queen I.: Four years and out of those four years I did three in the snake pit.

C.S.: What's that?

Queen I.: It's a four by four room, no bed . . . [respondent pauses and takes some deep breaths]

C.S.: Would you like to stop?

Queen I.: No, that's OK, I got it. I just . . . it bothers me when I have to go there. You get thrown in there. There's no light. There's no bed. You have a floor. You have rats. You have a sheet that's so light you can see right through it. And here it is 3 or 4 degrees below outside, you've got no heat in that room, and that's what you sleep with. And if you give a fuck they'll demand something from you and you have to fight them. They'll hose you down and let you freeze. I came out of there twice with pneumonia. The last time I came out I was weighing 86 pounds . . . That's why it's called the snake pit [Interview with Queen I., 4/2/1998].

Meanwhile, King S. recounts the same penchant for physical force by correctional staff.

King S.: I got a time cut for good behavior. I did like close to 2 years in the box. Then I was in Keep Lock.

D.B.: So you were in solitary?

King S.: That was solitary confinement. . . . You write to the superintendent and he gives you a time cut if he sees that you changed. Um, if you stood out of trouble. From there I went to Keep Lock. When I went to Keep Lock somethin' took place while I was in Keep Lock. I was involved. Everything, I was involved. These officers was out to get me, the correction was out to get me, cuz I beat the system. They don't like that. They brought me up to the box again. Um, they didn't feed me on time, my meals was cold, they gave me torture, they tortured me!

D.B.: What did they do?

King S.: They used to give me beatings. They said, "We're gonna get you. We're gonna get you good."

D.B.: So it would be like two or three officers would come in?

King S.: Two or three officers would come in, not only come in, you don't see they faces. They wore hoods. You know, hoods? Like Ku Klux Klan members. Well, the stories that you hear about Attica, yes, it's true. I took the beatings. I'm a livin' proof person that's tellin' you it's true. It goes on still as we talk, with hoods, masks, beating me down with hoses, you know, hoses? [Interview, 8/2/1998]

Who Looks After the Family?

But what happens to the families when the Kings or the Queens get put away? According to the rules of the organization, they should receive some assistance, especially if the member is in the leadership of the group. To some degree, it depends on the circumstances, but if the member runs afoul of the criminal justice system on account of his/her membership in the organization then the organization is supposed to take care of him/her by helping out with a lawyer and through providing a minimum of financial support. In some cases, the support was forthcoming and the local tribe would make collections for the brother or sister and some money might be put aside from the group's box (i.e., its treasury). However, this policy was not always followed through on, and imprisonment, as for most poor and working-class people, not only involved extreme privation for the inmate but was an enormous burden on the family left behind.

> Queen N.: Well, my King, when he was in jail, he was picked up in a sweep and . . . he was in there for seven months and I asked the Nation . . . but it was a fight to get that money, you know what I'm sayin'? He was in there and they gave him like a hundred and fifty dollars for the whole seven months he was in there, and where he was at you had to buy everything, you couldn't bring nothin', so it was like every five days I was dishin' out fifty dollars, thirty dollars 'cuz it's phone calls, his food, you know? It was hard. It was hard. But, like it gets to a point where the Nation will actually tell you that's y'all personal business. "You gotta handle that. When he go in jail he gotta be a King, he gotta do what he gotta do to make his money" [Interview, 5/27/1998].

"Where Have All My Friends Gone?"—The Emptying of the Community

With the inmate population hovering around two million in state, local, and federal institutions, researchers are beginning to write about the dislocations caused to whole communities who have lost so many of their male members (Rose and Clear 2002). The impact is felt on multiple levels: families are bereft of their breadwinners, children lose their parents, the pool of eligible men for marriage diminishes substantially, the number of one-parent families increases, as does their poverty rate.

In the lives of many respondents, this phenomenon, the criminalization and the consequent emptying out of entire communities, was experienced very close to home. The loss of so many friends and family members made them feel fatalistic, mistrustful, paranoid, impotent, and resentful, all of which helped to cement their bonds to the ALKQN.

> L.B.: OK, so are the people you hang out with the same people that you went to school with or they are different people?

> King T.: No. People that I grew up with on my cousin's block, like my cousin,
> like mostly everybody that I grew up with . . . is in jail. And my cousin
> . . . he comes home this month, you know, in July. He comes home. He
> did 2 years. My friend, Babe . . . he got locked up like for good, like
> maybe last year, and my other brother, Nat, they all got locked up and
> they doin' like 25 years. So it's like the people I really grew up with, they
> all gone, you know? So it's like my man, Chino, he doin' 2 years. It's like
> everybody's gone [Interview, 12/2/1997].

Then there were those who for so long had fed the system—in effect, they
were the system's raw material. At a certain point in their cognitive development, such respondents finally drew the obvious conclusion: they were engaging in behavior that (1) would most probably kill them, and (2) was wors-
ening their own oppression, both collectively as part of the community and
individually.

> King F.: So bein' in the gangs just got me in and out of prison and every time
> I came out I always noticed that anybody that was in the gang with me,
> they were dead, or they were in jail doin' life, or they just overdosed.
> They died of something, so every time I came out it was like a new gen-
> eration. It was like, "I'm not getting any younger, I'm just getting older."
> So I became a Latin King on January 16, 1991, about a year after I was
> in the institution [Interview, 10/2/1998].

As we can see, the members of the ALKQN are quite diverse on a number
of levels. In age, there were a substantial number between fifteen and
nineteen who appeared to represent the bulk of the new recruits during our
research. However, there were also many members in their twenties and thirties who often filled the leadership positions, providing the kind of organizational experience and emotional stability that the group needed. Education-
ally, the members varied both in terms of their positive and negative
experiences of schooling and their attainment of credentials, but all agreed
with the group's conviction that education was the key to bettering both their
own life's chances and that of the community. Involvement with the criminal
justice system also ranged widely. Many older members who had served time
in state and/or federal penitentiaries were now on a quest to convince the Nation's youth that "crime doesn't pay," while others had little direct experience
of "the system" and wanted to keep it that way.[7] And finally, the twin concepts of family background and social class also varied. Some members re-

counted horribly deformed and abusive familial relationships while being raised in the depths of urban poverty, while others told of a very mainstream two-parent upbringing and remembered few instances of hardship during their formative years.

Certainly, this diversity among the members was a basic ingredient of the organization's dynamism and ensured that issues such as the group's identity (see chapter 10), its social agenda, its politics, and its structuring were kept at the fore of the efforts to reform and pursue the goals of social movement building (see chapter 11). At the same time, we should not lose sight of what the members had in common. They were all Latino/a, primarily Puerto Rican and Dominican, and they had all experienced some form of marginalization that they attributed to the white-dominated system of economic, political, and cultural power. Further, they were all from working-class backgrounds— the sons and daughters of primarily blue-collar workers who, perhaps a generation before, would have been rural peasants. Finally, their circumstances were the result of a fairly recent process of social and geographical displacement, their parents having migrated for economic reasons to the United States, leaving their children to figure out their cultural place in the world.

CHAPTER 10

IDENTITY AND COLLECTIVE RESISTANCE

Is it possible that we are facing a new diaspora of collective action? What happened to the analysis in this quarter century? Why have we become aware only recently of the new diversity of action? Are we dealing with new actors and the new social practices or, rather, with old actors utilizing new practices? Perhaps these questions are too limiting to permit an answer, except in the most ambivalent terms. But we cannot overlook the fact that the social movement of twenty-five years ago had strong state/political orientations and that, in contrast, many of today's actors are searching for their own cultural identities and spaces for social expression, political and otherwise.

Calderón, Piscitelli, and Reyna, 1992:23

Why should I deny who I am and what I believe in? We've gone back to an era of McCarthyism in the United States.

King R., 10/05/1998

Introduction

In the process of liberation, all social movements in some way have the ability to claim, deconstruct, construct, and reconstruct their identity. According to the literature, there is some consensus that a relationship exists between the construction of identity and collective action (Melucci 1989; Calhoun 1991; Calderon, Piscitelli, and Reyna 1992; Escobar 1992; Castells 1997; Della Porta and Diani 1999). This finding accords with our own analysis of the ALKQN and distinguishes our work from the tradition of mainstream psychology, which limits its analysis of identity issues to the causal properties of individual deviance.

In contrast to the prominent analytical position that identity occupies in the social movements literature, there is little such attention paid to this aspect of group process in the gang literature. Quite the contrary; for the most part, the importance of identity is restricted to the contemporary notion of "risk factors" (Branch 1997), especially since gangs have increasingly been perceived and defined as socially pathological. As Branch (1997) states, for all the gang's multifunctional qualities, it has never been viewed as a "protective factor" in any marginal youth's path of social and/or psychological development; i.e., it has never been seen as the kind of support system that would foster a gang member's transition to mainstream life.

The primary focus in this chapter takes up the question which Branch and others have posed: can a collective identity emerge from a street subculture that makes possible their social transformation? Our approach to this question approximates the work of social movement students who declare that identity is a process of meaning construction, both for individuals and for collectivities, by which certain "sources of meaning" (Castells 1997:6) are prioritized over others and eventually become internalized, leading to: "the formation of communes, or communities [and] . . . forms of collective resistance against otherwise unbearable oppression"[1] (Castells 1997:9).

In the discussion that follows, we apply this concept of identity as a collective resistance to respondents' narratives and to the various texts and observations that emerged from our participation in the group's day-to-day endeavors. Based on these data we have developed three identity-related themes to guide the analysis: (1) the Latinization of identity; (2) identity and hope; and (3) identity of the spirit.

The Latinization of Identity

I'm always gonna be Boricua no matter what. American or no American, that's my heritage. That's where I was born at. If they think that because Puerto Rico is a part of the States—that they control some of that . . . I'm still one hundred percent Boricua, I would never say, I'm American. No, cuz I know where I come from [Queen H., 10/25/1997].

As Queen H. describes, Latino identity is of paramount importance to both the members' and the organization's worldview and helps to shape many of their everyday organizational practices. Yet the claims to their ethnic identity are not simple and straightforward but emerge out of the specific experiences of their own personal, collective, and subcultural histories. This process is dynamic and not at all mechanistic, as might be construed when one first hears expressions of cultural affiliation that appear to be essentialistic. In the following, we organize the analysis of the ALKQN's ethnic reclamation into two subthemes: (1) the affirmation of Latino heritage; and (2) against invisibility.

Affirmation of Latino Heritage

The respondents in our sample were very much social agents struggling to recognize what liberation theologists describe as their own "realidad humana."[2] In so doing, as we have seen throughout this book, they became increasingly aware that they were struggling against a dominant culture that sought to both neutralize them politically and assimilate them culturally. Many respondents, particularly those of the second generation, discussed the quest for their own ethnicity with reference to the traditions and struggles of their parents:

> I tried actually not to assimilate to American culture because I'm proud of my Puerto Rican and Dominican heritage. I'm proud of all Latinos and I try to keep that in mind. I know that I live in America and I should get used to the way they do things, but some of my family is very strong when it comes to their culture and they like it. They're proud of it and they try to instill that in me and I try not to forget that. You know I may not be from the islands, but I still have that in me. It's in my blood and I try not to forget where my family came from [Queen J. 6/20/1998].

These assertions of ethnic self-affirmation and continuity, while reflecting efforts to resolve identity issues at the level of the individual, are carried out in conjunction with the entire membership and form an integral part of the group's collective agency. This point is crucial and, in many ways, distinguishes the ethnopolitical development of this group from other street subcultures that, while also claiming their members' ethnic solidarity, leave it undeveloped, parochial, and particularistic (see, for example, the notions of "mi barrio," or "cholismo" among West Coast Chicano gangs[3]). In the following, King C. discusses what happens when the group and the individual start to get other ideas about their ethnic trajectory:

> Well, my own personal opinion is that the white people don't agree with what the Latin Kings are doing because they notice that Latins are getting along with Latins and together they're helping each other in all ways—in school, education, neighborhoods, and we are reaching our goal of uplifting Latino

communities, and I think they really mad at us. But deep down they really fear us because we are rising to power and we are doing what we said we were gonna do, which is protect the weak and uplift the Latino community [King C., 11/6/1997].

In King C.'s experience, ethnicity is fine until it calls into question the distribution of power in a city that is famed for its cultural pluralism at the bottom and its highly concentrated and homogeneous hold on wealth (and decision-making) among the white elite at the top. King C., in fact, underscores three important points that are consistent with the group's approach to identity issues. First, the struggle for identity, if it is taken to its logical conclusion in a racially divided society, must always involve a breach of the ethnic status quo, leaving no resolution or accommodation at the individual level. Second, King C. is part of a group that, while appearing to be peripheral to the city's power matrix, actually exposes the deep cleavages in the fabric of class and ethnic life (Touraine 1989). Third, the audacity of the group, along with its ethnic claims to represent the community, contradict the tendency, so rampant in the popular discourse on American social justice, to view human and political rights as essentially a black and white "thing" (Muñoz 1989).[4]

Thus, it was in this contentious manner that respondents spoke of promoting those cultural values that are related to their Latino/a heritage and, in particular, to their Puerto Rican/Dominican backgrounds. This orientation was prevalent not only in the life history narratives and beliefs of the individuals, but also in the rituals present throughout the group's organizational and written practices.

For example, in monthly Universal Meetings, the stage was often decorated with two Puerto Rican flags: the "Grito de Lares," which is the flag associated with the Puerto Rican independence movement, and the official flag of the currently colonized Puerto Rico. Toward the end of the research period, however, the stage for the meeting was decorated with a third flag, that of the Dominican Republic. This move toward a more conspicuous ethnic pluralism within the group reflected both the leadership's recognition of the increasing importance of the Dominican membership and its claim that the ALKQN was obscuring its presence, just like the dominant society.

Further, in *El Grito*, the official newsletter of the ALKQN (1996–1999), many articles were dedicated to memorializing and promoting Latino culture with numerous articles reporting on the conditions and circumstances of Puerto Rican political prisoners and highlighting grassroots movements (see also Moore and Garcia 1978).

" El Grito "

April 1998

Volume 1, Issue 3

A big shout out to the Almighty Queens

This is a shout out to all the Almighty Queens of this Almighty Latin King & Queens Nation. Thank You for being at our brothers sides in good & bad. For you all hold the key to our existence, for without the key of reproduction we cannot reproduce. Thank You for taking the time to help in the Universal preparations. We all are greatful and on this Day we dedicate this Grito to all of the Almighty Queens of this Almighty Nation. Amor De Rey to all my Sisters and Amor de Rey to my personal Queen, Maggie.

A·D·R· King Jose

A Prayer for our Queens*****

A.

"Almighty Father King of Kings" Allow our race to be plentiful. Magnify our glory, so that the fruits of our Queens may elevate to the fullest. Show her the way with your Almighty seeing eye, of the Golden Path, for it is together as one that we will build our Almighty Kingdom. The Almighty Latin Kings & Queens Nation. Through the seed in which our Queens nuture, shall we always see the "LOVE" of our existence. Through the Queens "LOYALTY" we rise and not fall and through her "OBEDIENCE" shall the Nation always exist in the Golden Light of our Crown.

Almighty Father King of Kings, give our Queens the strength through "LOVE" to always be at our side until no end. Allow her "LOYALTY" and "WISDOM" of your Third Eye. That she may not be deceived to turn against her King. Let this be done through the "LOVE" for her King and Nation.

Almighty Father show her the way and "RESPECT". Yesterday, Today, Tommorrow and Forever*****

Amor De Rey * * * * *

FIGURE 10.1 Front Page from *El Grito*.

Therefore, the group encourages members to discover the source of their Latinness through a variety of means that are relevant to the building, re-building, and preservation of their community. In addition, the group itself is the vehicle through which members' Latino heritage is recognized and af-firmed, becoming a repository for ethnic memory and ethnic innovation. This search for meaning in everyday life inevitably involves them not only in the development of their Latino/a identity but in a search for role models against whom they can measure their own and their community's evolution. However, as many members reported, this thirst for ethnic knowledge is not quenched by the city's school curriculum, which leaves many of the younger members grateful for the group's weekly culture clubs (see chapter 7):

> They [the culture classes] just show you a little bit more about yourself, about things they don't teach you in school, which is about Latinos, how they came about, how Latinos created a lot of things [Queen A., 6/12/1998].

Against Invisibility

On a range of ideological, organizational, and cultural levels, the ALKQN was dedicated to resisting and ending processes of social-psychological subju-gation that are the modus operandi of colonial social control (Fanon 1965). One important facet of this resistance orientation was the commitment of the group's members to: (1) make themselves and "their people" visible again, and (2) reject all attempts by the dominant culture to successfully label the group as criminal and pathological. These tasks were extremely difficult, given the history of political and economic subordination of most Latinos in New York City, the number of members returning to civil society from incarcerated set-tings, and the past actions of the group, which haunted its every move.

> King B.: When we go out there and find out that we got a felony, well, we can't work. When you go out there to get a job, you have to stand there all day busting your ass working, excuse my language, busting, you know, doing your thing. For what? For five dollars an hour?
>
> Interviewer: Five dollars twenty-five.
>
> King B.: Yeah, five twenty-five. And you realize you're cleaning your life away for five twenty-five an hour. Where could you go with that in a week? Not rent, there's nothing out there. And if there is, they're not giving it to us, you know because we're Latin Kings. We're criminals, you know. I see a lot of youth in our Nation that want something out of life. But no,

you see a cop, you see the FBI, and everybody just assumes that we're doing something wrong [Interview, 12/10/1998].

"We haven't completed our goals yet. We haven't yet arrived to where we want to arrive. It's that we are not accepted how we are . . . we are not accepted because we were in jail, because we robbed before, because we used to use drugs, because before we did this and that and the other bad. But accept us now because we changed. Leave our pasts in the past. Don't bother with the past because we don't bother with yours, you understand me? We don't go in the street to say, "Oh, look! Fulana was a crook before and she is an artist now," you know? Don't look at our past, look at us now and we don't do anything bad. We defend ourselves because everybody is putting us down. That's it [Queen D., 11/21/1997].

The response of the leadership to such experiences of King B. and Queen D., above, was that rescuing one's identity had to be a primary goal of the group, and that the struggle to do so was essentially one of life and death[5]:

They want to destroy us by taking away our identity. We will demonstrate that we are Latinos/Latinas, and not only that, we will fight against anyone who has the intention to make us invisible by giving us another identity [King Tone, speech at universal meeting].

Queen M.: We know how it is to live without. We are survivors. This is what we have (the Nation); no one can take that away! I don't want to use a messed up past as an excuse, but as a motivation to keep on going. If we don't fight for Latinos, who is going to do it? (4/6/1997].

For Tone, as for many Kings and Queens, the pride that one feels for one's ethnic culture can only be achieved by being a member of the ALKQN, given the level of mistrust for the mainstream institutions of their community that have failed to protect their interests both economically and culturally. In effect, the ALKQN, members are "coming out" as Latinos/as, unafraid to represent who they are in any social gathering. This is done in various ways, but in particular it is carried out through their cultural style (Hebdige 1979), including their: (1) attire (e.g.,black-and-gold bandanas; black, gold, and sometimes red beads; yellow and gold shirts sometimes with black ribbing, yellow leather boots, sometimes with black laces, etc.); (2) demonstrative hand gestures, greeting rituals, and prayer performances; and (3) verbal self-identifications (e.g., "Amor de Rey," or "ADR").

The members' refusal to be coy and camouflaged about their public selves, although they strategically chose to keep their identity concealed at

FIGURE 10.2 A young Latin King with his son, both of whom wear the group's colors. (Photo by Steve Hart.)

different times,[6] is their way of refusing to be content with an annual cele-bration of ethnic pride, such as the Puerto Rican and Dominican Day Pa-rades, which mostly reject them in any case.[7] This struggle waged by the ALKQN against the invisibility of Latinos, pitting the group against techni-cians of the dominant culture and those collaborators within their own com-munity, was not lost on the younger members of the organization. Listen, for example, to the resilient words of King F.: "My life is . . . it's not all good, but I maintain my life as a man that I feel that I am. My name is King F. . . . I'm 16 years old. I'm a Latin King and that's it" (King F., 7/3/1998).

King F.'s simple statement echoes what the younger generations of the sub-jugated classes have consistently recognized when actively searching for respect in this exclusionary and colonizing society (Flores 2000; Young 1999; Bourgois 1995): claiming one's identity despite its negative connotations is an act of social and political defiance. In King F.'s case, he is proclaiming himself to be: (1) a man, despite the enormous structural pressures denying him his (gendered) role in the political economy; (2) a youth, in a world where his kind of generation inspires fear in adults (Males 1996); and (3) a Latin King, one of the most "spoiled" identities in any subculture.

King F.'s defiance is part of the general recognition among the ALKQN that, consciously or unconsciously, Latinos have the power to resist and even to change the rules of an oppressive sociopolitical system.

> The Latino can draw additional strength from another force too, if he has the will and the faith. Anonymous millions of brown men and women have given their life in the fight for liberation. They have fought against colonialism, hunger and ignorance and for the human dignity of our people. They have drawn from one another, through unity, a force of fortitude—brown force—the force which provides the splendor and growth of hope in oppressed people. The seed they cast into the founding of a Nation—The Almighty Latin King/Queen Nation—has withstood the trials of time. Drawing upon the endurance and fortitude of brown force, we continue our quest to unify and insure free political and cultural expression among third world people and among the commonwealth of individuals. We are the people's liberating force—brown force—the foundation of the Nation [ALKQN Manifesto, p. 15].

In this late-capitalist society, for the most part, power is increasingly measured not only by access to economic but also to symbolic resources (Bourdieu 1989), particularly in the form of validated knowledge and self-serving imagery. However, there are other ways to demonstrate power, which the ALKQN continually promote, e.g., indigenous knowledge, self-organization, and group spirituality. Above, the notion of a "brown force" is a metaphor for the potential solidarity of Latinos, much like "black" has been an empowering signifier for the social and cultural aspirations of African-Americans. But the process of "becoming" requires a combination of energy, persistence, and consistency, as King H. reminds us:

> It took 500 years to get my people to this type of sickness here, it ain't gonna take five years or even three years to bring us out of that sickness. So, for every two steps we take forward, you know, sometimes we take three back, sometimes we take two back, but we keep goin' forward, we keep tryin'to go

forward, except now we're like that hamster in that little hamster cage—just doin'a lot of energy like when you hustlin', but stayin' in the same spot, you know? [1/30/1998]

Thus, for the ALKQN, becoming visible, while it involves striking out against "the system" through a collective embrace of one's neighborhood and community allies, also involves tackling and engaging the many different processes of institutional socialization, particularly schooling (see chapter 8 and Brotherton 2003). This repossession of oneself and one's culture is not only the power to say "who I am" but "who I am not." According to many members, this recognition and validation of distinctiveness needs to be heard, first as they reaffirm to themselves who they are within the group, and then as they aim their words and actions at the "oppressors."

But the quest for identity is not met solely by affirming who one is within and through one's subculture, even though such activity is an important first step. Neither can the search be satisfied simply by taking advantage of the representational spaces provided by corporate media channels. Rather, being a Latin King/Queen immediately raises one's status, a "social fact" that has often been difficult for them to achieve in the mainstream. This is done through the notion of royalty in the belief system of the organization.

Thus, in the King's Manifesto, they are "the Yahweh Latin American Tribe" and the Latino and Latina children of God. This makes them Kings and Queens and the "chosen ones," in direct contradiction to the designation they receive under the gaze of the criminal justice system and through their collective label as "minorities" by the dominant society. In short, while the ruling classes have been labeling them and treating them as colonized subjects for generations, they are magically transformed into royalty through their own system of status provision.

Finally, another important feature of their quest for visibility involves paying attention to tradition. In this they have not only their ethnic but also their subcultural traditions (as described in chapters 3, 4, and 5) to help undergird their presence. Below, King M. is describing how he understands the ritual of the circle, one of the most important ways the group demonstrates its solidarity to itself and to the outside world:

They made a circle, they kept it tight, you know, and the leader would go in the middle and address the circle, so there's a lot of traditions that we follow that we don't even—I don't even know where—that they're ancestral. It just seems to happen, you know, just like the color of our hair, just like our mannerisms, you know? It's like part of our DNA, and, uh, the 360, again, that is one of our—it's holy to us. The circle, the whole circle, is always holy to us. Forever we protect the lives inside of the circle, but now we're becoming aware of the other side of the circle, which is the outside of the circle, so sometimes we could be facin' it, at each other, but sometimes the circle is still there but we must face out [King M., 1/30/1998].

Identity and Hope

I love being a Queen. It gives me hope, it makes me proud to say that I've got family that I know I can always count on and no matter what happens in my life, I know they'll always be there for me and they may not physically be there, but I know them spiritually and I know they will be there. You know, I've been in gangs, I've been in other nations, I've been in a lot of things, and I've never felt so at home as I have when I joined the Queens [Queen J., 6/20/1998].

Queen J., above, expresses a sentiment that ran through many of the respondents' narratives: declaring one's identity as a King or Queen, by fully embracing one's ethnicity and humanity, cleared the psychological and cognitive paths to feelings of hope and spirituality. Consequently, reclaiming one's identity through the group was a powerful riposte to the deep feelings of fatalism that many of the members felt prior to joining the organization. In other words, as we have seen in chapter 8, members who had weathered such experiences as racial prejudice, physical and sexual abuse, imprisonment, drug addiction, educational failure, poverty, and/or menial labor had come to expect this daily barrage of negativity to be their lot in life. Nonetheless, with the adoption of a new self, the feeling of status that comes with being baptized into an organization of street royalty, or the solidarity that is felt among hundreds of other similarly motivated members of the Latino community, a new era for the individual is announced and, probably for the first time, the subject looks toward the future with a demonstrated level of self-control and a socially valued place in the world.

In the work of the critical pedagogue Paulo Freire, recognition of the interrelationship between identity and hope is of paramount importance and is viewed as the cornerstone to a politics of liberation aimed at bringing previously alienated and highly marginalized individuals into the struggle for a more inclusive democracy. As Freire states:

It would be horrible if we were sensible to pain, hunger, injustice, and violence without perceiving the reasons for all this negativity. It would be horrible if we could feel the oppression but could not imagine a different world. It would be horrible if we could dream about a different world as a project but not commit ourselves to the fight for its construction. We have made ourselves men and women by experimenting in the dynamic of these understandings. Freedom cannot be gained as a present. One becomes richer in the fight for it, in the permanent search for it, even if there can be no life without the presence, however minimal, of it. In spite of that, we cannot acquire freedom for free. The enemies of life threaten it all the time. We must fight to maintain it, recover it, and expand it [Freire 1996:186].

What Freire and Queen J. have in common is their recognition that critically engaging the historical context of one's life is the starting point for a consciousness bound to action and aimed at both self- and social transformation. The Queens hint at these transformations in these short excerpts from their monologues:

We know how it is to live without. We are survivors. This is what we have [the Nation]; no one can take that away!
I don't want to use a messed up past as an excuse, but as a motivation to keep on going. If we don't fight for Latinos, who is going to do it? . . .
My history is my inspiration. You got to know where we come from to fight. History repeats itself. Without the knowledge we are destined to commit the same mistakes.

Such an orientation to everyday life, Freire claims, requires an "imagination" and the capacity to dream beyond the boundaries of our enforced social, economic, and cultural location. This impetus is captured below, by King S. and Queen A., who have begun envisioning their "own people" in top decision-making positions which, in reality, is almost unthinkable given the sociocultural impediments facing most poor Latinos/as:

Interviewer: What sort of government would you like to see?

King S.: I would like to see my brothers and sisters well educated, to see one of my brothers and sisters become the Federal Justice, which is the biggest court in the White House. I wanna see my sisters work down in 1 Federal Plaza, you know? Be the next Mary Jo White [Federal District Attorney for New York City].

Queen A.: Instead of the media tryin' to discriminate against us, we become the media. Instead of actually like lawyers prosecuting us . . . we could become one of them . . . after some of them has their degrees and things like that they can become part of it. But we can't because of what the Nation was about before. But we go to school now, we do what we have to do in order to get to that stage. When they see a lot of strong people, Latinos, they'll have no other choice. They cannot deny us no more [Interview, 5/1/1998].

For the most part, however, "hope" by members was expressed in terms of achieving the "American Dream"; moving out of the projects; sending their children to decent schools; getting an education for themselves (i.e., finishing their General Education Diploma, aspiring to college, or finishing college); having a government (usually at the city level) that is accountable to the people; and surviving the rigors of debilitating and sometimes fatal diseases:

Interviewer: How would you describe your life up to now?

King D.: Great. I mean, you gotta remember I'm HIV positive but today I'm a positive person. I would not let nobody tell me, no doctor tell me, I'm gonna die, cuz I ain't gonna die, see? . . . as long as I keep the positive mind . . . and talk to people freely, let people know how I feel and don't be shy because I'm HIV positive and you cannot get it unless you did the things that I did. You know, I could relate back to the days when I couldn't relate to people. That's when I used drugs, because drugs made me feel comfortable. Today, I feel comfortable with myself and with people. I like people today [Interview, 6/1/1998].

Thus "hope" was not particularly utopian, even though the rhetoric of the group was relatively grandiose. Rather, it was related to accomplishing goals in members' everyday lives—small, incremental achievements that would make their existence that much more comfortable and assured. Sometimes, the leadership would grow impatient with these limited ideals and might charge the rank-and-file with complacency:

What is Kingism? Why are we here? What's . . . the whole point other than just, you know, a term like unity. Unity for what sake? You know, unity for the sake of political power, economic empowerment! We lack a collective vision . . . there's one guy that has a dream which is not a vision, and there's another guy who just talks about this. But when you have a vision, you have to have a plan of action [King H., 1/30/1998].

Nonetheless, to habitually approach the world from a position of optimism instead of defeatist resignation, or to harbor a set of expectations in which the individual member routinely sees him or herself as an agent in the creation of the everyday (Flacks 1988), was still an extraordinary psychosocial development for most members and, as we observed, infused the entire organization with an upbeat mood during the first two years of the study. But there is a third aspect to this analysis of identity that has to be addressed and helps to further explain how the political animus of the group was maintained over time.

Identity and Spirituality

And the movement took on. And I started, you know, putting in religion. I started using King's lessons and using the Bible as a concordant. So everything I learned in Kingism I would match a story from the Bible, I would preach it to the kids and break it down in knowledge and it started working on them. They started getting a sense of spirituality; they got a sense of belonging. They got a sense that I didn't want them, like the pastor, to be Jesus. I just wanted them to try and walk like he did [King Tone, 10/21/1997].

In the construction of their identity, the ALKQN does not restrict its spiritual practice to mere contemplation or a series of internal abstractions—rather, it very consciously uses this aspect of its identity construction to urge members to reflect on their "realidad humana" through rituals and ceremonies which highlight the daily experiences of poverty, unemployment, police brutality, and racism. This approach to cementing the group's identity on the members' religiocultural histories[8] (see chapter 4) played an important role in the reform process and helped to reinforce key tenets of the group's doctrine:

Interviewer: Can you describe some of your spiritual and religious practices?

Queen C.: Um, I personally, I'm a Christian. Well, that's from the religion of my family. Kingism is a mix of Catholic, Born-Again Christians, and . . . we read the Bible. But we're not a cult like people say we are! We all have our different religions . . . it really has nothing to do with it. The main fact of Kingism is that we emphasize our humility, we are one and we're supposed to be there for each other no matter what [Interview, 3/4/1998].

For King Tone, the group's leader and former street preacher, the discourse and rhetorical style used to expand this politicization are often borrowed from standard religious practices, and they became his stock-in-trade as an innovative promoter of the group's ethnospiritual project:

> I pray that You make these few many and that You bless them with the power of knowledge and the word that you have given us. Give us no limitations. Teach us not to send boundaries and walls that'll keep us from achieving the goal of eternal life. Give us the power to teach our children how to believe in oneself and the things that can be accomplished if one believes in his brother more than he believes in himself. Give us the examples to teach our children how to stand with each other. Even when society says "abandon," we say, "take in." Let us not be the judge of this world, but people who serve it in a righteous way (a prayer offered by King Tone during a Sunday church mass at which both Latin Kings and Queens and the lay congregation of Father Barrios' Latino/a ministry were present).

In meeting after meeting, Tone provided countless renditions of biblical narratives in the form of prayers, anecdotes, and parables to refer indirectly to some of the tensions facing the group internally, to illuminate challenges to the group from external sources, and to emphasize the need of the organization to keep focused on its possibilities for growth and regeneration. This process of linking the group's collective and individualized identity to the pursuit of a radical and action-oriented spirituality was a determining characteristic of the organization and proved an effective strategy for solidifying the identity of members and helping the group to withstand the pressures of the struggle.

Thus, in our analysis, spirituality is one of the main driving forces behind the group's collective identity, encouraging members to engage in an ongoing reflexive relationship with the structures of their everyday life through a "human reencuentro"[9] with the creation of God. How is this carried out? First, by giving members permission to seek an alternative consciousness; second, by convincing them of the moral need to subvert the present social order; and third, by making them responsible for dismantling their *realidad humana*—e.g., their political oppression, helplessness, exploitation, and exclusion. In other words, the foundation of the group's spirituality is always manifested in a specific time and space and grounded in the struggle for dignity, justice, and respect in daily life. Spirituality, therefore, is an integral part of the meaning systems through which a resistance identity is constructed and regenerated, and it functions as a powerful bulwark against the pressures of the dominant society's ideological penetrations and corrupting moralities.

In liberation theological terms (Barrios 2003), this spirituality is seen as: (1) not limited to the practice of a formal religion, and (2) encouraging a radical form of solidarity in which people change as a result of their psychological and material engagement in a liberation movement. The ALKQN's spirituality, therefore, is an experience of empowerment solidarity in which the group, on the one hand, is urging its members toward a critical class consciousness, and on the other hand, is prompting the sociopolitical transformation of the organization by subverting oppressive circumstances despite the overwhelming odds against doing so (Barrios 2000, 2003). The manifesto of the ALKQN is fairly unequivocal about the need of members to engage in this contest:

> The new King recognizes that the day of resurrection is here. A time for the appearance of a new manifestation of truth. The rising of the dead means the spiritual awakening of those who have been sleeping in the graveyard of ignorance. The day of the oppressor must now be judged by the oppressed [The King's Manifesto, p. 10].

In the above, we have seen the multiple forms that identity construction in the ALKQN can take. A substantial part of our data shows that both the collective and individual identities that emerge out of members' commitment to the group are embedded in a resistance project that Castells has begun to highlight, but no one has yet applied to the case of gangs. These findings point again to significant gaps in the gang research literature where identity formation is largely considered a window into group and/or individual acculturation processes rather than a novel psychosocial pathway into communal levels of empowerment. Based on our research with the ALKQN, and in direct contrast to received wisdom, we have observed socially labeled deviants: (1) engage in endlessly ingenious ways to plumb their ethnicity, transforming themselves into culturally competent social agents; (2) launch a frontal attack on cynicism and fatalism over time, as part of an effort to change members' self-perception and convince themselves of their unfulfilled and potential agency; (3) embrace unabashedly their spirituality through reacquainting themselves with their own religiopolitical biographies; and (4) experience a collective "we-ness" that inspires individuals to transcend the semblance of their material limitations by reviewing and renewing their commitment to a new morality.

CHAPTER 11

GOALS VERSUS ACTS

I want to end by just talking about some people who are not with us. I want to talk about Anthony Baéz, Frankie Arzuaga, 15 years old shot in the back of the head in Los Sures, in Williamsburg. I wanna talk about Anibal Carrasquillo who was shot in the back in Flatbush area. These are all folks. These are our blood. Their families were like our families. They weren't political. Their families in many cases didn't approve of the things their sons were doing. But nobody hast the right to take us away like that. Their mother came into the struggle for social justice and formed a group called Parents Against Police Brutality. Many of you participated in the struggle to get justice for Anthony Baéz and for the other families. We couldn't have made the progress that we made without the support of the Almighty Latin King and Queen Nation.

Mr. P., Universal Meeting, 1/7/1999

Introduction

In the gang literature, there are few attempts to fully understand or document the qualitative changes in a gang's subcultural practices, which emerge when such a group begins to reshape its core identity. The closest treatment to such a project comes from the insightful autobiographical work of Dawley (1982), in which the author records his organizing experiences with the Chicago Vice Lords during the later years of the civil rights movement.[1] Other treatments from social scientists have generally dismissed the possibility that gangs can achieve any meaningful transformation, arguing that the gang essentially remains a primordial group, bound by tradition, whose members evince a parochial, lumpen consciousness that precludes aspirations of community leadership.

So far we have charted the social, cultural, and political history of the group, tracing how it emerged under a specific set of circumstances in the prison system and spread to the streets, where it virtually imploded from the internecine strife caused by internal factionalism that had little to do with social and/or political goals or communitarian sentiments. Thereafter the group went through fundamental changes; its leadership was removed by the criminal justice system and the void was filled by new personnel who had quite different visions of the group's identity, potential achievements, and direction for the future. Thus, the group was being shaped as much by exogenous as endogenous factors, and this continues throughout the research as we shall see in chapter 12. But what was the reality of the new rhetoric? To what extent could the leadership deliver on their many promises to the rank-and-file? What legacies of the old Latin Kings remained that prevented a thoroughgoing change not only in outlook but in behavior?

This chapter therefore deals with the contradictions of the organization and, in many ways, subjects the group to an empirical test of its social-movement credentials. The analysis will be divided into the following themes, through which we will consider the goals that the group set for itself and trace the difficulties and successes that it met in trying to achieve them: (1) shifting the group toward a political direction; (2) empowering the Queens; (3) taking up the cudgels for education; and (4) ending the group's violent traditions.

Shifting the Group toward a Political Orientation

In 1996, there was no shortage of members, especially among the leaders, who were quite content to have the organization remain wedded to its internal and local concerns, keeping it firmly embedded within the enclosed, boundary-conscious worlds of New York street gangs and others throughout the United States. Yet the general aim of the new leadership to bring the group closer to the concerns of the community meant moving the group in a progressive political direction. This is not to say that the group had never experienced a political encounter or that its members rarely thought about systems of power and privilege or ways to engage the status quo.[2] But, as a group, their experiences were bittersweet, and as far as most Kings were concerned, most politicians were opportunists who could not be trusted. Politics, therefore, was a game played at the local level by community hustlers and at the national level by white elites who did nothing but conspire to keep the lower orders in check. Yet, at the end of 1997, two years after the reform movement had begun, a leader of the group gave this summary of the year's activities.

H.: Last January we were still defending ourselves from the cop being shot—the captain who was shot in the 46th precinct. That's how our year started. Come February, they sentenced King Blood, our Godfather. How many of y'all were there 200–300 deep in the rain? Amor de Rey!

M.: Amor de Rey!

H.: What did they do afterwards? Tony told us, "H., take us to City Hall." But what did they give us? A whole train express from Chambers Street to 125th Street. Amor De Rey!

M.: Amor de Rey!

H.: In March we didn't go and hide like roaches into the cupboards, we came out for racial justice. They told us we ain't goin nowhere, and alongside with The Congress of Puerto Rican Rights and all this we kept the struggle goin'. Palante! Siempre palante! April, we kept doin' our thing. We marched alongside brothers in the Gay Men's Health Center in the AIDS Walk, and we kept doin' our thing. Then came the summer months, summer months that maybe all of us don't wanna remember. Names like King B., King S., and other things. I kept thinking of Tone every time I saw the Eveready Battery Rabbit. Every time he keep tickin'. Tony kept tickin' his and kept moving, kept bringin' the Nation forward and in the middle of all of that, in the Puerto Rican Day Parade, four blocks deep, thousands of brothers in black and gold, side by side, 360 strong, unbreakable. Amor de Rey!

M.: Amor de Rey!

H.: And leading in to the end of the summer, come September, school started. Here it come again. Brother Roman, we stood by his side as we took on operation "Red Bandanna" and all that other stuff. I'm not gonna do what Giuliani did and promote it, but Rafaél Cancel Miranda, one of the brothers who fought for our independence in the Blair House, was invited to St. Mary's church and spoke. And Rafaél Cancel Miranda said, "I am the Latin King of my time and Lolita Lebrón was the Latin Queen of her time." Amor de Rey!

M.: Amor de Rey!

H.: Come October, we stood side by side with our brothers in the Nation of Islam to commemorate a day of youth, a day of atonement, and we stood on 125th Street side by side with our brothers and once again, with brother Benjamin Mohammed and brother Mohammed Abdula, again, across the nation, we stood for peace. Tony kept us on the path. Come now, in October, we led the march across the country of all Latinos, of all immigrants' rights as we body-guarded Lolita Lebrón ourselves. Amor de Rey!

M.: Amor de Rey!

H.: And I come here in November because Tone will now tell you about his business of where we goin' in '98, but we started a new chapter. A chapter of economic empowerment with new allies such as Father D. and others that believe in us. Others that will stand by our side because they see in the light how we shine and how we comin' through, you know, and with that, that was that year. Next year we'll still be here together twice as big, with our own building. Amor de Rey! (King H., universal meeting, 11/27/1997)

King H., above, is clearly of the opinion that the group has turned a corner and is optimistic about how quickly the ALKQN was achieving some of its goals. Not only has the group honed a path of open resistance, declaring itself in active solidarity with Puerto Rican *independentistas*, Louis Farrakhan's Million Youth March at the United Nations, the Puerto Rican Day Parade, and the gay-led National AIDS walk, but it was now talking about institution-building and entering the very serious field of economic empowerment. For a street gang, made so infamous for its macabre way of keeping internal order, it would seem to be quite unprecedented.

But how deep did the politicization of the group go? Did all members consider themselves political agents, ready to align themselves against an opposition manifested at so many different levels of society? These related questions are quite difficult to answer since we interacted consistently with only about fifty to sixty of the two thousand or more members. If we had been allowed to administer some form of survey that focused on political consciousness and orientation we could have developed a more comprehensive analysis, but this was not the case. However, in the sections that follow we have noted a number of relationships between goals and actions.

Raising the Consciousness of the Rank-and-File

The group had long claimed that it was committed to raising the consciousness of its members and certainly in the interviews most subjects stated that they had developed a heightened level of political interest since they had joined. Thus, it was clear that during the 1996–1999 period, new and old members alike had been encouraged and indeed obligated to participate in a variety of political activities that ranged from internal discussions about community-related matters to protest actions such as demonstrations, picket lines, rallies, and voter-registration drives. This ongoing political mobilization of the group ensured that members developed positions on a variety of moral and philosophical issues, such as gay rights, drug abuse, racial equality, women's emancipation, abortion, freedom of religion, civil rights, and so forth—issues that not all the members were particularly versed in when they first joined.

Yet this did not mean that the group always took a "progressive" stand, nor did it mean that all the tribes were equally politically developed. In fact, it could be said that there was an uneven development in political activity across the group that grew out of both the disparate quality of leadership and the specific cultural histories of the local area. This finding is highlighted by the following field report, provided by one of our Long Island field researchers:

While the New York chapter of the Latin Kings was developing a public, political persona, the Long Island tribes voiced approval and lent support in various ways, but ultimately did not follow suit. Their circumstances were indeed very different. Part of the problem was a lack of community support and the absence of natural allies. Thus, members who were especially politically conscious and motivated spent a lot of time in the city. On Long Island, Kingism stood for resistance to racism and exploitation, as well as an alternative to "gangs," among other things. The attitude of resistance, put in the language of "sacrifice," was widely shared and cut across regional differences. The idea of achieving social change through either legitimate channels or direct participation remained controversial with the majority of members on Long Island with whom I spoke; whereas the meaning of "sacrifice" was not. Nor was there anything vague about the types of situations in which loyalties were tested. Hardship and disappointment thus yielded the conclusion that a "true King" is one who is willing to risk everything all the time, one who offers his head on a platter, like John the Baptist, as King Tone said in his sermon at St. Mary's Church. This standard undoubtedly resonates with a certain fatalism. But in another setting it can also provide for the opposite, namely, an engagement in high-risk activity to effect social change (Kontos 2001).

Consequently, although the leadership tried to emphasize politics as much as possible in members' everyday lives, it was not always successful, and the failure to come to terms with this dynamic could lead to actions that were destabilizing. There was no better example of this than the apolitical sentiment that was often expressed by inmates of the state and federal prison systems:

> Tone is talking on the phone with someone about rumors of a plot to overthrow him. During the course of my visit, over the next few hours, this rumor is confirmed by at least six members who pass by, all but one offering help. King T. and Queen Y. are supposedly planning the overthrow. King S., Inca of prison system, was given his position by Blood. Queen Y. was given her position by Blood, and Tone was asked to take care of her. She went to see King S. and became his woman. Tone describes the process as "prisoners selling dreams." She had a "universal" in a park with the women without Tone knowing about it. The women were sworn to secrecy but many of them reported to him what had happened. Tone plans to settle this on Sunday at St. Mary's. He plans to have a universal and preach from the teachings of the group instead of the bible. This has a special significance which is not clear. He then plans to confront the coup leaders.
>
> According to Tone, there is basically a single reason for the effort which is assumed to be underway to overthrow him, namely: power. The argument which Tone presents is as follows: the older set, among which would be King T. and Queen Y., have little to gain from the new direction of the group, whereas previously, they could make money illegally and also had a lot of power as the girlfriends of powerful leaders. According to Tone, he's been propositioned by all of them. He claims to have made his three-year-old daughter the First Lady of the Nation ("Luna") in order to "freeze" the position and thereby offset rivalry for it (L. K., field note, Latin Queen Overthrow, 9/29/1998).

The Continuity and Discontinuity of Reform

Although the leadership hoped that it could instill sufficient idealism in the organization to carry it through even the most difficult of times, the demise of King Tone in 1999 led to its opposite. In the period following the Inca's incarceration, the group fell into a state of confusion and disorientation; no solid political power base emerged that could continue to take the group forward on the same communitarian path of reform. The absence of any new credible leadership produced the conditions for the group to splinter into local spheres of influence that often reverted to the practices of the group prior to its reform years. The worst example of this post-reform revanchism was the antipolitical gangsterism of a group that called itself "Gangster Killer Kings," which worked mainly in the Brooklyn area. Its leader, King J., had formerly been a devout supporter of reform, but with the heightened attention of law enforcement and the successful conviction of their leader, he had become disillusioned and seemed to have given up on most of his own ideals about community uplift and pan-Latino resistance:

> I've had enough of this political shit. I've had enough of all these outsiders coming in and telling us what to do . . . all these reporters, priests, professors. We're the Latin Kings and we don't want no help from nobody and anyone wanna disagree with that has to come up against me. . . . I'm in charge now. . . . Its this politics that's got us into this shit in the first place. All of you get out of here, leave us alone [King J., 4/1/1999].

The Politics of Indigenous Cultural Production

An important goal of the organization was to generate and regenerate its own culture and to develop the self-confidence in members to take the messages of the group into an array of evolving cultural spheres. To this end, the group engaged in an extraordinary range of cultural practices, from the writing of texts in the form of manifestos, newsletters, prayers, and leaflets, to its participation in public debates and protests. But it also did what few other grass-roots groups seem any longer to be interested in carrying out, and that is extending its counter-hegemonic profile through artistic media such as plays, poetry, documentary film, photography, and music.

Following, we see one example of the group's involvement—a Latino theater production by Pablo Figueroa and Verónica Calcedo, which used the Latin Kings and Queens to tell the Oedipus story. Such an activity was quite irregular for so-called gang members, i.e., becoming involved in a function normally associated with high culture. The group, in effect, had inspired different community artists through its "in-your-face" resistance and they, in turn, responded by capturing a range of Latin King images through various media and narrative devices. Consequently, the group participated in a documentary called, appropriately, "Black and Gold" (Big Noise Productions, 1999) that located the organization in the context of the Puerto Rican community's history and civil rights struggle, and three photographic exhibits.

Below, King M., an early leader of the Pee Wees, described his entree into the organization precisely through his creative pursuits.

> M.: Yeah, I was a freshman in high school. I was in the debate team, and it was the only public school in the whole league, the rest was Catholic. We

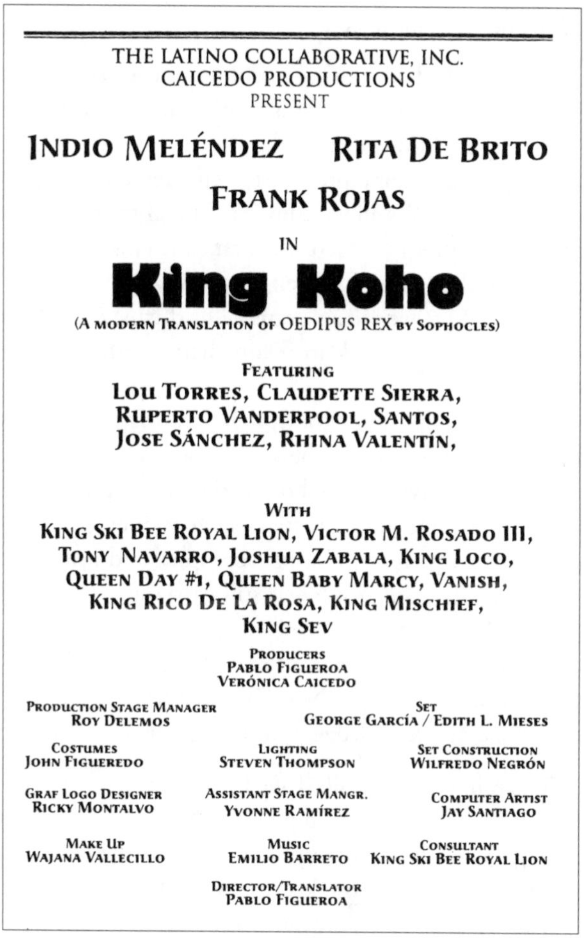

FIGURE 11.1 Flyer from a theater production.

were like the only minority group, everybody else was white, and we used to take such a different perspective on the arguments. Little by little I started getting more and more conscious of certain things, and on November 13th of '93, I went to my first rally, and there, you know, I got roughed up by a cop, and I looked around and I saw like 400 or 500 cops in riot gear against 200 unarmed protesters for the budget cuts, and that was like a wake-up, and from that point on, I started writing poetry—that's how I met King H., through my poetry [Interview, 8/1/1998].

Creating a Culture of Openness

The group had long talked of limiting its subterranean secret practices, which had, in part, allowed regimes of internal authoritarianism to go unchecked. To this end, the organization opened the doors wider to outside inspection than any Latin Kings had done previously, with researchers, journalists, political supporters, and friends all welcome at general meetings. As part of this liberalization, internal dissent was for the first time encouraged and members were constantly asked to fight for their position and hold their leaders accountable. In Figure 11.2 we see an example of this new culture as the organization's youngest members seek to retain their youthful autonomy in the group.

Perhaps the most important proof of the group's commitment to openness is the extent to which it could be said to be involved in crime as an organized activity. Illicit activities based on intrigue, conspiracy, and subterfuge implicitly undermine democratic practices such as open communication and goals-means transparency. Yet this issue is complex and it is important to remember the baggage that the group was still carrying.

> J.E.: So you think like for instance some of you or King Tone or someone else, some other King in the New York chapter would be . . . able to contribute to the new knowledge or to change the knowledge . . .?
>
> King L.: Oh, yeah, yeah. Actually Tone has modified the Nation, you know? Ever since he took control he flipped the Nation upside down, you know, according to how we carry ourselves. Now, in the lessons he changed a lot of things, too, you know, because we had shadow lessons before. Just like we had golden rules, golden lessons, which is the one to our eyes, King Blood also had something called shadow lessons and that's considered organized crime, you know. So they seized all that. Tone, in another way, took the Nation to another level. We kind of modified our lessons. We all come from the same root. But we've modified it, and it has developed throughout the years and it will continue . . . because, let's say I have a proposal, I put the proposal to the proper procedures, which it will go to the councils and all that, and if its majority vote "yes," then it will be added on to the manifesto constitutions [Interview, 6/12/1998].

But what did the group do in practical terms to move beyond its crime relations? How did it guard against such relations influencing the group in the future? The answers to these questions are somewhat opaque. On the one hand, the leadership in the various tribes with the support of King Tone and

<u>**A.L.K.Q.N.**</u>

We pee-wee queens in Cacique Tribe feel that we wish to stay in cacique untill we turn 18. We still feel that at the age of 18 we still don't have the understanding to be with the adults. The adult queens has there own problem and pee-wee queen's hasn't been through those problem. We will reach those problem at one time but right now we wish to fall and grow with our brothers by our side as pee-wees. The sisters has learn to respect the brother and also be respectal by the brothers. Together we are learning from eachother. The brothers feel that they like having there sisters by there side in the 360. Mission is a good leader and he has build alot of strengh in us. With this letter we are doing what our leader K.Mission, K.Tone, & K.Hector has taught us to ask for what we want and to never give up. We are asking to stay in cacique tribe untill the age of 18 and even longer. We feel that the adult queens should give us the oppertunity to grow and learn by our brothers side with the understanding that at all time the adults will be there for when we need them. Understanding that a tribe does not divide our Brothers, Sisters, Crown, & Nation but makes us learn different thing in life and in ourself.

FIGURE 11.2 Letter from Pee Wees.

the Supreme Team sought to remove a number of members who were drug dealers. They were essentially asked to end their drug activity or risk being purged from the organization. On the other hand, we know that certain individuals were still involved in the drug trade through primarily selling marijuana and that this activity was tolerated as long as the member had no other means of support. However, we have no empirical data explaining why some individuals were allowed to retain their membership while others were expelled. We can only speculate that some individuals in this position might have (1) been long-time friends of the leadership, (2) declared themselves open allies of the reform process, (3) vowed to remove themselves from the underground political economy as soon as possible, and/or (4) been helping the organization financially.

Empowering the Queens

As we mentioned earlier, increasing the autonomy of the Queens and bolstering their position in the overall power structure of the group was a critical goal of the new ALKQN, whose claims of being revamped would mean little without addressing the low status position of women in the organization. Consequently, some of the declared goals of the group were to increase the presence of women, increase the decision-making power of females in the group, and bring as many women as possible into leadership roles committed to the Latino/a community.

How did the group fare in these achievements in an organization renowned for its male hierarchies? At the level of recruitment, the membership of the Latin Queens significantly increased from the early 1990s, when internal written accounts of the group stated that there were no more than fifty females at most. This contrasted with the second half of the 1990s, when we estimated that 150–200 female members had joined throughout the New York City area.[3]

In terms of the structure of the group, we have already commented on changes to the constitution that ruled out some of the sexist prerogatives of the males (e.g. the allowance of mistresses) and the language of the Queens' constitution, which began to reflect more modern feminist concerns.

> Queen N.: The biggest fight now is to get the lessons changed or to have new constitution lessons written for us because it states in our lessons we have to reproduce. Our main concern to this Nation is to reproduce. Don't tell me I'm gonna be here just to reproduce, cuz then that's the way they

put it, you know, the way the Kings say it. It's like, "No, no, no." And then the King could have a mistress and this, this, da, da, da. No, no, no, no, no. That shit don't fly with me and it don't fly with a lot of the Queens, let me tell you. It don't fly! It don't fly at all! [Interview, 3/2/1998].

On the subject of female leadership, the group had also made some headway. In 1997, the first female was brought into the Supreme Team, the highest decision-making body in the New York City area, and given the title Secretary of State, and a year later, a female was named head of the Pee Wee tribe for the first time in its New York history. A further indication of the increased role of females could be gauged at the New York State universals (general meetings), where both the leadership and the rank-and-file were powerfully on display. On many occasions we observed that at least a quarter of the speakers who addressed the multitude were female members, even though they were often outnumbered ten to one in the audience.

One Step Forward, Two Steps Back

On a number of measures the actions taken by the group to increase the power of the Queens were significant. However, we must be clear that efforts of the group failed to adequately address and challenge the overwhelming male culture of the organization which, considering the history of the group and the male-dominated nature of street subcultures (Bourgois 1995; Maher 1997) whence it came, is hardly surprising. Ironically, at the end of the reform period, the group had established its first "coeducational" tribe, out of which a powerful cadre of young men and women was emerging. One of these members, below, exemplifies the growing self-confidence of females during that period:

C.S.: So, as a Queen, if you fall in love with an outsider you have to leave the Nation?

Queen N.: If we gettin' down to lessons, it says we can't have no outsiders, but if I break up with my husband and an outsider's gonna be there for me and he's a man who's gonna take care of me and take care of my kids and he's got a little job and he treats me like the woman I'm supposed to be treated like, then they can't tell me who to love and who I can't love. They can't tell me that, so that right there is . . . they can't tell me who to love, straight up and down. Or they can't tell me as a woman who to sleep with either, you know? So, it's always gonna bump heads. They can't kick me out the Nation for that [Interview, 3/2/1998].

Unfortunately, within a few months of the above interview, Queen N. was expelled after a picture of her kissing another King other than her husband came to light. Despite her assertion that the photograph was not contemporary, the act was judged a transgression of the Queen's code of fidelity and showed the degree to which the ingrained chauvinism of the group held sway over the process of deciding membership. Such a case speaks volumes about the contradictory state of gender relations within the Nation and within the Queens themselves. Below, we discuss a few of them as they relate to the organization and to the broader society.

The Price of Ending Invisibility

Undoubtedly, for the Queens to get involved in an ethnic political movement gave them a shared sense of fulfilment, bringing both individual and collective agency into their own lives and the lives of their children. In their eyes, they were taking an assertive step, perhaps for the first time, toward changing the patterns of abuse and neglect that they had long endured, and their growing fealty to the group symbolized that there was no turning back. At the same time, however, they were joining a group that was often associated with the new female threat (Chesney-Lind 1997). Thus, their emergence from the conditions of invisibility was risky. On the one hand, as newly reformed Queens they could be considered examples of strong, inner-city women, while to others they were nothing more than savage, slutlike tomboys or vamps (Campbell 1984).

Defending Ethnicity Yet Recharging and Resisting Sexist Traditions

Even though the principle of gender equality has been accepted by much of society, both recent and not-so-recent Latino/a immigrants still carry with them the customs and practices of traditional gender roles reinforced by their countries of origin. In many instances, as the Queens sought to declare their ethnic solidarity and distinctiveness, they also held on to traditional concepts of gender almost as a form of stubborn resistance to white modernity. Embracing their culture, therefore, could also compromise their freedom, alienating themselves from themselves and relegating them to positions that further rationalized their care-taking and domestic duties. Nonetheless, in interviews the older Queens all said that they had achieved great strides in liberating themselves from the male-dominated rules of the Nation, citing, for example, early incarnations of the ALKQN, when women were not allowed to leave the house unless escorted by at least one man. In contrast, the Queens today held their own meetings and moved freely without escort, even though male members still insisted on providing "protection" during Queen meetings.

Remaining Loyal, but Where's the Reciprocity?

Loyalty was a primary goal of the organization and they did everything possible to emphasize the need for brothers and sisters to remain committed to one another as a way of increasing Latino solidarity. This emphasis on loyalty is both a class and ethnic characteristic and stands in contrast to the primary importance placed on individual mobility, competition, and the "getting-ahead" corporate mentality that is so prominent in middle-class ideological systems taught in schools, universities, and throughout our commodified culture. In contrast, most orthodox criminological texts generally consider loyalty as an adolescent predilection for peer-group affinities, as if it were an act of nature or an ingrained trait of certain societal types. Among the Queens, however, loyalty was given a particularly gender-based rendition:

> We are willing to follow our Kings till the end—every King or Queen of this Nation are our brothers and sisters so we will be there every time we are needed [First line in the Queens' opening and closing prayer].

In addition to acknowledging their vital role of providing the Nation with a sense of family, performing traditional matriarchal responsibilities when together, Queens refer to themselves as "the backbone of the organization." This reflects the realization that the Queens are expected to stand by the Kings under all circumstances, "through good or bad," but the same obligation is not expected of the Kings. Thus, many times the Queens have expressed their distress over this unquestioning allegiance, in particular when they have felt powerless to prevent their Kings from participating in potentially risky situations. Their objection is a reasonable one, for it is they who must take care of the children and support them in every way possible while the Kings are away, "doing time."

Taking up the Cudgels for Education

I wanted to thank you, King Tone, for bringin' me to the light and showin' me the right path, and I also wanted to thank my tribe right now. We are representing the "Coppauge" tribe who bring me in their hearts and directed me first to the light. And I also wanted to leave you with this. My mother always told me that you can't take care of your girlfriend if you can't take care of yourself. So what I wanna say is, how can you tutor somebody if you can't go to school yourself? How can you try to teach somebody if you can't read or write? So you have to elevate yourself before you can elevate anybody else. Amor de Rey! (King R. of Long Island, from a speech at a general meeting)

The importance of education for the ALKQN cannot be overestimated, as we have discussed throughout this book and elsewhere (see Brotherton 1999, 2002; Brotherton and Salazar 2002). This fact alone makes the ALKQN quite distinctive from other street subcultures and should alert the "outsider" to the fact that, if nothing else, the group is fundamentally atypical of gang formations. Rather, it is a group that is postcolonial in nature, refusing to be pigeonholed into any imagined pattern of adaptation, acculturation, or assimilation, as is presented in most modernist narratives of inner-city subcultural life. In the visions and practices of the Kings and Queens we not only see the extraordinarily conscious efforts to empower from below, but other more hidden though unmistakable developments such as the ordering and reordering of urban boundaries and the struggle for "third spaces" (see Soja 1996; Bhaba 1994, among others).[4] Therefore, what did education mean? Why was it so intrinsic to its new identity? What actions were taken to ensure that educational goals were achieved both individually and collectively? And what were the obstacles faced by the group in achieving these goals? We have tried to address these questions in the discussion below.

The Multiple Meanings of Education

You have chosen to join our Nation because of the promise you have shown in past endeavors. These are your lessons and your laws. Learn them well and engrave them in your hearts and mind. . . . Our goal is to build a strong nation within society. A Nation where our children will never experience any kind of hunger because we are there to feed them. Where they, as Latino children, will have the same opportunity as the rest because we are the keys to their doors and to ensure them success because we are their guides [From the founding manifesto of the New York City chapter of ALKQN].

Education was constantly referred to in the texts and speeches of the group and became primarily interpreted in formal and informal spheres as encompassing both the instrumental and the political.

Instrumental

A path to individual and collective social mobility: The ALKQN thought quite correctly that without formal credentials in education there was no way that their members could advance in today's society. It was well known that poor Latinos/as and particularly Puerto Ricans had fared badly in the city's public school system and, at least anecdotally, the group knew from the experience of its own members that failure in school, even among those who had promising beginnings, was widespread. At the same time, the group was committed to overcome many of these educational and job barriers as part of its primary ideological goal of uplifting the Latino community.

A way to improve the leadership: As the group's membership grew and changed, with more working-class members from stable family backgrounds entering the organization, demands on the leadership became more complex and intense. It was not enough anymore for leaders to have street credibility and know how to put down rebellions in the ranks. They were now called upon to speak to public audiences, lead discussions in the group on new policy proposals, and deal with a range of constituencies as the group attempted to be more democratic. Thus, a key to changing the leadership qualitatively was to ensure that more of them were educated or at least were committed to move their membership in that direction.

A way to extend the reach of the groups: As the group began to move in different circles, speaking in front of college students, providing interviews for television, newspaper, and magazine reporters, engaging in talks with leaders of the community, and attempting to negotiate with law-enforcement personnel on issues regarding the social control of its members, the different layers of the leadership found themselves confronted with new kinds of communication that they had to master or at least come to understand. This meant that they: (1) had to engage in a rapid process of self-education, (2) had to confer increasingly with outsiders who could help explain the new terrain, and (3) needed to utilize the most educated members in the group, particularly those who had college experience.

A vehicle for self-control: A primary goal of membership in the group was to put one's life in order. Chaos often was the context of many members' lives when they joined and by their own admission they were tired of the daily ups and downs, with so little control over their futures. Problems associated with drug use, dysfunctional relationships, economic insecurity, the criminal justice system, and life in high-risk environments had convinced many of them that they had to learn more about the sources of their own volatility—and education, both formal and informal, was one way this could be achieved. Thus a critical subgoal of the group was to increase knowledge of the self that would promote, complement, and condition members' individual and social responsibility.

Political

Showing the capabilities of Latinos/as: As stated earlier and as borne out in the general demographics of the Puerto Rican and Dominican populations of the city and the membership, educational expectations for poor and working-class Latinos/as were abysmally low. As a result, in the group's texts and in interviews, two parallel themes emerged: (1) the need to disprove and confound the stereotype of Latino/a underachievement, and (2) the imperative of increasing the visibility of Latinos/as in the professional classes. Naturally, the group reasoned that access to formal education, particularly at the highest level, was a key to achieving its foremost political goal: Latino/a power.

Raising the collective consciousness of the group: All the reform-minded members realized that for the group to succeed in its newfound quest for respectability and legitimacy a different way of seeing the world was necessary. The group had to emerge from its focus on internal and local concerns and begin to view itself as reciprocally linked to a larger social and political construct. In order to do this, the group literally needed to be educated, particularly with regard to politics, philosophy, religion, and the law, which were the areas that most related to its members' practical, discursive (Giddens 1979), and historical consciousness.[5] This turn toward a highly politicized form of education essentially supported the group's efforts to redefine the role of citizenship for its members and move it more visibly into the wider world. Eventually, the group hoped that this broad engagement with education would help create a different form of collective consciousness and further consolidate the reforms that had been made.

Connecting members to their history and culture: One interpretation of the group's embrace of reform was that a critical mass of members had begun intuitively to understand something about its postcolonial location in the broader realm of resistance and resistance movements. This meant that members who had come to understand and resent their disappearance from such grand U.S. narratives as "the American dream" or "the melting pot" were not simply satisfied to learn about their repressed histories and attendant cultures but they were prepared to actively repossess and reconstruct them. Education in this context was a way to capture and rekindle both individual and collective memory, which meant rescuing the histories of the two colonized nations from which most of the members' families had originated, Puerto Rico and the Dominican Republic.[6]

Educational Actions, Not Words

How did the group put into practice its educational commitment? As far as the younger members of the group were concerned, according to the interviews and our observations of many local chapters, it did so through: (1) keeping a check on the school attendance records of school-age members; (2) enforcing 10 p.m. curfews on members under sixteen years of age during the week; (3) establishing informal tutoring programs to help younger members with their homework; (4) encouraging students who are having disciplinary problems at school to bring their problems to the attention of senior members; (5) ensuring that school-age members do not get caught up in local intergroup conflicts, either at school or on the streets, that could disrupt their school careers; and (6) collaborating with the parents (where possible) regarding the school career of the son or daughter.

Of course, not all of these efforts were totally successful, but all of the tribes in the New York City area attempted to put in place to various degrees all of the above policies. As one local leader in the Bronx put it:

> King W.: We push education, actually, because, for the younger Kings, they have to bring us their report cards, they have to be doing the right thing if they wanna be associated with the Kings now. If they're not doing anything with their life, you're not helpin' yourself. If you're not allowing us to help you then you're just what I consider dead weight.

But what about the older members? Those of postschool age who perhaps never graduated or who left school with low-level skills or who had spent a great deal of time behind bars and were essentially prison-educated? With these older members the group had less influence and had to rely on moral support and encouragement and on the ideology of self-betterment that was intrinsic to the group's doctrine. However, the group worked hard to meet the needs of members who had the least educational training, raising where they could those individuals' human, social, and cultural capabilities:

> B.: I seen a lot of mothers suffer. I seen a lot of people get killed. I heard a lot of things. Come on now . . . and I don't wanna get shot. I don't wanna

go to jail. I don't want these guys to put me away for trying to help these kids, at the same time helping myself. I just wanna do the right thing. But you know, I learned to walk away from that. I learned to walk away because all this knowledge. . . . Remember, four years ago I couldn't read. I couldn't read [emphasis]. I didn't even know how to add. This word here [he holds a leaflet in front of him that advertises a conference on the death row inmate, Mumia]. Maybe I still drop some words like this, "explosive" [he points to the word on the leaflet]. Now that word "explosive." You think four years ago I would remember that word?

D.B.: So where did you learn it?

King B.: By bein' in the Nation . . . study, culture classes. You know what I'm sayin'? 'Cause our lessons teach us that, you know. It also teaches us not only to become a man but to become a King. And when you become a King, you have responsibilities, you have self-esteem, you have self-respect, you have belief. You know? (King B., a New York City Latin King, forty-seven years old, originally quoted in Brotherton 2003)

How Much Can We Overcome Without Cultural Capital?

For all the educational rhetoric of the group and its concerted efforts to implement proeducational policies throughout the Nation's practices, there was a host of contradictions that flowed from such a bold move. Below, we discuss five areas of tension that arose around the centrality of education in the new ALKQN's agenda.

The Risks of Crossing Cultural Boundaries

The primary culture of the group was still wedded to the streets. The displays of colors, the hand signals, the locations for social hangouts, the experiences of members raised in barrio/ghetto neighborhoods, all of these properties determined the everyday life, practice, and image of the group and continually reaffirmed that it was a grassroots-street movement. Consequently, the group was immersed in the dynamics and meaning systems of a "low culture," i.e., a working-class and subworking-class street and prison culture, with its interlocking symbolic signifiers, rituals, and knowledge bases, and a nonstreet/prison culture that grew out of everyday domestic proletarian life. In contrast, embracing education often means valuing a "high culture," with its emphases on white bourgeois learning and middle-class tastes, which represent distinctly different symbolic and cultural capitals (Bourdieu and

Passeron 1977). Inevitably there is a clash between these two cultural spheres, even though they often intersect and overlap as seen in music, dress styles, and language. Thus it was sometimes difficult to convince members to cross these cultural boundaries and embrace a terrain that is largely unknown or that has systematically excluded them. Therefore members expressed not only ambivalence but also hostility toward the "educational" turn, and saw it as too compromising and risky to their proud ethnic and class roots.

The Establishment Still Rejects the Organization

For all the efforts to reach out to the educational establishment—meeting with school principals, developing relationships with individual teachers and even explaining their group's philosophy to district superintendents—the organization was unable to develop any long-lasting rapport with educational "officials." Quite the contrary, the Board of Education had declared in 1997 that official school policy toward "gangs" was one of "zero tolerance," just like it was toward drugs and other public scourges. Since the ALKQN was classified as a gang by the New York Police Department, this ensured that the School Security Administration would do the same (see chapter 12) and therefore all "official" dealings with such a group were strictly off limits.

Can "Good" Students Be on the "Front Lines"?

It must not be forgotten that the group was still in transition and that its identity was essentially a hybrid one. Thus, while it wanted to leave behind its history of internal struggles and street/prison conflicts, the reality of doing so was still in the future and it was very much involved in an ongoing process to reimagine and restructure itself under conditions, both political and subcultural, that were constantly shifting. There were some members who could bridge the worlds of violence and learning quite effortlessly, but others were not so successful, since it required a very different sense of self to earn respect in the street as opposed to the classroom. King H., below, articulates some of these tensions:

> King D. has gotta be a man, he's gotta stand up for himself. It's OK telling the Pee Wees what to do and what not to do. He's good at telling 'em they gotta go to school, they gotta go to college, but he can't back down when some brother comes after him. You can't come running to the Kings to sort out your problems, we're not gonna be used that way. . . . So, when he called on the brothers to help him they stood back. Now the brother's been stripped but he'll come back, he has to learn, that's the Kings way [Interview, 3/12/1998].

*The Contradiction Between the Promise of Individual Advancement
and the Commitment to Group Solidarity*

Ostensibily, there was a conflict between the pursuit of education, which promises individual mobility and status, and the twin goals of the ALKQN to promote Latino/a social and ethnic solidarity and thereby uplift the whole community. While at times these notions of empowerment conflicted in the thinking of individual members, they oftentimes overlay each other as if the contradictions could be avoided or they did not apply to them.

> Our goal is to strive for more knowledge, more kids, more of our brothers goin' into schools without being kicked out for being a King. Becoming lawyers, doctors, cops, becoming all these things that we're striving for, but right now it's still hard. It'll eventually get there no matter how many of us get locked up, there's always gonna be more to replace.

Ending the Group's Violent Traditions

While nonviolence was certainly a major goal of the organization, how was it possible to implement it? How seriously was the group turning in a peaceful direction and away from the earlier corporeal regimes of discipline and authority? How could they entirely reject the very real lure of street dramas and the retaliatory impetus that is such an integral part of gaining respect in hard-bitten neighborhoods? How would the group control the multiple forms of machismo and toughness (Katz 1988) which are characteristic of all street players and "street elites"? What were the incentives to make such thorough-going changes to the customs and strategies of the group?

We stated earlier that there was every incentive to stop the blood-letting in the group after the indictment of many of the top leadership. The truth is, however, there are many gangs in which the leaders are busted and the group left behind never makes any changes to its practices or worldviews. Thus there had to be a qualitative difference with the ALKQN indicating it had become something else and was transforming in a way that was making perfect sense to its members while allowing it to exploit and develop its rich internal social resources.

> King F.: It's no longer about gangbanging, it's about getting involved in the community. It's something we should have done years ago, you know? But thanks to the new leaders we have, they've made it possible. To see that change, to see that dream come true . . .

DB.: Let me ask you, how have you seen the organization change?

King F.: We've come a long way. We're into rallies, we're into marches, we got a beautiful church that we can have some peace in, and that's a lot! That's a lot for us compared to what we had, which was nothin' you know? And I like that feeling. It makes you feel like you don't have to watch your back any more. You don't have to worry about the Feds or the police coming to harass you because you ain't doing nothing wrong. You're having a peaceful protest and nobody got hurt, so you go home and you relax. And that's a good feeling. I don't ever wanna go home and have to chain and bolt my door down in order that something won't harm my company [Interview, 6/1/1998].

Whatever strategy a particular tribe used to address conflict situations, the results were impressive. During the three-year research period we could not find a single homicide reported as a result of intragroup conflict. Further, we heard few reports of beat-downs for disciplinary infractions and only three or four interpersonal confrontations among members that resulted in physical injury. At the intergroup level, we recorded one death of a King, who was killed in his capacity as small-time drug entrepreneur, not as a Latin King, and several woundings, mostly in altercations with the Bloods street gang (see chapter 11).

As we have stated, by and large, the group did not retaliate under strict instructions from the prevailing Inca; rather, group members were urged to press charges against the perpetrators and wait for the criminal justice system to do its work. Of course, this commitment to nonviolence by the membership was part of a process of deep change not only for the identity and behavior of the group but for the individual members who still had to live everyday in fluid, high-risk environments where threats of violence were normalized. Queen M., a seventeen-year-old Pee Wee, articulately explains this:

Interviewer: What are the main goals of the organization?

Queen M.: To get a new reputation for ourselves . . . because the reputation right now is that we're a gang, we do drive-bys, we carry guns, we carry knives. I'm not gonna lie, like carrying somethin' like a little knife even if they don't use it. The simple reason is, even if you're not a King or Queen, if you have a fight with somebody and they pull out something, you gotta defend yourself regardless. . . . We're not good friends with other . . . street gangs. Why . . . don't they get along with us? Because we're not a gang and they feel, "Why are they better than us?" Like the

Bloods, that's a gang. Even though they have their lessons, that's a gang. Really, that's all they do, they stay on the corner and sell their drug and start trouble. We don't get along at all. Why? Cuz they killed two of our brothers for no apparent reason . . . But we didn't retaliate and start cuttin' them up and start killin' them, no! We're not gonna stoop to that level. Why? Cuz we're not a gang. That's what a gang does.

Interviewer: What are you going to do?

Queen M.: About that? . . . Hopefully if they see us mature. It takes time. the thinking process and the maturing process takes time. I hope they see that they did it for no apparent reason. Just because you believe in one thing and I believe in another or just because we're one thing, we are an organization, we are a Nation!

However, it was difficult to rein in all the members and some were still involved in administering traditional forms of street justice. In the following, a leading King of a local tribe candidly explains what his solution is and why, although it is preferable, peaceful negotiation might not always work.

L.B.: In your organization you have to deal with conflict.

King T.: Yes.

L.B.: So how you do this?

King T.: Well, it depends on the problem. It depends upon how they disrespected one of my brothers. Like if one of my brothers gets shot, I have to go and, I think, well, go back and do the same thing they did to my brother, you know? It's only right, you know, because it's just like friends, you know? It's just like friends. If I have a friend and my friend gets shot, it's the same thing like me going back over there and doing the same thing for my brothers. How I react to it? I make a plan . . . we'll go in the cars, and we'll look at everything, and we'll look at the people that did it, and we'll look at where they're at, and then we just be like, "One be over there, one be over here." And then we just catch 'em in the middle, you know? But if it has to do with like gunplay, the only one that would go would be like my head chief, and that would be like me and my five pearls. And my five pearls would go and do it and I would stay looking from a corner to see if they did anybody.

L.B.: So what kind of problems do you have to deal with?

King T.: Most of the time it's usually like fighting or cuttin'.

L.B.: So how do you solve those problems?

King T.: Well, usually, they don't want problems cuz they know we're too deep or probably because like they see two of my brothers walking and they figure that they're only two deep right now, so "Let's get them now." So they would jump 'em and then they'd be like later "Yo, we didn't know he was a King. Boom, Boom. We're sorry. We don't want no problems." But like once they jump my brother and my brothers come back and tell us, we usually go handle it the same day, and then we flip on 'em. And then they'll be like, "Yo, we don't want no beef." But we make sure one of them get hurt before anything happens, you know? That's how I see it.

L.B.: OK. Do you think that there's a better way to solve these conflicts?

King T.: Yes, there is.

L.B.: By what?

King T.: By talking. But sometimes you can't talk because if you always talking, the person that you're talking to is gonna be like, "These Kings is punks," and then they gonna try to take advantage of that and then the next time it happens, they will see, they gonna be shedding blood. Cuz I think that's the only thing people do nowadays is like they just shedding blood. They don't care. They don't care what happens no more [Interview, 11/15/1998].

Thus the struggle to end the violence of the group was a difficult one and consumed an enormous amount of energy and time among the leadership, who were committed to instilling an alternative sensibility in the group. To what degree this more violent side of the group coexisted with the peacemaking process is hard to say. We think it reasonable to assume that if such a violent regime were widespread, many more injuries would have been brought to our attention and the media would have given it much more coverage. To help counter the culture of violence that so many of the members had grown up with, a range of policies and strategies was tried and implemented.

Goals and Actions

We have already noted in passing how different internal and external conflicts were being handled by the group during its reform phase. Below, however, we offer a more pointed discussion of how this central aim of the group was achieved.

Conflict Resolution

A range of different conflict-resolution techniques was put into place through-out the organization: third-party interventions, one-on-one counseling, talk and negotiations between conflicting parties, fractionating problems, and so on. Certainly, these were typically resorted to when interpersonal issues arose in branch meetings and effective intervention strategies were required. But what happens on the streets when the character of the conflict is more fluid and the risk of escalation is high? Below, King J. describes an incident in which he found himself making an effective "intervention," probably pre-venting a member from going to jail.

> J.E.: OK. Have you ever been trained in conflict resolution techniques?
>
> King D.: Yeah.
>
> J.E.: Oh, you have? Do you think that these are useful skills?
>
> King D.: Of course. Because when you could talk a guy out of a fight. . . .
>
> J.E.: Do you like having this skill? How do you use it?
>
> King D.: A couple of weeks ago. I had a brother that had an incident with some guy, and him and the guy were ready to fight in the street. The guy was walkin' with his girl and the bro saw him. The bro was walkin' with his sister, you know? Him and the guy looked at each other. The guy ended up sayin' somethin' and he walked back to the guy and they were ready to fight, so I came in and I looked at the guy and I looked at the bro and I asked the guy if he had a problem with my brother. The guy said no, so I told the guy to keep on walkin'. The brother was upset cuz he was like he wanted to fight the guy, but then I told him, "Open your eyes, stupid, and look across the street." There was a cop car there wait-in' for him with two cops right across the street from him. There was no car blockin' him, they was just right there lookin' at him, parked. If he would've fought he would've went to jail right then and there. So I saved him. That conflict resolution shit, it worked! [Interview, 7/25/1998]

Nonetheless, for all the undoubted talents and commitment among the membership for negotiating rather than fighting their way through street set-tlements, the organization's leaders realized that if this evolution of tech-niques was to be taken to the next level, outside expertise was needed. Thus, in addition to consulting Latino community leaders who, over time, had be-come highly influential, the leadership also agreed to attend training sessions given by professionals—sessions focusing on community development, sustaining processes of individual and group empowerment, and nonviolent problem-solving.

The Installation of New Forms of Authority

Aside from the emphasis on developing tried and tested leadership skills and group dynamics that have long worked for rank-and-file movements across the political spectrum, the organization had to change its culture at the top, particularly if it wanted to show that the leaders were not endorsing one strategy in public and implementing another in private. But how would the leaders in their everyday interactions pursue a nonviolent path in the face of so many macho-dominated rituals? More specifically, how do you create face-saving solutions to conflict when so many "hard" male reputations and identities are on the line?

> Tone tells me that the previous night there had been a fight between one of the member's wives and another girl. The fight was vicious and she got her brother to confront Tone. Apparently her brother was a body builder. People joked about him not having a neck, and joked about the way he didn't really want trouble, only to stand up for his sister; he said that he would ram an uzi up Tone's ass for her. Tone said that after talking with this guy, he discovered that the guy needed a way out without losing face. (Apparently, the fact that Tone was the leader of the Latin Kings made it even harder for the guy to back down, because then it would seem certain to everyone that he did so out of fear.) Tone said that all he needed to do was make it seem to everyone that they hit it off and they both realized there was no reason to fight. He laughed and said, "I actually did hit it off with this guy." I asked Tone what would've happened if this strategy had failed. He said, "Well I guess one of us would be dead right now" [L.K., Field notes, 11/18/1998].

Changing the Culture of Violence in the Group

But changing the behavior of the leadership was only part of the solution. The chief task was to change the culture of the group through institutionalizing new forms of behavior and rituals, particularly those that constituted key stages of a member's career. Thus, the obvious place to start would be the practices associated with entering and leaving the organization.

> Interviewer: What did you do to become a member?
>
> King R.: Well . . . I had to take a five-minute physical. I had to get hit by two people, you know, I couldn't hit back, but they don't hit me in my face. Everywhere else but the face and once I did that I went through

the lessons and stuff like that. He [his cousin] taught me a little bit, you know. And I became a Latin King.

Interviewer: Did you get in this way because of the Latin Kings' constitution or because that was the way your cousin learned it in Chicago?

King R.: Well, in Chicago, actually, yeah. In Chicago, that's the way it was back in those days. In Chicago they wanted to see if you were a man. If you were able in a fight to take the pain or run. So that's the way they were.

Interviewer: So, how is it here?

King R.: Here, you have to go through probation. They put you on five-alive, you gotta study your notes, read your lessons, they wanna see if you can knock a person out with your mind, you know, than with your hands [Interview, 3/22/1997].

Consequently, entering the group had clearly become a different proposition from the way it was in the Chicago Motherland. Gone were the beat-ins and the various forms of physical testing that were so part and parcel of gang lore across the country. However, the group was notorious in all its franchises for ensuring that membership entailed a lifelong commitment and that their slogan, "Once a King always a King," was more than just empty rhetoric. Removing this central element of fear and control over the membership was essential to the internal peace process—especially as it became evident to the leadership that the best members were those who remained in the group voluntarily, and that coerced membership often had the opposite effect, masking an insincere form of group cohesion and fostering levels of resentment among members that could be easily exploited by law enforcement (e.g., in the recruitment of snitches; see chapter 12).

In 1998, the group came up with a solution that was unprecedented. It introduced what it called the "golden gate"—an official ALKQN document showing that a member had voluntarily left the organization or had been summarily dismissed and that henceforth he or she was not acting as a member of the group. The form had to be witnessed by a second King and was usually signed in front of a superior. During the years 1998–1999 we estimate that there were at least fifty "golden gates" and the effect on the organization was noticeable in a number of ways. First, it significantly improved the public perception of the group; second, it increased the legitimate authority of the leadership; and third, it reduced reservations among younger members who might have been hesitant to join if they thought it would be so difficult to leave.

GOLDEN GATES

DISMISSAL/RESIGNATION
FROM THE
ALMIGHTY LATIN KING/QUEEN NATION

This is to certify that on this _____15th_____ day of the month of __November__, in the year __78__, I ▇▇▇▇▇▇▇▇▇▇▇▇▇▇▇▇ known in the ALMIGHTY LATIN KING/QUEEN NATION AS KING/QUEEN _K. Eley_ residing at ▇▇▇▇▇▇▇▇▇▇▇▇▇▇▇▇▇▇▇▇▇

And whose social security number is ▇▇▇▇ - ▇▇▇▇ - ▇▇▇▇ has been expelled/dismissed from the ALMIGHTY LATIN KING/QUEEN NATION, and am no longer a member of this most precious tribe of people(A.L.K.Q.N.), for reasons of either violation of our laws; code of ethics or voluntary leave. I am leaving as I came in, contrary to others beliefs, with no physical abuse or assault but rather with love and the A.L.K.Q.N.'s blessings. In either case, to whom ever it may be concerned be informed/advised that any action that I may take, from this day on through the rest of my life on this earth, on this planet, in this universe are in no way affiliated with or to be reflected upon the ALMIGHTY LATIN KING/QUEEN NATION or any member or affiliate of the A.L.K.Q.N.. Be also informed/advised that any supposed A.L.K.Q.N. information, literature or symbols that I may present to any person, place, animal, agency or institution is to be deemed false and incorrect. I now on this day sign as confirmation that I have not now or ever have witnessed any criminal activity executed by anyone in this nation (A.L.K.Q.N.). I now confirm that I have only seen and am witness to the fact that only good deeds, which do not conflict with the laws of this state, have been done by the A.L.K.Q.N. and its affiliates. I now give up my rights to disclose any A.L.K.Q.N. information, literature, symbols, customs or names of any members to any person, place, thing, agency, institution or organization on this earth in this universe from today on through the rest of my entire life, by signing my name to this document.

NAME: _Tyrone Sanders_   DATE: _11/15/58_

WITNESS: _K. Annel_

FIGURE 11.3 Example of a "Gold Gate" form.

D.B.: When someone breaks one of the rules, one of the different codes for the Kings, do you meet as a group, the five leaders in the Aztec Tribe or whatever, and then say, "What are we gonna do?"

King R.: We put our heads together. If we can't make a decision we take it to the whole body. Let them help us out cuz we're all leaders, like I said, and whatever final decision comes up, comes up, you know what I mean? We always give the brother a fair trial. We don't just strip brothers like that. We give 'em a fair trial. Some brothers beat it, some don't. Most of the brothers that don't beat it, we don't see them no more. It's not like we got rid of them or anything, they just don't hang out with us no more, and I feel that instead of takin' someone's colors away from them and hurting them, it's more damaging taking their colors away and saying, "Bye, you're not no more a King," because once that person leaves he's gonna be missing out a lot, man, cuz we got a good family here and he's gonna be all by himself and he's gonna say, "Wow, I can't go to this any more."

D.B.: Do you see that a lot?

King R.: Yes, I do.

D.B.: People are being stripped.

King R.: Yeah, they're being stripped.

D.B.: Are they being given golden gateways?

King R.: Yeah. Golden gates. Now you can see them. They're like to themselves. It's not like the same. They don't have that big family, they don't have that support there no more. A lot of them become drug addicts and then they're like lost or a lot of them, it's like they're lost, like they need that—that unity, they need somebody to say, "Yo. I don't have a brother. Can you help me out?" Cuz, see, all my life, like I said, I got a brother and a sister, so I'm the oldest, so I had to protect them all my life. When is somebody gonna help me? I don't have big brothers, now I got about 150 big brothers. So if I need somebody to talk to I go to one of my brothers and I talk to him. It's good to have that family [Interview, 10/1/1998].

In this chapter we have traced some of the goals and the corresponding practices that the group struggled to implement during the transition period. We have argued that, for the most part, the group was seriously engaged in trying to become something quite new as far as street subcultures were concerned, but also something quite traditional when it came to the history of social movements. In Touraine's language, the group was functioning as if this "new" Nation were the continuator and "mutator" (Touraine 1988) of a radical and even revolutionary history, and it was not afraid to turn to outsiders for advice and support to develop this history. Did this mean, however, that the group was progressing without stumbling over the many contradictions contained in its own gang history? Quite the contrary, the organization openly conceded that it could not transform itself overnight and that its links to Chicago, to the prison system, and to the street both compelled it and constrained it from making the kind of radical changes that a bona fide social movement required before it could proudly declare its new identity to be firmly in place.

CHAPTER 12

PERCEIVED ADVERSARIES

Interviewer: OK. What kind of things do leaders of your organization like to speak about at your open meetings?
Queen C.: The leaders, they like to be inspiring us to keep on going forward in life. They like to inspire us . . . even though the government, federal, mostly like the FBI, CIA, or whatever, like they're tryin' to bring us down, but we have to keep on goin'.

Interview, 7/8/1997

King J.: I think it's just ever since we've been having these rallies they've been attacking us like this, so, you know, they're scared of something, that's all I gotta say. And, apparently, it ain't nothin' to do with violence. They're scared we might get somewhere, somewhere they don't want us to be.

Interview, 10/2/1998

King S.: We're here to help all Latin people that wanna be helped, that wanna join this beautiful organization that we belong to, to fight and struggle against our problems which is not us! We have to live in poverty, we have to deal with each other every day in the street . . . no, our problem is the Giulianis, the Mary Jo Whites, the Government, that's out problem! City Hall is our problem, Shafer is our problem, gettin'. . . more money to the budget so they could get more brothers educated and so sisters could go to school, go to John Jay, go to Harvard, so they could get into law, and they could get into those classrooms and teach our youth. That's the problem, not us! Then we could build more decent buildings and we could get the brothers that don't have education, but they have talent. They good with they hands, they could do construction work, they're good laborers. They have work. That's with whom our beef is, not the Bloods, not the Crips, not no gang. My beef is with the government, changing life, changing the way our government is, that's my problem.

Interview, 7/9/1997

Introduction

The notion of adversaries in Touraine's schema is critical for the impetus of social-movement building and is a key to any movement's claim to historicity. In order to have a coherent sense of itself (what Castells calls its "resistance identity"; see chapters 1 and 9) the movement has to have a somewhat articulate grasp of its adversaries, otherwise it is difficult to see how a process of identity construction that claims to be oppositional can proceed with any momentum. In the world of gang literature, such an intrinsically political process with regard to oppositional conflicts is almost entirely absent, as we have discussed in earlier chapters, although the role of conflict itself is one of the central tropes of gang research. Traditionally, the enemies most frequently cited are other local gangs (Decker and VanWinkle 1996; Sanders 1994), which provide both real and symbolic targets of fear and loathing so that gangs always have sufficient identifiable foes against which to organize, recruit, and develop their internal solidarity, if only to socially implode at the community level.[1] Occasionally, studies report individual gang members' expressing an intuitive dislike for members of other social classes (Jankowski 1991) and other racial and ethnic groups, but such tensions never lead to collective mobilizations in which gang members' class and social antipathies for the logic(s) of domination (Castells 1997) are articulated and transformed into social action.

In our study of the ALKQN, however, these real and symbolic conflicts between the group and a range of interconnected forces that are instrumental to what might loosely be called the "dominant society" were precisely one of the most visible and defining elements of its political and subcultural trajectory. At the same time, the group's participation in these struggles was not limited to itself but rather was (1) part of the community's general efforts to respond to some extremely oppressive policies and actions by the state at the local level and (2) related to the restructuring of the political economy as New York became increasingly the site of global interactions of capital, labor, and technology (Sassen 1998).[2]

Nonetheless, there were other adversaries that were particular to the group, and these, at first glance, appear to have more in common with what is typically thought of as gang behavior. But even these "enemies," it could easily be argued, emerged out of a set of socioeconomic dynamics and ideological processes that define the existence of a "dominant society": discrepant income distribution, unequal access to education, residential segregation, and so on. Hence, in this final chapter, our analysis will concentrate on delineating both the external and the internal forces with which the group was preoccupied and, where possible, suggest their interconnections within a sociohistorical context. As we do so it should become clearer how these forces helped shape the group's identity and provided both the constraints and the impetus for its collective evolution.

External and Internal Adversaries

In the bible of the ALKQN, the primary opposition to the group is seen in the form of white society and those who would oppress the Latino masses, keeping them in poverty, denying them opportunities to achieve their potential, and devaluing or hiding from them their true culture and history. What these structures and symbols of oppression constitute is not made explicit, although at various points it could be construed as the "government," the criminal justice system, colonialism, the materialism and antispiritual nature of modern capitalism, and the prejudicial treatments and discriminatory practices of white-dominated institutions in general. For example, in one section, it states: "The white man will not put our children in college for us. Because they are afraid that we will take over." And then in another:

> We are not AMERICAN, we are one of 22 million Puerto Ricans who are victims of Americanism. One of the 22 million Puerto Ricans who are victims of democracy. Nothing but disguised hypocrisy . . . and we see America through the eyes of the victim. Brothers and Sisters I am telling it like it is then and now. America is a prison for Puerto Ricans and other oppressed people. And we come from those oppressed people. And they look to us and others for leadership. It was for our uncompromising stand and for giving voice to the deepest feelings of the most oppressed that our good brothers and sisters were hounded and finally assassinated by agents and white folks. . . . We are Revolutionary Nationalists but we are remembered as proletarian internationalists, heroic fighters in the struggle against oppression and imperialism.

These composite constructions of the oppressor represent early efforts by the group to define its political opponents. In these texts there are no data to buttress the claims and no sustained arguments to convince the reader of a just cause, only the barbed renderings of frustrated, angry subjects "naming" (Freire 1970) the sources of their historical exclusion and issuing a call for organized, from-below resistance. Cited alongside the various incarnations of the external foe are a number of internal adversaries, generally referred to as "fakers," traitors, and cowards. These are group members who function as Trojan horses, weakening the solidarity of the organization and threatening to prevent the group from reaching its individual and collective goals. Taking this discussion further, a systematic interpretation of what members felt were the real and symbolic obstacles to their self-empowerment agenda is provided below.

External Adversaries

The bulk of the data for this analysis are drawn from respondents' answers to the question: What difficulties do you face in reaching your goals? Of the total sample, sixty-five answered unhesitatingly that powerful, interconnected societal forces were conspiring not simply to undermine their organization but to destroy it.[3] Some might interpret such a consensus as an indication of collective paranoia brought about by the group's conspiratorial outlook and history of subterranean practices, yet we found the members' views to be both varied and discerning; they based their opinions not on what they had heard or been told but on what they had experienced first-hand. However, before discussing at length the individual themes that emerged, we will bring up several points worth mentioning about the character and overall thrust of members' views.

First, most members often held contradictory positions when discussing their adversaries. On the one hand, they complained that bitter experience had proved that compromise and negotiation with "the enemy" was next to impossible; on the other, they sought to respond to and reach out to those same forces, in search of an illusory middle ground. In fact, many members believed in the same threats to social control as the social controllers themselves, despite the obvious irony inherent in such a position.

Second, the range of adversaries perceived by most members was surprisingly limited. This seemed to reflect the still localized development of the members' consciousness and their transitioning into a more complex and unbounded worldview. Furthermore, considering the array of forces that was pitted against the group during what is one of the most conservative political eras of the twentieth century, there was a degree of optimism about the group's trajectory that often seemed to bear little relation to reality.

Third, there were some differences between the genders regarding which adversaries were the worst. For example, according to thirty respondents from the Kings, the primary problem was the police, in their many different guises. In contrast, more than half the Queens (sixteen) cited that "the media" was their chief adversary, although they often saw the police working in collusion with the tabloids and television news reporters.

This difference can most obviously be explained by a differing set of ascriptions given to each of the subgroups. For both law enforcement and the political establishment the Kings were viewed as an all-too-conspicuous version of "social dynamite" (Spitzer 1975) that, if left unchecked, would increasingly appeal to the city's lower-class male youth. Further, the Kings were also seen as the epitome of in-your-face, organized, barrio masculinity that competed with the other exemplars of working-class, street masculinity, namely, the police department itself. The Queens, on the other hand, were still seen by the police as the more restrained female "auxiliaries" and, to that extent, the police resisted the media-created stereotype of the new violent female (Chesney-Lind 1997).

The other adversaries mentioned were, in order of frequency: (1) the New York City mayor, Rudolph Giuliani; (2) the New York City street gang, the Bloods, (3) white society, (4) the Board of Education, and (5) the upper classes. In the following, we organize our discussion around the four adversaries most commonly cited: the police, the media, the mayor and the Bloods. Where appropriate we incorporate the other three—white society, the Board of Education, and the upper classes—into this discussion as well.

The Police

The literature on gang members' views of the police, perhaps surprisingly, is rather thin. Most studies concur with the findings of Decker and Van Winkle (1996:210) that: "Our subjects obviously do not like the police. Even those that said they had "good" relations often meant only that they themselves were not being harassed at this particular time." Jankowski (1991) deviates from this perspective, arguing that gang members' negative view of law enforcement is mediated by community dynamics and traditions that directly affect the dialectics of the gang-police relationship. For example, in large cities such as Los Angeles and New York, he found that the former's lack of civic culture allowed paramilitary solutions to the "gang problem" to be the norm as reflected in the "Ramparts" scandal (see Hayden 2001), while for the latter, its history of community participation in local politics kept such draconian responses to some extent in check. This at least was the case until the era of the Giuliani administration.

Among our respondents, we found a generalizable contempt for law enforcement based on (1) negative personal and group experiences with representatives of local and national police forces and (2) the widely held community view that the police, still one of the least diverse forces in the nation (Amnesty International 1996), are essentially an outside, illegitimate authority whose role is to protect the white power structure. At the same time, however, there were some members who expressed a certain amount of empathy, at the individual level, for the police officer's lot and at times there was even room for a modicum of cooperation between the two seemingly opposing sides.

HANGING OUT, BEING PICKED ON, AND SYSTEMATIC HARASSMENT
As working-class youth in poor areas of the city, many of the Kings and Queens spent time on the streets as part of their normative childhood experiences. Thus, socializing with friends and taking in the dramas of a city famed for its democratic street life (Jacobs 1961) was not just about the lure of street culture. Rather, it was related to the traditions of the city itself, where for almost two centuries citizens young and old have participated in the social parades on urban thoroughfares that have given neighborhoods their particular cultural "feel" and residents their sense of place and interconnectedness.[4] At the same time, however, there are powerful class, race, and gender influences that overdetermine this predilection for the streets. For many poor youth living in overcrowded housing, growing up in disruptive and sometimes abusive households, and/or being socialized into ultramasculine gender roles (see chapter 4), the street can be a place of refuge, a space to be oneself, and a terrain for honing one's identity.

Nonetheless, while the street has always been a natural extension of the living quarters of the urban lower orders (and both authors have their own life histories to verify this), a wide array of laws has been created to contain and prevent them from assuming the nightmarish form of the "dangerous classes." Consequently, laws and ordinances such as "unlawful assembly," "disorderly conduct," "mob action," "loitering," "antidrug-trafficking," "vagrancy," and "youth curfews" have been applied to individuals and collectives for the purposes of bringing about a certain type of social order (Chambliss 1970; Conquergood 1993), primarily in poorer neighborhoods. In such neighborhoods visions of "disorder" (Skogan 1990) and "disorganization" register every emotion from scorn and contempt to sympathy and curiosity from outsiders (Gans 1962). This experience of containment and social control at the hands of law enforcement is what many of the Kings expressed both in formal and informal exchanges:

D.B.: Have they picked you up before?

King J.: Yeah. This is always happening. Everywhere we go they pick us up and blame us with hanging out in the corner, "Oh, you're loitering," bull-crap charges, you know, just to make you go through the system and give your life a livin' hell, you know?

D.B.: How many times have you been picked up for this?

King J.: About 3 or 4 times.

D.B.: Three or four times? All in Brooklyn?

King J.: Yeah.

D.B.: Are they different officers each time?

King J.: Yeah. They mostly, um, different officers that I've seen.

D.B.: Now, King Tone said that this was also going on in the Bronx. Have you heard this?

King J.: Yeah. In the Bronx, almost every borough they be doin' this. They be comin' from the Bronx, the same people you see in every borough, so we seen 'em in the Bronx, in Brooklyn, they'll pop up anywhere. They're always there. That's harassin' [Interview, 7/1/1998].

During the research, there was no specific law aimed at so-called street gangs and it was not illegal to belong to such a group whatever its ideology or defining characteristics, yet many of the male respondents reported being constantly harassed for doing little other than being with their fellow members. In interviews with respondents from different tribes, the same comments were heard, signaling that it must have been police policy to contain the group wherever it demonstrated its presence. Such a strategy had to be decided upon at the highest level, otherwise it would be difficult to see how its enactment would be so uniform. For the most part, such "harassment" happened in local public social spaces, such as street corners and/or neighborhood parks, although the police reserved the right to appear at any time, anywhere:

C.S.: OK. In what ways have you had difficulties in reaching these goals?

Queen B.: Cops.

C.S.: Why?

Queen B.: I don't know. It's like cops hear that you're a Latin King and all this and that. Right away they think bad. Right away you're doin' somethin' wrong. Like we get in the train from a universal—first, they don't do nothin' bad, we're just sittin' there all together, we're all tight, tryin' to go home. It's a long journey from here to upstate. Cops started thinking of followin' us, you know? Why you gotta do that for? It's like besides that, I don't know, sometimes you can't get a job because they find out you're a King or something or you can't do this or they won't let you go here or you're not allowed in there. Stuff like that [Interview, 8/1/1998].

FIGURE 12.1 New York City Police raid an ALKQN "universal" at Broadway Temple United Methodist Church, with Fr. Barrios (coauthor) in attendance.

Clearly, one purpose of all this police attention was to impose strict boundaries on the group's movements, perspectives, and actions, and through such highly charged interactions the police were constantly reaffirming the group's deviant gang status, which, whether the members sought it or not, had become their "master status" (Jankowski 1991). More important, however, what members experienced was not that they were simply a part of the universal "gang problem," against which police forces and criminal justice systems across the nation had been technologically and ideologically mobilized (Klein 1995),[5] rather, members felt that the law and order war against them had deep political roots:

I met with Professor L. today, he told me that one of his students, a Puerto Rican, has been working on the gang task force. According to the student,

during a recent meeting of representatives from a range of police units dealing with the "gang problem" in New York City, the Latin Kings' involvement
in politics and, in particular, in the Puerto Rican independence struggle was
the center of discussion. At the meeting, many leading officers and administrators, who described themselves not only as experts on gangs but also on
"terrorists," felt that the course this group was taking was "deeply disturb-
ing." The problem they felt was not the group's involvement in crime but its
turn to radicalism. As one person at the meeting phrased it, "there's no way
we're gonna let a bunch of gangbangers think they're the Panthers or the
Young Lords" [DB, Field notes, 1/18/1998].

GATHERING INTELLIGENCE, PROVOCATIONS, AND THE CULTURE OF
SURVEILLANCE As the war on the organization gathered steam and the motives behind the assault revealed more political than criminal concerns, a
range of specialized units and personnel came to play an expanding role.
Consequently, both ALKQN members and their families discussed not only
their interactions with local police officers, but their many dealings with the
Gang Task Force, the Federal Bureau of Investigation, the Drug Enforcement
Agency, and state marshals. For a while, it seemed as if no amount of resources would be spared to bring down the group's leadership, sow dissension
among the ranks, disintegrate its structure, and sap the membership's will to
struggle. In many ways, the character of the campaign resembled that of
counterinsurgency techniques used in paramilitary circles (Kitson 1960), and
it certainly bore a great many similarities to the COINTELPRO policies of
the J. Edgar Hoover years, when black and Latino radical movements and the
New Left were the chief targets (Churchill and Vander Wall 1986).

D.B.: When they were interrogating you, was it like endless questions?

King J.: Yeah, just a lot of questions, just to try to confuse you and stuff.

D.B.: And they had you all separate, right?

King J.: Yes.

D.B.: And how long did the questions last for?

King J.: Around 15 minutes.

D.B.: So they kept you in there for like 15 minutes at a time?

King J.: Mmmm, hmmm. Maybe some longer.

D.B.: And did they say that their main purpose was to get you to inform?

King J.: Yeah, they was like, um, they were offering money, they were asking like "Do you have a job? How much do you get? We could double that, or . . .," you know, "We'll pay you to work with us," stuff like that [Interview, 9/2/1998]

The campaign of systematic harassment, phone taps, constant surveillance, recruitment of "snitches"[6] and infiltrators, and periodic sweeps produced the desired results, as many of the members became unsure who to trust and who to believe. The targets, however, were not just restricted to the group but to anyone who had a close working and supportive relationship with its members, as is made clear by the following interview with a member of the clergy who employed a number of Kings and Queen in his nonprofit organization:

Father D.: So K. [the group's lawyer] asked me to go upstairs with him and talk with gang intelligence. The first time I was there they didn't have anything to do with me. . . .

D.B.: Do you know their names?

Father D.: No, I don't but now they sit around with me, they'll talk with you about their children or whatever. It can be quite cordial and friendly. We just don't talk about Tone or about the Nation. But my lines get tapped, my telephone lines, the whole nine yards! Although a lot of that has subsided. I don't hear the taps anymore. They're terrible at tapping, they really are. You hear the music playing in the background and people talking and stuff like that. It gets ridiculous after a while.

D.B.: Why do you think they are changing their focus?

Father D.: There's nothing on me. I have no felonies, I pay my taxes. I mean, I'm not a jaywalker, I don't walk on the grass, I'm like so clean it's pitiful [Interview, 10/1/1998].

But while the role of the police in its many guises was to disrupt, corrupt, and contain, it also had to ensure that sufficient illegal actions were committed and that proof was forthcoming for the eventual prosecutorial debacle.

D.B.: How do the snitches work?

King M.: They find out all your skeletons in the closet and then they work on them. You know, if you've been off drugs for a while and trying to get straight then they'll offer you something. If you've left the drug trade and started to go legit, they'll come up with an offer you can't refuse. That's the way it works, I've seen it over and over again. They prey on the weak, and we have a lot of brothers who are trying to build a new life, so they are vulnerable [Interview, 5/1/2000].

Several months after the research period ended, a leading King, his words almost seeming to be scripted by state agencies wanting to get the message across to other would-be street radicals, had this to say:

King H.: The Kings are only one part of me and right now it's a small part. When I joined they were a big part, they were going somewhere but not now and I don't think they can ever change. You know why? Because the way the government has got us, with all the paid snitches and informers, we can't get around. I was very naive. I used to think that the informers were all about getting intelligence but most of what they do is provoke situations and this brings us right down and we can't get out of it. That's the way I see it right now and I don't see really how its gonna change.

BUT THERE MUST BE CONTRADICTIONS IN THIS RELATIONSHIP! Indeed there were. As is often the case between social controllers and the subjected class, there is a negotiated social relationship in which mutual interests can be recognized and a certain form of collaboration can be found. Jankowski (1991), for example, claims that although police insist their goal is to eradicate gangs, the operational relationship between police and gangs is one of accommodation and regulation. He argues that the power of community politicians, especially in places like New York and Boston, would not allow the police to make a relentless paramilitary assault on gangs, and neither is it in their self-interest to do so. Gangs, for Jankowski, provide the police with useful intelligence as well as the pretext to expand their specialized resources. In the following, we see an example of the police in their accommodationist mode. This is not to assert that there was too much trust between the two parties, just that in specific contexts, the two could find a common approach to a problem and both sides seemed genuinely appreciative of the other when it happened.

Luis and I go to Brooklyn to meet with Tone—he's not there but a driver, King B., is waiting for us in a red Cadillac. He says he's going to take us to the X precinct where Tone is dealing with a case involving two Kings. When we arrive at the precinct King H. is waiting for us. He is talking to a member of the Gang Unit, a white guy with red hair in his late 20s. King H. is saying, "Now, you know we have to work together. We don't want things to get out of control over nothing." The other guy seems to be agreeing with him. It is obvious there is some kind of working relationship here. A few minutes later Tone appears, looking agitated, "It's fucked up. They are accusing two members of the Nation of rape against these girls who are under age. The brothers say it was consensual and that these girls are running scared of their mother. She's a junkie and has seven kids and they are all running wild all over the place. One of the brothers has just gotten off the rock [Riker's Island] after a year. He just beat a twenty-five-year rap and now this has to happen. I've got an agreement with Sergeant L. that he won't go after them until tomorrow, so we have to go talk to them and see what we can do. But he [the police officer] is cool, you know. Their photos are up on the wall and he could go looking for them now and put out a warrant but he wants to work with us. We have a good relationship with him . . . you might want to talk to him some time [D.B., Field notes, 7/29/1997].

THE FINAL ACT Despite the occasions when cooperation and interdependence characterized at least part of the relationship, there was a core antagonism that was especially driven by the criminal justice politics of the day. During much of 1998, the members were being prepared at both public and private meetings for a grand jury indictment against the group that would authorize all the paramilitary forces to go into action and produce one grand final celebratory sweep of the organization. Such talk and rumor reinforced to everyone that no matter how hard members tried to reform, they would always be singled out as criminal deviants. It was an impossible contradiction since, as we have seen, the very key to members' resolving many of their "issues" was the organization that was causing them to be labeled. Yet, based on our observations, few people left the group due to these fears and considerations. In fact, it seemed to be quite the opposite; the nearer the group came to the mass round-up, the more youth, in particular, appeared to be joining. King Tone, below, recollects the day, May 14, 1998, when Operation Crown entered its concluding stage:

> They came for us at around four in the morning. Dozens of cops from the Feds, NYPD, DEA [Drug Enforcement Agency] and I even saw someone from Giuliani's [the mayor of New York City] team. After they threw us in handcuffs they took us all to a military barracks at Fort Hamilton, Brooklyn. We were greeted with a big banner that said "Welcome Latin Kings." They had black and gold balloons everywhere, coffee and donuts all laid out . . . for them it was like a big victory celebration. We were all processed and then taken off to different precincts.

The irony, arrogance, and gamesmanship of the police as described in the account, above, powerfully indicate the level of rivalry that existed between the two groups. But what was it a celebration of? Who had the "good guys" defeated? What large-scale crimes had the group committed? The Commissioner of the New York City Police Department had this to say, directly challenging the new identity of the ALKQN:

In spite of the Latin Kings' attempts to portray themselves as a benign, community-oriented organization, this gang has always been, and continues to this day to be, a dangerous group of criminals. While their leaders may speak of peace initiatives, day care and scholarships, our investigation shows that they continue to be involved in a wide range of very violent crimes that erode and destroy the communities rather than improve or build them [*New York Times*, 5/15/1998:B-3].

In reality, less than half of the ninety-four arrested were actual members of the organization and "while more than half of the state and Federal charges filed . . . were felony charges, there were no homicide allegations and many of the charges were misdemeanors" (*New York Times*, 5/15/1998:B-3). The sociological reality and absurdity of the drama notwithstanding, a stoic, square-jawed police commissioner continued to assert in front of the cameras that another successful action in the endless crusade against the city's organized street criminals had just occurred: "Today's arrests have effectively dismantled the command structure of the Latin Kings organization by effectively removing the so-called supreme king, who supervised all of New York State, and each of the borough leaders, who are called crowns" (*New York Times*, 5/15/1998:A-10).

Six days after the incarceration of many of the group's local and regional leaders, approximately three hundred Latin Kings and Queens gathered to hold their monthly meeting in a church on 179th Street in the Washington Heights neighborhood of Manhattan. Although the mood among the members was definitely somber, and in private conversations there was great consternation about the future activities of the group, a large body of the membership remained committed to the organization. As one leading member put it, "They did it to the Young Lords, they did it to the Panthers and now they doing it to us. Well we ain't runnin' and we ain't going nowhere. And you know why? Cuz we the community. That's what they don't get. We not just the Latin Kings we the community and we're righteous."

The Corporate Media

Was the transformation of the Kings and Queens simply a ruse, a legerdemain designed to pull the wool over the public's eyes, as the police, who have

FIGURE 12.2 Several days after the biggest sweep since prohibition, Latin Kings wait outside Broadway Temple, United Methodist Church, Washington Heights, for their general meeting to begin. (Photo by Steve Hart.)

followed this group for more than ten years, maintained? Or were they genuinely taking the path to reform and simply being maligned by an establishment in search of enemies? This debate over the apparent twin personae of the group was played out in the local and national media as journalists from major corporate-owned tabloids, magazines, and television networks presented stories of both depictions. In response, members had an ambivalent attitude toward the process of news construction in which they were heavily featured. On the one hand, the majority condemned "the media" for its coverage of the group, which they felt stigmatized all current members as gangbangers. On the other hand, the group's leaders looked to media workers for some form of honest accounting, as if such workers could opt out of their occupational cultures and play the role of unprejudiced observers.

BEING DEMONIZED AND SCAPEGOATED

> C.S.: OK. What kind of difficulties has your organization had in reaching those goals?
>
> Queen G.: What difficulties? The media. The media puts us down like we're gangbangers, killers, you name it, and that's what we were, you know, but they don't see what we are doing now. As the more good we doin' the more bad they're gonna give us our names, but you know what? We learned, in our own studies, we learned that we don't have to listen to the media because we're gonna go higher and higher. The more they put us down, the more we gonna attempt to go up and to uplift this Nation [Interview, 8/13/1998].

This process of demonization and criminalization to which Queen G. refers has been repeatedly analyzed by sociologists and criminologists who have pointed to the government-media stereotyping of young inner-city populations as a practice stretching back through much of this century (Gilbert 1986). What many of the studies have found is that the violent, bestial, and primitivistic stereotypes of gang youths (Conquergood 1992) have been constant themes in crime and community reports and play a powerful role in constructing the symbolic reality for a mass audience, most of whom have little real contact with actual gang members. In effect, such reporting has been an effective tool in fueling "moral panics" (Cohen 1972) at various stages of the economic cycle, reflected in successive waves of antigang legislation at local, state, and federal levels (Jackson and Rudman 1993; Kessel 2003). Thus, around such populist concerns as urban decay, rising immigrant populations, juvenile crime, the drug culture, failing public schools, and youth immorality, gangs have been "tagged" (Young 1971) as a leading factor contributing to the problem rather than as a primary symptom of a broader set of social, economic, and political contradictions.

In Erikson's (1966) terms, the use of such "enemies" is an effort by the dominant order to restore society's social boundaries by ensuring that the threatening Other is managed and brought into line (Spitzer 1975). Not surprisingly, many Kings and Queens felt that they were, wittingly or unwittingly, another example of "blaming the victim" in U.S. urban social policy.

> C.S.: So the organization's main goals are rallies and demonstrations?

Queen T.: Like demonstrations, like food drives, you know, to bring people of like Latin descent and now other ethnicities as well, together to show that we should stop fighting each other, we shouldn't kill each other because that's what the government wants, or exactly what the media loves seeing. We should expose the real enemy and, I mean, I wouldn't say that just like the government is the enemy, but certain people in the government that target us, you know, as a youth gang or whatever they wanna put it, you know? . . . they're really trying to use us as scapegoats. When they're really doing illegal activities they tryin' to divert attention from what they're doing wrong and trying to focus the attention on us.

This "structured feeling" (Williams 1965) of being persecuted by media agents working in tandem with the criminal justice system was evidenced in the many stories surrounding the group, particularly during the early to mid-1990s. It seemed to the members that the manifesto's claim about a bloc of interests out to scuttle their efforts was true. Later, as the group actively entered the newsmaking process, taking steps to blunt the hegemonic thrust of crime stories as ideology (Fishman 1978), a different set of dynamics could be detected between the organization and the media industry. The group began to tread a path that was unique among street subcultures and raised a number of issues about resistance possibilities among subaltern classes, including the production of their own images, if not their own voices (Spivak 1988).

CAN THE MEDIA BE CHALLENGED BY A STREET ORGANIZATION? After years of meeting in the shadows of the barrio, many Kings and Queens still remained skeptical about media intentions, and yet they continued to carefully negotiate the representational terrain even with the most powerful news and multimedia corporations, such as the *New York Times*, the *Daily News*, ABC, NBC, and the Fox News Network. Consequently, representatives of the group appeared in a number of lengthy feature articles as well as television investigative reports, and despite the obvious cynicism that pervaded some of these accounts, the group made remarkable headway against the semiotic equation that gangs = violence = drugs = Latin Kings. In doing so they were engaging in an effort to actively make the news themselves, a feat similar in some respects to Barak's (1988) notion of "newsmaking criminology" and Gitlin's (1980) reading of the contradictory relationship between the media and radical social movements in the 1960s.[7] To highlight the effectiveness of the group's new relationship to those who would represent them, we have reviewed the headlines from twelve feature-length articles that appeared from the early nonreform period in 1994 to the later reform period in

1998. The first and second set of headlines are drawn from the mainstream press, while the third comes from a range of more liberal news sources. While this brief media analysis is no substitute for a thoroughgoing treatment of the representational data,[8] it suffices to underscore our claims about the quality and impact of the group's resistance.

Mainstream Headlines Pre-Reform

20 MEMBERS OF HISPANIC GANG INDICTED IN MULTIPLE KILLINGS—A FEDERAL LEGAL ASSAULT ON REALM OF LATIN KINGS

—New York Times, 6/22/1994

DIARY OF A STREET GANG: MORE THAN 20,000 PAGES OF LETTERS, STANDING IN EVIDENCE AGAINST A SCORE OF LATIN KINGS AND QUEENS

—Newsday, 6/28/1995

CHARGED WITH MURDER, TELL BRUTAL TALES OF LIFE AND DEATH ON THE STREETS OF NEW YORK

—Newsday, 6/28/1995

ALL THE QUEENS' MEN: LIKE SO MANY OF THE LATIN KINGS AND QUEENS, STREET GANG'S SOVEREIGN ZULMA AWAITS A MURDER TRIAL BEHIND BARS, UNDONE BY HER KING—AND HER OWN WORDS

—Newsday, 6/28/1995

Mainstream News Headlines During Reform Period

SECRETS OF THE KINGS: HAVE THE LATIN KINGS, THE CITY'S MOST NOTORIOUS STREET GANG, FORSAKEN THEIR VIOLENT PAST? THEIR LEADER KNOWS

—New York magazine, 2/17/1997

KINGS ON THE STREET: A Look at the 2 Faces of the City's Most Notorious Gang

—Newsday, 10/27/1997

TOP LATIN KING'S INTENT IS AN ISSUE: He offers Image of Peace as Police See Man of Violence

—New York Times, 11/20/1997

An Inside Look at a Gang's Grisly Drama: Trial of a Deposed Leader Offers Contrasting Views of the Latin Kings

—New York Times, 11/18/1996

Non-Mainstream Headlines During Reform Period

KING OF NEW YORK

—Village Voice, 10/10/1996

HAS KING ATONED?

—Brooklyn Bridge, March 1997

How the Gangs Made Peace in New York's Ghetto

—London Weekend Guardian, 1/2/1999

THE POWER OF KING LOVE

—Spin, September 1996

ANATOMY OF KING TONE

Vibe, July 1997

A BID FOR THE CROWN: The Latin Queens, the female branch of New York's notorious Latin Kings, try to play a part in the group's drive to reform before the media and the city

—Latina, January 1998

COMMENTS ON THE PRE-REFORM AND REFORM FEATURE HEADLINES
In the first group of headlines, we see several common themes that bear out essentially what Jankowski (1991) states is the striking similarity of gang-media stories. First, the nature of the group is linked explicitly to "killings," "murder," and brutality, and it is presented in such a way that involvements are seen as a defining characteristic of the group. This is done in the first headline by mentioning the indictment of the federal government, which in the public's mind denotes legitimacy, while in the second headline it is done through mentioning the 20,000 pages of written evidence, and in the third it is achieved through telling the reader that a leading Queen has indicted herself, in "her own words." The second theme is the ironic use of the notion of royalty, which invokes the notion of bloody, aristocratic in-fighting and delusions of grandeur. In sum, there is nothing in these headlines that conjure up any doubt in the reader's mind that this group is guilty as charged, that its

members are pathologically motivated, and that they represent a real (and not imagined) threat to society.

In comparison, the second group of headlines contain much more equivocation and ambivalence as to the nature of the group. Here we see references to the group's past rather than present as violent. In addition, there is talk of peace, intent, and self-reform, which are all terms that denote positive agency and a different quality of seriousness. At the same time, such a soft focus for the group is counterposed by references to the group's notoriously secret world, and participation in a "grisly drama." Clearly, these headlines are designed to demonstrate to the reader that the jury is still out on the legitimacy of this group's new orientation—a notion bolstered by competing quotes from members of the group and law enforcement "experts."

Finally, the third collection of headlines hardly features any of the evocative, inflammatory vocabulary of the other groups. For the most part, they have short captions without any explanatory bylines, and though they also use royalty as a key descriptor, it is not done cynically but rather suggestively, leaving the reader to digest the article before making any assumptions.

Thus, the above texts provide a powerful example of the extent to which the ALKQN was able to effectively intervene in its own representation over time, not only by affecting the content of the news but by impacting one of the vital instruments of media story-telling: the headline. The importance of headline construction is emphasized in the work of van Dijk (1988), who calls them the semantic macrostructure of news narratives.

The relevance of van Dijk's analysis of media-ethnic relations to our own treatment of gangs and, in particular, the ALKQN, should be clear. In basic terms, we are arguing that the media conceptualization of "the gang" and of the ALKQN has been a not very subtle form of race and/or ethnic derogation (Murji 1999). This process is captured by Conquergood in his commentary on the representational treatment of the Chicago Latin Kings:

> "Gang" has become a fantasy-fetish of primitivism that is co-extensive with other colonialist tropes deployed to erect barriers between Self and Other. In our postcolonial world the alien Other has migrated from the margins of empire and is now, in an ironic twist of history, colonizing our cities. The figure of the gang member in multicultural late twentieth-century urban America is an ethnic male member of the migrant and un- and underemployed classes. Like the representations of "natives" in the colonies, representations of "gangs" in the cities are deployed to contain and control the "dangerous classes," as urban primitives [Conquergood 1992:4].

The Mayor

> I don't think that youth programs will help the Bloods, the Crips, the Latin Kings, the Zulu Nation, MS13. These are gangs that begin in jail and in prison. These are violent repeat career criminals and I don't think that giving them sewing lessons is going to help. So we have a major disagreement about how you approach crime. I believe that social programs are important: they are valuable, they can help. But when you are dealing with hardened criminals like the members of the Bloods, the Crips, the Latin Kings, and the Zulu Nation, it is almost an inappropriate thing to start talking about youth programs for them [Mayor Giuliani during a debate with his Democratic challenger, Ruth Messinger. *New York Times*, 10/10/1998].

It is usually the case that oppositional social movements include some apparatus of the state in the panoply of foes against which they are organizing and strategizing. Certainly, for most lower-class social movements, a city's mayor is probably the closest its members come, both physically and conceptually, to anything that resembles an institutional body dispensing services or seeking to legitimately contain the citizenry. Therefore, in general, any mayor could be expected to figure in an urban grassroots movement's worldview, but the erstwhile mayor of New York City, Rudolph Giuliani, was, even by New York standards, an extraordinarily controversial public figure whose uncompromising stances on "crime," welfare, public education, civil rights, the arts, property development, and health care inspired both hatred and adulation from the populace (Barrett 2000).[9]

Consequently, it was little wonder the mayor was cited in almost every public speech made by a leading or rank-and-file member of ALKQN as an example of anti-Latino, anti-working-class bias. In the eyes of the group, it was as if the mayoral administration was engaged in a personal vendetta against the organization, as he whittled away at every vestige of New York's welfare state tradition while insinuating his law-and-order apparatus into every facet of social life for the poor and the working classes. Most ALKQN members agreed that this man would not back down, would never seek a middle ground, and would prosecute his real and imagined enemies into extinction.

C.S.: What difficulties has your organization had in reaching those goals?

Queen S.: Giuliani. That's our main problem . . . right there. So I gotta figure out something. We could succeed if, you know, if we knock down that wall. We're gonna knock that wall down, you know? So far . . . we're takin steps. They're not that big, but Giuliani he's doin' everything to stop us [Interview, 10/22/1998].

In the following discussion, we look at some of the group's objections to this major player in local and national politics, focusing on two areas that Giuliani saw as key to the success of his tenure: criminal justice and education.

CRIMINAL JUSTICE   The ALKQN, by its very nature, was opposed to the mayor's vision of criminal justice and its unwavering reliance on punitive and coercive systems of social control, ranging from his assault on "quality-of-life crimes" and his antidrug crusades (which included proposals to shut down all the methadone clinics in the city) to the saturation-policing of so-called crime "hot spots," nearly all of which were found in the city's ghettos and barrios. To many in the group, his policies on crime were spurious and represented a cover for his authoritarian agenda, which aimed to boost the power of the white elite that still controlled most of the city's economic wealth. His efforts to make New York governable again—while applauded by many of the group's leaders who had been through the crack epidemic and who desired no return to that period—involved criminalizing vast numbers of Latinos/as and blacks. It was no coincidence that while spending on the state's prisons and the city's jails mushroomed, investments in the City University of New York, the most publicly accessible university in the nation, plummeted by almost equal amounts.

> King T.: Like I said, the community shouldn't let Giuliani run the city without giving one black a position . . . what I'm tellin' the community, "Are we gonna let it happen again? Yeah, I love the safe city, I love all this, but now that it's safe, why are the beds in jail still full? Now that it's safe, why did he hire another 15,000 cops? If it's so safe why aren't we investing . . . taking that money that they saved, put it in crime-prevention . . . in schools, with youth counselors, youth prevention. Get out the metal detector machines and start workin' with the kids and show 'em why it's a safe city and doin' it for the jail-mates when they come out of re-entry programs so they won't have to go back to parole [King Tone's oral diary, 1998].

The ALKQN recognized early on that much of his effort to shift resources away from the working class of the city would be managed through his control of the crime debate (Chambliss 1994). The only question was, who was controlling whom? Did Giuliani lord it over the police or had the police grown so strong politically that it held the mayor in the palm of its hands?

EDUCATION A second major set of objections to the mayor related to his handling of the thorny problem of public education in the nation's largest school district (1.4 million students). As far as the ALKQN were concerned, access to quality public schooling was essential if the Latino community was ever to empower itself and break the vicious circle of delinquency and poverty. However, as many members saw it, the public school system was starved of funds, short of good teachers, and run by a bureaucracy that rationalized discriminatory practices in poor neighborhoods. Many of the group's members had their own children in the public school system and knew first-hand many of the problems the schools were facing. They also believed that they could play a positive role in some of the social conflicts developing in school environments and that in some schools the group's leaders were already being called in to mediate intergroup conflicts, often to great effect.

But the open involvement of the group in such a visible public institution could not be countenanced by an administration whose reputation hinged on its ability to tame deviant young New Yorkers by identifying, prosecuting, and crushing any hint of nonconformity with the law (although such a policy was never applied to the police department).

> Interviewer: What do you think could be done to improve the relationship between your organization and the schools?
>
> Queen I.: Get Giuliani out of office. I'm being honest! Get that man out of office and let us sit down with these principals, let us sit down with the Board of Education, you know, and let us show them what we're doing and what we could do. It's not about gangbanging. Them days are over.

Those "days," however, would never be over as far as the mayor was concerned, and in late 1997 the mayor launched a crusade against gangs in the city that coincided with an investigation by the Board of Education into gang infiltration in the school system. Aided and abetted by the *New York Post*, which ran a full-page "exclusive" story[10] seven months earlier on a school security guard who was a Latin King (see 3/17/1997 issue, p. 3), the Special Commissioner of Investigation for Schools,[11] Edward Stancik, began an inquiry into the proliferation of deviant groups and the complicity of school personnel in their emergence. The investigation became a major news item and contributed handily to the mayor's campaign for a second term of authoritarian populism against his liberal challenger, Ruth Messinger.

Recommendations to the Board of Education from the Special Commissioner of Investigation, New York City School District, October 1997

The Chancellor, working with appropriate city officials, should adopt a uniform antigang program for the schools. This program must be thoroughly disseminated and enforced throughout the school system. We favor a "No Tolerance" approach, which should include the following:

- Prohibiting gang related graffiti, known as "tagging," gangwear, and other elements essential to gang recruiting and intimidation strategies in the schools. Where tagging occurs, it should be removed as soon as possible and those responsible should face strong disciplinary action.
- Gang-related offenses should be reported to the police without delay. This step is of critical importance and may prevent injury or death.
- Gang-related offenses should be given special priority in the school's disciplinary system. School officials should proceed quickly and forcefully, applying fair, firm, and consistent penalties.
- School officials, including school safety officers, should not meet with gang leaders or members to "mediate" gang-related disputes. While mediation can be, and already is, a successful method of handling many student disputes in the public schools, it should not apply to gang-related matters. When gang members and issues are involved, "mediation" by the school lends an air of legitimacy to these criminal organizations and might well end up with schools overlooking gang-related offenses as a means of appeasing the gangs. Further, affording gang members or leaders an official status, which is likely to be well-known to the student body, puts pressure on students to join. We recommend that the schools give no legitimacy to gang leaders or to the gangs themselves.

Precisely at the moment that the liberal democratic candidate was finally beginning to make some headway by focusing on the parlous state of so much public schooling in the city, the above recommendations were released to the press. The effect on the campaign was immediate, and it shifted the focus from a meaningful debate on the quality of education to one about gang students and deviant personnel. In every respect it was a classic witch hunt, timed to derail the challenger's more liberal agenda and forcing her back to the center.

As far as the ALKQN were concerned, the mayor had done it again. Using groups such as themselves as red herrings, he launched a series of antigang initiatives, focusing on schools (he assigned 200 officers to move against gangs in 40 schools) and parolees (he urged the state to pass laws forbidding parolees to associate with known gang members). Still, the issue that most galled the group's members was the mayor's inference that the Kings and Queens were quintessential "outsiders" (Becker 1963), neither wanted by nor belonging to the mainstream of any ethnic group.

The Bloods

> J.E.: Is this like internal problems or external problems in the Nation?
>
> King F.: This is like a forever problem cuz Bloods is out there, I can't lie. Bloods is out there and Bloods, they are dangerous. I can't lie about it. If there was none of that bullshit out there, none of that, then we'd be fine. But we got problems to take care of [Interview, 6/18/1998].

Although a small minority (twelve) of the sample pointed to the threats posed by other street groups, principally the Bloods, as one of their biggest obstacles, it was clearly an issue that more members were forced to deal with on a daily basis. Was this, therefore, proof that the group was still enmeshed in its gang persona, unable to see beyond its competitive subcultural context or resist the existential allure of the street (Katz 1988)? Would the group therefore always be in conflict with itself? This reading is, of course, part of the "truth" about the organization, but as we have emphasized, the threat of other groups, and in particular of the largest "other group" in New York City, featured as a secondary external adversary and was not understood as a key to its own identity formation—i.e., it did not use the real and symbolic war with the Bloods as a way of enhancing and solidifying its own identity (what Conquergood [1992] calls "affirmation through negation").

But why the Bloods? How had they come to see themselves as the enemy of the Kings? Or was the feeling mutual? Although the history is somewhat murky, according to Blood leaders, the group had formed in the early 1990s in the Riker's Island Correctional Facility precisely at a time when the Kings were in the ascendancy on "the island." As the Bloods would have it, the Kings controlled the "phones" and had much of the power within the facility. By forming the United Blood Brotherhood, African-American inmates sought an organizational solution to the dominant Latino presence. Ironically, the Bloods tell a similar story to that of the Latin Kings, who, it should be remembered, were formed by Latinos after challenging the power of the 5 Percent Nation, an African-American inmate group in Collins Correctional Facility.

Nonetheless, the struggle with the Bloods took many forms. While the leadership was cognizant of the problems coming primarily from young Bloods wanting to make a name for themselves at the expense of Latin Kings, they did not allow an outright gang war on the streets, such as the internecine conflicts frequently witnessed in Los Angeles and Chicago. In fact, many Kings had little trouble moving among the Bloods members, many of whom they had grown up with and were even working alongside in legitimate occupations:

> D.B.: You've also dealt with Bloods in this nonprofit, how do they get on with the Kings?

> Father D.: You know, Bloods teach Kings how to do their jobs and Kings teach Bloods how to do their jobs and there's no problem. But the Bloods are organized differently. They are very reluctant to step forward. . . . It's my impression that Bloods who are ready to live legally are a bit ashamed of speaking about it. Compare that to King S. on Saturday [at a general meeting] just standing up front, just pounding the pulpit and, you know, pushing that line left and right. [Father D. is a director and founder of a large nonprofit organization in New York that employs many men and women with criminal records.] [Interview, 10/1/1998].

Moreover, there were constant attempts to negotiate truces both inside Riker's Island and on the street, with the Nation even striking up a relationship with leading Bloods from the Los Angeles area who were trying to improve relations between the two groups in New York.

> D.B.: I wanna ask you what brought you here to New York City?

> B.: There was a lot of contributing factors that made me decide to come out here. One of them was when I met with King H. in Kansas [the National Urban Peace and Justice Summit for gang members in 1998], and I seen that we was on the same page, bein' that he's still a member of the Latin Kings and he still does positive things, you know? . . . He's one of the brothers that agrees with me, so that's why I was willing to work with him. To try to bring some peace to the streets [Interview, 12/6/1998].

Despite these very complicated intergroup and interpersonal negotiations, there were also Kings who were simply convinced of the Bloods' inferiority and depravity. In the mind-set of such members the only answer was to "pay back" whenever they had the opportunity. This activity of the Kings was kept hidden from the research team, although such actions did not seem to be condoned by the leadership.[12] In the following interview, a young Pee Wee reveals his profound antipathy for Bloods, even though he seems to share a similar physical and cultural space with them in his neighborhood.

C.S.: Do the Bloods attack you too?

King T.: Yeah, right. They're supposed to be killers. The only people they attack is innocent people that can't do shit. They like to jump girls, cut pregnant ladies in their stomach, cut little kids. I have yet to meet one that steps to [challenges] me. When I see them on the train I always start with them, always start with them. I see them on the train I start throwin' it up, start throwin' they sign down, disrespectin' them, callin' them slobs and tomatoes, killer tomatoes. I'm a Blood killer. They don't do shit, they never do. I think way too many people be scared of them. You know, I hang out with a lot of them. They don't do nothin when I wear my rag. I dress up in their colors. They don't do nothin about it. I dress up in they colors and look just like them. I ask them what they gonna do about it—they can't do shit [Interview, 8/2/1998].

Internal Adversaries

It is difficult to talk authoritatively about the internal enemies of the Nation because of the simple fact that, while we heard about factional infighting and attempts on the life of the leader, King Tone, we were unable to interview anybody who openly identified themselves as having an oppositional tendency. Nonetheless, we can broadly describe the social types and underlying issues that, according to the data, were behind most of the conflicts that were a constant concern to the leadership during the transitional period. As we stated earlier, from the perspective of those who did not want to see the ALKQN succeed in their political ambitions, the more internal adversaries there were the better. Constantly putting out the fires of intragroup, often interpersonal, disputes and defusing situations before they could escalate to higher-level conflicts, with the increase in interested parties that inevitably results, were important functions of the leadership at all levels of the organization.

The Sway of Local Leaders and Their Reputations

It was well known within the organization that most of the opposition to the King Tone leadership—and therefore to the reforms—came from the Bronx. Repeatedly, different leaders complained about the wayward nature of that tribe, and there were at least several attempts on King Tone's life, one of which was supposedly intercepted by the police, although the circumstances were very unclear. But what was prompting such a consistent recalcitrance?

Based on formal and informal interviews, we surmise that certain local leaders, who already had a powerful street reputation before they became Kings, had been used to a high degree of autonomy to run their tribes under previous regimes. The conflict, therefore, seemed to revolve around the degree to which street leaders would (1) subordinate themselves to a central authority, and (2) agree to channel their street influence in a political direction.[13]

> They tried to kill me again last night. I can't understand these people, I just don't understand them. I went out there to the Bronx, they called me outside and up they come in a car. I was gonna meet one of them, you know, the same ones I told you about, and he shows up with three of his people. I walk up to the car and pull the door open and there he is with a gun in his trousers. He goes to pull the gun out and I grab, I pull the gun off him. "So you gonna smoke me mother fucker? You gonna smoke King Tone?" In the back seat he has other people and my people come round both sides and they put one of them in a sleep hold until he drops his gun. Now, a bunch of people could have been killed and merciful Lord the cops didn't come and bust us. They came after it was all over and we got rid of all the guns by then, but this kind of shit was crazy! [Conversation with King Tone taken from DB's field notes, 7/17/1997.]

Doing the Job on Behalf of Prison Kings

We have already seen (in chapter 6) some of the problems caused by recently released inmates who have been given instructions by imprisoned Kings to bring down the civilian leadership. Certainly, it is in those first few weeks after leaving prison that many members have to be watched closely, for it is difficult to know the degree to which prison intrigues are going to be played out on the street or how paranoid and vengeful ex-inmates can be after years in such restrictive conditions, where the truth of the outside world can be highly manipulated by movement leaders.

Snitches

Earlier in this chapter we dealt with the problem of "snitches" and how they formed a tangible threat to the stability of the group. We know that hundreds of thousands of dollars were paid to dozens of members who had done deals with prosecutors and the police to inform, provoke, and set up conspiracies which would satisfy the grand juries. The practice was so common that even the *New York Times* was moved to print an article on the subject. Based on a story about a key Latin King informant who had now been deserted by his former police employers, the article highlighted the growing reliance of the criminal justice system on "snitch" testimonies and the enormous risk to inmates if their willingness to betray their former comrades backfires. Nonetheless, it is difficult to assess the extent of the infiltration of the group except to say that very few layers of the organization seemed to be infiltrator- or informer-free.

Drug Dealers

We stated earlier that a number of drug dealers were purged from the organization while others remained. It is still difficult for us to understand the complex set of risk-assessments and negotiations that this arrangement consisted of, but since numerous dealers became ex-Kings and therefore lost a certain amount of protection, prestige, and "community," it is safe to say that a number of them must have harbored grudges against the new regime. But what becomes of their animosity? For some, there were probably opportunities to inform on their erstwhile colleagues in the neighborhood for the price of a sentence-reduction or a straightforward dollar compensation, and then there were the much-talked-about "ghost tribes" (see "The Ghost Tribes" section below) that they could purportedly join or even establish. On one occasion we were privy to a case where a member of the crown structure who was also a crack dealer was expelled. In a very messy, exiting process that involved the criminal justice system, the expelled member ordered his sellers to go to war against the organization. At the last moment the "showdown" was avoided and a face-saving truce was negotiated. Nonetheless, it was a powerful reminder of the risks involved in dishonoring certain men who have reputations to protect and the weaponry to retaliate.

"Knuckleheads"

Many of the leaders talked about the young "knuckleheads" that still opted to join the organization but who were reckless and clung to the "street thug" persona. For such youth the new policy of nonviolence was difficult to live by and the ALKQN must have seemed somewhat of a letdown. Such youth, who had difficulty controlling their rage and/or aggression or who were too immature for their responsibilities, were subjected to a great deal of discipline and control by the older members. Nonetheless, they were still considered an endless source of needless, increased conflict both with other groups and with the police.

The Ghost Tribes

Of all the internal adversaries, it is the ghost tribes that we have not as yet mentioned in previous sections of the book. Although we failed to interview any of their members, we have sufficient data to make a number of observations about this interesting product of another subculture.

In Figure 12.3 we see an example of a ghost tribe manifesto that is taken from a group of ex-Latin Kings who have formed their own breakaway tribe. As can be seen, there are certain similarities to the language of the ALKQN's bible although it has no open affiliation with the group—rather it is a secret society of youth who have decided to go their own way. There was much talk of the ghost tribes in the court cases of several Latin Kings who were being tried for threatening assaults on ghost tribe members. As far as the ALKQN is concerned the ghost tribes cannot be allowed to exist. They threaten the authority of the organization and they create the pretext for more police attention, since ghost tribe members often wear the same attire as the official Kings and Queens. The troubling question, however, is how should the group deal with such "pretenders." In one of his last interviews from jail before being taken to the maximum security federal penitentiary at Leavenworth, Kansas, King Tone spoke about his approach to the ghost-tribe problem.

> D.B.: Can you tell me about the ghost tribes? How much of a problem were they to the Kings?
>
> King T.: You know, the ghost tribe is only as strong as you make them. That's how I figure, so I pay no mind to the ghost tribe. To me, the ghost tribe is people who are ignorant and not informed or they're being informed by the wrong people. So, what it takes is time. It takes patience, and it takes giving them the love and knowledge . . . I have a letter here from a King whose father was with me. He goes, "The ghost tribe told me you're a snitch and that you were teaching them in your rooms that you didn't want Blood to be known." So I say to him, "Look here's the number, call if you know the truth and then you decide." The ghost tribe is just people who wanna live according to their own rules. They wanna sell drugs, they wanna do things that we don't allow. But these people pay too much attention to them. You can't encounter all enemies in the same way. Some enemies are a true threat, some enemies are just sent, and some enemies represent the negligence in there and don't got the knowledge . . . they kids who come out of jail, all young, misinformed, and they need time to be taught [Interview, 3/28/1998].

By Bad Boy King Hand Rock

Bad Boys By Lavvs

I - the study and practice of the 1-10 is,
in order to maintain bad boy status. failu
so will result in bearing the Mark of the su
II - Bad Boys need no green light. either you're the hu
the prey. (unless otherwise mentioned by sup.
structure.) III - As a true bad boy, No excuses will
tolorated what so ever for any reason or matter
- IV - No ~~time~~ Member of this tribe is a gangster, so
the time comes always remember that true bad
move in silence at all times...
V - No bad boy is allowed to Violate another bad boy.
bad girl shall Violate another bad girl or bad boy
penalty will bring down the Mark of the swon
VI - A bad boys Castle is sacred ground and shall
Violated under any circumstances!!!
VII - When seeing or ~~meeting~~ another bad boy, yo
salute him, no Matter who's in your surround
VIII - all internal situations concerning bad bo.
shall be addressed to the Supreme structure.
~~VIII~~. IX - all bad boy by lavvs shall be writte
authorized by bad boy Supreme Structure. an
lavvs written shall Meet bad boys standards

FIGURE 12.3 A Manifesto of the Bad Boyz Ghost Tribe.

This chapter has discussed the many different adversaries envisioned and identified by the members. These foes are both social actors and institutional forces that have had a hand in preventing the group from making the kind of progress it desired. Some of these oppositional forces are predictable, since they belong to the broad network of social-control apparatuses whose raison d'etre is to fight what the ALKQN represented. This is particularly so in a period of extreme political conservatism, which we witnessed during the 1990s and which is continuing into the new millennium. Such forces have been harnessed to the crime-fighting bandwagon that has been growing in strength ever since the late 1960s (Parenti 1999; Garland 2001), and they essentially mask an enormous shift in political and economic power—not only away from the working classes and most vulnerable sections of society, but away from the middle classes as well. The ALKQN to some extent understood this truism of the current political economy and did their best to keep their energies focused on the major players that were determining their future. Thus, we found that the three major political opponents that fueled the group's ire and which heavily influenced its organizational strategies were the institution of law enforcement, the mayor, and the media. In contrast, the role of another rival street gang, the Bloods, came in a distant fourth, which indicated to us that the group had come a long way from the more localized gang mentality that often characterized its earlier beginnings.

In addition, we have pointed to some internal adversaries, some of which we have discussed in earlier chapters. Such forces actually operated in the less patrolled border areas of the group, i.e., in sociocultural spaces inhabited by ex-members or disgruntled members, or in the secret networks of state-sponsored surveillance systems, where conspiracies are hatched, intelligence is gathered, and self-survival is negotiated.

Day after day, children are denied the right to be children. The world treats rich kids as if they were money, teaching them to act the way money acts. The world treats poor kids as if they were garbage, to turn them into garbage. And those in the middle, neither rich nor poor, are chained to televisions and trained to live the life of prisoners. The few children who manage to be children must have a lot of magic and a lot of luck.

Galeano, 2000:11

No class society is a society of pure dominance. . . . Faced with dominance, the dominated always somehow offer resistance.

Maduro, 1982:75

In this final chapter, we want to reiterate briefly and perhaps add to some of the major findings and lessons of our study that we have outlined in the previous pages. Although we have essentially come to the end of this part of the journey, we are sure that we will be spending many more years with our friends and acquaintances on the streets of New York as they struggle to do what they think is best for themselves and for their community. While we cannot predict with any certainty the future of the group, one thing is for sure: the political will within our current society to marginalize the poor and working classes continues unabated and has become more of a permanent trend than should be possible in any functioning democracy. Consequently, the kind of political subcultures that have been introduced to the reader in the preceding analyses will likely become more the norm than the exception in the ensuing years.

ALKQN Exceptionalism?

The two questions we are asked most often are: (1) what caused the ALKQN to transform itself in the ways we have claimed? and (2) why has this political development not been observed and recorded in gangs elsewhere? In answer to the first question, we have to give a fairly complicated response that rarely satisfies the inquirer. The problem is that, based on the data, it is difficult to unravel where the influence of one factor starts and another ends; rather, there are a number of factors that converged to enable this rare moment in a street organization's history when it succeeded in engaging the political establishment.

In answer to the second question, we are not sure we can fully provide an answer without an empirically grounded study of such organized street/prison groups as the Bloods and Crips in Los Angeles, or the Latin Kings and Gangster Disciples in Chicago, to provide the kind of comparative study necessary to address such an important issue. Certainly, we have some ideas about the distinctive nature of the ALKQN in New York that we shall shortly discuss in a little more detail. However, we should also remind readers that during the last decade a number of "street gangs" have developed political activities and ambitions among the membership, and they have been engaging in a variety of community projects and protest movements that deserve much more analysis. For example, both the Bloods and the Crips in Los Angeles have been involved in longstanding efforts to forge urban peace treaties in the wake of the Los Angeles uprising (Esteva 2002); in Connecticut, groups such as Los Sólidos and the Latin Kings have at various times participated in community movements during the 1990s (see DiChiara and Chabot 2002); in Chicago, the Black Gangster Disciples made headlines as they developed political pretensions and united behind certain candidates (Curry and Decker 2002); and in New York, the Ñetas have long been involved in Puerto Rican political-prisoner campaigns (Brotherton 2003). Were all such developments the result of impression management by backstage gangster leaders? This is possible, but highly unlikely. What is probably closer to the truth is that street gangs have often contained memberships with political aspirations, but it is only in certain periods and under specific conditions that a critical mass of such members emerges and the first steps toward a resistance movement are attempted. What makes the case of the ALKQN particularly difficult to grasp for outsiders is that this movement occurred during a period when few mass mobilizations were visible and society was moving inexorably toward the right in almost all spheres of life.[1]

In the following discussion, we isolate seven of the major factors that help explain the reformist changes in the organization and make some comparative remarks based on what we know about gang cultures in other parts of the U.S.

Prison-to-Street Gang Origins and the Effects of Increased Punishment

As we have noted, the federal and state's "war on drugs" dramatically increased the rate of incarceration for black and Hispanic males during the 1990s in New York, with the vast majority of those convicted coming from just a few zip codes in New York City. As Latino inmates, who are often underrepresented in the statistics, were released from the prison system, they took with them their gang identities. During the early 1990s, this caused the street membership of the Latin Kings and the Netas to grow significantly, with ex-inmates disseminating their prison-based ideologies to street youth searching for an ethnic identity and a strong organization to take back their neighborhoods from the many drug gangs and posses that had overrun local public spaces. This dialectic between the prison subculture and the highly receptive street youth never developed into a territorial focus such as New York's "jacket gangs" of the 1970s or the ethnic "fighting gangs" of the 1950s. We surmise that this was due to two factors: (1) the subcultural flow behind the organization was from the prison to the streets, rather than vice versa (as has often been the case in Chicago and Los Angeles), and (2) youth wanted to escape the restrictive and bordered environment brought about by the street drug wars within which they had grown up.

In addition, many ex-inmates, facing increasingly severe sentences by the mid-1990s, were not willing to readily go back "inside"—but neither were they willing to leave the organization to which they had been affiliated while "doing time." As a result, a critical mass of nonrecidivists emerged, seeking to extend the functions of the group beyond maintaining ex-prisoner support networks to promote social, economic, and political goals that would increase their chances of becoming legitimate members of society. Important too is the fact that the emerging agenda of the Latin Kings and Queens during a crucial period of its political growth was not sufficiently compromised either by territorial gang feuds or by ex-inmates who felt unable to function outside of criminalized and violent street worlds.

Anticolonial Consciousness and the Continued Marginalization of Barrio Youth

Both in the prison and on the street, the continued cultural, social, educational, and economic marginalization of barrio and ghetto youth fostered an anticolonial consciousness that should not be underestimated. In the case of the ALKQN in the prison system, these latent sentiments, laced with Puerto Rican nationalism, became channeled into a form of in-group/out-group exceptionalism that bolstered the group's internal discipline and secured its cohesiveness in relation to other groups. These same sentiments, which were also given full expression in the group's New York manifesto, were translated by the new reformist leadership into an ideology and identity of empowerment. However, instead of this new solidarity being a reaction to the prison administration or other prison gangs, it instead found an external target, e.g., the city's Republican mayor, the prison-industrial complex, the corporate-dominated media, the sell-out local politicians, the substandard public school system, and so forth. At the same time, the reformist leadership sought alliances with a wide range of community radicals, including churches, to aid this transition and help break the group out of its parochial and outlaw-based isolation (cf. Short 1980:250). Despite some resistance from the more apolitical elements, the group managed to change its strategy as well as its consciousness in a remarkably fluid process. There have certainly been other instances where street gangs have sought to politicize themselves; however, it is rare to see them form such powerful alliances with civic groups and allow themselves to be so democratized as a result of this encounter.

The Timely Influence of "Matured-out," Politicized Elders and the Pragmatic Need to Change the Image

Although little attention has been paid to the positive influence of "old gang heads" on a gang's younger members, this phenomenon is an important factor in the street organization's development. In the Latin Kings, for example, after the leadership void created by the federal prosecutions, the group was ripe for a takeover by a new "matured-out" stratum of street-seasoned elders. King Tone, the new leader, was, of course, pivotal in this process, but he also needed a strong cadre of confederates to protect and support him. The fortunate appearance on the scene of a talented group of men and women occurred precisely at the time that the group was in need of a drastically different public image. For, it was reasoned, this was the only way to influence the life chances of King Blood. In fact, even after he had been sentenced to more than 100 years, with half a century in isolation, the group still maintained that its new identity was important in the battle for public opinion, believing that any increase in the standing of the group could be used somehow to ameliorate Blood's conditions in prison.

The Quality and Quantity of Leadership

Nearly all successful social movements, irrespective of the "ripe" objective conditions, contain at least one powerful subjective component, namely leadership. In the ALKQN, this came in the form of a charismatic leader and an engaged cadre who were able to develop and mobilize a constituency over a sustained period of time. With King Tone they were fortunate to have a street-wise president who not only was unafraid to take political risks but relished the task, who allowed himself to learn from others (something leaders rarely do), and who could place his own role and that of his organization in a broader perspective. Such movement actors do not come along very often, but when they do, they attract other talented, aspiring members of the same community who have been yearning to throw in their lot, regardless of the gang label that might come with membership. Consequently, the ALKQN could boast, at the height of its popularity, a rare assortment of ambitious, skilled and energized members who combined to form a visionary leadership prepared to experiment with innovative organizational strategies while practicing a high level of reflexivity.

The Changing Nature and Organization of the Drug Trade Meets the "Booming" Economy

The group managed to make most of its major changes during an era when the organized market for drugs was changing significantly. As Curtis and others have explained, by the end of the 1980s, crack use in the city was sharply decreasing (Curtis et al 1998; Golub and Johnson 1997; Egan 2001). Although this was followed by an increase in the market for street heroin (Curtis 2002; *New York Times Magazine* 2002; Spunt 2001; Wendel and Curtis 2002), the drug market itself had become more vertically integrated and the system of ownership more consolidated; and the importance of Puerto Ricans in the drug trade had been superseded by Dominicans (Curtis 1999).[2] In effect, this restructuring of the drug trade lessened the opportunities for Puerto Rican members, i.e., the bulk of the group's membership, redirecting their attention to job opportunities emerging within the expanding economy.

The Evolution of Nonviolence Among Street Youth

A strong argument can be made that the generation of youth that joined the ALKQN during the late 1990s has learned that violence is not the only way to resolve conflicts. In New York City, as in many other cities, youth experienced a critical mass of suffering brought about by the incessant assaults on barrio and ghetto communities during the Reagan and Bush years and the introduction of "crack" as a new means to escape the indignities of everyday life. In contrast to predictions that burgeoning youth crime would continue throughout the 1990s (Fox 1998; Bennet, DiLiulio, and Walters 1996) and that a more remorseless breed of street youth would emerge, the opposite was the case. In New York City, serious youth crime fell, in line with serious adult crime (Correctional Association 2000), and reflected what Males (1995) has pointed to as the modeling effect, which is critical in understanding the longitudinal trends of deviant youth behavior. As the doors of the ALKQN opened to more and more neighborhood youth and adults, this culture change was reflected in the quality of the membership and increased the consensus within the organization that the time was ripe to effect a less self- and community-destructive pathway of development.

The Influence and Changing Role of Women Within These New Subcultures

During the late 1980s, when the street organizations were still in their old-style gang phase, there were few roles for women. By the early 1990s, females started to enter the organization in increasing numbers and over time began to articulate a set of concerns specific to their own interests. These early steps toward some form of semi-autonomy gained more widespread support almost immediately after the reformist phase was instituted. This new look on the part of the Latin Queens, in which self-respect, independence, ethnic identity, and self-empowerment were trumpeted characteristics, attracted a wide variety of young barrio women who had been drug-addicted, victimized, and/or neglected by family, spouses, and partners through much of their lives. The growing involvement of such females, searching for a new life in the group, encouraged both leaders and the rank-and-file to become more nurturing, more cognizant of family matters, more inclusive in the sharing of power, and less coercive in the group's use of discipline and rhetoric. All of these female-based influences inevitably strengthened the reform process, bringing the group a great many more supporters from outside the organization. While we have seen female groups develop in other gangs, for example, in sections of Sur Trece, Mara Salvatrucha, the Bloods and Crips in Los Angeles, and the Latin Queens in Chicago, we have not seen them be allowed to play such a leading role in their respective male-dominated organizations. Neither have we seen the institution of the family being so wholly embraced by the entire organization as happened in the ALKQN.

And the End of the Movement?

Naturally, there is a third question that we are continually asked: why did the movement stop? To answer this we can point to a number of structural problems with the organization: (1) the fact that it was still too vertically organized, which left it vulnerable when the leadership was removed by the state; (2) the group needed, perhaps, more powerful backers in the community, which could have provided it with more resources to assist and develop its activities; (3) the state succeeded in filling the group with "snitches" and provocateurs, and this had a devastating impact on the activities and the morale of the group; (4) without a larger radical movement developing in the surrounding community, it was difficult to maintain the momentum of this lone voice of resistance; (5) the internal contradictions were perhaps too great, i.e., there was still a large faction of the group that had a "gangsta" mentality. We could go on and on enumerating the reasons for the group's political demise, and it is an issue that we need to think about seriously in the next stage of our research with this group or any other group. In the following, however, are some "insider" thoughts from one of the authors, Luis Barrios, regarding the contributory factors in the decline of the ALKQN's extraordinary experiment:

I remember when Fr. Castle told me to end the ALKQN's sanctuary at St. Mary's Church. It was very difficult for me to understand his motivation and I reminded him how dangerous this decision was for the Nation and for our community ministry. But I realized I was not going to change his mind. He was the senior priest, my supervisor, and he was intent on demonstrating that he was in charge. I prayed and meditated, looking for the best way to share this bad news with the ALKQN leadership. I was angry because this arbitrary and racist decision would give the police and other enemies of the Nation an opportunity to dismantle what had been created in the last few years. Removing this physical space was one of the most effective ways to create chaos and destroy the collective identity of those resisting oppression. I didn't know what to do. Fr. Castle was and is an incredibly progressive priest. He was there for the Black Panthers and he is a person who knows how to take risks and how to challenge the status quo. Yet, he was making a unilateral decision, stating that these Latinos are growing too large in number and one of these days they are going to take over the church. I went back into my many years of experience in the struggle and began thinking of how often it is that white progressives, when it is time to give power to those who are being oppressed, want to continue with their paternalistic approaches. I concluded that this was the source of his reasoning. His decision was devastating to the movement and contributed to the negative changes that befell the ALKQN in the following months. This was when they started to move away from a progressive community and political agenda. You can imagine, King Tone was in prison and we don't have a sanctuary in which to meet. As a result of the spiritual and leadership vacuum, we never had an opportunity to bring healing to this Nation. The Nation could have taken one of the blows but both of them coming together were too much. We continued meeting in the parks and in different basements of churches but the police and FBI agents did their best to harass us and to stop us from working together as a community. They knew exactly what they were doing. After Fr. Castle's decision, he also told me that the Latino congregation had to go. He said that the church was an African-American beacon and that he didn't want to lose that. Consequently, I also had to leave and search for a new church, which I still haven't found [L.B., field note and recollection, 7/1/2002].

Rethinking Policy

On so many fronts, the prosocial activities of the ALKQN help us to see more clearly the resistance of the dominant society to any long-term commitment to increase the opportunities for the barrio poor and working classes or to negotiate any other form of participatory democracy. Instead, we have witnessed more than two decades of failed repressive techniques, including more specialized police, more jail time for gang members, the widespread use of intelligence gathering, zero tolerance in schools, anticombination laws, special prisons for gang members, all of which have done little if anything to prevent youth and adults joining gangs (Geis 2002). Garland (2001) has traced this ascendancy of the culture of control, showing that it occurred not only because the political elites and the law enforcement establishments wanted it, but also because the public perceived that such measures were "common sense." Thus, we can learn immensely from those who, against the prevailing wisdom, struggle to create their own societies in the belly of one that shows little inclination to meaningfully include them.

Family Life

Current welfare policies toward the poor are punitive, destructive, and designed to separate the undeserving from the deserving (Katz 2001). There needs to be a reversal of much of this neoclassical thinking on how to manage working-class and poor families from above and provide the social, cultural, and economic supports that are desperately needed to strengthen from below. Certain provisions—such as free child care; income allowances for children; free and decent health care; strong legal sanctions against domestic and child violence; affordable, quality housing; and welfare rights—should be fundamental supports for all citizens instead of the workfare penury that is replacing the social safety net. In addition, much more needs to be done to support families who have lost one or more adults to the criminal justice system. Frequently, it is the children and the spouses of inmates who suffer inordinately when the only breadwinner is taken away or when the emotional ties of parents and children are so abruptly broken. In their own small way, the ALKQN did their best to address each of the above, which, of course, should be the function and responsibility of the state in a just and caring society.

Education

Public educational standards in the city are still mired at levels of underachievement that are reflected in the consistently high dropout rates for blacks and Latinos/as and the appallingly low scores on both English and math exams for fourth and eighth grades in the poorest school districts. Members of the ALKQN repeatedly told us about the low-tier schooling they had to endure simply because of their zip code, or of the different ways they had become dispirited by their school experience, which increased the lure of the streets. Yet they were all adamant that education was now a primary goal for themselves and for their children. The most obvious policy corrective on education in New York City is to fund fully the city's schools, bringing the Board of Education's budget up to the level recommended by Judge La Grasse in his historic judgment on the unequal funding provisions for New York schools. Further, a concerted effort needs to be made to bring in more minority faculty, inject the curriculum with large doses of cultural relevancy, provide sufficient spaces for early childhood education, address the English language deficiencies of so many immigrant and nonimmigrant students, and bridge the gaps between communities and schools through a sustained campaign of outreach to students' parents and families, e.g., by offering weekend classes to family members as a means of increasing the school's standing in the community. Finally, much more investment needs to be made in the City University of New York, the largest urban public university in the country, so that the college experience for these poorer youth prepares them for careers other than the entry- and mid-level positions where many of them find themselves after graduation.

Jobs

As we have reported, work for adult Puerto Ricans and Dominicans in the city is often low-paid, low-status, and insecure, and for those returning from prison the task of finding worthwhile employment is even more daunting. For minority lower-class youth, the prospect of unemployment is a fairly safe bet, which increases the certainty that they will be spending much of their time on the streets with little money and lots of frustration, surrounded by a society that saturates them with the images of conspicuous consumption. The answer is the same one that has been advocated for many years: greater public investment in job-creation plans that produce needed facilities for the community and that are protected by union wages and conditions.

Criminal Justice and Prisons

It is a sad but telling commentary on the state of contemporary U.S. society that at the beginning of the new millennium many minority and working-class youth are more certain of going to prison than they are of attending college. Yet this is the oft-repeated fact after twenty years of mass prison expansion, most of which is predicated on the supposedly successful resolution of the so-called "war on drugs." Consequently, it should not surprise us that more is now spent on corrections in New York State than on New York City's public university system and, of course, a similar trend can be seen in California, Illinois, and numerous other states. The ghettoization of the prison (Wacquant 2002) is and will continue to have a deleterious impact on race and class relations, on family structures, and, contrary to simplistic beliefs about deterrence, on the crime rate. Certainly, the determinate prison sentences for multiple offenders changed the consciousness of some adult Latin Kings in a more positive direction, but these same changes could have occurred if the present prison system were still actively premised on rehabilitation rather than on punishment and social exclusion.

Further, there are many lessons to be learned from King Blood's story. No amount of solitary confinement, "supermax" punishments, and conspiratorial "sweeps" will put an end to such "enemies of society." Quite the contrary, such measures will only exacerbate the fertile conditions from which the street and prison gangs emerge, even though the state will continue to claim that it is winning the war. One of the many tragic ironies of King Blood's current and past state is that the more the authorities sought to contain him, the more dangerous and influential he became. On this score, nothing has changed, for King Blood is still revered as a hero by many street youth and the ground whence his followers came is being constantly tilled.

To reverse the irrational waste of hundreds of millions of tax dollars and the squandering of countless productive lives, some simple yet effective reforms can be introduced, as called for by the oldest prison watchdog organization in the United States: the Correctional Association. In its recent report, based on visits to twenty-five facilities during the period 1998–2001, the organization recommended the following policy changes, among many others:

Downsize the Prison System

With the inmate population beginning to fall (from 1999 to 2001 the number of state inmates declined from 71,466 to 67,500 and is projected to fall to 64,400 by 2003) and the crime rate maintaining its downward trend, it is clear that a dramatic scaling back of the incarceration industry is required. This is particularly necessary in a period of scarce resources, as the local, national, and international economy heads into extremely troubled waters.

Expand and Restore Vocational, Educational, and Substance-abuse Treatment Programs to Inmates

It has been shown repeatedly that education and vocational training for inmates has had the most powerful influence on recidivism rates. With so many thousands of inmates returning to civilian life each year, it would seem to be a very rational policy to have them as prepared as possible to reintegrate into society and to allow them to become part of the legitimate workforce as quickly as possible.

Restrict the Use of Disciplinary Units

More and more inmates are being kept in isolation cells for longer and longer periods. The use of extreme punishments, such as special housing units, etc., has become commonplace and is now almost the rule rather than the exception in many facilities. Resorting to such measures is often unjustified and has serious consequences for the mental health of inmates that few studies have begun to address.

Monitor and Address Staff Misconduct

While no one is underestimating the difficult and stressful work carried out by correctional officers, there is a long history of abuse and misconduct by prison personnel throughout the system—particularly in the maximum-security facilities. In the last decade, the rights of inmates have been severely curtailed and the importance of grievance procedures restricted, allowing many prisons to operate without sufficient oversight, accountability, or professionalization.

Expand Services for Inmates with Mental Illness

With 11 percent of inmates diagnosed as suffering from some severe form of mental illness, there is a clear need for a major investment in treatment facilities to address this growing issue. Yet, as the report states, there are only 210 beds available for 1,300 inmates who the system itself has classified as requiring intensive mental health services. The number of inmates with mental health problems has dramatically increased as psychiatric facilities available to the poor have been dramatically reduced in the society at large.

Politics

We have seen that many of the members, young and old, were interested in political participation and playing their roles as engaged citizens in a democratic society. But in response to questions about who they felt represented them there was usually silence. In New York, as in most other states, there are few elected candidates in either state or federal assemblies that are attractive to people at the lower end of the class divide, although a little more political variation exists at the city council level. For the most part, therefore, those in this stratum of society simply do not feel adequately represented, which is demonstrated repeatedly by poor, working-class youth and adults being consistently absent from the polling booths. This alienation from the representational process is compounded by a cynical disregard among the political elites for principles and morality, as was evidenced by the Clinton era of corporate favors and the morass of scandals afflicting the early Bush administration. The combined effect of a lack of real political alternatives and the ongoing legitimacy crises of government powerfully undermines democracy's credentials. Nonetheless, what the ALKQN showed was that there is nothing endemically apolitical about these lower-class constituencies, and that they can be mobilized very effectively for radical democratic action if political movements take the trouble to address their concerns, value their input, and give them the respect and power to change their lives.

Constructing Theory

This book is an answer to all those who argue that the gang, despite its many variations, cannot sustain a political essence. This argument, based on the presumption that the gang is formed and driven by a convergence of pathological forces, is in need of serious revision. Taking a cue from Burawoy (1991) and his work in the tradition of extended case study analysis, we see the case of the ALKQN as an "anomolous outcome," whereby tensions between the existing literature and the empirical world are evident. To address some of these tensions we have suggested a number of theoretical propositions that may contribute to nudging the field away from its orthodox complacency.

First, there is the problem of the gang as a sociological concept. In our eyes, it simply did not fit the data and we needed to invent a new working term, what we have called a "street organization," to proceed with the analysis. However, in general terms, we think that the "gang" is in great danger of being overused and applied to many groups that do not deserve the attention. In contrast, we think that this alternative sociological construct can have continuing relevance as we enter a new and vitiated culture of street politics, particularly as more and more youth reject and are rejected by mainstream politics and the bankrupt morality of our contemporary capitalist democracy becomes painfully apparent.

Second, we have introduced, probably for the first time, the notion that street subcultures can be looked at as social movements. This has helped us to understand the resistant core that characterizes many of the group's thought processes, rituals and practices, almost all of which have been obscured, denied, and understated in the dominant literature. Thus, the role of religion, the importance of spirituality, the prevalence of social reciprocity and grassroots forms of welfare, all of these have been critical to the group's emerging radical identity. We have done our best to illuminate these areas, but we see it merely as a first step; much more needs to be done to highlight the many different meaning systems being constructed at the street and prison levels.

Third, we see divergent processes of empowerment or, to paraphrase Touraine (1988), historical self-production, among different subcultures. Typically, in gangs, members go through interrelated stages of adaptation and accommodation; in street organizations, because of their rhetorical and practical commitments to the accumulation of knowledge and to the greater historical designs of "the community," these processes are much more contradictory. Further, we must add two more stages, those of resistance and transformation, which open up a vast, new, unexplored area of street research.

Fourth, we need to recognize that this new period of globalized and decentered capitalism has transformed all social actors in ways that are difficult to comprehend. Thus, continuing to limit gang research to studies of local pathological deviance, a trend that is guaranteed by the commitment of most federal research funds to uncritical research designs, leaves virtually uncharted the relationship between the observed realities and possibilities of so many marginalized groups at the local, national, and international levels. Rarely, today, do we get to examine street subcultures and their new spatial and geographical properties. Nor do we conceive of them with their own histories replete with bodies of indigenous knowledge, or as organizational models that defy their stereotypical representations. Having said this, however, we do recognize that there is a growing trend toward dissent. As new and old researchers, trained in the orthodox traditions but working in the critical margins, look to different disciplines for some alternative explanations,[3] they point to a crisis of meaning not only in regard to what we do, both epistemologically and methodologicially, but why we do it. What is the continued relevance of the countless studies on urban violence and its many internal causal connections to "gangs," without acknowledging a shred of agency at the individual, group, or community levels? And what can be the relevance of such studies outside of their global contexts? Such questions, we predict, will be at the center of many future endeavors in the field.

Doing Research

At the beginning of the book we briefly discussed our approach to this work and coined the term "collaborative," which we freely borrowed from the principled community studies carried out by Joan Moore (1978) and her associates in the 1970s. We believe that this kind of ethnographic research, based on a trusting and open relationship with the subjects, is the best and perhaps only approach to studies of this kind, where reaching a holistic understanding of a stigmatized group is the task at hand. Of course, we were fortunate in two ways: (1) the group was at a particular point in its development that made it receptive to our social-scientific overtures, and (2) a social and spiritual relationship between the group and one of the authors, Luis Barrios, was already quite advanced by the time the study was launched. With these foundations in place, we could set about a relatively long-term commitment to the inquiry and, with the financial support of the Spencer Foundation, were able to begin recruiting and training field researchers who needed to be innovative, resilient, culturally sensitive, and exhaustively curious. Such personal and intellectual qualities are the basics for all researchers if they are to proceed with "thick description" projects, and we were blessed in finding some of the best young interviewers and observers to conclude the work.

A Short Postscript

Nowadays, not too much is reported about the antics and practices of the ALKQN in New York. There is a different mayor at the helm, who seems not to relish the constant need for conflicts with scapegoats in order to bolster his political standing. Meanwhile, the group is still very much in existence, meetings are taking place in the respective boroughs, and there are some tentative moves to reestablish the broader city-wide structure that so characterized its reform phase and to reassert some of its political goals that were at the forefront of the King Tone era. At the same time, a number of "gangsta" Kings have been picked up and charged with crimes reminiscent of the early-1990s rendition of the group. This tension between the group's criminal, subproletarian elements and its communitarian, political wing continues. However, no legitimate leadership has emerged to make good on its promised potential and carry through with plans and strategies for community renewal that were so much a part of the transitional stage. Still, this is a new period of gestation, and with sentiments like the following, coming from a former Pee Wee, the future for the group may be once again "up for grabs."

> We are reestablishing ourselves, getting our house in order. We are not where we were but the brothers and sisters are still holding true in a lot of the tribes. We have a lot of ideas where we wanna go and I've never seen so many youngsters coming around. There's a thirst, see, they wanna know who they are and no one else is giving it to them. The media and them, they all thought we were dead or something. We weren't dead but we were disorganized. Now we're back but we gonna do it quietly this time. We're gonna build the brown force like we were supposed to. Nothing's changed as far as that's concerned [Interview, King M., 5/2/2001].

Introduction

1. Among the hundreds of newspaper and magazine articles on the New York Latin Kings and Queens from the period 1989–1999 that we reviewed (see chapter 12), only one did not describe them as a gang (the London *Guardian*, 1/12/1999) and only three engaged the political, social, and economic issues behind the group's efforts to transform itself into a community-based social movement.

Chapter 1: The Study

1. Notable exceptions are: Bourgois (1995), Conquergood (cited above), and Sharff (1998).

2. This dominant, almost hegemonic, strain in urban gang studies has for the most part reduced gang members to an aggregate of attitudes and behaviors (Venkatesh 1997), while the definition of the gang itself has become hotly disputed, ensconced in the pragmatic theoretical debates and unannounced agendas of "neutral experts."

3. We recognize that complete equality between the researcher and the subjects is impossible, but the collaborative method is as close to an ethical and effective paradigm of research for this type of study as we have found. In an effort to ensure that not all the royalties from this work will be going to the authors, some of the proceeds will be used to establish a fund to aid the rehabilitation process of ex-inmates.

4. This method, also sometimes referred to as participant action research (Whyte 1943, 1991), involves the researchers in a highly interactive relationship with the subjects that strives to construct as holistic a picture of the subjects' world as possible.

5. Aside from Whyte's (1943) study of a street-corner society in the slums of Philadelphia, other studies on marginalized communities, such as Kenneth Clarke's *Dark Ghetto* (1965), Joan Moore's *Homeboys* (1978), and John Hagedorn's *Peoples and Folks* (1988) are good examples of this now established tradition.

6. Until this time, other than work done in Chicago by Dwight Conquergood, there was no record of any successful ethnographic relationship with this group. In fact, the group had long prided itself on the fact that it was a secret "elite" society, and that its members had no business revealing any information to outsiders, be it reflections on members' lives or any of its closely guarded rites and rituals. As Conquergood (Conquergood 1992)

states: "I had been in the field almost a year before I even had heard about 'the Book,' and then it was always shrouded in secrecy."

7. Having previously worked on a street gang study in San Francisco (Brotherton 1996a, 1996b, 1994; Waldorf 1992), Brotherton had been struck by the respondents' low level of political consciousness (with the exception of several female respondents), particularly considering their experiences of both direct and indirect state violence (Salmi 1993). For example, many of the youth spoke of having fled from U.S.-supported Central American dictatorships and civil wars, had been tortured by Mexican federal agents, experienced physical abuse by U.S. border guards, were constantly harassed by the local police, had been shunted around the educational system by administrators and teachers, or were working in some of the lowest-paying labor positions in the city.

8. It is worth quoting Schwandt's (1994:128) description of this method or paradigm: "It is interpretive and fosters comparing and contrasting divergent constructions in an effort to achieve a synthesis of same. They strongly emphasize that the goal of constructivist inquiry is to achieve a consensus (or, failing that, an agenda for negotiation) on issues and concerns that define the nature of the Inquiry."

9. Of course, some critics will contend that this strategy is tantamount to "going native" and only pollutes the data. It is reasoned that you cannot trust such a stakeholder to be truthful. But this is the risk of the collaborative process and to counter such problems we have constantly employed different methods of triangulation to verify accounts and gain alternative perspectives on processes and events. Nonetheless, the benefits of this strategy were enormous and it would have been impossible to carry out one tenth of the research without the active participation of the organization's principal leader.

10. All future field notes and some interviews will contain a reference to one of these authors through their initials, i.e., DB (David Brotherton), LB (Luis Barrios), JE (Juan Esteva), CS (Camila Salazar), and LK (Louis Kontos). The Rev. María Isabel Santiviago, Ms. Lorinne Padilla, and Marcia Esparza focused mainly on face-to-face interviews.

11. Nearly all of the demographic statistics for the city are broken down into White, Black, Hispanic, and Asian. This practice, of course, subsumes many different ethnicities under the same umbrella terms.

12. In 1998, the U.S. Census Bureau calculated that the Latino/Latina population was nearly 30 million, representing approximately 11.1 percent of the total United States population. By 2050 Latinos/as will reach 22 percent of the population, or 90 million residents (Day 1993) and will become the second-largest ethnic group in the United States.

13. According to the Task Force Report, "Many parents are equating the program [i.e., the health insurance program] with welfare and do not believe their children are entitled to coverage."

14. These figures are starkly different not only for whites (16.6 percent have no high school diploma, 4.9 percent no high school) but also for African-Americans (30.8 percent have no high school diploma, 8.1 percent no high school).

15. Lately, the prison population has begun to fall, and in the latest tally the numbers had fallen to 67,500 as a result of the drop in crime.

16. "A number of studies have examined these correlates [age, race, and socioeconomic status] and ones that do include the issue of age. Gang members range across a wide va-

riety of ages, but typically they are teenagers. It is not easy to pinpoint a single age as the 'average' age of gang members, but a number of studies identify seventeen or eighteen as the average age of members in their sample" (Curry and Decker 2003:78).

17. There were others, of course, such as those in school who lived at home and were supported by their parents.

18. During the late 1990s New York City had the lowest recorded gang-related homicide record of any major city in the United States (Brotherton 1999). Both according to media reports and whatever information we could glean from the secretive New York Police Department, Latin King-related homicides or Latin King fatalities were extremely rare. We counted three Latin King deaths from 1997 to 1999 that were due to street-related altercations.

19. None of the Queens reported being introduced to the group via a female relative, not even a sister!

Chapter 2: The Theory of Gangs

1. This is important to underscore, for the role that texts play in the shaping of human behavior and in the construction of criminal-justice and social-service agendas is often ignored, forgotten, or underestimated (Best 1989).

2. The Chicago School approach, although quite radical at the time, has come to be equated with the notion of mainstream criminology. By this we mean the plethora of theories purporting to explain the causes of crime that are often based on assumptions about the criminogenic conditions of everyday life. Such theories, while highlighting failures in the socioeconomic order, never call into question either the ideological or material foundations of the political economy nor address the glaring contradictions that emerge within its social system.

3. The paradigms in the first three of the four epochs are generally consistent with other literature reviews (see Bursick and Grasmick 1996; Jackson 1989). Only the paradigm—social and economic contingency—in the 1990s is our invention.

4. Nonetheless, the contradictions of society's hierarchical dynamics were left untheorized. As Pfohl has stated:

In one grand sweep of sociological imagery, the Chicago theorists dismissed both the sentimental longings of the nativists and the structural critique of the radicals. By conceiving the negative consequences of rapid change as a deviant reaction of the naturally disorganized, rather than as a discontented reaction of the structurally or historically disadvantaged, the Chicago school contributed to a depoliticized image of social problems [Pfohl 1985:143].

5. Larkin (1979:47) sums up this period as follows:

The youth of the 1950s lived in a context that on the one hand extolled youth as the ideal state of humanity, while on the other hand, resented the young for being youthful. Juvenile delinquency had become a serious problem. The 1960 White House Conference on Children has as its central focus the alienation and isolation of youth (Beck 1973). The major issue was juvenile delinquency. The family was evidencing an inability to control its own young and the burden was falling ever harder on public authorities: teachers, counselors, social workers, and the police. Yet the adolescent "rebellion" was not a collective phenomenon, with the exception of the inner-city gangs.

6. This revanchism has been rationalized by a very different type of Chicago School theorist. These are the supporters and adherents of people like Milton Friedman and Gary Becker, both supporters and originators of "trickle-down" and supply-side economics.

7. In many respects, the underclass was a combination of what Spitzer (1971) a decade earlier had referred to as two kinds of surplus populations, social dynamite and social junk.

8. See also Huff (1991), Klein (1995), Moore (1988), Padilla (1992), Skolnick (1992), Taylor (1991), and Vigil (1988).

9. Of course, an argument can be made that among gang members little political consciousness is present, but this "finding" is itself an intensely political statement—although it is rarely considered as such.

Chapter 3: Politics and Gangs

1. Thrasher considered the gangs-politics connection an important aspect of the formal and informal distribution of power in the industrial urban setting he was studying. In fact, he devoted an entire chapter to the subject, which has rarely been repeated in subsequent studies. Recently, Curry and Decker (2002) also drew some attention to the history of this connection, reminding us that some important urban players have graduated from gang subcultures, citing the case of former Chicago mayor Richard Daley, who had been a longstanding member of the Hamburg gang as a youth.

2. Such a conclusion can be easily explained by the literature when we consider the gangs as: (1) hegemonically subordinate to the dominant culture (Laclau and Mouffe 1987), (2) socially isolated from the "working"-class community (Wilson 1987), and (3) primarily concerned with activities that reinforce and maintain their own particular status system over actions that promote the general interests of the oppressed class (Jacobs 1977).

3. Fanon, of course, was the originator of the thesis that the lumpen proletariat, so apparently dismissed by Marx and Engels as revolutionary potential, could be the "most spontaneous and most radically revolutionary forces of a colonized people" (Fanon 1965: 103).

4. Therefore, in many ways, it would appear not only that gangs are somewhat subversive, but Conquergood himself might be considered in the same deviant light in certain circles.

5. Morris says very explicitly: "The significance of outside resources, in this view, lies in the help they can give in sustaining movements. However, our evidence suggests that they are not a causal determinant, because they are triggered by the strength and force of indigenous movements" (1984: 283).

6. Much orthodox thinking about social movements suggests that a movement's success depends on the generosity of external supporters rather than the self-reliance and self-sacrifice of a movement's members.

7. McAdam showed not only how these movements impact the community, creating different levels of tension, but how the community shapes and impacts the social movement.

Chapter 4: Who Are the Almighty Latin King and Queen Nation?

1. For example, during the period from January 1997 to April 1997, the Latin Kings leadership suspended all interviews with the research team, due to what they considered a breach of trust by the two authors (see chapter 1 on methodology for a detailed account of this development).

2. The Chicago Latin Kings are a Peoples-aligned gang along with the Vice Lords, Bishops, Gaylords, etc. This alliance is opposed to the Folks-aligned gangs, such as the Black Gangster Disciples, Simon City Royals, and Imperial Gangsters, among others. For a more detailed explanation of these alliances and the power dynamics that are involved see Conquergood's (1993) "Homeboys and Hoods: Gang Communication and Cultural Space."

3. Kingism, and also Queenism, are the philosophy and sets of practices that fundamentally bind the ALKQN (Barrios 2003]).

4. This is not to say that "outsiders" are not engaged in trying to decode these practices. For the most part, however, this engagement is being done in the service of social control rather than social inquiry. One obvious example is that of law enforcement's approach to graffiti. In this particular case the outsider's interest is: (1) to end this practice of gangs defacing private property, or (2) to use the information contained in the cryptic messages as part of police intelligence-gathering. Another example is that of school officials who see the language of the streets as a threat to the legitimate authority of the administration. In this case, graffiti is immediately painted over for fear it will: (1) encourage students to challenge the establishment, or (2) stimulate/perpetuate tensions between student groups.

5. The exact nature of the relationship between New York and Chicago throughout the project has been mostly an organizational secret.

6. For example, talking to the media, permitting "outsiders" to attend "universals" (meetings) and allowing the group to be part of a collaborative research project would all be impossible under Chicago rules. In addition, there were periods during the ALKQN's reform era when relations between the New York City chapter and leaders of the Motherland were reported to be tense.

Chapter 5: The Traditions of King Blood

1. The institution, located in the small, white, working-class town of Helmuth, near Buffalo, N.Y., is some 200 miles north of Manhattan. At the time of Blood's stay, the institution held 999 inmates, 210 categorized as Latinos, 501 as blacks, 279 as whites and 9 as other. In three years, the total inmate count had increased to 1,255 (by roughly 25 percent) and the racial-ethnic breakdown was now: Latinos, 305; blacks, 630; and whites, 304 (Personal communication from the Department of Correctional Services, 2000).

2. Century (1999:87) describes the Five Percenters as

an offshoot of the Nation of Islam, [which] arose on the Harlem streets in the mid-60s under the leadership of Clarence 13X Smith (1928–1969). A Korean

War veteran and former member of the NOI's elite Fruit of Islam security force, Smith (aka Pudin') was expelled from the NOI's Harlem Mosque Number 7 in 1963 by Malcolm X, reputedly because he refused to forgo his fondness for dice games.

In another sociological account, Campbell writes:

The Five Percent Nation considers itself a religious and cultural movement directed toward young blacks, aiming to teach them the correct ways of Islamic life. Its name derives from the members' belief that 10 percent of humanity controls and exploits 85 percent of the poor and uninformed; the remaining 5 percent are those "civilized people also known as muslims and muslims' sons," whose task is to educate fellow blacks in their true religion [1984:176].

3. "In New York State, there are three types of disciplinary housing: (1) 'keeplock,' where inmates are confined to their cells or to a special keeplock area in the prison, typically for thirty days or less; (2) longer-term solitary confinement in a prison's Special Housing Unit (SHU), located in a separate area of the prison or in a freestanding building; and (3) supermax housing in fully automated, freestanding, high-tech control units" (Correctional Association, 2002).

4. Pedro Albizu Campos and Lolita Lebrón are two of the most important revolutionary nationalist figures in Puerto Rican history. Lebrón emerged from prison on September 6, 1979, after serving twenty-five years for her part in the armed attack on the United States Congress in 1954. In 1998, she took part in a demonstration in front of the United Nations; the ALKQN provided her with security in New York City.

5. Trial transcript, *United States v. Luis Felipe*, pp. 543 and 555.

6. King Blood's son, Duane, who lives in Spain, would be allowed to see him, but he refuses to recognize his father's existence.

7. There is, however, a certain similarity between the demonic nature of Blood's criminal-justice-generated profile and eventual lifetime encagement and that of Larry Hoover, the leader of Chicago's Black Gangster Disciples, who was sentenced to two life terms. It is also worth noting that Hoover also had semiradical political pretensions for his street gang, although drugs were always part of the official capital of the group, which in New York was never really the case.

8. Barrios provides a version of one such request:

The judge got straight to the point, asking me what I wanted. I explained that I wanted him to authorize me to visit and write to Luis Felipe. One of the FBI agents then started interrogating me. "What is your affiliation to the ALKQN?" "Are you a member of the gang?" "Are you one of the leaders?" "Why do they have meetings in your church?" I answered, "you know who I am," and that I was not there to answer such questions. I then told the judge that Luis Felipe was very depressed and that he could commit suicide due to his isolation. He asked me how I knew. I told him that as a clinical psychologist, I can perceive the signs of depression in his writing. The judge was angry. He wanted to know "how the hell" I received a letter from Luis Felipe! I explained that Luis Felipe had managed to pay a correctional officer to bring the letter out. "Are you aware," I asked the judge, "that if Luis Felipe commits suicide you are responsible for his death?" He told me that he was going to get back to me. When I returned to my office there was a phone message from the judge saying. "OK, Fr. Barrios, here is the deal. You can write and visit Luis Felipe. However, I need to read the letters that you are sending him and the ones he is sending you." I called him and thanked him for his understanding [LB field notes, 5/97].

9. Prison gangs, as Parenti (1999) notes, have increasingly been used by prison authorities to socially control the inmate populations. This has been a pragmatic policy, despite strenuous denials, necessitated by the impossible task of maintaining order in prison facilities that are frequently filled to almost twice their expected capacity. But Jacobs (1977) also makes the important point that gangs in the 1970s, during their political heyday in Chicago, could make or break the status quo, and they were very adept at exploiting the "organizational crisis" of the prison system.

10. To get closer to the nature of gang leadership requires a much deeper immersion into gang life. For example, basic empirical issues—such as: (1) the actual versus stated power that certain individuals profess, (2) the talents that leaders need, (3) the process by which leadership is achieved—can only be addressed if one has access to multiple forms of data.

11. The most obvious example of this was the Mafia, which, Jankowski (1991) asserts, was seen by gangs as a powerful model, with its history of providing an alternative opportunity structure and its system of rational bureaucracy and brash disregard for the law.

12. Evidence of King Blood's democratic side might be: (1) the frequency of member meetings, (2) Blood's need to constantly consult with both the leaders and the rank-and-file, (3) Blood's exhortations to leaders to behave responsibly and not to abuse their power, and (4) Blood's own efforts to be humble and play down his autocratic potential.

13. Article 78 refers to section 78.01 of the New York Civil Practice Laws and Rules. An Article 78 proceeding allows New York prisoners to ask the State Court to review a decision or action of a New York State official or agency which the prisoner believes was unlawful.

14. C.M.C. stands for Central Monitoring Case, which means that an inmate is being closely watched by the facility's central office.

15. An example of some leadership autonomy is the following:

Please correct me if I'm wrong. *Now* I want to know how did King G. fake the funk on brother L.? What did he do that you made me take King G. out the family? Remember King Blood, nobody's perfect, everybody make their mistakes, King G. made a little mistake and now he's out the family [Letter to King Blood from King L. 8/21/1993].

16. Although, in his letters, he constantly entertains the thought of one day gaining his freedom, "I was day dreaming that if we get together in New York we'll definitely flip

New York outside down . . . $$$," he writes to a leader of Riker's Island. But beneath this whimsical bravado is the sad fact that he has already fully adapted to his caged condition, with its relentless structures of time, space, and movement.

17. This is primarily done through the 25–30 letters a week he receives from his members, including the reports from his supremas, i.e., the leaders of the various prison chapters.

18. This development in the group raises some intriguing questions we are still unable to answer: Did the leaders understand that the FBI and the New York Tactical Narcotics Squad were building a case to eventually launch a grand jury inquiry into the organization? Why were they so open about many of their activities in their communications? Why had the organization been able to kill so many of its members when all of the intragroup letters were photocopied by the authorities?

19. Of course, we also have to remember that it was a white, middle-class judge passing sentence on an infamous, lower-class Latino. If the defendant had been of the same race and the same class as the judge, would the sentence have been the same? A recent article in *Newsday* pointed out that no Mafia members are currently on death row, compared to the dozens of street gang members who are awaiting their fates. This is despite the fact that Mafia hit men are usually guilty of many more homicides than street gangbangers (*Newsday*, 5/12/02, p. 5).

Chater 6: Nongang Traditions I

1. In the minutes of group meetings during this period, the only conflicts that are repeatedly reported are with two gangs: Unity and the Ruffnecks, both of whom seem to have been more active in the Bronx than anywhere else in the city. This is a far cry from the web of allied gangs that the Chicago Latin Kings have had to deal with on a day-to-day basis (see Conquergood 1993).

2. McRobbie makes a not so dissimilar point with regard to the presumption that deviant youth subcultures are by their nature socially isolated:

On what grounds did these sociologists assume segregation? Was it not more likely, as I argued in a critique of subcultural theory in the early 1980s, that the male sociologists, like the journalists, restricted their gaze to the streets and other sites of public display and never thought to follow the deviants home at night, to their families and to the more mundane activities which they also took part in, like shopping, eating, and going to college or to work, and even getting married? [1994:204]

3. Tone, at the age of thirty-three, has still not been tested for dyslexia. Based on the many letters we have exchanged with him, this seems to be at least one of his learning "disabilities."

4. According to Tone's May 10, 1999 pre-sentence report,

The defendant reported completing the eleventh grade at Franklin K. Lane High School in Brooklyn in 1984, and left school to get a job. School officials report that the defendant completed eighth grade before being discharged on June 3, 1985, because he was over seventeen years of age. They rated the defendant's scholastic standing and attendance as "poor."

5. According to Tone's pre-sentence report,

On April 15, 1992, the defendant was observed by the police to be retrieving vials of cocaine from a brown paper bag on top of a pile of garbage. The defendant then walked away with a group of people. He later returned to the brown paper bag and was arrested without incident. The defendant was in possession of 35 vials of cocaine with a weight of 21.5 grains. In post arrest statements, the defendant admitted possessing the vials of cocaine and added that each vial cost $12.00 [United States District Court, East District of New York, 5/10/1999].

6. Mary Jo White was the United States Attorney for the Southern District of New York.

7. This is Ron Kuby, King Tone's defense lawyer.

Chapter 7: Nongang Traditions II

1. Even though a leading theory of gangs posits that delinquent cultures (Shaw and McKay 1969) are transferred from generation to generation.

2. Both the notions of mentalities and structural feelings have not been easy to define. Basically, the former refers to the "study of the mediations and the dialectical relationship between the objective conditions of men's lives and the way in which they tell about it and even how they live it" (Vovelle, quoted in Tarrow 1992:179); the latter refers to what Giroux (1983:127) describes as "class . . . viewed less as a structural than an interpersonal medium through which people define experience and respond to conditions under which they live."

3. Historians Burrows and Wallace (1999:xxiv), explain this dialectical relationship between past and present as follows:

We believe that the world we've inherited has an immense momentum; that actions taken in the past have bequeathed us the mix of constraints and possibilities within which we act today; that the stage onto which each generation walks has already been set, key characteristics introduced, major plots set in motion; and that while the next act has not been written, it's likely to follow on, in undetermined ways, from the previous action. This is not to say that history repeats itself. Time is not a carousel on which we might, next time round, snatch the brass ring by being better prepared. Rather we see the past flowing powerfully through the present and think that charting historical currents can enhance our ability to navigate them.

4. But, while the environmental conditions were very similar, the differences in the membership and the contents of the group were also striking. The Black Panthers and the Young Lords drew on a lot of working-class and lower-middle-class students while the gangs almost exclusively came from working-class nonstudents. The gangs were mainly male, with almost all-male leaderships and female attachments (see Miller 1973; Campbell 1984; Fishman 1995; Harris 1985). Although the females played a more important

role in the gangs than most traditional criminologists have admitted, they nonetheless were made to be and feel subordinate in a male-centric culture or in a culture whose priorities were geared to addressing the problems of working-class masculinity construction (see Schneider 1999). Meanwhile, the radical groups were also mainly male but with strong, vocal contingents of females who were actively embracing and creating the many versions of feminism during this era. Nonetheless, the radical groups were still predominantly run along male-centric lines of societal critique and organizational hierarchy. A further important difference between the gangs and the radical groups was that the latter's founding visions and ideologies of structural change contrasted with the former's socially oppositional, yet politically underdeveloped and even conformist view of societal transformation (see Schneider 1999 and chapter 11 of this book).

5. "Stalked by fear, seized by rage" was one quote from the *New York Times* in Gale 1977:252.

6. During such episodes a range of speakers at the group's meetings would refer back to the days of COINTELPRO and the harassment of both Martin Luther King and Malcolm X and the systematic infiltrations of the Panthers and the Young Lords.

7. The Workers World Party (WWP) was one of the groups most consistently present at ALKQN meetings. In fact, the ALKQN's banner, emblazoned with the head of Luis Felipe and always displayed when the ALKQN participated in rallies or held its meetings, was made by Carlos, a leading member of the WWP and a member of the decolonization and independence movement for Puerto Rico.

8. Ms. Lebrón was convicted of "seditious conspiracy" along with Rafaél Cancel-Miranda, Irving Flores, and Andrés Figueroa-Cordero who, on March 1, 1954, led a revolutionary action against the U.S. Congress in Washington, D.C. This demonstration was to condemn the U.S. military invasion of, and colonialization of, Puerto Rico on its 100-year (July 25, 1898) anniversary.

9. This relationship between radical parents and children in the Nation is a somewhat different interpretation of Cohen's notion of "parental culture" (1972), although what is present is still the notion of defiance among the children.

10. Gramsci was the first theorist to coin this phrase in the service of Marxism. In his early formulation he described such an intellectual as follows:

> Every social group, coming into existence on the original terrain of an essential function in the world of economic production, creates together with itself, organically, one or more strata of intellectuals which give it homogeneity and an awareness of its own function not only in the economic but also in the social and political fields [1971:5].

11. There are currently six political prisoners, five men and one woman, incarcerated in the United States for their opposition to U.S. colonialism on their island and categorized as "terrorists" by the courts and the Federal Bureau of Prisons. President Clinton in 1999 pardoned eleven Puerto Rican political prisoners after they agreed to renounce any violence in their continued political opposition to the subjugation of Puerto Rico.

12. The U.S. government, meanwhile, because of its Cold War alliance with these Central American dictatorships, wanted to send them back to their probable deaths (Chomsky 1985).

13. This is the name of God in Yahwism and later in Judaism.

14. Maduro (1978:76) locates the achievement of religious autonomy in a process of ongoing struggle for independence between the powerful and powerless:

> The subordinate classes in achieving maximal autonomy, material and symbolic, vis-à-vis the dominating classes, includes a certain tendency to achieve religious autonomy. That is, it involves a tendency to construct a system of religious thought and practices that favor the subordinate classes' objective interests.

This conception is much in line with our own interpretation of religious practice in the ALKQN.

15. In two important ways, this is similar to the group's view of education (Brotherton 2003). First, the group encourages members to take education seriously, not only as a way to develop the individual, but as part of the group's long-term agenda to end the marginalization of working-class Latinos/as at all levels of society; and second, the group urges members to question their teachers and not to succumb to the "banking method" of education (Freire 1970; Barrios, 2001, 2002c), i.e., training students to be passive and to master the art of recall for tests, rather than to think critically.

Chapter 8: The Level of Organization and Structure of the Latin Kings

1. In these treatments, we see the gang as a way to discover the deep-seated interrelationships between individual, subcultural, and community histories with gang structures deemed secondary to systems of meaning, interpersonal relations, and the restructuration of the political economy.

2. For example, Klein and Maxson (1996) have coined the terms *traditional, neotraditional, compressed, collective,* and *specialty* to describe gang structures. As schematic constructs these terms usefully describe patterns of reported criminality and membership flows courtesy of police department chroniclers. On the other hand, they do little to deepen our understanding of what makes a gang a gang through the "life worlds" of gang members, community residents, and the myriad social actors that constitute a gang and its environment. Even the recent work of Miller (2001), who effectively uses the Klein and Maxson typologies to order her empirical data, lacks any complex discussion of context, consciousness, history, or agency to inform the debate on organization.

3. The number five is a key symbolic figure in the Latin Kings and is seen in the five-point crown, which is the focal insignia of the group; in the five senses, which are supposed to orient the member's behavior; and in the five points of knowledge, which refer to the key principles of membership. Consequently, the titled leadership of the various bodies of the group always consisted of five individuals.

4. It should be remembered that for many members who lived on welfare or who had minimum-wage jobs, the payment of dues was a significant sacrifice.

5. We have found only one written report of females forming a ganglike group with an articulated ideology and some clearly defined goals (other than the Latin Queens),

which is contained in Campbell's (1984) study of the Five Percent Nation in New York City.

6. For example, the Queens exhibited organizational characteristics very similar to those of the Kings, including their crown structure, dues, regular meetings, comparable initiation rituals, and prayers.

7. We have focused our attention here on gender-based power relations within the group, but there were other sources of internal social conflict that should also be noted. For example, there were several members of the group who were gay males but were afraid to "come out" among the rest of the members due to the history of homophobia in the organization. In discussions between the authors and King Tone on this issue, the group's leader suggested that they, the gay members, should bring it to the membership and let it become a topic of debate regardless of the controversy. A second area of note was the domination of the group by second- or third-generation Puerto Ricans, who conducted the meetings almost exclusively in English and who mostly allowed only Puerto Rican flags to be displayed. The Dominican membership, many of whom were first-generation and spoke mainly Spanish, often complained about this bias on the part of the group and it was only later in the group's transition phase that this issue began to be addressed.

8. Heterosexism is another discriminatory relation that we also identified (e.g., homophobia). However, the rejection was more against gay men than lesbians.

9. To this day, according to informants, the New Jersey Latin Kings are using a version of New York's bible (manifesto) that was compiled during the leadership of King Tone.

10. This estimate comes from observations of general meetings, political rallies, and social events.

Chapter 9: Membership

1. A major critique we have of many delinquency studies is that they rarely treat subjects as if they were in the act of "becoming." Rather, the tendency is to accept the self-definition of the youth/adult and the fatalistic approach to life that are often part of their consciousness.

2. It should be noted that the absence of fathers was not simply a result of male irresponsibility; it also had to do with long antisocial working hours in the highly segmented labor force.

3. These memories of Queen G. and King Pol. were also partly borne out in field observations at three inner-city schools which many of these respondents had attended. Brotherton (1996b) found a lack of Puerto Rican and/or Dominican representation in the faculty, in the symbols that adorned the public spaces and walkways, and in the curriculum itself, into which the social and cultural histories of these countries could easily have been incorporated.

4. The era of gangs to which these respondents referred was called "flying cut sleeves," as in the documentary of the same name (Chalfant and Fecher 1989). The gangs themselves had flamboyant, outlawlike, and pseudo-upper-class names that reflected both their playful character (most members at that time referred to these groups as "club") and the somewhat conscious aim to undermine the hegemony of the dominant race-class culture, i.e., they appropriated aristocratic-sounding names, fraternity clothes, and radical rheto-

ric to create a stylistic pastiche (Hebdige 1979) through which they subculturally organized their resistance.

5. When recalling this era, many of the respondents spoke of their long-held desire to be part of a communitarian movement that would counter the vapidity caused by intergenerational poverty and constantly high levels of youth unemployment and underemployment during the late Reagan era.

6. At the same time, a number of respondents reported that they had attended Alcoholics Anonymous and Narcotics Anonymous meetings.

7. If time had permitted us, this issue of the relationship between the younger and the older members would have been important to pursue, since the "ex-cons" received a great deal of respect in the organization and yet they were keen to be seen as role models based not on their lives of crime but rather on their successful efforts to change, become "rehabilitated," and lead the new Nation through this challenging period.

Chapter 10: Identity and Collective Resistance

1. A fuller version of the quote here reads:

> The seasonal type of identity-building, identity for *resistance*, leads to the formation of communes, or communities, in Etzioni's formulation. This may be the most important type of identity-building in our society. It constructs forms of collective resistance against otherwise unbearable oppression, usually on the basis of identities that were, apparently, clearly defined by history, geography, or biology, making it easier to essentialize the boundaries.

2. This Spanish term literally means "human reality," which refers to the underlying sociohistorical context in which life is being lived on a day-to-day basis. The use of the term implies a process of consciousness development, or as Freire (1970) calls it, "conscientization," in which power relations are critically recognized and possibilities for individual and collective empowerment are increasingly engaged.

3. Vigil (1988:168) writes: "Through various means, a positive self-identity has failed to materialize among certain Chicano youth. Because of this, some have sought what Erikson has labeled "a greater sense of identity in being withdrawn or in being delinquent" (1956:9). The multiple roots and origins of this identity-ambivalence become especially troublesome during adolescence, when the street gang takes over. To manage the crisis, the ego integrates itself with the barrio (group) ideal and the gang provides role expectations and functions to shepherd a person through this "psychosocial moratorium."

4. In other words, as we have been increasingly discovering in the stirrings of the working classes in Los Angeles recently (Davis 2001), the Latinos are coming and they bring with them a long history of popular organization, struggle, and resistance.

5. Of the Puerto Rican experience, Flores (2000.162) writes:

> For Puerto Ricans, the "blessings" of American citizenship have been even worse than mixed. Under the constant sway of colonial machinations, it has been a setup for stigmatization and pathological treatment, more than outweighing, over the long haul, their advantageous exemption from the most pressing of immigrant woes.

6. For example, in schools and sometimes during high levels of street tension when they do not want to attract police attention or add to conflicts with other street groups (see chapter 11).

7. In fact, for several years, beginning in 1996, the group requested permission to walk in the parade but was rejected by the parade's organizers, who finally only allowed them to march in their colors in 1998, positioning them toward the back of the mile-long throng. As far as we know, the Dominican branch of the ALKQN never openly marched in their official day of ethnic celebration.

8. Out of the sample, not a single respondent claimed to be an atheist. All the subjects asserted that they believed in God, with many coming from a Catholic or a Pentecostal tradition.

9. In Spanish, the term literally means human re-encounter.

Chapter 11: Goals Versus Acts

1. According to Dawley,

The Vice Lords had converted grants into jobs and community service, but storefronts and programs were only the visible surface of deeper changes. . . . In two years, the outlaws of the ghetto had moved into business development and direct political action—the kind of tough and legitimate fighting for social change that propelled Chicago's Irish into power. So when the Vice Lords helped to form a vanguard of a coalition that closed deals worth $100 million of construction to negotiate more blacks into the trade unions, Mayor Daley understood the deeper political message [Dawley, 1982:193].

2. Only recently one of the group's tribes in Manhattan had been approached by a prospective candidate for local office and had worked diligently on his campaign, almost helping to deliver him a victory.

3. This estimate is based on combining the female members of the Naia tribe (the Latin Queens' only tribe) and those females in the Pee Wee tribe, and then asking several leading Queens to estimate the numbers of inactive members that might also be calling themselves Latin Queens. The highest figure we recorded at any one sitting was seventy-one, which occurred at a general meeting during 1998.

4. Bhaba's postcolonial discourse is especially illuminating in describing the ALKQN's organizational, spiritual, and ideological hybridity and the necessity to adopt a very flexible analytical approach in trying to understand it. Addressing the tension between the notion of cultural hybridities and the modernist concept of multiculturalism, he says: "we should remember that it is the 'inter'—the cutting edge of translation and negotiation, the 'in-between' space—that carries the burden of the meaning of culture.' And by exploring this Third Space, we may elude the politics of polarity and emerge as others of our selves" (1994: 38–9, quoted in Soja 1996: 141).

5. We use Giddens to describe the three types of consciousness as follows: (1) practical consciousness, "tacit stocks of knowledge which actors draw upon in the constitution of social activity" (Giddens 1979:5); (2) discursive consciousness, "involving knowledge

which actors are able to express on the level of discourse" (Giddens 1979:5); and (3) historical consciousness, the "consciousness of history as a progression of change, rather than as the constant reenactment of tradition, and the availability of 'exemplars' located differentially in time or space for current processes of transformation" (Giddens 1979: 222).

6. Both countries have been badly represented in the media and the public imagination has rarely been forced to think of either country as little more than two empty though pernicious sound bites: "vacation paradise" and "welfare sinkhole" (González 2000:247).

Chapter 12: Perceived Adversaries

1. Most studies argue that the gangs' main enemies are members of the same social class, gender, and ethnic/racial group.

2. Both Jankowski (1991) and Venkatesh (1997) similarly found that under specific cultural, historical, and structural conditions inner city street gangs can function as agents of community resistance in the struggle for day-to-day survival. Whereas these authors highlight the relationship of the gang to the informal economy, we argue that the ALKQN provided the community with a different set of resources.

3. Only four of the sample felt that their goals were being accomplished with little opposition, and these were members who had only recently joined the group in what was its heyday.

4. Conquergood (1993) explains this active interpretation of one's locale vis-à-vis Chicago gang members: "The communicative task of the gang group is to transform marginal, somewhat forbidding urban space into a hood—to make a world of meaning, familiarity, adventure, and affective intensity through ritual, symbol, and dramaturgy."

5. Many if not most researchers agree with Klein's assessment of anti-gang strategies that rely almost exclusively on law-enforcement action:

> Suppression programs . . . are short-term. They do little to nothing about the forces that foster gang development. But by focusing on gang-qua-gang problems, they can and—I'm convinced—do serve to reinforce gang identity. . . . Legislation that increases penalties for gang-related crimes makes prosecutors happier, but it leads cops to play the gang game with even more vigor. It's counterproductive" [1995:233].

6. The role of snitches in the organization cannot be underestimated. Neither can the amount of resources spent by city, state, and federal agencies in recruiting and maintaining this form of intelligence. The following are field notes taken at a federal trial hearing (1/12/99):

> King M. is charged with conspiracy to murder, what the federal prosecution says is a case of "murder-for-hire." The three star witnesses are King B., an ex-Latin King and leader of a "ghost tribe" (see chapter 12), KJ, and FB. In the morning session Detective F., under questioning, talked about the background of the witnesses. He told the court that they were all being held in Riker's Island on various drug charges and that they had all signed cooperation agreements to reduce their own sentences. The detective was asked if these witnesses had been working as informers for the government. He replied that they had and that King B. had been working in such

a capacity for almost a year. The defense attorney asked the detective how much they had been paid. The detective replied that King B. had been paid $55,000 and that the other two informers had received approximately $21,000 each. The detective added that they were normally paid $150 per day for their work and that the money came from funds confiscated under the drug seizure laws.

7. Gitlin essentially argues that while social movements widely used the media to disseminate their message(s) to a mass audience, they were having their agendas set by these same outside agencies. Thus, while the relationship was instrumental to the movement's need for propaganda, it was also dangerous and brought with it the tendency for co-optation.

8. We found more than 300 articles devoted to the New York State Latin Kings and Queens during the period 1992–2002 in the Northeast region alone. Of these, we counted seventy-five separate stories—in other words many stories were covered multiple times by different news outlets in a display of what some have referred to as "pack journalism."

9. Almost all the mayor's major policy initiatives, while they bore discernible fruit for his primarily white, conservative, and moneyed backers (Fitch 2002), were extremely divisive for the city as a whole. At the end of his eight years in office, with the crime rates down and with a more robust economy, the poor were as poor as ever, the public schools were still underperforming, affordable housing was almost nonexistent, and civil liberties had been systematically undermined (Barrett 2000). "Freedom," said the mayor who put snipers on the roof of City Hall for an AIDS demonstration, "is the willingness of every single human being to cede to lawful authority a great deal of discretion about what you do and how you do it" (Barrett 2000:6).

10. The article had every property of the typical sensationalist scoop. The banner headlines read: "Latin Kings Infiltrate Our Schools," under which appeared, in large, bold type, "JUST ONE OF THE GANG," and then in smaller type, "Safety officer is, & teacher may be." Just in case the reader was unclear about what they were supposed to think, the paper also included two large photographs, one of the guard making a Latin King hand signal while wearing his "beads," and another smaller one with the same person in his school security uniform standing outside a school.

11. This office is almost unique in schools management. It was set up in 1990 under Mayor David Dinkins but grew out of the Gill Commission, which operated during the mayoralty of Ed Koch to look into rampant corruption in the school system. The role of investigator "was given extraordinary independence for an appointed official: the office has no term limits, and the investigator can be removed only for cause by the city's commissioner of investigation" (*New York Times*, 3/13/02:B-1). During Stancik's tenure, he was accused of focusing on sensationalistic crimes within the school system (i.e., sex scandals, gangs, etc.) and in 1997, former Chancellor Rudy Crew accused him of spreading "panic through the system" by releasing exaggerated reports to the news media before the Board of Education had an opportunity to respond.

12. Most likely, the fact that it was happening showed that the leadership did not have full control of the membership, and this ran counter to the image they were trying to maintain not only to us, the researchers, but to themselves and the public in general.

13. An interesting subject for research with regard to the social actors who were in opposition would be to compare their traits to those Sanchez Jankowski has described as the "defiant individualist," i.e., the "ideal typical" organized gang member (see Jankowski 1991:26–28).

Chapter 13: Conclusion

1. This is not to say that no new significant social movements have emerged during the last few years, for one of the most notable efforts at resistance has been the widespread antiglobalization protests that have dogged world financial and economic leaders wherever they have attempted to rendezvous.

2. Curtis (1999:5) describes the history behind the ethnic competition in the drug market as follows:

In New York City, criminal drug distribution had been vertically organized since the prohibition of alcohol, and it was the exclusive domain of European-American gangsters. Heroin, an illegal substance since 1914, was incorporated by them in the 1920s and 1930s on Manhattan's lower east side. After World War Two, African-American subordinates were franchised to distribute it in their neighborhoods. In the 1950s, drug distribution and use were widely suspected to be part of a subversive Chinese communist plot to undermine America, and a series of harshly punitive laws were enacted. At an infamous meeting in upstate New York in the late 1950s, organized crime "Dons," wishing for greater legitimacy, withdrew their "families" from drug distribution. Puerto Rican freelance distributors filled the vacuum. As the drug became popular in the heroin-injecting epidemic of 1964–1972, they quickly cornered the street-level sales in many neighborhoods and their incipient organizations grew in size and complexity. When the epidemic ended, just a few Puerto Rican "owners" had consolidated the market and, throughout the late 1970s and early 1980s, served an aging, increasingly impoverished clientele. Located in selected latino neighborhoods, these businesses remained an exclusively Puerto Rican enterprise. By 1992, one Puerto Rican and three Dominican "owners" ruled over crack distribution at the northern end of Bushwick. Each had a trademark, or the color of the "tops" of the crack vials they sold: white, blue, brown, and pink. Dominican families monitored the day-to-day operations of the largest three. Younger family members and close non-kin "associates" directed street sales, while older family members, entirely removed from the street scene, were the "executives." When there were not enough family members, owners employed persons who shared a similar background. The practice earned them the resentment of street-level workers, particularly among the Puerto Ricans who had controlled distribution throughout the 1970s and early 1980s (and had similar policies), only to be topped by the Dominicans in the late 1980s.

3. See, for example, presentations at the "Globalizing the Streets Conference," John Jay College of Criminal Justice, May 2001, and the seminar, "Gangs in the Global City," Chicago, May 2002. Also see Kontos, Brotherton, and Barrios, eds., 2002; Hagedorn, ed., in press, and the expanding field of cultural criminology (Ferrell and Saunders 1995).

Acland, Charles R. 1995. *Youth, Murder, Spectacle: The Cultural Politics of "Youth in Crisis."* Boulder, Colo.: Westview Press.

Adorno, Theodor. 1973. *Negative Dialectics.* New York: Seabury Press.

———. 1976. "On the Logic of the Social Sciences" In T. W. Adorno et al, eds., *The Positivist Dispute in German Sociology.* London: Heinemann.

Agus, Carole. 1995. Diary of a Street Gang. *New York Newsday* (June 28): B4-5.

Amnesty International. 1996. *United States of America: Police Brutality and Excessive Force in the New York City Police Department* (June). New York: Amnesty International.

Anderson, Elijah. 1990. *Streetwise: Race, Class, and Change in an Urban Community.* Chicago: University of Chicago Press.

———. 1999. *Code of the Street: Decency, Violence, and the Moral Life of the Inner City.* New York: W.W. Norton.

Arnold, William. 1966. "The Concept of a Gang." *Sociological Quarterly:* 7: 59–75.

Asbury, Herbert. 1990 [orig. 1927]. *The Gangs of New York: An Informal History of the Underworld.* New York: Paragon House.

Baer, Justin, and William J. Chambliss. 1997. "Generating Fear: The Politics of Crime Reporting." *Crime, Law & Social Change* 27: 87–107.

Bakhtin, Mikhail. 1981. *The Dialogic Imagination.* Edited by M. Holquist. Austin: University of Texas Press.

Barak, Greg. 1988. "Newsmaking Criminology: Reflections on the Media, Intellectuals, and Crime." *Justice Quarterly* 5: 565–87.

Barrett, Wayne. 2000. *Rudy: An Investigative Biography of Rudolph Giuliani.* New York: Basic Books.

Barrios, Luis. 1998a. "Santa María as a Liberating Zone: A Community Church in the Search of Restorative Justice." *Humanity & Society* 22, no. 1 (February): 55–78.

———. 1998c. "Amor de rey, amor de reina." *El Diario La Prensa* (February 12): 16.

———. 1998d. "Ñeta, ñeta, ñeta: De corazón." *El Diario La Prensa* (March 27): 20.

———. 2000. *Josconiando: Dimensiones sociales y políticas de la espiritualidad.* Santo Domingo, República Dominicana: Editora Aguiar, S.A.

———. 2001a. "Educando para embrutecer." *El Diario La Prensa* (November 4): 8.

——. 2001b. "La cultura del miedo." *El Diario La Prensa* (December 9): 10.

——. 2002a. ¡Hablando de derechos humanos! *El Diario La Prensa* (May 19): 8

——. 2002b. "La psicología del terror." *El Diario La Prensa* (May 26): 8.

——. 2002c. "Hay la necesidad de enseñar a razonar." *El Diario La Prensa* (June 2): 8.

——. 2003. "Spirituality and Resistance in the Latin Kings and Queens." In L. Kontos, D. Brotherton, and L. Barrios, eds., *Gangs and Society: Alternative Perspectives.* New York: Columbia University Press.

Barrios, Luis, and Richard Curtis. 1998b. "The Impact of the War on Drugs on Puerto Ricans: A Lost Generation." In Jefferson M. Fish, ed., *How to Legalize Drugs,* pp.102–128. Northvale, New Jersey: Jason Aronson.

Bearak, Barry. 1997. "Top Latin King's Intent Is an Issue." *New York Times* (November 20): B1-4.

Becker, Howard. 1963. *Outsiders: Studies in the Sociology of Deviance.* New York: The Free Press.

Bellah, Robert. 1986. *Habits of the Heart.* New York: Harper and Row.

Benjamin, Walter. 1969. *Illuminations,* ed. by Hanna Arendt. New York: Schocken.

Bennett, William J., John J. Diliulio, Jr., and John P. Walters. 1996. *Body Count—Moral Poverty and How to Win America's War Against Crime and Drugs.* New York: Simon and Schuster.

Berger, Peter, and Thomas Luckman. 1966. *The Social Construction of Reality—A Treatise in the Sociology of Knowledge.* Garden City, N.Y.: Doubleday.

Betto, Frei. 1992. *Fidel y La Religión: Conversaciones Con Frei Betto.* La Habana, Cuba: Editorial SI-MAR, S.A.

Bhabha, Homi. 1994. *The Location of Culture.* New York: Routledge.

Biernacki, Patrick, and Dan Waldorf. 1981. "Snowball Sampling: Problems and Techniques of Chain Referral Sampling." *Sociological Methods and Research* 10: 141–163.

Big Noise Productions. 1999. *Black and Gold.* Documentary film. www.bignoise.com.

Block, Carolyn R., and Richard Block. 1993. "Street Crime in Chicago." In *Research in Brief* (December). Washington, D.C.: Office of Justice Programs.

Blumer, Herbert. 1971. "Social Problems as Collective Behavior." *Social Problems* 18: 298–306.

Bogardus, Emory. 1926. *The City Boy and His Problems.* Los Angeles: House of Ralston, Rotary Club of Los Angeles.

Bourdieu, Pierre, and Jean-Claude Passeron. 1977. *Reproduction in Education, Society, and Culture.* Beverly Hills, Calif.: Sage.

Bourgois, Philippe. 1989. In Search of Horatio Alger: Culture and Ideology in the Crack Economy. *Contemporary Drug Problems* 16(4): 619–49.

——. 1995. *In Search of Respect: Selling Crack in El Barrio.* New York: Cambridge University Press.

Brake, Mike. 1985. *Comparative Youth Cultures: The Sociology of Youth Culture and Youth Subcultures in America, Britain, and Canada.* London: Routledge and Kegan Paul.

Branch, Curtis. 1997. Clinical Interventions with Gang Adolescents and Their Families. Boulder, Colo.: Westview Press.

Brotherton, David C. 1994. "Who Do You Claim?: Gang Formations and Rivalry in an Inner City High School. *Perspectives on Social Problems* 5: 147–171.

——. 1996a. "'Smartness,' 'Toughness,' and 'Autonomy': Drug Use in the Context of Gang Female Delinquency." *Journal of Drug Issues* 26: 261–277.

——. 1996b. "The Contradictions of Suppression: Notes from a Study of Approaches to Gangs in Three Public High Schools." *Urban Review* 28(2): 95–120.

——. 1997. "Socially Constructing the Nomads: Part One," *Humanity and Society.* 21(2): 1–21

——. 1999. "The Old Heads Tell Their Stories," *Free Inquiry in Creative Sociology* 2(1): 1–15.

——. 2003. "The Role of Education in the Reform of Street Organizations in New York City." In L. Kontos, D. Brotherton, and L. Barrios, eds., *Gangs and Society: Alternative Perspectives.* New York: Columbia University Press.

Brotherton, David C., and Camila Salazar. 2003. "Pushes and Pulls in the Resistance Trajectories of the Latin Queens." In L. Kontos, D. Brotherton, and L. Barrios, eds., *Gangs and Society: Alternative Perspectives.* New York: Columbia University Press.

Brune, Tom. 2001. "The Two Faces of Death Penalty: Minority Gangs Face It, White Mobsters Do Not." Washington Bureau, *Newsday* (June 13): A-6.

Brzezinski, Matthew. 2002. "Re-engineering the Drug Business." *New York Times Magazine* (June 23): 24–55.

Burawoy, Michael. 2000. *Global Ethnography: Forces, Connections, and Imaginations in a Postmodern World.* Berkeley, Calif.: University of California Press.

——. 1991. *Ethnography Unbound.* Berkeley: Berkeley, Calif.: University of California Press.

Burns, Haywood. 1971. "Introduction" in *Look for Me in the Whirlwind: The Collective Autobiography of the New York 21,* pp. 7–15. New York: Random House.

Burrows, Edward G., and Mike Wallace. 1999. *Gotham: A History of New York City to 1898.* New York: Oxford University Press.

Bursick, Robert J., and Harold G. Grasmick. 1996. "Defining Gangs and Gang Behavior." In M. Klein, C. Maxson, and J. Miller, eds., *The Modern Gang Reader.* Los Angeles: Roxbury.

Calderón, Fernando, Alejandro Piscitelli, and José Luis Reyna. 1992. "Social Movements: Actors, Theories, Expectations." In Arturo Escobar and Sonia E. Alvarez, eds., *The Making of Social Movement in Latin America: Identity, Strategy and Democracy, pp. 19–36.* San Francisco: Westview Press.

Calhoun, Craig. 1994. "Social Theory and the Politics of Identity." In Craig Calhoun, ed., *Social Theory and the Politics of Identity,* pp. 9–36. Malden, Mass.: Blackwell Publishers Inc.

——. 1991. "The Problem of Identity in Collective Action." In J. Huber, ed., *Macro-Micro Linkages in Sociology,* pp. 51–75. London/Beverly Hills, Calif.: Sage.

Campbell, Anne. 1984. *Girls in the Gang.* London: Blackwell.

Carrere d'Encause. 1993. *The End of the Soviet Empire: The Triumphs of Nations.* New York: Basis Books.

Castells, Manuel. 1997. *The Power of Identity.* New York: Blackwell.

Castells, Manuel, and John H. Mollenkopf. 1991. *Dual City: Restructuring New York.* New York: Russel Sage Foundation.

Chalfant, Henry, and Rita Fecher. 1989. *"Flying Cut Sleeves."* New York: Cinema Guild.

Chambliss, William 1964. "A Sociological Analysis of the Law of Vagrancy." *Social Problems* 12 (Summer): 67–77.

——. 1994. "Policing the Ghetto Underclass: The Politics of Law and Law Enforcement," *Social Problems* 41(2): 177–194.

Chesney-Lind, Meda. 1997. *The Female Offender: Girls, Women, and Crime.* Thousand Oaks, Calif.: Sage.

Chomsky, Noam 1985. *Turning the Tide: U.S. Intervention in Central America and the Struggle for Peace.* Boston: South End Press.

Churchill, Ward, and Jim Vander Wall. 1989. *The COINTELPRO Papers: Documents from the FBI's Secret Wars Against Dissent in the United States.* Boston: South End Press.

Citizen's Committee for Children of New York. 1993. *"Keeping track of New York City's Children."* 1st ed. New York: Citizen's Committee for Children of New York.

——. 1998. *"Keeping track of New York City's Children."* 4th ed. New York: Citizen's Committee for Children of New York.

——. 2000. *"Keeping track of New York City's Children."* 5th ed. New York: Citizen's Committee for Children of New York.

Clarke, Kenneth. B. 1965. *Dark Ghetto: Dilemmas of Social Power.* New York: Harper.

Clifford, James. 1988. *The Predicament of Culture: Twentieth-Century Ethnography, Literature, and Art.* Cambridge: Harvard University Press.

Cloward, Richard A., and Lloyd Ohlin. 1960. *Delinquency and Opportunity.* New York: Free Press.

Coffield, Frank, C. Borrill, and Sarah Marshall. 1986. *Growing Up at the Margins.* Philadelphia: Open University Press.

Cohen, Albert. 1955. *Delinquent Boys.* New York: Free Press.

Cohen, Phil. 1972. "Subcultural Conflict and Working-class Community." Working Papers in Cultural Studies 1. Birmingham, U.K.: University of Birmingham, Center for Contemporary Cultural Studies.

Cohen, Stanley. 1972. *Folk Devils and Moral Panics: The Creation of Mods and Rockers.* London: McGibbon and Kee.

Collins, Herbert. 1979. *Street Gangs: Profiles for Police.* New York: New York City Police Department.

Collins, Patricia Hill. 1989. "The Social Construction of Black Feminist Thought." *Signs: Journal of Women in Culture and Society* 14(4): 745–773.

Conquergood, Dwight. 1992. *"On Reppin' and Rhetoric: Gang Representations."* Paper presented at the "Philosophy and Rhetoric of Inquiry Seminar," University of Iowa.

——. 1993. "Homeboys and Hoods: Gang Communication and Cultural Space." In Larry Frey, ed., *Group Communication in Context: Studies of Natural Groups,* pp. 23–55. Hillsdale, N.J.: Lawrence Erlbaum.

——. 1997. "Street Literacy." In James Floord, Shirley Brice Heath, and Diane Lapp, eds., *Handbook of Research on Teaching Literacy Through the Communicative and Visual Arts,* pp.354–375. New York: Simon and Schuster Macmillan.

Conquergood, Dwight, and Taggart Siegel (co-producers/directors). 1990. *The Heart Broken in Half.* Videotape. New York: Filmmakers Library.

Correctional Associaton of New York. 2000. *Correctional Association Bulletin* 1(1). New York: The Correctional Association of New York.

——. 2002. *State of the Prisons: Conditions of Confinement in 25 New York Correctional Facilities.* Report by the Prison Visiting Committee of the Correctional Association of New York.

Cox, Oliver. 1970 [orig. 1942]. *Caste, Class, and Race.* New York: Modern Reader.

Curry, G. David., and Scott H. Decker. 2003. *Confronting Gangs: Crime and Community.*2d ed. Los Angeles, Calif.: Roxbury.

Curtis, Richard. 1998. "The Improbable Transformation of Inner-City Neighborhoods: Crime, Violence, Drugs, and Youth in the 1990s." *Journal of Criminal Law and Criminology,* (88)4, Summer: 1233–1276.

——. 1999. *"Gangs and Violence,"* Sociology Colloquium, John Jay College of Criminal Justice (February 8).

——.2003. "The Role of Gangs and Drug Distribution in New York City in the 1990s." In L. Kontos, D. Brotherton, and L. Barrios, eds., *Gangs and Society: Alternative Perspectives.* New York: Columbia University Press.

Dahl, Robert. 1970. *After the Revolution? Authority in a Good Society.* New Haven: Yale University Press.

Davis, Angela. 1983. *Women, Race, and Class.* New York: Vintage Books.

Davis, Mike. 1990. *City of Quartz: Evaluating the Future of Los Angeles.* New York: Verso.

Dawley, David. 1992. *A Nation of Lords: The Autobiography of the Vice Lords.* 2d ed. Prospect Heights, Ill.: Waveland Press.

De Certeau, Michael. 1984. *The Practice of Everyday Life.* Berkeley: University of California Press.

Decker, Scott, Tim Bynum, and Deborah Weisel. 2001. "A Tale of Two Cities: Gangs as Organized Crime Groups," in Jody Miller, Cheryl L. Maxson, and Malcolm Klein, eds., *The Modern Gang Reader.* 2d ed., pp.73–92. Los Angeles: Roxbury.

Decker, Scott H., and Van Winkle, Barrik. 1996. *Life in the Gang.* Cambridge, England: Cambridge University Press.

Della Porta, Donatella, and Mario Diani. 1999. *Social Movements: An Introduction.* Malden, Mass.: Blackwell Publishers.

Denzin, Norman. 1989. *The Research Act.* Englewood Cliffs, N.J.: Prentice Hall.

Devine, John. 1996. *Maximum Security: The Culture of Violence in Inner-City Schools.* Chicago: University of Chicago Press.

DiChiara, Albert, and Russel Chabot. 2003 "Gangs and the Contemporary Urban Struggle: An Unappreciated Aspect of Gangs." In L. Kontos, D. Brotherton, and L.Barrios, *Gangs and Society: Alternative Perspectives.* New York: Columbia University Press.

Donziger, Steven R., ed. 1996. *The Real War on Crime: The Report of the National Criminal Justice Commission.* New York: Harper Perennial.

Douglas, Mary. 1982. *In the Active Voice.* London: Routledge.

Egan, Timothy. 2001. A Drug Ran Its Course Then Hid with Its Users. *New York Times* (January 9): A-1.

Empey, LaMar T., and Mark C. Stafford. 1991. *American Delinquency: Its Meaning and Construction.* Belmont, Calif.: Wadsworth.

Erlanger, Howard. 1974. "The Empirical Status of the Subculture of Violence Thesis." *Social Problems* 22: 280–91.

Erikson, Erik H. 1965. "Youth, Fidelity and Diversity." In E. H. Reikson, ed., *The Challenge of Youth.* New York: Anchor.

Erikson, Kai. 1966. *Wayward Puritans: A Study in the Sociology of Deviance.* New York: Wiley.

Escobar, A. 1992. "Culture, Economics, and Politics in Latin American Social Movements Theory and Research." In A. Escobar and S. E. Alvarez, eds., *The Making of Social Movements in Latin America: Identity, Strategy and Democracy,* pp. 62–85. Boulder, Colo.: Westview Press.

Esteva, Juan. 2003. "Urban Street Activists: Gang and Community Efforts to Bring Justice to Los Angeles' Neighborhoods." In Louis Kontos, David Brotherton, and Luis Barrios, eds., *Gangs and Society: Alternative Perspectives.* New York: Columbia University Press.

Fagan, Jeff. 1996. "Gangs, Drugs and Neighborhood Change." In C. Ron Huff, ed., *Gangs in America,* pp.39–73. Thousand Oaks, Calif.: Sage.

Fanon, Franz. 1965. *Wretched of the Earth.* New York: Grove Press.

Fine, Michelle. 1991. *Framing Dropouts.* New York: SUNY Press

Fine, Michelle, and Lois Weis. 1998. *The Unknown City: The Lives of Poor and Working-Class Young Adults.* Boston: Beacon Press.

Finnegan, William. 1999. *Cold New World: Growing Up in Harder Country.* New York: Random House.

Fishman, Laura. T. 1995. "The Vice Queens: An Ethnographic Study of Black Female Gang Behavior." In Malcolm W. Klein, Cheryl L. Maxson, and Jody Miller, eds., *The Modern Gang Reader,* pp. 83–92. Los Angeles: Roxbury.

Fishman. Mark. 1978. "Crime Waves as Ideology." *Social Problems* 25: 530–43.

Fitch, Robert. 2002. *The Assassination of New York.* New York: Verso.

Flacks, Richard. 1971. *Youth and Social Change.* New York: Rand McNally.

———. 1992. *Making History: The American Left and the American Mind.* New York: Columbia University Press.

Fleischer, Mark. 1998. *Dead End Kids: Gang Girls and the Boys They Know.* Madison: University of Wisconsin Press.

Flores, Juan. 2000. *From Bomba to Hip-Hop: Puerto Rican Culture and Latino Identity.* New York: Columbia University Press.

Fordham, Cynthia. 1996. *Blacked Out: Dilemmas of Race, Identity, and Success at Capital High.* Chicago: University of Chicago Press.

Foucault, Michel. 1977. *Discipline and Punish: The Birth of the Prison.* New York: Vintage Books.

Fox, James Alan. 1998. *Homicide Trends in the United States.* Washington, D.C.: U.S. Department of Justice Programs.

Franklin, Bruce. 1971. *From Movements Toward Revolution.* New York: Van Nostrand Reinhold.

Freire, Paulo. 1970. *Pedagogy of the Oppressed.* New York: Seabury Press.

——. 1996. *Letter to Cristina: Reflections on My Life and Work.* New York: Routledge.

Fusco, Coco. 1998. "A Bid for the Crown." *Latina Magazine,* (January): 54–58.

Gale, William. 1977. *The Compound.* New York: Rawson Associates.

Galeano, Eduardo. 1977. *Open Veins of Latin America: Five Centuries of the Pillage of a Continent.* New York: Monthly Review Press.

Galeano, Eduardo. 2000. *Upside Down: A Primer for the Looking-Glass World.* New York: Metropolitan Books.

Gang Intelligence Task Force. 1999. *Handbook of the Latin Kings.* New York: New York Police Department.

Gans, Herbert. 1962. *The Urban Villagers.* New York: The Free Press.

——. 1995. *War Against the Poor: The Underclass and Antipoverty Policy.* New York: Basic Books.

Garland, David. 2001. *The Culture of Control: Crime and Social Order in Contemporary Society.* Chicago: The University of Chicago Press.

Geertz, Clifford. 1983. *Local Knowledge: Further Essays in Interpretive Anthropology.* New York: Basic Books.

Geis, Gilbert. 2002. "Ganging Up on Gangs: Anti-Loitering and Public Nuisance Laws." In C. R. Huff, ed., *Gangs in America,* pp. 257–270. Thousand Oaks, Calif.: Sage.

Giddens, Anthony. 1979. *Central Problems in Social Theory: Action, Structure, and Contradiction in Social Analysis.* Berkeley: University of California Press.

Gilbert, James. 1986. *A Cycle of Outrage: America's Reaction to the Juvenile Delinquent in the 1950s.* New York: Oxford University Press.

Giroux, Henry. 1983. *Theory and Resistance in Education.* South Hadley, Mass.: Bergin and Garvey.

Gitlin, Todd. 1980. *The Whole World Is Watching.* Berkeley: University of California Press.

Glasgow, Douglas G. 1981. *The Black Underclass: Poverty, Unemployment, and Entrapment of Ghetto Youth.* New York: Vintage Books.

Goffman, Erving. 1961. *Asylums: Essays on the Social Systems of Mental Patients and Other Inmates.* New York: Anchor.

——. 1963. *Stigma: Notes on the Management of Spoiled Identity.* Englewood Cliffs, N.J.: Prentice-Hall.

Golub, Andrew, and Bruce Johnson. 1997. *Crack's Decline: Some Surprises Across US Cities.* National Institute of Justice: Research in Brief 6(July).

González, Juan. 2000. *The Harvest of Empire.* New York: Viking.

Goode, Eric. 1984. *Deviant Behavior.* Englewood Cliffs, N.J.: Prentice Hall.

Gould, Stephen Jay. 1981. *The Mismeasure of Man.* New York: Norton.

Gouldner, Alvin W. 1970. *The Coming Crisis of Western Sociology.* New York: Basic Books.

Gramsci, Antonio. 1971. *Selections from the Prison Notebooks.* New York: International.

Gross, Jane. 1999. "Lawyer Is Solitary Killer's Reluctant Pen Pal." *New York Times* (March 25): B-2.

Hagedorn, John. 1988. *People and Folks.* Chicago: Lake View Press.

——. 2002. "Gangs and the Informal Economy." In C. Ron Huff, ed. *Gangs in America,* 3rd ed. Thousand Oaks, Calif.: Sage, pp. 101–120.

——, ed. [In press]. *Gangs in the Global City.* Chicago: University of Illinois Press.

Hall, G. Stanley. 1904. *Adolescence: Its Psychology and its Relations to Physiology, Anthropology, Sociology, Sex, Crime, Religion, and Reducation.* New York: Arno Press.

Hall, Stuart, and Tony Jefferson, eds. 1975. *Resistance Through Rituals.* London: Routledge.

Hall, Stuart, Tony Jefferson, Chas Crichter, John Clarke, and Brian Roberts. 1978. *Policing the Crisis: Mugging, the State, and Law and Order.* New York: Holmes and Meier.

Haraway, Donna. 1991. *Symians, Cyborgs, and Women: The Reinvention of Nature.* New York: Routledge.

Hardt, Michael, and Antonio Negri. 2000. *Empire.* Cambridge, Mass.: Harvard University Press.

Harris, Mary G. 1988. *Cholas: Latino Girls and Gangs.* New York: AMS.

Hartocollis, Anemona. 1998. "9 Percent of City's Public Schools are Failing Says State." *New York Times* (November 14): B-1.

——. 2002. "Calls to Limit Powers of Next Schools Investigator." *New York Times* (March 13): B-1.

Harvey, David. 2000. *Spaces of Hope.* Berkeley, Calif.: University of California Press.

Hayden, Tom. 2000. "LAPD: Law and Disorder." *The Nation* (March 22): p. 4.

Hebdige, Dick. 1979. *Subculture: The Meaning of Style.* London: Methuen.

Hernández, Ramona, and Francisco Rivera-Batiz. 1997. *"Dominican New Yorkers: A Socioeconomic Profile."* New York: Dominican Research Monographs–The CUNY Dominican Studies Institute.

Hevesi, Dennis. 1998. Racial Disparity Seen in Immigrant Housing. *The New York Times* (November 27): B-8.

Hoffman, Jan. 1997. Testing the Limits of Punishment: Unusually Severe Life Sentence vs. Society's Need for Safety. *New York Times* (October 26): 31.

Hollingshead, August B. 1949. *Elmtown's Youth.* New York: Wiley.

Huff, C. Ron. 1996. "Youth Gangs and Public Policy." *Crime and Delinquency* 35: 524–537.

Hunt, Geoffrey, Kathleen McKenzie, and Karen Laidler-Joe. 2000. "'I'm Calling My Mom': The Meaning of Family and Kinship Among Homegirls." *Justice Quarterly* 17(1): 1–31.

Inciardi, James. A. 1990. "The Crack-Violence Connection Within a Population of Hard-Core Adolescent Offenders." In M. de la Rosa, E. Y. Lambert, and B. Gropper, eds., *Drugs and Violence: Causes, Correlates and Consequences.* Rockewell, Md.: National Institute on Drug Abuse Research Monograph.

Inciardi, James A., Ruth Horowitz, and Anne Pottieger. 1993. *Street Kids, Street Drugs, Street Crime: An Examination of Drug Use and Serious Delinquency in Miami.* Belmont, Calif.: Wadsworth.

Irwin, John. 1980. *Prisons in Turmoil.* Boston: Little, Brown.

Jackson, George. 1969. *Blood in My Eye.* New York: Random House.

Jackson, Patrick. 1989. Theories and Findings About Youth Gangs. *Criminal Justice Abstracts* (June): 312–329.

Jackson, Patrick, and Cary Rudman. 1993. "Moral Panic and the Response to Gangs in California." In Scott Cummings and Daniel J. Monti, eds., *Gangs: The Origins and Impact of Contemporary Youth Gangs in the United States,* pp. 257–275. Albany: SUNY Press.

Jacobs, Jack. B. 1977. *Statesville: The Penitentiary in Mass Society.* Chicago: University of Chicago Press.

Jacobs, Jane. 1961. *The Death and Life of Great American Cities.* New York: Random House.

Jankowski, Martín S. 1991. *Islands in the Street: Gangs in American Urban Society.* Berkeley: University of California Press.

Joe, Karen A., and Meda Chesney-Lind. 1995. "'Just Every Mother's Angel': An Analysis of Gender and Ethnic Variations in Youth Gang Membership." *Gender and Society* 9: 408-430.

Johnson, Bruce D., Terry Williams, Kojo A. Dei, and H. Sanabria. 1990. "Drug Abuse in the Inner City: Impact on Hard Drug Users and the Community." In Michael Tonry and James Q. Wilson, eds., *Drugs and Crime,* vol. 13. Chicago: University of Chicago Press.

Johnson, Dirk. 1997. A Jailed Chicago Gang Leader Is Charged as a Drug Criminal. *New York Times* (September 21): 23.

Jónasdóttir, Anna G. 1994. *Why Women Are Oppressed.* Philadelphia: Temple University Press.

Katz, Jack. 1988. *Seductions of Crime: Moral and Sensual Attractions in Doing Evil.* New York: Basic Books.

Katz, Michael. 2001. *The Price of Citizenship: Redefining the American Welfare State.* New York: Metropolitan Books.

Kelly, Delos H. 1978. *How the School Manufactures Misfits.* South Pasadena, Calif.: Newcal.

Keniston, Kenneth. 1960. *Youth and Dissent: The Rise of a New Opposition.* New York: Harcourt Brace.

Kessel, Philip. 2003. "The Gang Crackdown in Massachusetts' Prisons: Arbitrary and Harsh Treatment Can Only Make Matters Worse." In L. Kontos, D. Brotherton, and L. Barrios, eds., *Gangs and Society: Alternative Perspectives.* New York: Columbia University Press.

Kincheloe, Joe L., and Peter L. McLaren. 1994. Rethinking Critical Theory and Qualitative Research. In *Handbook of Qualitative Research,* pp. 138–157. Thousand Oaks, Calif.: Sage.

Kitson, Frank. 1971. *Low-intensity Operations: Subversion, Insurgency, Peace-keeping.* London: Farber.

Klein, Malcolm. 1971. *Street Gangs and Street Workers.* Englewood Cliffs, N.J.: Prentice Hall.

——. 1995. *The American Street Gang: Its Nature, Prevalence, and Control.* New York: Oxford University Press.

Klein, Malcolm, and Cheryl Maxson. 1989. "Street Gang Violence." In Marvin Wolfgang and Neil Weiner, eds., *Violent Crime, Violent Criminals,* pp. 198–231. Beverly Hills, Calif.: Sage

——. 1996. "Gang Structures, Crime Patterns, and Police Responses." *Final Report to the National Institute of Justice.* Los Angeles, Calif.

Klein, Malcolm, Cheryl Maxson, and Jody Miller. 2000. *The Modern Gang Reader.* 2d ed. Los Angeles, Calif.: Roxbury.

Knox, George. 1997. "An Update on the Latin Kings." *The Gang Journal* 5(1), Fall: 63–76.

Kontos, Louis. 2001. "The Politics and Culture of the Long Island Latin Kings." Unpublished manuscript. New York: Long Island University.

Kontos, Louis, David Brotherton, and Luis Barrios, eds. 2003. *Gangs and Society: Alternative Perspectives.* New York: Columbia University Press.

Kornhauser, William. 1959. *The Politics of Mass Society.* Glencoe, Ill: The Free Press.

Kozol, Jonathan 1967. *Death at an Early Age: The Destruction of the Hearts and Minds of Negro Children in the Boston Public Schools.* Boston: Houghton Mifflin.

——. 1995. *Amazing Grace: The Lives of Children and the Conscience of a Nation.* New York: Harper Perennial.

Laclau, Ernesto, and Chantal Mouffe. 1987. *Hegemony and Socialist Strategy: Towards a Radical Democratic Politics.* London: Verso.

Ladner, Joyce, ed. 1973. *The Death of White Sociology.* New York: Vintage.

Larkin, Ralph, W. 1979. Suburban Youth in Cultural Crisis. New York: Oxford University Press.

Lather, Patti. 1991. *Getting Smart: Feminist Research and Pedagogy within the Postmodern.* New York: Routledge.

Lefebvre, Henri. 1971. *The Production of Space.* Oxford: Blackwell.

Lewis, Oscar. 1965. *La Vida: A Puerto Rican Family in the Culture of Poverty—San Juan and New York.* New York: Random House.

Lincoln, Yvonna S., and Egon G. Guba. 1985. *Naturalistic Inquiry.* Newbury Park, Calif.: Sage.

Lusane, Clarence. 1991. Pipe Dream Blues: Racism and the War on Drugs. Boston: South End Press.

Macleod, Jay. 1995. 2d ed. *Ain't No Makin' It.* Boulder: Westview Press.

Maduro, Otto. 1982. *Religion and Social Conflicts.* Maryknoll, New York: Orbis.

Maher, Lisa. 1997. *Sexed Work: Gender, Race, and Resistance in a Brooklyn Drug Market.* Oxford: Oxford University Press.

Males, Michael. 1996. *The Scapegoat Generation: America's War on Adolescents.* Monroe, Maine: Common Courage Press.

Marcuse, Herbert. 1960. *Reason and Revolution.* Boston: Beacon Press.

——. 1964. *One Dimensional Man.* Boston: Beacon Press.

——. 1978. "On Science and Phenomenology." In A. Arato and E. Gebhardt, eds., *The Essential Frankfurt School Reader*. New York: Urizen Books.

Martin, Douglass. 1994. Legislative Candidate Turns to Gang for Help. *New York Times* (September 13): B-5.

Marx, Gary. 1988. *Undercover: Police Surveillance in America*. Berkeley: University of California Press.

McAdam, Doug. 1982. *Political Process and the Development of Black Insurgency 1930–1970*. Chicago: University of Chicago Press.

McFaden, Robert D. 1999. "94 in Latin Kings Are Arrested Citywide. *New York Times* (May 14): B-4.

McLaren, Peter. 1993. 2d ed. *Schooling as a Ritual Performance: Towards a Political Economy of Educational Symbols and Gestures*. New York: Routledge.

McRobbie, Angela. 1994. *Postmodernism and Popular Culture*. New York: Routledge.

Melucci, Alberto. 1988. "Social Movements and the Democratization of Everyday Life." In J. Deane, ed., *Civil Society and the State: New European Perspectives*. London: Verso.

——. 1989. *Nomads of the Present*. Philadelphia: Temple University Press.

——. 1996. *Challenging Codes: Collective Action in the Information Age*. New York: Cambridge University Press.

Merton, Robert. 1938. "Social Structure and Anomie." *American Sociological Review* 3: 672–682.

——. 1949. *Social Theory and Social Structure*. Glencoe, Ill.: Free Press.

Miller, Jerome. 1996. *Search and Destroy: African-American Males in the Criminal Justice System*. New York: Cambridge University Press.

Miller, Jody. 2001. *One of the Guys: Girls, Gangs, and Gender*. New York: Oxford University Press.

Miller, W. B. 1958. "Lower-Class Culture as a Generating Milieu of Gang Delinquency." *Journal of Social Issues*. 14: 5–19.

——. 1973. "The Molls." *Society* 2: 32–35.

——. 1976. "Youth Gangs in the Urban Crisis Era." In J. F. Short, ed., *Delinquency, Crime and Society*. Chicago: University of Chicago Press.

Mills, C.Wright. 1959. *The Sociological Imagination*. London: Oxford University Press.

Mollenkopf, John. 1992. *Dual Society: Restructuring New York*. New York: Sage.

Monti, D. 1994. *Wannabe: Gangs in Suburbs and Schools*. Cambridge, Mass.: Blackwell.

Moore, Joan. 1988. "Introduction." In John Hagedorn, ed., *Peoples & Folks*, pp. 3–17. Chicago: Lake View Press.

——. 1991. *Going Down to the Barrio: Homeboys and Homegirls in Change*. Philadelphia: Temple University Press.

Moore, Joan, and Robert García. 1978. *Homeboys: Gangs, Drugs, and Prison in the Barrios of Los Angeles*. Philadelphia: Temple University Press.

Moore, Joan, and John M. Hagedorn. 2001. *Female Gangs: A Focus on Research*. Washington, D. C.: U.S. Dept. of Justice, Office of Justice Programs, Office of Juvenile Justice and Delinquency Prevention.

Morales, Ed. 1996. "King of New York." *Village Voice* (December 10): 40–42.

Morris, Aldon D. 1984. *The Origins of the Civil Rights Movement.* New York: The Free Press.

Muñoz, Carlos. 1989. *Youth, Identity, Power: the Chicano Movement.* New York: Verso.

Murji, Karim. 1999. "Wild Life: Constructions and Representations of Yardies." In Jeff Ferrell and Neil Websdale, eds. *Making Trouble: Cultural Constructions of Crime, Deviance and Control,* pp. 179–202. New York: Aldine de Gruyter.

Murr, Andrew. 1999. "L.A.'s Dirty War on Gangs." *Newsweek* (October 11): 72.

Muwakkil, Salmi. 2000. "The New Black Leadership: Gang-Related." In Joy James, ed., *States of Confinement: Policing, Detention, and Prisons.* New York: St. Martin's Press.

Myrdal, Gunnar. 1944. *An American Dilemma: The Negro Problem and Modern Democracy.* New York: Harper.

New York City Department of Planning. 1994. *Puerto Rican New Yorkers in 1990.* New York: The City of New York.

New York City School District. 1997. *"An Investigation into the Latin Kings: No Tolerance for Gangs in Public Schools."* New York: Special Commissioner of Investigation for the New York School District, New York City Board of Education.

New York Post. 1999. "A Thug in Sheep's Clothing." Editorial (June 19): 14.

New York Times. 1997. "Race for City Hall: Candidates in Mayoral Race Touch on Education, Gangs, and Unemployment." Metropolitan Desk (October 10): B-4.

Oakes, Jennie. 1985. *Keeping Track: How Schools Structure Inequality.* New Haven: Yale University Press.

Oberschall, Anthony. 1973. *Social Conflict and Social Movements.* Englewood Cliffs, N.J.: Prentice-Hall.

Office of Juvenile Justice and Delinquency Prevention. 1998. *1998 National Youth Gang Survey.* Washington, D.C.: U.S. Department of Justice, Office of Justice Programs.

Padilla, Felix. 1992. *The Gang as an American Enterprise.* New Brunswick, N.J.: Rutgers University Press.

Parenti, Christian. 1999. *Lockdown America.* New York: Verso.

Parsons, Talcott. 1957. *The Structure of Social Action.* New York: McGraw-Hill.

Pfohl, Stephen. 1985. *Images of Deviance and Social Control: A Sociological History.* New York: McGraw-Hill.

Pfohl, Stephen, and Avery Gordon. 1986. "Criminological Displacements: A Sociological Deconstruction." *Social Problems* 33(6) (December): 94–113.

Piven, Frances Fox, and Richard Cloward. 1970. *Poor People's Movements: Why They Succeed and How They Fail.* New York: Vintage Books.

Platt, Anthony M. 1969. *The Child Savers: The Invention of Delinquency.* Chicago: University of Chicago Press.

Puerto Rican/Hispanic Task Force 2001. *Where Do We Stand Today?* The 2001 Annual Report of the New York State Assembly.

Reiman, Jeffrey. 1998. *The Rich Get Richer and the Poor Get Prison: Ideology, Class, and Criminal Justice.* Boston: Allyn and Bacon.

Richardson, John H. 1997. "Secrets of the Kings." *New York Magazine* (February 17): 30–37.

Richardson, Lynda.1996. An Inside Look at a Gang's Grisly Drama. *New York Times* (November 18): B-1, B-8.

Rist, Ray. 1977. *The Urban School: A Factory for Failure.* Cambridge: MIT Press.

Rivera, Lucas. 1997. "Has King Atoned?" *Brooklyn Bridge* (March): 43–46.

——. 1997. "Anatomy of a King." *Jibe* (July): 167–169.

Rodríguez, Luis. 1994. *Always Running: La Vida Loca, Gang Days in L.A.* New York: Touchstone Books.

Rosaldo, Renato. 1989. *Culture and Truth: The Remaking of Social Analysis.* Boston: Beacon.

Rose, Dina, and Todd Clear. 2000. *Drugs, Incarceration, and Neighborhood Life: The Impact of Reintegrating Offenders into the Community.* Final Report. Washington, D.C.: U.S. Department of Justice.

Roszak, Theodore. 1969. *The Making of the Counteculture: Reflections on the Technocratic Society and Its Youthful Opposition.* New York: Doubleday.

Said, Edward. 1979. *Orientalism.* New York: Vintage Books.

Salmi, Jamil. 1993. *Violence & Democratic Society: The Need for New Approaches to Human Rights.* London: Zed Books.

Sánchez, Raymundo. 2000. *My Bloody Life: The Making of a Latin King.* Chicago: Chicago Review Press.

Sanders, W.G. 1994. *Gangbangs and Drive-bys: Grounded Culture and Juvenile Gang Violence.* New York: Aldine de Gruyter.

Sarup, M. 1983. *Education, State Crisis.* London: Routledge.

Sassen, Saskia. 1998. *Globalization and its Discontents.* New York: New Press.

Schlossman, Stephen. 1978. "The Crime of Precocious Sexuality: Female Juvenile Delinquency in the Progressive Era." *Harvard Educational Review* 48 (February): 65–94.

Schneider, Eric. 1999. *Vampires, Dragons, and Egyptian Kings.* Princeton, N.J.: Princeton University Press.

Schumpeter, Joseph. 1942. *Capitalism, Socialism, and Democracy.* New York: Harper.

Schwandt, Thomas A. 1994. "Constructivist, Interpretivist Approaches to Human Inquiry." In N. Denzin and Y. Lincoln, eds., *Handbook of Qualitative Research,* pp.118–137. Thousand Oaks, Calif.: Sage.

Selznick, Philip. 1960. *The Organizational Weapon.* New York: Free Press.

——. 1970. *Institutional Vulnerability in Mass Society.* New York: Wiley.

Sharff, Jagna W. 1998. *King Kong on 4th Street: Families and the Violence of Poverty on the Lower East Side.* Boulder, Colo.: Westview Press.

Sharkey, Alix. 1999. A Bronx Tale: How the Gangs Made Peace in New York's Ghetto. *The Guardian,* London (January 2): 8–12.

Shaw, Clifford R., and Henry D. McKay. 1931. "Social Factors in Juvenile Delinquency: A Study of the Community, the Family, and the Gang in Relation to Delinquent Behavior." Report of the National Commission on Law Observance and Enforcement (Wickersham Commission),vol. 2, no. 13. Washington, D.C.: U.S. Government Printing Office.

Shaw, Clifford R., and Henry D. McKay. 1969. *Juvenile Delinquency and Urban Areas.* 2d ed. Chicago: University of Chicago Press.

Sheldon, Randal G., S. K. Tracy, and W. B. Brown. 1997. *Youth Gangs in American Society*. New York: Wadsworth.

Shoemaker, Donald. 1985. *Theories of Delinquency*. New York: Oxford University Press.

Short, James F. 1967. "Delinquency Theory and Recent Research." *Journal of Research in Crime and Delinquency* 4: 35.

Short, James F., and Fred. L. Strodtbeck. 1965. *Group Process and Gang Delinquency*. Chicago: University of Chicago Press.

Sibley, David. 1995. *Geographies of Exclusion*. London: Routledge.

Silva-Gotay, Samuel. 1983. *El Pensamiento Cristiano* Revolucionario *en América Latina*. Rio Piedras, Puerto Rico: Cordillera/Ediciones Sígueme.

Skogan, Wesley. 1990. *Disorder and Decline: Crime and the Spiral of Decay in American Neighborhoods*. Berkeley, Calif.: University of California Press.

Skolnick, Jerome. 1992. "Gangs in the Post-Industrial Ghetto." *The American Prospect* 8 (Winter): 109–120.

Smelser, Neil. 1962. *Theory of Collective Behavior*. New York: Free Press.

Snodgrass, John. 1976. "Clifford R. Shaw and Henry D. McKay: Chicago Criminologists." *British Journal of Criminology* 16 (January): 1–19.

Soja, Edward. 1996. *Third Space: Journeys to Los Angeles and Other Real-and-Imagined Places*. Oxford: Blackwell.

Spergel, Irving. 1995. *The Youth Gang Problem: A Community Approach*. New York: Oxford University Press.

Spitzer, Steven. 1975. "Toward a Marxian Theory of Deviance." *Social Problems* 22 (June): 641–651.

Spivak, Gayatri C. 1988. "Can the Subaltern Speak?" In C. Nelson and L. Grossberg, eds., *Marxism and the Interpretation of Culture*. London: MacMillan.

Spunt, Barry. 2001. "Heroin and Crime in New York City." In Andrew Karmen, ed., *Crime and Justice in New York City*. Rev. ed. Vol. 1 , pp. 90–96. Belmont, Calif.: Wadsworth Custom.

St. Clair, Drake, and Horace R. Clayton. 1962. *Black Metropolis: A Study of Negro Life in a Northern City*. New York: Harper and Row.

Sullivan, Mercer. 1989. *Getting Paid: Youth Crime and Work in the Inner City*. Ithaca, N.Y.: Cornell University Press.

Sutherland, Edwin H., and Cressey, Donald. 1966. *Principles of Criminology*. 7th ed. Philadelphia: J. B. Lippincott.

Suttles, Gerald. 1968. *The Social Order of the Slum*. Chicago: University of Chicago Press.

Tabor, Mary B. 1994. "20 Members of Hispanic Gang Indicted in Multiple Killings," *New York Times* (June 22): B-1.

Tallty, Stephan. 1996. "The Power of King Love." *Spin* (September): 61–66.

Tannenbaum, Frank. 1938. *Crime and the Community*. Boston: Ginn.

Tarrow, Sidney. 1992. "Mentalities, Political Cultures, and Collective Action Frames: Constructing Meanings Through Action." In Aldon D. Morris and Carold McClurg Mueller, eds., *Frontiers in Social Movement Theory*, pp. 174–202. Newhaven, Conn.: Yale University Press.

Task Force on the Education of Children and Youth at Risk. New York, 1996.

Taussig, Michael. 1987. *Shamanism, Colonialism, and the Wild Man: A Study in Terror and Healing.* Chicago: University of Chicago Press.

Taylor, Carl. S. 1990. *Dangerous Society.* East Lansing, Mich.: Michigan State University Press.

Terry, Don. 2000. U.S. "Child Poverty Rate Fell as Economy Grew, But Is Above 1979 Level." *New York Times* (August 11):A-10.

Thomas, Jim. 1993. *Doing Critical Ethnography.* Newbury Park, Calif.: Sage.

Thomas, William.I., and Frederick Znaniecki. 1920. *The Polish Peasant in Europe and America,* vol. 4. Boston: Gorham Press.

Thrasher, Frederick. 1927. *The Gang: A Study of 1,313 Gangs in Chicago.* Chicago: University of Chicago Press.

Touraine, Alain. 1971. *Post-Industrial Society.* New York: Random House.

———. 1981. *The Voice and the Eye: An Analysis of Social Movements.* New York: Cambridge University Press.

———. 1988. *Return of the Actor.* Minnesota: University of Minnesota Press.

Turner, Victor. 1977. *The Ritual Process: Structure and Anti-Structure.* Ithaca: Cornell University Press.

U.S. Department of Commerce. 1996. *March 1996 Current Population Survey* (October). Washington, D.C.: Bureau of the Census.

———. 1997. *March 1997 Current Population Survey* (October). Washington, D.C.: Bureau of the Census.

———. 1999. *March 1999 Current Population Survey* (October). Washington, D.C.: Bureau of the Census.

U.S. District Court Eastern District of New York. 1999. *United States versus Antonio Fernandez,* presentence investigation report. New York: U.S. Department of Probation.

Van Dijk, Teun. 1988. "How They Hit the Headlines: Ethnic Minorities in the Press." In G. Smitherman-Donaldson and T. van Dijk, eds., *Discourse and Discrimination,* pp. 221–262. Detroit: Wayne State University Press.

Venkatesh, Sudhir A. 1997. "The Social Organization of Street Gang Activity in an Urban Ghetto." *American Journal of Sociology* 103(1): 82–111.

———. 2000. *American Project: The Rise and Fall of an American Ghetto.* Cambridge, Mass.: Harvard University Press.

———. [In press.] "A Note on Social Theory and the American Street Gang." In L. Kontos, D. Brotherton, and L. Barrios, eds., *Gangs and Society: Alternative Perspectives.* New York: Columbia University Press.

Vigil, James Diego. 1988. *Barrio Gangs: Street Life and Identity in Southern California.* Austin: University of Texas Press.

Wacquant, Loic. 1997. "Three Pernicious Premises in the Study of the American Ghetto." *International Journal of Urban and Regional Research* (July): 341–353.

———. 1998. "From Welfare State to Prison State." *Le Monde Diplomatique* (July 4): 1–14.

———. 2002. "Deadly Symbiosis." *Boston Review* (May 1): 1–25.

Waldorf, D. 1992. "Crack Sales, Gangs and Violence." *Final Report to the National Institute on Drug Abuse.* Alameda, Calif.: Institute for Scientific Analysis.

Warner, Lloyd S., and Paul S. Lunt. 1941. *The Social Life of a Modern Community.* New Haven: Yale University Press.

Weber, Max. 1978. *Economy and Society: An Outline of Interpretive Sociology.* Edited by Guenther Roth and Claus Wittich. Berkeley: University of California Press.

Weinstein, Corey, and Eric Cummins. 1996. "The Crime of Punishment: Pelican Bay Maximum Security Prison." In Elihu Rosenblatt, ed., *Criminal Injustice: Confronting the Prison Crisis,* pp. 308–321. Boston: South End Press.

Wendel, Travis, and Curtis, Richard. 2002. "The Heraldry of Heroin: Dope Stamps and the Dynamics of Drug Markets in New York City." *Journal of Drug Issues* 30(2): 1–34.

Werthman, Carl. 1969. "Delinquency and Moral Character." In D. R. Cressey and D. A. Ward, eds., *Delinquency, Crime, and Social Process,* pp. 613–632. New York: Harper and Row.

Whyte, William F. 1943. *Street Corner Society.* Chicago: University of Chicago Press.

——. 1991. *Participatory Action Research.* London: Sage.

Williams, Raymond. 1961. *The Long Revolution.* London: Penguin.

Willis, Paul. 1977. *Learning to Labor: How Working-Class Kids Get Working-Class Jobs.* Westmead, U.K.: Saxon House.

Wilson, William J. 1987. *The Truly Disadvantaged.* Chicago: University of Chicago Press.

Wynn, Jennifer. 2001. *Inside Rikers.* New York: St. Martin's Press.

Yablonsky, Lewis. 1963. *The Violent Gang.* New York: Macmillan.

Yinger, Milton. 1982. *The Promise and Peril of a World Turned Upside Down.* New York: Free Press.

Young, Jock. 1971. *The Drugtakers: The Social Meaning of Drug Use.* London: MacGibbon and Kee.

——. 1999. *The Exclusive Society: Social Exclusion, Crime, and Difference in Late Modernity.* London: Sage.

Zatz, Marjorie. 1987. "Chicano Youth Gangs and Crime: The Creation of a Moral Panic." *Contemporary Crises* (11): 129–158.